T0281043

Lecture Notes in Computer Science   14706

Founding Editors

Gerhard Goos
Juris Hartmanis

Editorial Board Members

Elisa Bertino, *Purdue University, West Lafayette, IN, USA*
Wen Gao, *Peking University, Beijing, China*
Bernhard Steffen, *TU Dortmund University, Dortmund, Germany*
Moti Yung, *Columbia University, New York, NY, USA*

The series Lecture Notes in Computer Science (LNCS), including its subseries Lecture Notes in Artificial Intelligence (LNAI) and Lecture Notes in Bioinformatics (LNBI), has established itself as a medium for the publication of new developments in computer science and information technology research, teaching, and education.

LNCS enjoys close cooperation with the computer science R & D community, the series counts many renowned academics among its volume editors and paper authors, and collaborates with prestigious societies. Its mission is to serve this international community by providing an invaluable service, mainly focused on the publication of conference and workshop proceedings and postproceedings. LNCS commenced publication in 1973.

Jessie Y. C. Chen · Gino Fragomeni
Editors

Virtual, Augmented and Mixed Reality

16th International Conference, VAMR 2024
Held as Part of the 26th HCI International Conference, HCII 2024
Washington, DC, USA, June 29 – July 4, 2024
Proceedings, Part I

 Springer

Editors
Jessie Y. C. Chen
U.S. Army Research Laboratory
Adelphi, MD, USA

Gino Fragomeni
U.S. Army Combat Capabilities
Development Command Soldier Center
Orlando, FL, USA

ISSN 0302-9743 ISSN 1611-3349 (electronic)
Lecture Notes in Computer Science
ISBN 978-3-031-61040-0 ISBN 978-3-031-61041-7 (eBook)
https://doi.org/10.1007/978-3-031-61041-7

© The Editor(s) (if applicable) and The Author(s), under exclusive license
to Springer Nature Switzerland AG 2024

This work is subject to copyright. All rights are solely and exclusively licensed by the Publisher, whether
the whole or part of the material is concerned, specifically the rights of translation, reprinting, reuse of
illustrations, recitation, broadcasting, reproduction on microfilms or in any other physical way, and transmission
or information storage and retrieval, electronic adaptation, computer software, or by similar or dissimilar
methodology now known or hereafter developed.
The use of general descriptive names, registered names, trademarks, service marks, etc. in this publication
does not imply, even in the absence of a specific statement, that such names are exempt from the relevant
protective laws and regulations and therefore free for general use.
The publisher, the authors and the editors are safe to assume that the advice and information in this book
are believed to be true and accurate at the date of publication. Neither the publisher nor the authors or the
editors give a warranty, expressed or implied, with respect to the material contained herein or for any errors
or omissions that may have been made. The publisher remains neutral with regard to jurisdictional claims in
published maps and institutional affiliations.

This Springer imprint is published by the registered company Springer Nature Switzerland AG
The registered company address is: Gewerbestrasse 11, 6330 Cham, Switzerland

If disposing of this product, please recycle the paper.

Foreword

This year we celebrate 40 years since the establishment of the HCI International (HCII) Conference, which has been a hub for presenting groundbreaking research and novel ideas and collaboration for people from all over the world.

The HCII conference was founded in 1984 by Prof. Gavriel Salvendy (Purdue University, USA, Tsinghua University, P.R. China, and University of Central Florida, USA) and the first event of the series, "1st USA-Japan Conference on Human-Computer Interaction", was held in Honolulu, Hawaii, USA, 18–20 August. Since then, HCI International is held jointly with several Thematic Areas and Affiliated Conferences, with each one under the auspices of a distinguished international Program Board and under one management and one registration. Twenty-six HCI International Conferences have been organized so far (every two years until 2013, and annually thereafter).

Over the years, this conference has served as a platform for scholars, researchers, industry experts and students to exchange ideas, connect, and address challenges in the ever-evolving HCI field. Throughout these 40 years, the conference has evolved itself, adapting to new technologies and emerging trends, while staying committed to its core mission of advancing knowledge and driving change.

As we celebrate this milestone anniversary, we reflect on the contributions of its founding members and appreciate the commitment of its current and past Affiliated Conference Program Board Chairs and members. We are also thankful to all past conference attendees who have shaped this community into what it is today.

The 26th International Conference on Human-Computer Interaction, HCI International 2024 (HCII 2024), was held as a 'hybrid' event at the Washington Hilton Hotel, Washington, DC, USA, during 29 June – 4 July 2024. It incorporated the 21 thematic areas and affiliated conferences listed below.

A total of 5108 individuals from academia, research institutes, industry, and government agencies from 85 countries submitted contributions, and 1271 papers and 309 posters were included in the volumes of the proceedings that were published just before the start of the conference, these are listed below. The contributions thoroughly cover the entire field of human-computer interaction, addressing major advances in knowledge and effective use of computers in a variety of application areas. These papers provide academics, researchers, engineers, scientists, practitioners and students with state-of-the-art information on the most recent advances in HCI.

The HCI International (HCII) conference also offers the option of presenting 'Late Breaking Work', and this applies both for papers and posters, with corresponding volumes of proceedings that will be published after the conference. Full papers will be included in the 'HCII 2024 - Late Breaking Papers' volumes of the proceedings to be published in the Springer LNCS series, while 'Poster Extended Abstracts' will be included as short research papers in the 'HCII 2024 - Late Breaking Posters' volumes to be published in the Springer CCIS series.

I would like to thank the Program Board Chairs and the members of the Program Boards of all thematic areas and affiliated conferences for their contribution towards the high scientific quality and overall success of the HCI International 2024 conference. Their manifold support in terms of paper reviewing (single-blind review process, with a minimum of two reviews per submission), session organization and their willingness to act as goodwill ambassadors for the conference is most highly appreciated.

This conference would not have been possible without the continuous and unwavering support and advice of Gavriel Salvendy, founder, General Chair Emeritus, and Scientific Advisor. For his outstanding efforts, I would like to express my sincere appreciation to Abbas Moallem, Communications Chair and Editor of HCI International News.

July 2024   Constantine Stephanidis

HCI International 2024 Thematic Areas and Affiliated Conferences

- HCI: Human-Computer Interaction Thematic Area
- HIMI: Human Interface and the Management of Information Thematic Area
- EPCE: 21st International Conference on Engineering Psychology and Cognitive Ergonomics
- AC: 18th International Conference on Augmented Cognition
- UAHCI: 18th International Conference on Universal Access in Human-Computer Interaction
- CCD: 16th International Conference on Cross-Cultural Design
- SCSM: 16th International Conference on Social Computing and Social Media
- VAMR: 16th International Conference on Virtual, Augmented and Mixed Reality
- DHM: 15th International Conference on Digital Human Modeling & Applications in Health, Safety, Ergonomics & Risk Management
- DUXU: 13th International Conference on Design, User Experience and Usability
- C&C: 12th International Conference on Culture and Computing
- DAPI: 12th International Conference on Distributed, Ambient and Pervasive Interactions
- HCIBGO: 11th International Conference on HCI in Business, Government and Organizations
- LCT: 11th International Conference on Learning and Collaboration Technologies
- ITAP: 10th International Conference on Human Aspects of IT for the Aged Population
- AIS: 6th International Conference on Adaptive Instructional Systems
- HCI-CPT: 6th International Conference on HCI for Cybersecurity, Privacy and Trust
- HCI-Games: 6th International Conference on HCI in Games
- MobiTAS: 6th International Conference on HCI in Mobility, Transport and Automotive Systems
- AI-HCI: 5th International Conference on Artificial Intelligence in HCI
- MOBILE: 5th International Conference on Human-Centered Design, Operation and Evaluation of Mobile Communications

List of Conference Proceedings Volumes Appearing Before the Conference

1. LNCS 14684, Human-Computer Interaction: Part I, edited by Masaaki Kurosu and Ayako Hashizume
2. LNCS 14685, Human-Computer Interaction: Part II, edited by Masaaki Kurosu and Ayako Hashizume
3. LNCS 14686, Human-Computer Interaction: Part III, edited by Masaaki Kurosu and Ayako Hashizume
4. LNCS 14687, Human-Computer Interaction: Part IV, edited by Masaaki Kurosu and Ayako Hashizume
5. LNCS 14688, Human-Computer Interaction: Part V, edited by Masaaki Kurosu and Ayako Hashizume
6. LNCS 14689, Human Interface and the Management of Information: Part I, edited by Hirohiko Mori and Yumi Asahi
7. LNCS 14690, Human Interface and the Management of Information: Part II, edited by Hirohiko Mori and Yumi Asahi
8. LNCS 14691, Human Interface and the Management of Information: Part III, edited by Hirohiko Mori and Yumi Asahi
9. LNAI 14692, Engineering Psychology and Cognitive Ergonomics: Part I, edited by Don Harris and Wen-Chin Li
10. LNAI 14693, Engineering Psychology and Cognitive Ergonomics: Part II, edited by Don Harris and Wen-Chin Li
11. LNAI 14694, Augmented Cognition, Part I, edited by Dylan D. Schmorrow and Cali M. Fidopiastis
12. LNAI 14695, Augmented Cognition, Part II, edited by Dylan D. Schmorrow and Cali M. Fidopiastis
13. LNCS 14696, Universal Access in Human-Computer Interaction: Part I, edited by Margherita Antona and Constantine Stephanidis
14. LNCS 14697, Universal Access in Human-Computer Interaction: Part II, edited by Margherita Antona and Constantine Stephanidis
15. LNCS 14698, Universal Access in Human-Computer Interaction: Part III, edited by Margherita Antona and Constantine Stephanidis
16. LNCS 14699, Cross-Cultural Design: Part I, edited by Pei-Luen Patrick Rau
17. LNCS 14700, Cross-Cultural Design: Part II, edited by Pei-Luen Patrick Rau
18. LNCS 14701, Cross-Cultural Design: Part III, edited by Pei-Luen Patrick Rau
19. LNCS 14702, Cross-Cultural Design: Part IV, edited by Pei-Luen Patrick Rau
20. LNCS 14703, Social Computing and Social Media: Part I, edited by Adela Coman and Simona Vasilache
21. LNCS 14704, Social Computing and Social Media: Part II, edited by Adela Coman and Simona Vasilache
22. LNCS 14705, Social Computing and Social Media: Part III, edited by Adela Coman and Simona Vasilache

https://2024.hci.international/proceedings

Preface

With the recent emergence of a new generation of displays, smart devices, and wearables, the field of virtual, augmented, and mixed reality (VAMR) is rapidly expanding, transforming, and moving towards the mainstream market. At the same time, VAMR applications in a variety of domains are also reaching maturity and practical usage. From the point of view of the user experience, VAMR promises possibilities to reduce interaction efforts and cognitive load, while also offering contextualized information, by combining different sources and reducing attention shifts, and opening the 3D space. Such scenarios offer exciting challenges associated with underlying and supporting technologies, interaction, and navigation in virtual and augmented environments, and design and development. VAMR themes encompass a wide range of areas such as education, aviation, social, emotional, psychological, and persuasive applications.

The 16th International Conference on Virtual, Augmented, and Mixed Reality (VAMR 2024), an affiliated conference of the HCI International Conference, provided a forum for researchers and practitioners to disseminate and exchange scientific and technical information on VAMR-related topics in various applications. A considerable number of papers have explored user experience topics including avatar design, walking and moving in VR environments, scene design and complexity, 360o immersive environments and the design of 3D elements, cybersickness, and multisensory feedback. Moreover, submissions offered a comprehensive examination of perception aspects, including our understanding of body image, self-presentation, visual realism, and awareness. A key topic that emerged was interaction in immersive environments such as haptic interaction, tangible VR, and gestures. Furthermore, emphasis was given to the application domains of VAMR including collaboration, cultural heritage, education and learning, health and well-being, but also software programming, crime data analysis, terrain exploration, and astronomical visualization. We are thrilled to present this compilation of VAMR submissions encompassing a wide range of topics and exploring the current state of the art, while also highlighting future avenues in the design and development of immersive experiences.

Three volumes of the HCII 2024 proceedings are dedicated to this year's edition of the VAMR conference. The first focuses on topics related to Perception, Interaction and Design, and User Experience and Evaluation. The second focuses on topics related to Immersive Collaboration and Environment Design, and Sensory, Tangible, and Embodied Interaction in VAMR, while the third focuses on topics related to Immersive Education and Learning, and VAMR Applications and Development.

The papers in these volumes were accepted for publication after a minimum of two single-blind reviews from the members of the VAMR Program Board or, in some cases, from members of the Program Boards of other affiliated conferences. We would like to thank all of them for their invaluable contribution, support, and efforts.

July 2024

Jessie Y. C. Chen
Gino Fragomeni

16th International Conference on Virtual, Augmented and Mixed Reality (VAMR 2024)

Program Board Chairs: **Jessie Y. C. Chen,** *U.S. Army Research Laboratory, USA,* and **Gino Fragomeni,** *U.S. Army Combat Capabilities Development Command Soldier Center, USA*

- J. Cecil, *Oklahoma State University, USA*
- Shih-Yi Chien, *National Chengchi University, Taiwan*
- Avinash Gupta, *University of Illinois Urbana-Champaign, USA*
- Sue Kase, *U.S. Army Research Laboratory, USA*
- Daniela Kratchounova, *Federal Aviation Administration (FAA), USA*
- Fotis Liarokapis, *CYENS - Centre of Excellence, Cyprus*
- Jaehyun Park, *Incheon National University (INU), Korea*
- Chao Peng, *Rochester Institute of Technology, USA*
- Jose San Martin, *Universidad Rey Juan Carlos, Spain*
- Andreas Schreiber, *German Aerospace Center (DLR), Germany*
- Sharad Sharma, *University of North Texas, USA*
- Simon Su, *National Institute of Standards and Technology (NIST), USA*
- Denny Yu, *Purdue University, USA*

The full list with the Program Board Chairs and the members of the Program Boards of all thematic areas and affiliated conferences of HCII 2024 is available online at:

http://www.hci.international/board-members-2024.php

HCI International 2025 Conference

The 27th International Conference on Human-Computer Interaction, HCI International 2025, will be held jointly with the affiliated conferences at the Swedish Exhibition & Congress Centre and Gothia Towers Hotel, Gothenburg, Sweden, June 22–27, 2025. It will cover a broad spectrum of themes related to Human-Computer Interaction, including theoretical issues, methods, tools, processes, and case studies in HCI design, as well as novel interaction techniques, interfaces, and applications. The proceedings will be published by Springer. More information will become available on the conference website: https://2025.hci.international/.

General Chair
Prof. Constantine Stephanidis
University of Crete and ICS-FORTH
Heraklion, Crete, Greece
Email: general_chair@2025.hci.international

https://2025.hci.international/

Contents – Part I

User Experience and Evaluation

Contents – Part II

Contents – Part III

Perception, Interaction and Design

The Effects of a Virtual Instructor with Realistic Lip Sync in an Augmented Reality Environment

Madeline Easley[1], Jung Hyup Kim[1(✉)], Siddarth Mohanty[1], Ching-Yun Yu[2], Varun Pulipati[2], Sara Mostowfi[1], Fang Wang[3], Kangwon Seo[1], and Danielle Oprean[4]

[1] Department of Industrial and Systems Engineering, University of Missouri, Columbia, MO 65211, USA
{mge6pp,kijung,smdqv,sara.mostowfi,seoka}@missouri.edu
[2] Department of Electrical Engineering and Computer Science, University of Missouri, Columbia, MO 65211, USA
{cytbm,vpccn}@umsystem.edu
[3] Department of Engineering and Information Technology, University of Missouri, Columbia, MO 65211, USA
wangfan@missouri.edu
[4] School of Information Science and Learning Technologies, University of Missouri, Columbia, MO 65211, USA
opreand@missouri.edu

Abstract. In this study, we explore the impact of incorporating a virtual instructor with realistic lip-syncing in an augmented reality (AR) learning environment. The study is particularly focused on understanding if this enhancement can reduce students' mental workload and improve system usability and performance in AR learning. The research stems from previous feedback indicating that a virtual instructor without facial movements was perceived as "creepy" and "distracting." The updated virtual instructor includes facial animations, such as blinking and synchronized lip movements, especially during lecture explanations. The study aims to determine if there are significant changes in mental workload and usability differences between the AR systems with and without the enhanced virtual instructor. The study found significant differences in the usability scores in some questions. However, there was no significant difference in the mental workload between them.

Keywords: Augmented Reality · Workload · Usability · Lip Sync · Virtual Instructor

1 Introduction

In the realms of education and training, augmented reality (AR) has proven to be an impressive learning platform. This is evidenced by its success in enhancing retention [1], boosting motivation [2], and facilitating significant learning gains [3]. A key strength of AR lies in its ability to foster a personalized 'learning by doing' approach [4]. However, AR-based learning requires further improvement to boost its effectiveness in student

© The Author(s), under exclusive license to Springer Nature Switzerland AG 2024
J. Y. C. Chen and G. Fragomeni (Eds.): HCII 2024, LNCS 14706, pp. 3–12, 2024.
https://doi.org/10.1007/978-3-031-61041-7_1

learning. Wu, Lee [5] highlighted a critical challenge: students often experience cognitive overload in AR environments due to the influx of multiple information streams. To address this, introducing a virtual instructor equipped with realistic lip-syncing could mark a notable evolution in AR educational experiences. Such an integration promises to deepen student immersion in AR scenarios, offering an experience where virtual instruction mirrors the nuances of real-life human interactions. In this study, the participants were 37 students from an Ergonomics and Workstation Design course. The study was conducted over two consecutive fall semesters, with different groups each year. The participants went through lectures in an AR environment, guided by a virtual instructor, and their performance and subjective workload were measured.

2   Problem Description

In this study, we explored the advantages of incorporating a virtual instructor featuring a natural lip sync in augmented reality learning. In our previous study [6], we developed a virtual instructor without any facial movements. Participant feedback highlighted a shared concern: the facial expression of the animated instructor was deemed "creepy" and "distracting." To address this issue, the updated virtual instructor now includes facial animations, such as blinking and synchronized lip movements, especially during lecture explanations.

To evaluate the advantages of this enhancement, the experiment was structured to address the two research questions outlined below:

- What are the significant changes, if any, in mental workload following the implementation of an enhanced virtual instructor with realistic lip sync?
- How do the usability levels compare between the two versions of the virtual instructor, and is there a significant difference?

We hypothesized that the introduction of the updated virtual instructor could lead to a significant decrease in students' mental workload during this AR learning experience. Additionally, it is anticipated that the improvements in user experience might result in an increase in system usability. However, our findings revealed contrasting results.

3   Related Research

AR provides educators with the opportunity to present lessons in a new digital format. Learners would have the opportunity to handle information in a new and interactive format [5, 7]. AR can create an ease-of-use that has been proven to reduce students' cognitive workloads, which can encourage students to engage more with the content [1, 8–10]. This new way of educating students could help the content become more "fun and entertaining," allowing them to be more creative inside the AR environment. However, if the virtual content lacks naturalness, it could greatly affect student engagement during the learning process. To improve the impacts of learning outcomes and student engagement in VR/AR/MR environments, many studies are focusing on designing the virtual content based on gamification, which is about using game elements to engage that motivation [11, 12]. Gamification is not about creating complete games, but instead using game-thinking or mechanics to engage users to learn and solve problems. It will help to improve student motivation and engagement using game elements. According to the study done by Arnold [13], the ideal initiation for gamification lies in virtual or online learning, where students already accustomed to gaming, may find a smooth transition into educational contexts. This approach highlights the significance of maintaining a low workload and ensuring the naturalness of virtual content to enhance the learning experience. Radu further highlighted the importance of keeping workloads light, allowing students ample opportunity to interact with and adapt to the AR learning environment [1]. Because AR does not block students' view of their physical surroundings, and they are still able to interact with peers to discuss content [14]. AR also offers the capability to present students with experiences, such as visualizing complex subjects or simulating locations for field trips, aiding in their understanding of the topics being studied. A study conducted on marine education using AR found that students benefit from close-up examination through the features that AR offers, enhancing their understanding and motivation [15]. In AR-based education, the use of visualization can support differentiated instruction tailored to a variety of learners, a crucial aspect of lesson planning. AR can make the delivery of information more adaptive and personalized for education [16]. However, AR comes with certain limitations. Some students might perceive the new AR learning environment as complex, particularly if they encounter any technical issues associated with the virtual contents [3].

4 Methodology

4.1 Participants

The participants of this study (N = 37) were students in an Industrial and Systems Engineering Ergonomics and Workstation Design course at the University of Missouri–Columbia. Data was collected over two consecutive fall semesters. The first set of data, Year 1, was collected in Fall of 2022 during a 3-week period, October 17th to November 3rd, 2022. This first round of data collection had a total of 16 participants. In the second year of the study, data collection occurred over a period of 7 weeks, from September 18th – November 1st, 2023. The second set of data, Year 2 contains 21 participants. The ages of the participants ranged from 20 to 23 and consisted of Juniors or Senior college students. Lecture materials were directly related to the ergonomics class content.

4.2 Procedure

Participants completed two lectures during the experiment. Following the first lecture, they were required to complete the second lecture within a forty-eight-hour period. Lectures took place in an open space lab, which allowed free movement so participants could answer questions after each module on an unfixed table as they moved through the space. Participants were guided through two Biomechanics lectures within the augmented reality environment by a virtual instructor leading each session. The anticipated duration of each lecture was approximately sixty minutes; however, participants were encouraged to proceed at their own pace, allowing for content review or replay as needed (see Fig. 1). The initial lecture covered fundamental biomechanics and physics concepts, encompassing basic definitions and formulas (see Fig. 2). In contrast, the subsequent lecture applied these definitions, thereby elevating the difficulty level. Lecture 1 was segmented into seven modules, while Lecture 2 comprised of eight modules. Most modules concluded with participants answering a question related to the material, resulting in multiple questions within each lecture. Each lecture had seven questions. Following each response, participants provided a confidence rating indicating their level of certainty regarding the accuracy of their answer.

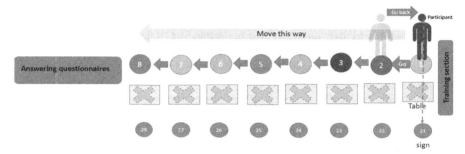

Fig. 1. Diagram of how participants traveled through the lab space.

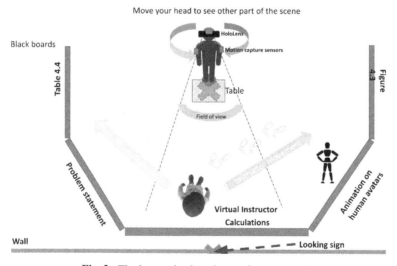

Fig. 2. The immersive learning environment [17].

At the conclusion of each lecture, participants were asked to fill out three survey forms. The NASA Task Load Index method [18] was used to evaluate and rank assessments of subjective demand considered by each participant. This survey asked participants to assign percentages (between 0–100) to predetermined workload dimensions (i.e., Physical Demand, Mental Demand, Temporal Demand, Performance, Frustration, and Effort) and then to rank those dimensions. Students also filled out a survey titled Student Satisfaction and Self-Confidence in Learning Scale (SCLS). This survey required participants to rate on a 5-point scale how much they agreed or disagreed with statements about learning in an Augmented reality environment. These questions included, but were not limited to, "The way the virtual instructor taught was suitable to the way I learn." And, "The teaching methods used in this Augmented Reality module were helpful and effective."

The main difference of the virtual instructor in Year 2 compared to Year 1 is with realistic lip sync, facial expression and more hand motions. Both versions of the instructor are shown in Fig. 3. While there are slight variations among these instructors in aspects like appearance, clothing color, and hairstyle, these differences do not significantly impact student engagement, workload, or usability. Virtual instructors, in contrast to human ones, reduce the likelihood of bias linked to appearance. A virtual instructor, created through 3D animation and powered by the Xsens motion capture system along with Murf AI, enabled realistic movements and synthesized a voice that sounded natural.

Fig. 3. Virtual Instructor in Year 1(left) and Virtual Instructor in Year 2 (right).

4.3 Apparatus

A HoloLens 2 AR headset was used to display the lecture modules (see Fig. 4). Motion-tracking sensors were attached to the upper bodies of participants. The lectures were conducted in a spacious lab environment. This setup enabled students to walk around the lab, activating different sections of the virtual lecture as they moved.

Fig. 4. A student participant wearing HoloLens and sensors in the testing area.

5 Results

Upon assessing the usability score over the two years, notable disparities were observed in the participants' answers to two out of the ten usability questions. A significant difference was particularly evident in the response to Question #3 on the survey. This particular question asked for participants' perspective on the system's user-friendliness. It read: "I thought the system was easy to use." (Fig. 5)

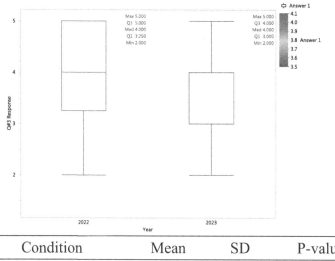

Condition	Mean	SD	P-value
Year 1	4.09	0.93	**0.0097**
Year 2	3.52	0.92	

Fig. 5. Statistical results of Usability Question #3 between Conditions.

The above figure illustrates a decline in participants' perceived ease of use in Year 2 as opposed to Year 1. The average score for the statement 'I thought the system was easy to use' dropped from 4.09 in Year 1 to 3.52 in Year 2. This decrease highlights that participant in Year 2 found the system to be relatively more difficult compared to those in the previous year.

The other question that showed notable differences was Usability Question #4, which asked "I think that I would need the support of a technical person to be able to use this system." (Fig. 6).

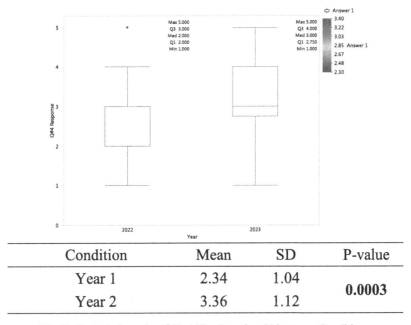

Condition	Mean	SD	P-value
Year 1	2.34	1.04	0.0003
Year 2	3.36	1.12	

Fig. 6. Statistical results of Usability Question #4 between Conditions.

This question shows a significant increase in students' ratings indicating a higher need for seeking assistance during the operation of this system. This once again implies that students perceive an increased complexity. Additionally, another survey extensively examined was the students' workloads, assessed using the NASA TLX. In a manner akin to the usability analysis, participants' workloads were compared year-to-year to observe any shifts in the data (Fig. 7).

This graph illustrates that there was no significant statistical difference between years. We believe the updated virtual instructor, which featured facial animations like blinking and synchronized lip movements, did not have a significant impact on the work-load.

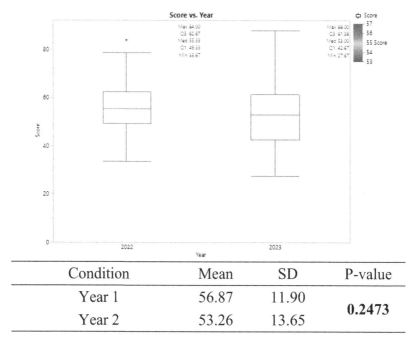

Condition	Mean	SD	P-value
Year 1	56.87	11.90	**0.2473**
Year 2	53.26	13.65	

Fig. 7. Statistical results of participants' workloads between Conditions.

6   Discussions and Conclusions

The analysis of usability results shows a consistent perception among participants that the Year 2 system is comparatively more complicated to use than its Year 1, as evidenced by participant responses to Question #3. Furthermore, responses to Question #4 further support the conclusion that the system is perceived as more challenging to use. There's a clear correlation: participants who perceive the system as harder to use are likely to feel an increased need for assistance. In other words, the participants in Year 2 perceived the AR classroom, enhanced with the upgraded virtual instructor incorporating facial animations such as blinking and synchronized lip movements, as not beneficial for AR lectures. A possible explanation for this phenomenon could be that participants are sensitive to any imperfections in realism, such as minor inaccuracies in lip-syncing or a limited range of expressions. These flaws might result in feelings of dissatisfaction or make it more challenging to engage with the AR content. Additionally, realistic animations demand considerable processing power and advanced software. Therefore, any constraints or deviations in the animations from actual human movements and expressions might interrupt the learning experience, thereby making it more difficult for users to concentrate on the educational material. Another possible explanation could be the realistic facial expressions and synchronized lip movements of a virtual instructor could unintentionally shift focus away from the educational content. Users may become more preoccupied with observing the instructor's animations rather than concentrating on the les-son itself. Furthermore, if students are not used to interacting with virtual instructors of this nature, the unfamiliar experience may initially seem more demanding.

Interestingly, even though there was a reported decline in the system's usability, the comparison of workloads between Year 1 and Year 2 did not reveal any statistically significant differences. According to the previous study [19], the observation that a virtual instructor in AR learning reduces workload compared to scenarios without one. However, in this study, a virtual instructor with facial expressions and realistic lip sync does not further reduce workload compared to a virtual instructor without these features. Despite the decrease in the system's usability, it's possible that the workload could have increased. Yet, no significant difference in workload results was observed. This suggests that while a virtual instructor can streamline learning through step-by-step guidance, the inclusion of realistic facial expressions and lip syncing may not significantly impact cognitive load.

This indicates that modifications like the updates to the virtual professor incorporating facial animations such as blinking and synchronized lip movements did not in-crease the workload or stress levels of the participants. Despite Year 2 students perceiving the system usability as more challenging, this did not lead to a rise in their workload.

In contrast to our initial hypothesis, the results did not support the idea that the introduction of the updated virtual instructor with realistic lip sync and facial expressions resulted in a significant change in students' mental workload during the AR learning experience. Furthermore, the anticipated improvements in user experience were not apparent based on the collected data. Hence, if the realistic animations do not offer extra educational value or enhance content comprehension, they may be viewed as unnecessary.

Although the data did not align with our initial predictions, there is still valuable in-sight to be gained from these results. These findings show the relationship between the perceived system difficulty and the impact on the workload and suggest further exploration is needed to understand the many factors that influence user experience.

The study concludes that while the virtual instructor with realistic lip sync may not have reduced cognitive load and improved usability as expected, it provides valuable insights into the complexity of user experience in AR education systems. This suggests a need for more research in this area to better understand and optimize AR learning environments. To enhance usability and lessen the workload in AR learning via modifications to the virtual instructor, we suggest opting for a simpler or more stylized design over hyper-realism. This approach can lower cognitive load and improve user-friendliness. Where realistic lip syncing and facial expressions are essential, it is vital to ensure their accuracy and naturalness to bypass the uncanny valley effect [20] and boost comprehension. Additionally, allowing for customization of the virtual instructor's appearance and behavior, if feasible, can render the learning experience more approachable and less intimidating for students. Finally, implementing a system where the virtual instructor adjusts to each student's learning pace and offers relevant feedback is key to making the learning process more effective.

Acknowledgments. This study was funded by the National Science Foundation (NSF).

References

1. Radu, I.: Why should my students use AR? a comparative review of the educational impacts of augmented-reality. In: 2012 IEEE International Symposium on Mixed and Augmented Reality (ISMAR). IEEE (2012)
2. Gutiérrez, J.M., Fernández, M.D.M.: Applying augmented reality in engineering education to improve academic performance & student motivation. Int. J. Eng. Educ. **30**(3), 625–635 (2014)
3. Akçayır, M., Akçayır, G.: Advantages and challenges associated with augmented reality for education: a systematic review of the literature. Educ. Res. Rev. **20**, 1–11 (2017)
4. May, D.B., Etkina, E.: College physics students' epistemological self-reflection and its relationship to conceptual learning. Am. J. Phys. **70**(12), 1249–1258 (2002)
5. Wu, H.-K., et al.: Current status, opportunities and challenges of augmented reality in education. Comput. Educ. **62**, 41–49 (2013)
6. Mostowfi, S., et al.: The Effect of Metacognitive Judgments on Metacognitive Awareness in an Augmented Reality Environment. Springer, Cham (2023)
7. Kim, J.H., Chan, T., Du, W.: The Learning Effect of Augmented Reality Training in a Computer-Based Simulation Environment. Springer, Cham (2015)
8. Guo, W., Kim, J.H.: How Augmented Reality Influences Student Workload in Engineering Education. Springer, Cham (2020)
9. Guo, W., Kim, J.H.: How Metacognitive Monitoring Feedback Influences Workload in a Location-Based Augmented Reality Environment. Springer, Cham (2021)
10. Guo, W., Hyup Kim, J.: Investigating academic performance using an AR-based learning environment with retrospective confidence judgments. In: Proceedings of the Human Factors and Ergonomics Society Annual Meeting. SAGE Publications, Sage CA, Los Angeles, CA (2022)
11. Buckley, P., Doyle, E.: Gamification and student motivation. Interact. Learn. Environ. **24**(6), 1162–1175 (2016)
12. Chapman, J.R., Rich, P.J.: Does educational gamification improve students' motivation? If so, which game elements work best? J. Educ. Bus. **93**(7), 315–322 (2018)
13. Arnold, B.J.: Gamification in education. Proc. Am. Soc. Bus. Behav. Sci. **21**(1), 32–39 (2014)
14. Galembeck, E., Magrini, M., Garzon, J.: Using augmented reality to bring interactivity to metabolism teaching. Revista de Ensino de Bioquímica **12**(1), 84 (2014)
15. Hsieh, M.-C.: Development and application of an augmented reality oyster learning system for primary marine education. Electronics **10**(22), 2818 (2021)
16. Aljowaysir, N., Ozdemir, T.O., Kim, T.: Differentiated learning patterns with mixed reality. In: 2019 IEEE Games, Entertainment, Media Conference (GEM). IEEE (2019)
17. Yu, C.-Y., et al.: Developing an Augmented Reality-Based Interactive Learning System with Real-Time Location and Motion Tracking. Springer, Cham (2023)
18. Hart, S.G.: NASA-task load index (NASA-TLX); 20 years later. In: Proceedings of the Human Factors and Ergonomics Society Annual Meeting. Sage publications, Sage CA, Los Angeles, CA (2006)
19. Kim, J.H., et al.: The effect of virtual instructor and metacognition on workload in a location-based augmented reality learning environment. In: Proceedings of the Human Factors and Ergonomics Society Annual Meeting. SAGE Publications, Sage CA, Los Angeles, CA (2023)
20. Seyama, J.I., Nagayama, R.S.: The uncanny valley: effect of realism on the impression of artificial human faces. Presence **16**(4), 337–351 (2007)

Assessing Body Dissatisfaction and Attentional Bias Towards the Body Using Eye-Tracking Technology in Virtual Reality

Jose Gutierrez-Maldonado[1]([✉]) [ID], Alejandra Rueda-Pina[1], Mariarca Ascione[1], Franck-Alexandre Meschberger-Annweiler[1], Marta Ferrer-Garcia[1], Maria-Teresa Mendoza-Medialdea[1,2], and Bruno Porras-Garcia[3,4]

[1] Department of Clinical Psychology and Psychobiology, Institute of Neurosciences, Paseo Valle de Hebrón, University of Barcelona, 171, 08035 Barcelona, Spain
jgutierrezm@ub.edu
[2] Universidad de Jaén, Jaén, Spain
[3] Brain Cognition and Behavior Research Group, Consorci Sanitari de Terrassa (CST), Barcelona, Spain
[4] Department of Basic Sciences, Universitat Internacional de Catalunya, Barcelona, Spain

Abstract. This study investigates body image perception, focusing on the impact of exposure to "ideal thinness" images on body dissatisfaction and attentional biases. Body image, shaped by beauty standards and sociocultural influences, significantly affects mental health, contributing to issues like depression, anxiety, and eating disorders. Body dissatisfaction extends beyond diagnosed cases, affecting the general population.

This research employs virtual reality (VR) and eye-tracking (ET) technologies to objectively analyze attentional biases before and after inducing body dissatisfaction. Hypothesizing that exposure to idealized body images increases dissatisfaction, the study reveals that women, after induction, exhibited longer fixations on areas unrelated to weight, indicating avoidance behavior.

Conducted with 40 women, using VR headsets and a virtual avatar, the study exposes participants to 15 "thin ideal" images. Results, measured through questionnaires and visual analog scales, show decreased body satisfaction and longer fixations on non-weight-related areas post-induction.

The findings confirm the efficacy of VR and ET technologies in objectively assessing body dissatisfaction and attentional biases. Exposure to thin-ideal images heightens dissatisfaction and triggers attentional biases, potentially reflecting short-term avoidance strategies. These results underscore the importance of understanding the complex relationship between body dissatisfaction and attentional biases, providing insights for future research and intervention strategies.

Keywords: Body Image · Body dissatisfaction · Attentional bias · Virtual Reality · Eye-tracking

© The Author(s), under exclusive license to Springer Nature Switzerland AG 2024
J. Y. C. Chen and G. Fragomeni (Eds.): HCII 2024, LNCS 14706, pp. 13–21, 2024.
https://doi.org/10.1007/978-3-031-61041-7_2

1 Introduction

Body image is a perceptual construct involving an individual's thoughts and feelings about their own body. It can be influenced by various factors such as beauty standards, natural and sudden bodily changes during adolescence, sociocultural influence through constant exposure to "ideal thinness" bodies in media [1] and, more recently, through the internet and social media [2]. These factors can lead women to internalize unattainable beauty and thinness ideals, resulting in excessive appearance concerns, social comparisons, and negative self-evaluation.

This heightened dissatisfaction with their bodies can lead to various negative consequences, including depression and anxiety, reduced self-esteem, and an increased risk of developing eating disorders [3, 4]. It is even considered a key symptom in the diagnosis of anorexia nervosa and plays a role in maintaining body image disorders [4]. Dissatisfaction with body image is not limited to individuals with diagnosed eating disorders; it affects a significant proportion of the general population [5]. Furthermore, research has shown that individuals with eating disorders exhibit both body dissatisfaction and attentional bias (AB) related to body size and shape. AB refers to the tendency to pay more attention to some bodily stimuli compared to other stimuli. Several studies suggest that even healthy individuals with high body dissatisfaction may display similar attentional biases, and these biases appear to be mediated by the degree of body dissatisfaction [6–8]. These attentional biases play a role in perpetuating body dissatisfaction [9]. Still, it is unclear whether these biases result from dissatisfaction or whether dissatisfaction arises from the biases. A recent study [10] has identified a causal relationship between body dissatisfaction and body-related attentional bias; however, further research and replications are needed to better delineate the connection between these two variables.

One way to study the potential causal role of body dissatisfaction in attentional bias is to manipulate dissatisfaction and observe its effect on bias. In this study, body dissatisfaction was manipulated by exposing participants to images of "ideal thinness". This induction procedure has been used before in some studies [11], which found that exposure to idealized body images led to decreased body satisfaction compared to a control group. However, previous research relied primarily on self-report questionnaires. By tracking eye movements with eye-tracking (ET) technology, this study aimed to provide more objective and behavioral evidence, thereby enhancing the validity of the procedure and its results. The use of ET in combination with virtual reality (VR) allows for direct and precise measurement of participants' visual patterns regarding body-related stimuli. Previous studies have indicated that eye tracking can reveal differences in fixation durations and latencies towards body images between groups with varying body dissatisfaction [8].

The study aimed to use VR and ET to evaluate attentional biases toward one's body both before and after the induction of body dissatisfaction. It was hypothesized that exposure to idealized body images would increase body dissatisfaction among participants and that, following this dissatisfaction induction, women would look longer at areas of their bodies unrelated to weight, as an avoidance strategy.

2 Method

2.1 Participants

The study was approved by the bioethics committee of the University of Barcelona, and informed consent was obtained from all participants before commencing the study. Initially, a total of 47 women agreed to participate in the study. Participants with recent anxiety disorders or eating disorders, epilepsy, or psychotropic medication use were excluded. After applying the exclusion criteria, seven of them were excluded, and 40 participants were finally included in the study. The mean age was 25.55 years (SD = 3.93, range: 22–40), and the average body mass index (BMI) was 21.93 (SD = 3.41, range: 17.65–33.67).

2.2 Measures and Instruments

HTC Vive Pro Eye headsets, featuring OLED screens and integrated Tobii eye trackers with a gaze data output frequency of 120 Hz and an accuracy range of 0.5–1.1 degrees, were employed as Head Mounted Display (HMD) to capture and record participants' eye movements during the virtual reality experience. VIVE 3.0 trackers were also used for full body tracking.

The virtual environment, created using Unity 3D software, consisted of an empty room and a large mirror positioned at 1.54 m from the participant, where they could see their reflected avatar. A virtual avatar was created using Blender and Unity 3D from a generic model of a Caucasian woman, which could be adjusted for height and body silhouette, as well as hair tone, shirt color, and pants to match those of the participant. This avatar was used to simulate the participant's image reflected in a virtual mirror, enabling the recording of their behavior in looking at different parts of the body.

To induce body dissatisfaction, 15 images representing the "thin ideal" were used. Each image was in color, displayed in full screen for 10 s, and featured women in bikinis, underwear, or body-hugging sportswear. Prior research has shown that this procedure reduces body satisfaction [12, 13]. These images were sourced from public Instagram accounts and Pexels, a free stock photo website. Three researchers independently reviewed a large pool of full-body images of women and selected those that met their subjective criteria for representing the "thin ideal." Afterward, the three sets of selections were compared, and a final set of images was chosen.

Assessing body dissatisfaction involved using a combination of questionnaires and visual analog scales. The Body Image States Scale [14], Spanish version (SBISS) [15], gauges current body dissatisfaction through a set of six 9-point Likert scale items, ranging from 1 (extremely satisfied) to 9 (extremely dissatisfied), with a robust Cronbach's Alpha of 0.92. Visual Analogue Scales (VAS) were utilized also to measure overall body satisfaction, with ratings on a scale from 0 (not satisfied at all) to 100 (very satisfied).

To assess anxiety towards different body parts, the Physical Appearance State and Trait Anxiety Scale (PASTAS) [16] was utilized, consisting of two subscales with 8 items each; one scale assesses anxiety associated with weight-related body areas (PASTAS-W), while the other evaluates anxiety linked to non-weight-related areas (PASTAS-NW).

The items are rated on a 5-point Likert scale, ranging from 0 (not at all) to 4 (extremely). Its Cronbach's Alpha is high, ranging from 0.82 to 0.92.

Assessing attentional bias involved participants gazing at their virtual mirror image for 30 s, with their arms and legs slightly apart (Fig. 1). AB related to the body was evaluated by recording each participant's visual fixations, a behavior involving maintaining gaze at a specific location for at least 100–200 ms. The corrected eye-tracking data were imported into the Open Gaze and Mouse Analyzer (OGAMA) software to calculate, on one hand, the number of fixations (NF), which is the sum of the times each body-related area of interest (AOI) is looked at, and on the other hand, the duration of each visual fixation in each AOI was added to determine the total fixation time (CFT). AOIs were divided into two groups (Fig. 2): those related to weight (W-AOIs: stomach, hips, waist, thighs, and legs) and those unrelated to weight (NW-AOIs: the rest of the body) [17]. The attentional bias scores were calculated by subtracting the number of fixations and the visual fixation time on NW-AOIs from W-AOIs. Consequently, these scores could be positive when the participant's visual attention was predominantly towards W-AOIs or negative when it leaned towards NW-AOIs.

2.3 Procedure

Body dissatisfaction and attentional biases towards the body were assessed before and after the induction of body dissatisfaction.

First, the participants' age, weight, and height were recorded to calculate BMI, and an avatar with the same body silhouette as the participant was created. Subsequently, participants completed the questionnaires. Following this, they were equipped with trackers

Fig. 1. Virtual representation mirroring the participant's reflected image.

and HMD. Within the virtual environment, participants were instructed to gaze at the avatar representing their reflected image in a mirror for 30 s. The recorded data from this observation were then employed to calculate pre-induction measures of attentional bias. Following this task, participants proceeded to complete the VAS scale.

Next, the VR equipment was removed to conduct the body dissatisfaction induction procedure. After the presentation of each photo, participants were encouraged to compare themselves with the models, aiming to enhance the impact of the images [18]. The second round of questionnaire assessments took place, and the VR equipment was reinstated. The post-induction attentional bias measure was recorded using the same procedure as before, followed by the completion of the VAS scale. Ultimately, all VR equipment was removed, marking the conclusion of the study. A debriefing was conducted to alleviate any residual discomfort that the induction of body dissatisfaction might have caused to the participant.

The comparison of measures obtained before and after the induction of body dissatisfaction was conducted using Student's t-tests.

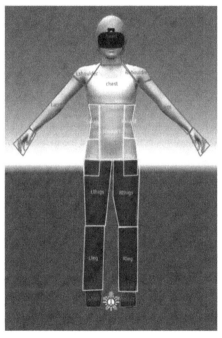

Fig. 2. Visual depiction of weight-related areas of Interest (highlighted in yellow) and non-weight related Areas of Interest (highlighted in blue) on the virtual avatar.

3 Results

Differences were observed between pre- and post-induction measures in the administered body dissatisfaction assessments, SBISS and VAS (see Tables 1 and 2). Specifically, a decrease in body satisfaction was noted in both measures after the induction, confirming the successful implementation of the body dissatisfaction induction procedure and achieving the anticipated effect. Additionally, differences were found between pre- and post-induction measures in body-related anxiety. A decrease in anxiety was observed in non-weight-related areas after the induction (PASTAS-NW), and no differences were observed in anxiety toward weight-related areas (PASTAS-W). In the VAS measures there is a sample of 37 individuals instead of 40, due to technical issues.

Table 1. Means (and standard deviations) of the body dissatisfaction (SBISS), satisfaction (VAS) and anxiety (PASTAS) measures before (pre) and after (post) the induction of body dissatisfaction.

Measure (N)	Pre	Post
SBISS (40)	5.45 (1.4)	5.56 (1.35)
VAS body satisfaction (37)	68.71 (23.25)	61.42 (25.67)
PASTAS-W (40)	4.1 (3.66)	4.4 (3.64)
PASTAS-NW (40)	2.35 (2.88)	1.85 (2.28)

Table 2. Significance of the observed differences in the body dissatisfaction (SBISS), satisfaction (VAS) and anxiety (PASTAS) measures before and after the induction of body dissatisfaction.

Measure (N)	Student's t-test (p)	r
SBISS (40)	2.67 (.011) *	.12
VAS body satisfaction (37)	3.06 (.004) *	.14
PASTAS-W (40)	−1.22 (.23)	.06
PASTAS-NW (40)	2.13 (.04) *	.10

Similarly, differences were found between the pre- and post-induction measures of visual attention. Specifically, longer fixation durations (CFT) were observed toward body areas not related to weight after the induction of body dissatisfaction. No differences were observed in the number of visual fixations (NF) (Tables 3 and 4).

Table 3. Means (and standard deviations) of the eye-tracking measures before (pre) and after (post) the induction of body dissatisfaction.

Measure (N)	Pre	Post
CFT (40)	−546 (5624.31)	−2429.25 (6041.69)
NF (40)	−1.45 (11.64)	−3.62 (10.92)

Table 4. Significance of the observed differences in the eye-tracking measures obtained before (pre) and after (post) the induction of body dissatisfaction.

Measure (N)	Student's t-test (p)	r
CFT (40)	2.03 (.04)*	.09
NF (40)	1.15 (.26)	.05

4   Discussion

Body image, the way individuals perceive and feel about their bodies, is shaped by various factors like societal standards, cultural influences, and exposure to idealized body images in media. This dissatisfaction with one's body can have negative consequences, impacting mental well-being and increasing the risk of developing eating disorders. Attentional bias, the tendency to focus more on some bodily stimuli, is linked to body dissatisfaction and plays a role in its persistence. While there's evidence of a causal relationship between body dissatisfaction and attentional bias, further research is required to fully understand this connection. To investigate the potential influence of body dissatisfaction on attentional bias, this study manipulated body dissatisfaction by exposing participants to images portraying an "ideal thinness" standard. Unlike previous research relying on self-reported measures, this study utilized eye tracking technology along with virtual reality for more objective and behavioral insights, enabling precise measurement of participants' visual patterns regarding body-related stimuli. The study aimed to assess attentional biases toward one's body before and after inducing dissatisfaction, hypothesizing that exposure to idealized body images would heighten dissatisfaction, leading to increased visual attention to areas unrelated to weight as a coping mechanism.

Consistent with findings in previous studies [10], the obtained results indicate that exposure to images reflecting the thinness ideal is a valid procedure for inducing dissatisfaction with one's body, and this dissatisfaction leads to an increase in attentional biases towards the body. Specifically, there is an increase in the time spent observing areas of one's body unrelated to weight. Additionally, we found that the induction of dissatisfaction has the effect of reducing anxiety experienced in relation to non-weight-related body areas. These two observations suggest that the attentional bias resulting from increased body dissatisfaction serves as a protective mechanism, aiming to reduce anxiety towards the body. Similar results have been found in other studies [19–22]. In contrast, some studies have presented different findings, proposing that greater dissatisfaction is linked to heightened focus on body areas perceived as unattractive [23]. The inconsistency in these results may be attributed to various factors discussed in a prior publication [10] and may be related to differences among participants in various studies, as some investigate patients with eating disorders while others involve healthy individuals.

In conclusion, these results demonstrate that the combination of virtual reality and eye-tracking technologies provides a valid method for assessing body dissatisfaction and attentional biases toward the body. These biases, particularly toward non-weight-related areas, appear to reflect defensive or avoidance behaviors, which may have a short-term protective effect but could potentially lead to negative long-term effects by hindering the habituation of anxiety associated with increased body dissatisfaction. These findings support the idea that an escalation in body dissatisfaction is linked to the development of attentional biases. The increased dissatisfaction appears to heighten sensitivity to appearance-related cues, leading to a deliberate avoidance of focusing attention on perceived flaws. However, the relationship between body dissatisfaction and attentional biases is intricate, and there's a potential for this connection to be bidirectional, contributing to a complex interplay between the two variables; therefore, further research is needed to delve into this topic.

Acknowledgments. This study was funded by "Fundació La Marató de TV3", Grant 202217-10.

Disclosure of Interests. The authors have no competing interests to declare that are relevant to the content of this article.

References

1. House, T., et al.: Is body dissatisfaction related to an attentional bias towards low weight bodies in non-clinical samples of women? A systematic review and meta-analysis. Body Image **44**, 103–119 (2023). https://doi.org/10.1016/j.bodyim.2022.12.003
2. Fardouly, J., Vartanian, L.R.: Social media and body image concerns: current research and future directions. Curr. Opin. Psychol. **9**, 1–5 (2016). https://doi.org/10.1016/j.copsyc.2015.09.005
3. Uchôa, F.N.M., et al.: Influence of the mass media and body dissatisfaction on the risk in adolescents of developing eating disorders. Int. J. Environ. Res. Publ. Health **16**(9), 1508 (2019)
4. Cerea, S., Doron, G., Manoli, T., Patania, F., Bottesi, G., Ghisi, M.: Cognitive training via a mobile application to reduce some forms of body dissatisfaction in young females at high-risk for body image disorders: a randomized controlled trial. Body Image **42**, 297–306 (2022). https://doi.org/10.1016/j.bodyim.2022.07.010
5. Timko, C.A., Juarascio, A.S., Martin, L.M., Faherty, A., Kalodner, C.: Body image avoidance: an under-explored yet important factor in the relationship between body image dissatisfaction and disordered eating. J. Contextual Behav. Sci. **3**(3), 203–211 (2014). https://doi.org/10.1016/j.jcbs.2014.01.002
6. Porras-Garcia, B., et al.: Body-related attentional bias as mediator of the relationship between body mass index and body dissatisfaction. Eur. Eat. Disord. Rev. **28**(4), 454–464 (2020). https://doi.org/10.1002/erv.2730

7. Meschberger-Annweiler, F.-A., et al.: An attentional bias modification task, through virtual reality and eye-tracking technologies, to enhance the treatment of anorexia nervosa. J. Clin. Med. **12**(6), 2185 (2023). https://doi.org/10.3390/jcm12062185

8. Cass, J., Giltrap, G., Talbot, D.: Female body dissatisfaction and attentional bias to body images evaluated using visual search. Front. Psychol. (2020). https://doi.org/10.3389/fpsyg.2019.02821

9. Talbot, D., Smith, E., Cass, J.: Male body dissatisfaction, eating disorder symptoms, body composition, and attentional bias to body stimuli evaluated using visual search. J. Exp. Psychopathol. **10**(2), 204380871984829 (2019). https://doi.org/10.1177/2043808719848292

10. Mendoza-Medialdea, M.T., et al.: Body dissatisfaction and body-related attentional bias: is there a causal relationship? J. Clin. Med. **12**(17), 5659 (2023). https://doi.org/10.3390/jcm12175659. MDPI AG

11. Carter, J.J., Vartanian, L.R.: Self-concept clarity and appearance-based social comparison to idealized bodies. Body Image **40**, 124–130 (2022). https://doi.org/10.1016/j.bodyim.2021.12.001

12. Slater, A., Cole, N., Fardouly, J.: The effect of exposure to parodies of thin-ideal images on young women's body image and mood. Body Image **29**, 82–89 (2019). https://doi.org/10.1016/j.bodyim.2019.03.001

13. Prefit, A.B., Cândea, D.M., Szentagotai-Tătar, A.: Effects of acceptance and reappraisal on body dissatisfaction: an experimental comparison of two adaptive emotion regulation strategies. Eat. Weight Disord. **25**(3), 803–809 (2020). https://doi.org/10.1007/s40519-019-00691-y

14. Cash, T.F., Fleming, E.C., Alindogan, J., Steadman, L., Whitehead, A.: Beyond body image as a trait: the development and validation of the body image states scale. Eat. Disord. **10**(2), 103–113 (2002). https://doi.org/10.1080/10640260290081678

15. Mebarak Chams, M., et al.: The Spanish body image state scale: factor structure, reliability and validity in a Colombian population. Front. Psychol. (2019). https://doi.org/10.3389/fpsyg.2019.02553

16. Reed, D.L., Kevin Thompson, J., Brannick, M.T., Sacco, W.P.: Development and validation of the physical appearance state and trait anxiety scale (PASTAS). J. Anxiety Disord. **5**(4), 323–332 (1991)

17. Porras-Garcia, B., et al.: An-vr-be. A randomized controlled trial for reducing fear of gaining weight and other eating disorder symptoms in anorexia nervosa through virtual reality-based body exposure. J. Clin. Med. **10**(4), 1–23 (2021). https://doi.org/10.3390/jcm10040682

18. Mills, J.S., Polivy, J., Herman, C.P., Tiggemann, M.: Effects of exposure to thin media images: evidence of self-enhancement among restrained eaters. Pers. Soc. Psychol. Bull. **28**(12), 1687–1699 (2002). https://doi.org/10.1177/014616702237650

19. Janelle, C.M., Hausenblas, H.A., Ellis, R., Coombes, S.A., Duley, A.R.: The time course of attentional allocation while women high and low in body dissatisfaction view self and model physiques. Psychol. Health **24**, 351–366 (2009)

20. von Wietersheim, J., Kunzl, F., Hoffmann, H., Glaub, J., Rottler, E., Traue, H.C.: Selective attention of patients with anorexia nervosa while looking at pictures of their own body and the bodies of others: an exploratory study. Psychosom. Med. **74**, 107–113 (2012)

21. Warschburger, P., Calvano, C., Richter, E.M., Engbert, R.: Analysis of attentional bias towards attractive and unattractive body regions among overweight males and females: an eye-movement study. PLoS ONE **10**, e0140813 (2015)

22. Lykins, A.D., Ferris, T., Graham, C.A.: Body region dissatisfaction predicts attention to body regions on other women. Body Image **11**, 404–408 (2014)

23. Rodgers, R.F., DuBois, R.H.: Cognitive biases to appearance-related stimuli in body dissatisfaction: a systematic review. Clin. Psychol. Rev. **46**, 1–11 (2016)

Bridging Tradition and Innovation: Exploring the Factors Influencing Students' Intention to Use Metaverse Technology for Chinese Calligraphy Learning

Yang Li[1] 🆔, Zhuoning He[1], and Yi Yang[2]([✉]) 🆔

[1] Department of Culture and Arts Management, Honam University,
Gwangju 62399, South Korea
[2] School of Art, Soochow University, Suzhou 215000, China
youngyear368@gmail.com

Abstract. With the continuous development of metaverse technology, various innovative ideas have been brought to traditional teaching methods. However, there is little attention paid to the impact and effectiveness of metaverse technology on university students' art curriculum learning. Therefore, The Technology Perception Experience (TPE) model was applied to investigate university students' willingness to use metaverse technology in a virtual reality environment. The research findings indicate that the technology perception experience, composed of perceived vividness, perceived interactivity, perceived novelty, and immersion, positively impacts Chinese university students' intrinsic and extrinsic motivation (perceived enjoyment and perceived usefulness) for learning. Additionally, there is a significant correlation between the intrinsic and extrinsic motivation of university students using metaverse technology for Chinese calligraphy learning and their willingness to use it. Furthermore, the research results prove that gender has a conditional effect between perceived enjoyment and perceived usefulness. These empirical findings provide valuable insights and implications for understanding the factors influencing Chinese university students' use of metaverse technology and exploring practical directions for development.

Keywords: Metaverse · Chinese calligraphy teaching · Virtual · TPE

1 Introduction

The preservation and development of intangible cultural heritage have become a globally significant concern [1]. Governments worldwide must enhance their awareness of the significance of intangible cultural heritage, especially when it comes to promoting it among the younger generation [2]. In 2009, Chinese calligraphy was inscribed in UNESCO's Representative List of the Intangible Cultural Heritage of Humanity [3]. While traditional culture gradually diminishes [4], people's attention to intangible cultural heritage has been on the decline. Incorporating intangible cultural heritage education into school curricula has become a crucial means of preserving and transmitting

© The Author(s), under exclusive license to Springer Nature Switzerland AG 2024
J. Y. C. Chen and G. Fragomeni (Eds.): HCII 2024, LNCS 14706, pp. 22–43, 2024.
https://doi.org/10.1007/978-3-031-61041-7_3

cultural heritage [5, 6]. Furthermore, intangible cultural heritage education can enhance students' understanding and interest in cultural heritage [7].

College students cannot avoid using technology for learning [8]. As a result, Chinese calligraphy courses can be improved using methods that integrate with new technologies to enhance students' learning experience and effectiveness. Based on previous research on new technology applications in education. For instance, using FPV drones can enhance students' experience of real environments and increase their interest in learning [9]. Students using of augmented reality in basic design courses can increase their immersion and learning intentions [10]. With the help of virtual reality technology, students can interact with concepts and objects visually and digitally, which effectively improves their learning outcomes in the context of active learning [11]. Using new technologies can significantly enhance the learning experience and thus stimulate students' willingness to continue learning [12]. In recent years, there has been an increase in research on using metaverse technology in education. Verified through an extended technology acceptance model that metaverse technology provides a new learning experience for teaching basketball that enhances the student's flow experience, thereby improving intention and effectiveness of learning [13]. In addition, the intention to use the Metaverse Education Platform plays an essential role in promoting and applying Metaverse technology in education [14].

However, there is no research on integrating Chinese calligraphy courses with metaverse technology. Metaverse Calligraphy, as an emerging form of calligraphy teaching, overcomes some of the limitations of traditional Chinese calligraphy teaching, especially the limitations of scenarios. Furthermore, teaching Metaverse Calligraphy can provide the same interactive experience as traditional Chinese calligraphy courses, enabling students to have a more authentically engaging learning experience. Although traditional teaching methods are still widely used in art courses, they have revealed some limitations as students' learning needs continue to increase. This study examines the possibility of integrating art instruction with metaverse technology. Additionally, it assesses the applicability of Metaverse Technology in a Chinese calligraphy courses and examines students' intention to use the technology. Simultaneously, this research serves as a valuable reference for scholars interested in integrating metaverse technology into art courses.

This study investigates the factors influencing Chinese college students' intention to use metaverse technology in Chinese calligraphy courses. This research analyzes the influential relationships between the technology perceptual experience, perceived enjoyment, perceived usefulness, and intention to use. Based on the previous studies, a new structural equation model and targeted recommendations for teaching metaverse calligraphy are proposed. In addition, Gender plays a significant role in influencing the application of technology [15], which considers it a moderator and explores the conditional effect of gender on the pathway. This study explores novel approaches to art teaching and offers design suggestions and references for integrating metaverse technology in art education.

2 Literature Review

2.1 Metaverse

The metaverse concept first appeared in Snow Crash, a science fiction novel published by an American novelist in 1992 [16]. Metaverse is a virtual community created using artificial intelligence, the Internet of Things, blockchain, video games, and high-speed internet technology [17]. Metaverse wearables are being perfected with the development of technologies such as VR and AR. In the metaverse, participants can achieve a high level of interactivity and immersion through devices such as VR glasses [18]. The educational field is experiencing a growing integration of metaverse technology, merging learning with virtual environments to create an immersive and authentic educational experience for participants [19].

2.2 Research on the Education of the Metaverse

Metaverse technology holds significant importance in the education field. While there is currently no independent reference application, related technologies and applications have demonstrated initial promise, showcasing its potential impact. Exceptional human-computer interaction and the integration of virtual reality technology enable real-time interaction with avatars, particularly in education and medicine. Augmented reality technology, in particular, enhances live online interactions, providing vivid and tangible experiences, and opening new possibilities for teaching [20, 21]. In education, the metaverse is gradually moving towards artificial intelligence. Students experience actual classroom elements in a virtual classroom, which is far more engaging than traditional online learning [22]. Additionally, Kye et al. applied metaverse technology to educational learning, which increased students' creativity and autonomy [23]. Wang et al. identified the advantages of the Metaverse Education Platform, which include ease of use, usefulness, contextualized teaching, personalized learning, and social needs, based on their investigation of users' intentions to use the platform. [24]. These results provide strong empirical support for the diffusion of metaverse technology in education. It is worth emphasizing that, with economic and technological development, metaverse technology is bound to reach its full potential [25].

2.3 Chinese Calligraphy Instructions

The purpose of teaching Chinese calligraphy is to enable students to understand the basics of calligraphy, the characteristics of calligraphic works of different periods and writing methods through the guidance of educators [26]. As art courses are improving with the times, art teachers are combining virtual reality technology with teaching Chinese Calligraphy to enhance the learning and teaching quality of Chinese Calligraphy courses through online learning media [27]. The Learning to Apply Media project significantly improved students' basic skills [28]. Additionally, combining play activities with instruction can effectively promote learning in middle school students while enhancing technical skills and personal performance [29]. Therefore, developing digital resources for teaching Chinese calligraphy has become an indispensable part of calligraphy education.

2.4   Perceived Vividness (PV)

Perceived vividness (PV) refers to the extent to which the technology is useful in creating a sensory media environment [30]. High vividness enhances the user's realistic experience [31]. Rich media design details can enliven the learning environment. In human-computer interaction, vividness positively impacts users' search and sharing behaviors [32]. Students may be more likely to achieve more active learning through HCI learning methods [9]. In this study, we used perceived vividness to assess the reality of the experience produced by the metaverse Chinese calligraphy courses in communicating the learning content to the students.

2.5   Perceived Interactivity (PI)

Perceived Interactivity (PI) is defined as the set of behaviors that humans exhibit when interacting with the environment, objects, or other people [33]. These interactional behaviors can affect the user's personal experience [34], making them an essential determinant of user behaviors [35]. Several studies have shown the impact of real-time interactive experiences in online environments on users' perceived interactivity [36]. Real-time interactive expertise refers to the interactive activities the user performs instantaneously, including the information exchange process, technical features, and user perception [37]. In this study, Perceived Interactivity (PI) refers to the psychological state experienced by users during their interaction with the Metaverse Chinese Calligraphy courses.

2.6   Perceived Novelty (PN)

Perceived novelty (PN) describes the user's perception of the technology as intriguing, novel, and distinct from what they have previously encountered or comprehended [38]. The perceived novelty of users has a significant impact on their technology acceptance [39]. Research has shown that when users experience new technologies, they may have a strong emotional response, including emotional experiences such as excitement, curiosity, and pleasure [40]. Innovations in learning styles are of great significance to the field of education, and by introducing new learning styles, educators can better satisfy students' interest in learning to stimulate their active participation [9]. In our study, perceived novelty (PN) refers to students' psychological experience of using metaverse technology for Chinese calligraphy courses that differs from traditional teaching methods.

2.7   Immersion (IM)

Immersion (IM) is the degree to which a virtual system engages the user's full attention in integrating into the virtual environment [41]. It is widely recognized as an essential factor in the gaming experience [30], and a key fulfillment goal in the information services domain [42]. Immersion is an emotional experience when a user interacts with a technology or service, allowing them to feel as if they are truly immersed in the virtual environment and energetically engaged [43]. In our study, immersion (IM) is defined as students' emotional experience when using metaverse technology for Chinese calligraphy courses.

2.8 Perceived Enjoyment (PE)

Perceived Enjoyment (PE) is defined as the degree to which a user's experience with a particular technology or service is pleasant [44]. Perceived enjoyment (PE) is considered to be one of the essential factors influencing the adoption of technology by users [45]. Online learning engages and motivates students to actively participate by providing exciting and interactive features that make learning activities more fun and pleasant [46]. Particularly noteworthy is the use of virtual reality technology in education to create immersive student learning experiences. Students perceived enjoyment of virtual reality technology experiences positively impacts learning outcomes [47]. Enjoyment plays an essential role in the use of technology. It emphasizes the user's focus on self-actualizing values and experiencing personal happiness and enjoyment rather than merely pursuing the utility of technological tools [48]. Accordingly, perceived enjoyment (PE) was defined in our study as students' intrinsic motivation in using the metaverse technology for Chinese Calligraphy learning.

2.9 Perceived Usefulness (PU)

Perceived usefulness (PU) is a critical concept in TAM [43]. It refers to the extent to which users help the information system in their work or study [49]. Perceived usefulness has an important role in the intention of U.S. residents to use innovative technology [50]. Therefore, it is an important factor influencing user acceptance and use of the system. In our study, PU is an extrinsic motivation defined as the degree to which the students evaluate whether using metauniverse technology improves their academic performance and efficiency.

2.10 Behavioral Intention (BI)

Behavioral Intention (BI) is the extent to which a user consciously decides on the specific future behavior of an individual [51]. When assessing the success factors of a service or product, behavioral intention is considered to be one of the important indicators [52]. Previous research has found that after completing an online course, students' online interactive behaviors significantly influence their willingness to engage further in online learning [53]. This paper investigates the behavioral intention of university students to use metaverse technology in Chinese calligraphy course learning.

3 Methods

An online survey was conducted with participants who had comparable experiences with interactive education through the Internet. This study did not involve the interactive teaching of subjects in an offline setting and therefore did not involve the process of human-computer interaction or healthcare-related ethical issues. Therefore, there is no statement applicable to institutional review boards. In Sect. 3.1, we first explain the rationale for the research question. In Sect. 3.2, we present the hypotheses about users' use of metaverse technology for the Chinese Calligraphy courses. Section 3.3 provides a description of the research study participants, and in Sect. 3.4, we present our ideas regarding the questionnaire design.

3.1 Research Subject

This study aims to investigate the determinants of Chinese college students' intention to use metaverse technology for calligraphy instruction. The study employed structural equation modeling to analyze the relationships between these factors. The questionnaire included an introduction to potential forms of future engagement with metaverse calligraphy, including videos of metaverse concepts and videos of current metaverse resources related to calligraphy. This paper investigates the determinants of students' intention to use metaverse technology in calligraphy courses, focusing on undergraduate art students enrolled in calligraphy courses.

College students possessing fundamental knowledge of metaverse-related products and technological expertise are more likely to make objective evaluations. Additionally, since calligraphy courses are exclusively offered to art majors, respondents from this major will have more exposure to calligraphy courses than those from other majors. Moreover, due to the objective factors of COVID-19, Chinese college students have gained considerable experience with online courses in recent years, allowing for more insightful comparisons upon their engagement with the Metaverse Calligraphy Education Project. Consequently, we selected Chinese college students majoring in art as our research participants.

3.2 Hypothesis Deduction

Figure 1 illustrates the research hypothesis proposed in this study. Research has shown that User immersion during interaction affects perceived enjoyment, perceived usefulness [40]. At the same time, perceived vividness, perceived interactivity, and perceived novelty also affect perceived enjoyment and perceived usefulness [54]. These four factors mainly influence the perception of an interactive product in interactive technology [40]. Thus, in the case of interaction products, a potential second-order construct may be added to these four variables. This second-order model relationship was validated using second-order validated factor analyses. Interactive technologies can have a positive impact on consumers, including positive perceived enjoyment and perceived usefulness [55]. Interactive teaching through metaverse technology allows students to have a learning experience different from traditional education. Therefore, we named the second-order construct the Technology Perception Experience Model. In summary, we propose the following hypothesis:

Hypothesis 1. Technological Perceptual Experience positively influences college students' perceived enjoyment when using metaverse technology for learning Chinese calligraphy.

Hypothesis 2. Technological Perceptual Experience positively influences college students' Perceived usefulness when using metaverse technology for learning Chinese calligraphy.

Perceived enjoyment is crucial in teaching as an essential support for learning [56]. According to previous research, perceived usefulness is positively influenced by students' perceived enjoyment [57]. It has been found that in self-directed learning, students' levels of perceived enjoyment are positively correlated with their levels of perceived usefulness [46]. Therefore, we propose the following hypothesis:

Hypothesis 3. Perceived enjoyment positively influences college students' Perceived usefulness in using metaverse technology for learning Chinese calligraphy.

Learning Chinese Calligraphy is a long-term cumulative process, and students need to maintain a continuous intention to learn throughout the course. Research has shown that when using sports-branded apps, consumers' perceived enjoyment positively influences use intention [58]. In informal English language learning, students' perceived enjoyment positively impacts their intention to use Chinese Web 2.0 tools [59]. In addition, one factor affecting behavioral intentions in learning from the curriculum is perceived usefulness [13]. Learning behavioral intentions were influenced by students' perceived usefulness during the use of the virtual classroom [14]. Therefore, we propose the following hypothesis:

Hypothesis 4. Perceived enjoyment positively influences college students' behavioral intention to use metaverse technology for learning Chinese calligraphy.

Hypothesis 5. Perceived usefulness positively influences college students' behavioral intention to use metaverse technology for learning Chinese calligraphy.

Additionally, to the above research hypotheses, this study tested the effect of using gender as a moderating variable on the model paths.

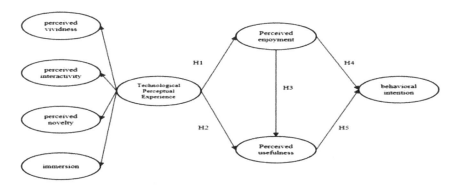

Fig. 1. Hypothetical model.

3.3 Demographic Characteristics

The results are shown in Table 1. The questionnaires were collected between April 2023 and June 2023 through online responses. All participants completed the questionnaire voluntarily and with full awareness. The study collected a total of 512 samples, from which 311 valid samples were obtained after excluding 201 invalid samples, resulting in an effective recovery rate of 60.74%. This study satisfies the maximum likelihood method proposed by Jackson, where the ratio of estimated parameters to the sample size (p:n) is greater than 1:10 [60]. And the data were counted with a valid sample of 311 undergraduate art students from Eastern, Middle, Northeastern, Western, Hong Kong, Macao and Taiwan regions of China. Among them, 105 were male students and 206 were female students.

Table 1. Basic information of interviewees.

Sample	Category	Number	Percentage
Gender	Male	105	33.8
	Female	206	66.2
Hometown	Eastern Region	97	31.2
	Middle Region	79	25.4
	Western Region	113	36.3
	Northeast Region	20	6.4
	Hong Kong, Macao, and Taiwan regions	2	0.6

3.4 Questionnaire Design

The questionnaire in this study is constructed using validated items from previous research and has been translated into Chinese. A seven-point Likert scale was employed, ranging from 1 (strongly disagree) to 7 (strongly agree). The questions in Table 2 were adapted to align with the intentions of college students learning Chinese Calligraphy through the Metaverse.

Table 2. Questionnaire composition.

Constructs	Coding	Item	Source
perceived vividness	PV1	The Chinese calligraphy visual display through the metaverse technology was clear	[54]
	PV2	The Chinese calligraphy visual display through the metaverse technology was detailed	
	PV3	The Chinese calligraphy visual display through the metaverse technology was vivid	
	PV4	The Chinese calligraphy visual display through the metaverse technology was well-defined	
perceived interactivity	PI1	I feel that I can take control of calligraphy learning through metaverse technology	[54]
	PI2	In my studies of Chinese calligraphy, I feel in some control of the metaverse technology that I wanted to learn	
	PI3	The metaverse technology had the ability to respond to my calligraphy learning needs quickly and efficiently	
perceived novelty	PN1	I found learning Chinese calligraphy using the metaverse technology to be a novel experience	[61]
	PN2	In my studies of Chinese calligraphy, Using the metaverse technology is new and refreshing	

(continued)

Table 2. (*continued*)

Constructs	Coding	Item	Source
	PN3	In my studies of Chinese calligraphy, Using the metaverse technology is a neat and novel way to learn	
immersion	IM1	Learning to Chinese calligraphy using the metaverse technology may cause me to lose focus on what is going on around me	[40], [62]
	IM2	With the use of metaverse technology, I expect I will lose my sense of time and feel like time flies when I learn Chinese calligraphy	
	IM3	When I learn Chinese calligraphy through the use of metaverse technology, I anticipate being very focused	
perceived enjoyment	PE1	I find using the metaverse technology on Chinese calligraphy learning to be enjoyable	[63]
	PE2	The process of using the metaverse technology on Chinese calligraphy learning is pleasant	
	PE3	In my studies of Chinese calligraphy, I have fun using the metaverse technology	
perceived usefulness	PU1	In my studies of Chinese calligraphy, I find the metaverse technology to be extremely helpful	[64]
	PU2	My studies in Chinese calligraphy have been enhanced by the use of metaverse technology	
	PU3	My Chinese calligraphy studies are facilitated by the use of metaverse technology	
behavioral intention	BI1	In the future, I intend to continue using metaverse technology for Chinese calligraphy learning	[65]
	BI2	My daily life will always involve using metaverse technology for the purpose of learning Chinese calligraphy	
	BI3	It is my intention to continue using metaverse technology for Chinese calligraphy studies on a regular basis	

4   Results

4.1   Research Subject

Table 3 describes the test results. Descriptive tests of the items showed that all aspects had a skewness of less than 3 and a kurtosis of less than 8 [66]. Therefore, the normal distribution assumption is satisfied and make it suitable for further analysis.

Table 3. Description of the test results

Constructs	Mean	S.D	Skewness	Kurtosis
PV	5.117	0.882	−0.572	1.115
PI	5.552	0.797	−0.493	0.254
PV	5.259	0.953	−0.588	1.366
PN	5.033	0.926	−0.511	0.634
IM	5.417	1.069	−0.564	0.685
PE	4.656	1.124	−0.491	0.236
PU	5.056	0.981	−0.342	1.091
BI	5.117	0.882	−0.572	1.115

4.2 Reliability Analysis

Table 4 presents the validation of the data using Cronbach's alpha and CITC in this study. The CITC for all aspects exceeded 0.5, and the Cronbach's alpha reliability coefficient surpassed 0.7, indicating high effectiveness. Thus, the scales utilized in this study exhibit internal consistency and are suitable for further analyses.

Table 4. Results of reliability analysis.

Items	Corrected Item Total Correlation	Cronbach's Alpha If Item Deleted	Cronbach's Alpha	Items	Corrected Item Total Correlation	Cronbach's Alpha If Item Deleted	Cronbach's Alpha
PV1	0.660	0.775	0.827	IM1	0.642	0.723	0.797
PV2	0.712	0.753		IM2	0.669	0.691	
PV3	0.606	0.802		IM3	0.612	0.749	
PV4	0.629	0.789		PE1	0.821	0.874	0.912
				PE2	0.861	0.840	
PI1	0.672	0.742	0.815	PE3	0.786	0.903	
PI2	0.719	0.692		PU1	0.764	0.779	0.861
PI3	0.617	0.797		PU2	0.717	0.819	
				PU3	0.727	0.812	
PN1	0.843	0.822	0.901	BI1	0.751	0.891	0.897
PN2	0.797	0.862		BI2	0.848	0.806	
PN3	0.77	0.887		BI3	0.792	0.857	

4.3 Exploratory Factor Analysis

Table 5 shows the results of the exploratory factor analysis. Exploratory factor analysis was performed in this study using SPSS 26.0, with a KMO value of greater than 0.7 for each construct, and a significance of significantly less than 0.05 for the Barlett's test of sphericity. As a result, exploratory factor analyses could be conducted [67]. Commonality, more significant than 0.5 for each construct, indicates a high degree of overlap, factor loadings greater than 0.6, and only one new factor with an eigenvalue more significant than one was identified, showing high-quality constructs [68].

Table 5. Exploratory factor analysis

Constructs	KMO	Bartlett's Sphere Test	Items	Commonality	Factor Loading	Eigenvalue	Total Variation Explained
PV	0.796	0.000	PV1	0.670	0.818	2.636	65.901%
			PV2	0.731	0.855		
			PV3	0.600	0.775		
			PV4	0.635	0.797		
PI	0.701	0.000	PI1	0.735	0.857	2.192	73.070%
			PI2	0.783	0.885		
			PI3	0.675	0.821		
PN	0.739	0.000	PN1	0.873	0.934	2.505	83.498%
			PN2	0.831	0.911		
			PN3	0.802	0.895		
IM	0.706	0.000	IM1	0.713	0.844	2.135	71.157%
			IM2	0.740	0.860		
			IM3	0.681	0.825		
PE	0.742	0.000	PE1	0.849	0.922	2.550	85.003%
			PE2	0.886	0.941		
			PE3	0.815	0.903		
PU	0.732	0.000	PU1	0.810	0.900	2.348	78.282%
			PU2	0.764	0.874		
			PU3	0.774	0.880		
BI	0.726	0.000	BI1	0.784	0.885	2.488	82.929%
			BI2	0.878	0.937		
			BI3	0.826	0.909		

4.4 Confirmatory Factor Analysis (CFA)

Table 6 shows the confirmatory factor analysis results. The variables in this study are correlated with each other, fulfilling the premise of path analysis. All the fitted values of the model are within the recommended range and hence the model is well fitted [69].

Table 7 shows that, Standardized factor loadings greater than 0.6, SMC greater than 0.4, significant p-value, reliability of the studied structural components (CR) greater than 0.7 and Average Variance Extracted (AVE) greater than 0.5 indicate that the construct has good convergent validity [69].

Table 8 displays the results of the discriminant validity analysis. The square root of each construct's AVE exceeds its correlation coefficient with the other constructs, affirming the good discriminant validity for each construct [69].

Table 6. Adaptation indices of the CFA model.

Common indices	χ^2	df	χ^2/df	RMSEA	GFI	IFI	CFI	TLI	SRMR
Judgment criteria			<3	<0.08	>0.9	>0.9	>0.9	>0.9	<0.08
Value	313.547	188	1.668	0.046	0.918	0.970	0.970	0.963	0.038

As shown in Table 9. This study conducted a second-order confirmatory factor analysis (CFA) on the model. The aim was to determine whether the application of metaverse technology in Chinese calligraphy has the potential to generate second-order effects on perceptual antecedent variables such as Perceived vividness, Perceived interactivity, Perceived novelty, and immersion. Based on the first-order confirmatory factor analysis (CFA), there is a high level of correlation among the four constructs, which also indicates the effectiveness of the second-order constructs [69].

4.5 Results of the Structural Equation Model

As shown in Table 11. The research model was validated by SEM. The research model has been correctly constructed and a standard fit has been achieved [69], $\chi^2/df = 1.700$, GFI = 0.913, IFI = 0.967, CFI = 0.966, RMSEA = 0.048, SRMR = 0.052.

As shown in Table 12, this study employs the Maximum Likelihood Similarity method to estimate the direct and indirect effects of various dimensions. Specifically, PE exhibits a significant direct influence on PU (ß = 0.136, p = 0.040). Furthermore, BI is directly influenced by both PE (ß = 0.437, p = 0.000) and PU (ß = 0.345, p = 0.000). The findings of this research indicate a positive causal relationship among college students learning Chinese calligraphy using metaverse technology, with PE, PU, and BI. Additionally, TPE has a direct and positive impact on both PE (ß = 0.465, p = 0.000) and PU (ß = 0.461, p = 0.001). Furthermore, TPE indirectly and positively influences BI (ß = 0.384, p = 0.000).

Table 7. CFA convergent validity.

Constructs	Items	Std	p value	SMC	AVE	CR
PV	PV1	0.735	0.001	0.540	0.549	0.829
	PV2	0.820	0.001	0.672		
	PV3	0.676	0.001	0.457		
	PV4	0.726	0.001	0.527		
PI	PI1	0.810	0.001	0.656	0.600	0.818
	PI2	0.818	0.001	0.669		
	PI3	0.690	0.001	0.476		
PN	PN1	0.899	0.001	0.808	0.756	0.903
	PN2	0.876	0.001	0.767		
	PN3	0.833	0.001	0.694		
IM	IM1	0.726	0.001	0.527	0.567	0.797
	IM2	0.778	0.001	0.605		
	IM3	0.755	0.001	0.570		
PE	PE1	0.879	0.001	0.773	0.778	0.913
	PE2	0.933	0.001	0.870		
	PE3	0.831	0.001	0.691		
PU	PU1	0.853	0.001	0.676	0.676	0.862
	PU2	0.790	0.001	0.624		
	PU3	0.822	0.001	0.728		
BI	BI1	0.812	0.001	0.857	0.751	0.900
	BI2	0.926	0.001	0.659		
	BI3	0.858	0.001	0.736		

Table 8. Discriminant validity.

Constructs	PV	PI	PN	IM	PE	PU	BI
PV	0.741						
PI	0.667	0.775					
PN	0.615	0.739	0.869				
IM	0.573	0.649	0.743	0.753			
PE	0.372	0.441	0.347	0.368	0.882		
PU	0.342	0.437	0.422	0.494	0.351	0.822	
BI	0.369	0.419	0.385	0.471	0.556	0.490	0.867

This research examines the moderating effect of gender. Table 12 presents the results of multiple group comparisons, indicating significant gender differences in one path: the impact of PE on PU, with no significant moderating effects in other paths. This suggests that male students are more sensitive to perceived enjoyment than female students.

Table 9. Assessment of second-order perceived coolness construct.

Second-order construct	First-order constructs[2]	Outer weights	p-values
Technology Perception Experience	Perceived vividness	0.727^{***}	0.000
	Perceived interactivity	0.842^{***}	0.000
	Perceived novelty	0.882^{***}	0.000
	Immersion	0.811^{***}	0.000

*** $p < .001$, ** $p < .01$, * $p < .05$

5 Discussion

This study investigated the intention of college students to use metaverse technology for Chinese calligraphy learning. A second-order construct was developed that integrates variables such as perceptual vividness, perceived interactivity, perceived novelty, and immersion. This second-order construct explains the drivers for using metaverse technology and has been named the Technology Perceptual Experience (TPE) model. Additionally, we performed correlation analyses for TPE, PE, PU and BI. Using gender as a moderating variable, we examined the effect on the inter-variable. The important aspect of this study is that the results provide new findings to the existing literature. It provides a reference for integrating metaverse technology in art teaching and learning projects. In addition, the study of validated models of perceptual experience with technology is not limited to metaverse Chinese calligraphy courses, and also has research value and applicability for human-computer interaction-related education.

H1 and H2 are supported, which showed that TPE positively affected the PE and PU of college students using the metaverse technology for Chinese calligraphy courses. The effect of TPE on college students' PE is higher than that on PU, which illustrates the critical role of technology perceptual experiences in education. Previous research on metaverse education has shown that, Yang et al. used the UTAUT2 model in basketball teaching to explore students' intentions to use metaverse technology [70]. Additionally, Al-Adwan et al. used the extended TAM model to investigate the intentions of college students to use the Metaverse educational platform [71]. Hence, this study complements previous research on metaverse education.

H3 is valid and proves that the PE of college students learning using metaverse technology in Chinese Calligraphy courses has a positive effect on PU. This confirms previous findings on the relationship between PE and PU [46]. The results also show that when college students prefer to use metaverse technology for learning, they believe that it will make learning more efficient. Therefore, PE is popular and beneficial to students' learning.

H4 is valid and indicates that the PE of college students learning using metaverse technology in Chinese Calligraphy courses has a positive effect on BI. This confirms the previous findings [59, 72]. Research has shown that PE plays an important role in BI. In addition, Deci et al. found that when people experience more interest and confidence, it improves their performance and creative power [73]. Therefore, significant PE is necessary to increase the BI of college students using metaverse technology.

H5 is valid, which showed that PU learned by college students using the metaverse technology had a positive effect on BI in Chinese Calligraphy courses, and this conclusion was consistent with the findings of previous studies. Notably, there was a significant correlation between PU and BI among college students in a virtual classroom setting during the COVID-19 pandemic [47]. The results of previous research have shown that the perceived usefulness of adopting WEB 2.0 technologies in the field of education positively influences behavioral intention [67]. Additionally, the use of new technologies in education is positively influenced by perceived usefulness [68]. College students show a high level of expectation and acceptance of new technologies, making them early movers in their adoption. For metaverse technology, college students show a higher intention to use it when they recognize its usefulness in learning, which provides educators and learners with more learning opportunities and options for learning styles.

With regard to gender differences. It was found that gender moderated the perceived usefulness of Chinese calligraphy courses for college students using metaverse technology. In contrast to previous research findings [69], this study found that male students are more susceptible to perceived enjoyment than female students, which can affect their perceived usefulness in using metaverse technology. Due to the differences between male and female students in terms of personality and interests, male students are more focused on learning Chinese calligraphy courses using new techniques or methods. They believe calligraphy courses through metaverse technology can be experienced as pleasurable with a new technology or service, which will have a more significant impact on the degree of usefulness of that technology or service. Female students are more inclined to focus on the practicality and functionality of the technology or service with relatively little impact. Gender has no moderating effect on other pathways when using metaverse technology in teaching and learning. Therefore, when using the TPE model proposed in this research to study metaverse education, designers need to pay special attention to male students, who are more likely to have better teaching and learning outcomes due to the perceived enjoyment of technology. More exciting features and pedagogical content can be added when designing the product (Fig. 2 and Table 10).

Table 10. Adaptability of SEM.

Common indices	χ^2	df	χ^2/df	RMSEA	GFI	IFI	CFI	TLI	SRMR
Judgment criteria			<3	<0.08	>0.9	>0.9	>0.9	>0.9	<0.08
Value	340.095	200	1.700	0.048	0.913	0.967	0.966	0.961	0.052

Table 11. Direct and indirect effects.

Path	Direct effect		Indirect effect		Total effect	
	β	Sig	β	Sig	β	Sig
TPE → PE	0.465***	0.000	/	/	0.465	0.000
TPE → PU	0.461**	0.001	0.063	0.094	0.524	0.001
PE → PU	0.136*	0.040	/	/	0.136	0.040
PE → BI	0.437***	0.000	0.047	0.095	0.485	0.000
PU → BI	0.345***	0.000	/	/	0.345	0.000
TPE → BI	/	/	0.384***	0.000	0.384	0.000

TPE Technological Perceptual Experience, *PE* Perceived enjoyment, *PU* Perceived usefulness, *BI* behavioral intention
***$p < .001$, **$p < .01$, *$p < .05$

Table 12. Results of multiple group comparisons based on genders

Hypotheses	Hypothesized path	Female group	Male group	Diff. Abs	df	CMIN	P
H1	TPE → PE	0.511	0.416	0.095	1	0.432	0.511
H2	TPE → PU	0.597	0.343	0.254	1	0.008	0.928
H3	**PE → PU**	**-0.019**	**0.274**	**-0.293**	**1**	**4.930**	**0.026**
H4	PE → BI	0.411	0.525	-0.114	1	0.058	0.810
H5	PU → BI	0.305	0.374	-0.069	1	0.132	0.717

Diff. abs = absolute difference; the bold rows = the paths have significant differences between male and female students

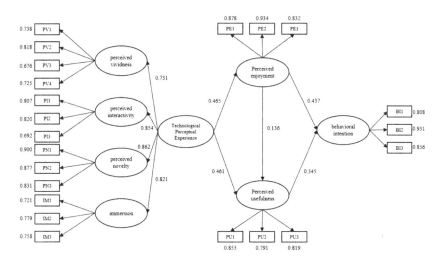

Fig. 2. Structural equation model.

6   Theoretical Implications

This study makes a significant theoretical contribution to the literature related to metaverse education. Firstly, various research has been done on metaverse education, but less research has been done on its application in the field of art. Therefore, this study contributes to the understanding of metaverse technology in the field of art. It provides a reference for future research on metaverse art education and enriches the existing literature research.

Secondly, this study integrates four variables: perceived vividness, perceived interactivity, perceived novelty, and immersion. The current theoretical models related to metaverse education are the TAM model, the UTAUT model and the UTAUT2 model [74]. Therefore, this study proposes a technology perceptual experience (TPE) model related to metaverse education. The model complements behavioral theories related to meta-universe education and enhances students' learning experience. Additionally, this study demonstrated the importance of technology perceptual experiences for developing extrinsic motivation PU and intrinsic motivation PE for students' learning using metaverse technology.

Finally, this study used gender as a moderating variable. The study showed male students were more sensitive to perceived enjoyment (PE). This finding lays the foundation for research related to male students.

7   Practical Implications

This study has significant practical contributions. Firstly, by combining the metaverse technology with the Chinese calligraphy teaching, teachers can have diverse ways of teaching calligraphy and at the same time, they can instruct and communicate with their students in a targeted way. Additionally, the use of diverse teaching methods and scenarios can enhance the student learning experience and help improve learning outcomes.

Secondly, research shows that developers should pay full attention to the perceived vividness, perceived interactivity, perceived novelty and immersion of the metaverse teaching and learning in order to stimulate students' interest and learning experience for educational purposes and help them maintain a positive intention to learn. In addition, developers can add more exciting content and gamified learning tasks to the metaverse calligraphy system to enhance students' enjoyment, thus increasing their perceived usefulness and intention to use, such as adding different writing scenes, styles of calligraphy in different periods, and the function of explaining the knowledge of calligraphy with the figures of ancient calligraphy masters.

Finally, metaverse teaching should pay special attention to the needs of male students. Research has shown that male students are more likely to embrace metaverse teaching as a way of learning and are, therefore, more likely to have a better learning experience. All factors encourage students to use metaverse technology for learning. Therefore, this is an essential reference for developing other disciplines of metaverse teaching.

8   Conclusion

With technology continuing to develop, student use of metaverse technology will likely be a dominant trend in the future of education. This study explored the factors contributing to college students' intention to use metaverse technology for a Chinese Calligraphy course. Additionally, the model test results in this study indicated that PV, PI, PE, and IM of the Metaverse Technology are essential factors in making students strongly Intrinsic Motivation PE and Extrinsic Motivation PU. Intrinsic motivation PE and extrinsic motivation PU are significantly related to college students' intention to use metaverse technology. Meanwhile, intrinsic motivation PE is more related to college student's intention to use it than extrinsic motivation PU. Moreover, inherent motivation PE has a direct effect on extrinsic motivation PU. This study also found that gender moderated the relationship between intrinsic motivation PE and extrinsic motivation PU, which other scholars may gain from this study. For teachers, using metaverse technology in the courses helps obtain more teaching resources and improve teaching effectiveness. For students, metaverse technology can enhance their learning experience. For developers, it can provide more available resources for the art teaching field by combining the characteristics of art teaching. This study has several limitations, which will be explored further below:

1. The study was conducted on Chinese undergraduate students. The sample is relatively unitary. Future research could consider students with different academic qualifications and grades. Additionally, the validity of this study could be enhanced by collecting data from student populations from different national cultures to validate the results of this study.
2. The research methodology is quantitative. Future research can combine quantitative and qualitative research methods, which can enhance the validity of the research and expand the perspective of the research.
3. Due to the low number of targeted resources related to metaverse technology, the testing resources for this study may have some shortcomings. Therefore, future research could incorporate the latest metaverse products to study and delve into the impacts, strengths, and weaknesses of their products, and such an exploration could help to fill in the possible gaps in current metaverse technology and provide guidance and support for its future development.

References

1. Tian, D., Wang, Q., Law, R., Zhang, M.: Of cultural identity on tourists' authenticity perception, tourist satisfaction, and traveler loyalty. Sustainability **12**, 6344 (2020)
2. Kurin, R.: Safeguarding Intangible Cultural Heritage in the 2003 UNESCO Convention: a critical appraisal. Museum Int. **56**, 66 (2004)
3. "UNESCO - Chinese Calligraphy." https://ich.unesco.org/en/RL/chinese-calligraphy-00216
4. Lu, Z., Annett, M., Fan, M., Wigdor, D.: In: Proceedings of the 2019 CHI Conference on Human Factors in Computing Systems, pp. 1–14. Association for Computing Machinery, New York (2019)

5. Olanipekun, W.D., Brimah, A.N., Rabiu, R.O.: Entrepreneurial and vocational education revolution: A catalyst for sustainable development. Kuwait Chap. Arab. J. Bus. Manag. Rev. **33**(2587), 1–9 (2015)
6. Abisuga-Oyekunle, O.A., Fillis, I.R.: The role of handicraft micro-enterprises as a catalyst for youth employment. Creat. Indust. J. **10**, 59 (2017)
7. Yan, W.-J., Li, K.-R.: Sustainable cultural innovation practice: heritage education in universities and creative inheritance of intangible cultural heritage craft. Sustainability **15**(2), 1194 (2023)
8. Zhao, G., Wang, Q., Wu, L., Dong, Y.: Exploring the structural relationship between university support, students' technostress, and burnout in technology-enhanced learning. Asia-Pacific Educ. Res. **31**, 463 (2022)
9. Gu, C., et al.: Examining the influence of using first-person view drones as auxiliary devices in matte painting courses on college students' continuous learning intention. J. Intell. **10**, 40 (2022)
10. Hsu, Y., Chen, J., Gu, C., Wu, W.: J. Design **26** (2021)
11. Fabris, C.P., Rathner, J.A., Fong, A.Y., Sevigny, C.P.: Virtual reality in higher education. Int. J. Innov. Sci. Math. Educ. **27** (2019)
12. Chen, J.-J., Hsu, Y., Wei, W., Yang, C.: Continuance intention of augmented reality textbooks in basic design course. Educ. Sci. **11**, 208 (2021)
13. Ren, L., Yang, F., Gu, C., Sun, J., Liu, Y.: A study of factors influencing Chinese college students' intention of using metaverse technology for basketball learning: extending the technology acceptance model. Front. Psychol. **13**, 1049972 (2022)
14. Huang, X., Zhi, H.: Factors influencing students' continuance usage intention with virtual classroom during the COVID-19 pandemic: an empirical study. Sustainability **15**, 4420 (2023)
15. Huffman, A.H., Whetten, J., Huffman, W.H.: Using technology in higher education: the influence of gender roles on technology self-efficacy. Comput. Hum. Behav. **29**, 1779 (2013)
16. Joshua, J.: Information bodies: computational anxiety in Neal Stephenson's snow crash. Interdiscip. Liter. Stud. **19**, 17 (2017)
17. Gokmi, K., Jeon, J.H.: A study on the copyright survey for design protection in metaverse period. Int. J. Adv. Smart Convergen. **10**(3), 181 (2021)
18. Mystakidis, S.: Metaverse. Encyclopedia **2**, 486 (2022)
19. Jeon, J., Jung, S.K.: Exploring the educational applicability of Metaverse-based platforms. 한국정보교육학회: 학술대회논문집361–368 (2021)
20. Genay, A., Lécuyer, A., Hachet, M.: Being an avatar "for real": a survey on virtual embodiment in augmented reality. IEEE Trans. Visual Comput. Graph. **28**, 5071 (2022)
21. Aguayo, J.M.B., et al.: Digital activism in students of a university in central Mexico in the COVID-19 era. Adv. Mob. Learn. Educ. Res. **2**(1), 297 (2022)
22. Tlili, A., et al.: Is metaverse in education a blessing or a curse: a combined content and bibliometric analysis. Smart Learn. Environ. **9**, 24 (2022)
23. Kye, B., Han, N., Kim, E., Park, Y., Jo, S.: Educational applications of metaverse: possibilities and limitations JEEHP **18**, 32 (2021)
24. Wang, G., Shin, C.: Education application platform: empirical evidence based on PPM and TAM models. Sustainability **14**, 17037 (2022)
25. Wiederhold, B.K.: Cyberpsychology. Behav. Soc. Netw. **25**, 1 (2022)
26. Yin, X.: On the application of virtual reality technology in public art teaching in colleges and universities. In: 2022 7th International Conference on Modern Management and Education Technology (MMET 2022), pp. 15–21. Atlantis Press (2022)
27. Li, P., Fang, Z., Jiang, T.: Research into improved distance learning using VR technology. Front. Educ.**7** (2022)

28. Riza, A.R., Azandi, F., Mawardinur, Manalu, N.: Development of basketball learning model based on e-learning and media applications in faculty of sports sciences (Fik) medan state university. In: 6th Annual International Seminar On Transformative Education And Educational Leadership, pp. 857–861. Atlantis Press (2021)
29. Hamidi, A.: Development model of learning basketball based modification games for secondary high school. JIPES – J. Indonesian Phys. Educ. Sport **4**, 118 (2018)
30. Bae, S., Jung, T.H., Moorhouse, N., Suh, M., Kwon, O.: The influence of mixed reality on satisfaction and brand loyalty in cultural heritage attractions: a brand equity perspective. Sustainability **12**, 2956 (2020)
31. Shin, D.: How do users experience the interaction with an immersive screen? Comput. Hum. Behav. **98**, 302 (2019)
32. Zeng, Y., Liu, L., Xu, R.: The effects of a virtual reality tourism experience on tourist's cultural dissemination behavior. Tourism Hospital. **3**, 314 (2022)
33. Heeter, C.: Interactivity in the context of designed experiences. J. Interact. Advert. **1**, 3 (2000)
34. Chi, H.-K., Huang, K.-C., Nguyen, H.M.: Elements of destination brand equity and destination familiarity regarding travel intention. J. Retail. Consum. Serv. **52**, 101728 (2020)
35. Reeves, T.C., Reeves, P.M.: Effective dimensions of interactive learning on the World Wide Web. Web-Based Instruct. **59** (1997)
36. Yang, S., Jiang, H., Yao, J., Chen, Y., Wei, J.: Perceived values on mobile GMS continuance: a perspective from perceived integration and interactivity. Comput. Hum. Behav. **89**, 16 (2018)
37. McMillan, S.J., Hwang, J.-S.: Measures of perceived interactivity: an exploration of the role of direction of communication, user control, and time in shaping perceptions of interactivity. J. Advert. **31**, 29 (2002)
38. Tokunaga, R.S.: Engagement with novel virtual environments: the role of perceived novelty and flow in the development of the deficient self-regulation of internet use and media habits: novel virtual environments. Hum. Commun. Res. **39**, 365 (2013)
39. Adapa, S., et al.: Examining the antecedents and consequences of perceived shopping value through smart retail technology. J. Retail. Consum. Serv. **52**, 101901 (2020)
40. Yim, M.Y.-C., Chu, S.-C., Sauer, P.L.: Is augmented reality technology an effective tool for E-commerce? An interactivity and vividness perspective. J. Interact. Mark. **39**, 89 (2017)
41. Palmer, M.T.: Interpersonal communication and virtual reality: mediating interpersonal relationships. Commun. Age Virtual Reality 277–299 (1995)
42. Nowak, K.L., Biocca, F.: The effect of the agency and anthropomorphism on users' sense of telepresence, copresence, and social presence in virtual environments. Presence: Teleoper. Virt. Environ. **12**, 481 (2003)
43. Park, E.: User acceptance of smart wearable devices: an expectation-confirmation model approach. Telematics Inform. **47**, 101318 (2020)
44. Ko, E., Kim, E.Y., Lee, E.K.: Modeling consumer adoption of mobile shopping for fashion products in Korea. Psychol. Mark. **26**, 669 (2009)
45. Lee, M.-C.: Explaining and predicting users' continuance intention toward e-learning: an extension of the expectation–confirmation model. Comput. Educ. **54**, 506 (2010)
46. Luo, Y., Lin, J., Yang, Y.: Students' motivation and continued intention with online self-regulated learning: a self-determination theory perspective. Z. Erziehungswiss **24**, 1379 (2021)
47. Shiau, W.-L., Luo, M.M.: PACIS 2010 Proceedings (2010)
48. van der Heijden, H.: User acceptance of hedonic information systems. MIS Q. **28**, 695 (2004)
49. Davis, F.D.: Perceived usefulness, perceived ease of use, and user acceptance of information technology. MIS Q. **13**, 319 (1989)
50. Chen, C., Xu, X., Arpan, L.: Between the technology acceptance model and sustainable energy technology acceptance model: investigating smart meter acceptance in the United States. Energy Res. Soc. Sci. **25**, 93 (2017)

51. Ramírez-Correa, P., Rondán-Cataluña, F.J., Arenas-Gaitán, J., Martín-Velicia, F.: Analysing the acceptation of online games in mobile devices: an application of UTAUT2. J. Retail. Consum. Serv. **50**, 85 (2019)
52. Teo, T.S.H., Srivastava, S.C., Jiang, L.: J. Manag. Inf. Syst. **25**, 99 (2008)
53. Zhu, Y., Zhang, J.H., Au, W., Yates, G.: University students' online learning attitudes and continuous intention to undertake online courses: a self-regulated learning perspective. Educ. Tech. Res. Dev. **68**, 1485 (2020)
54. McLean, G., Wilson, A.: Shopping in the digital world: examining customer engagement through augmented reality mobile applications. Comput. Hum. Behav. **101**, 210 (2019)
55. Kim, J.-H., Kim, M., Park, M., Yoo, J.: How interactivity and vividness influence consumer virtual reality shopping experience: the mediating role of telepresence. J. Res. Interact. Mark. **15**, 502 (2021)
56. Lumby, J.: Enjoyment and learning: policy and secondary school learners' experience in England. Br. Edu. Res. J. **37**, 247 (2011)
57. Wang, W., Ngai, E.W.T., Wei, H.: Explaining instant messaging continuance intention: the role of personality. Int. J. Hum.-Comput. Interact. **28**, 500 (2012)
58. Won, D., Chiu, W., Byun, H.: Factors influencing consumer use of a sport-branded app: The technology acceptance model integrating app quality and perceived enjoyment. Asia Pac. J. Mark. Logist. **35**(5), 1112 (2023)
59. Fan, C., Wang, J.: One country with two systems: the characteristics and development of higher education in the Guangdong–Hong Kong–Macau Greater Bay Area. Human. Soc. Sci. Commun. **10**, 1 (2023)
60. Jackson, D.L.: Revisiting sample size and number of parameter estimates: some support for the N:q hypothesis. Struct. Eq. Model. **10**, 128 (2003)
61. Wells, J.D., Campbell, D.E., Valacich, J.S., Featherman, M.: The effect of perceived novelty on the adoption of information technology innovations: a risk/reward perspective. Decis. Sci. **41**, 813 (2010)
62. Chen, C.-S., Lu, H.-P., Luor, T.: A new flow of location based service mobile games: non-stickiness on pokémon go. Comput. Hum. Behav. **89**, 182 (2018)
63. Davis, F.D., Bagozzi, R.P., Warshaw, P.R.: Extrinsic and intrinsic motivation to use computers in the workplace 1. J. Appl. Soc. Psychol. **22**, 1111 (1992)
64. Lam, J.M.S., Ismail, H., Lee, S.: From desktop to destination: User-generated content platforms, co-created online experiences, destination image and satisfaction. J. Destin. Mark. Manag. **18**, 100490 (2020)
65. Lee, S.M., Lee, D.: Healthcare wearable devices: an analysis of key factors for continuous use intention. Serv. Bus. **14**, 503 (2020)
66. Kline, R.B.: Principles and Practice of Structural Equation Modeling. Guilford Publications (2023)
67. Tao, D., et al.: Key characteristics in designing massive open online courses (MOOCs) for user acceptance: An application of the extended technology acceptance model. Interact. Learn. Environ. **30**(5), 882–895 (2022)
68. Hair, J.: Faculty and Research Publications (2009)
69. Fornell, C., Larcker, D.F.: Evaluating structural equation models with unobservable variables and measurement error. J. Mark. Res. **18**, 39 (1981)
70. Yang, F., Ren, L., Gu, C.: A study of college students' intention to use metaverse technology for basketball learning based on UTAUT2. Heliyon **8**(9), e10562 (2022)
71. Al-Adwan, A.S., Li, N., Al-Adwan, A., Abbasi, G.A., Albelbisi, N.A., Habibi, A.: Educ. Inf. Technol. (2023)
72. Ginzarly, M., Jordan Srour, F., Roders, A.P.: The interplay of context, experience, emotion at World Heritage Sites: a qualitative and machine learning approach. Tourism Cult. Commun. **22**(4), 321–340 (2022)

73. Deci, E.L., Ryan, R.M.: In: Nebraska Symposium on Motivation, pp. 237–288 (1991)
74. Roy, R., Babakerkhell, M.D., Mukherjee, S., Pal, D., Funilkul, S.: Development of a framework for metaverse in education: a systematic literature review approach. IEEE Access **11**, 57717 (2023)

AWARE^{S}CUES: Awareness Cues Scaling with Group Size and Extended Reality Devices

Vera M. Memmesheimer$^{1(\boxtimes)}$ ⓘ, Jannik Löber^2 ⓘ, and Achim Ebert^1 ⓘ

^{1} Human Computer Interaction Lab, RPTU Kaiserslautern-Landau, Kaiserslautern,
Germany
{v.memmesheimer,achim.ebert}@rptu.de
^{2} August-Wilhelm Scheer Institut, Saarbrücken, Germany
jannik.loeber@aws-institut.de

Abstract. The Covid-19 pandemic has strongly increased the relevance of remote collaboration such that online meetings are now well-established in many companies. However, the corresponding tools usually fail to share 3D content. Although Extended Reality (XR) technologies are known to support exactly such purposes, they are rarely applied in practical settings as existing solutions are designed for specific use cases or hardware and hence lack scalability. In this paper, we investigate the scalability of awareness cues such as head- and hand-rays that are typically suggested to support communication in XR meeting spaces. Based on seven heuristics we identify scalability limitations of existing awareness cues such as incorrect representations of user behavior and visual information overload. Addressing these issues, we present four collaboration support features named AWARE^{S}CUES which allow to individually activate awareness cues for nine different co-located and distributed collaboration styles involving head-mounted and handheld displays.

Keywords: Co-located collaboration · distributed collaboration · Awareness cues · Head-mounted displays · Handheld displays · Virtual Reality · Mixed Reality · Augmented Reality

1 Introduction

The Covid-19 pandemic has boosted the distribution and evolution of technologies that enable remote collaboration. This trend continues even in the post-pandemic era with various remote meeting platforms that are now well-established in many companies. Despite the widespread use of these platforms, most of them can only replace face-to-face meetings where at most 2D content is exchanged via screen sharing. As such, there are still many work processes which cannot be performed remotely, as the content that needs to be shared goes beyond 2D and therefore requires employees to be present at the same place. In this context, the application of Extended Reality (XR) technologies is deemed promising: XR technologies allow to immerse users in completely virtual

© The Author(s), under exclusive license to Springer Nature Switzerland AG 2024
J. Y. C. Chen and G. Fragomeni (Eds.): HCII 2024, LNCS 14706, pp. 44–59, 2024.
https://doi.org/10.1007/978-3-031-61041-7_4

environments or to virtually augment the real world and hence are predestined for sharing 3D content between distributed or co-located collaborators.

However, despite all the potential that has been assigned to XR technologies, they are still rarely used in the real world. As argued in [13,14], the adoption of XR technologies may be hampered by scalability limitations since existing solutions are often designed and developed for single use cases and involve specific hardware or interaction modalities. Regarding collaborative XR settings, previous research has proposed awareness cues such as rays indicating where someone is pointing or looking at to support the collaborators in correctly perceiving the activities of the other collaborators. These awareness cues are mostly evaluated in experiments with only two collaborators. Real-world use cases, however, often involve more than two collaborators and require users to switch frequently between different devices and degrees of virtuality. As for example outlined in [13], completely virtual environments may be favored at the beginning of product development processes when collaborators deal with fully virtual prototypes. As the product evolves, physically existing parts of the product can be augmented with virtual components in Mixed Reality settings. But even during these stages of the development process, people that are temporarily off-site may want to join their on-site collaborators remotely in a virtual replication of the physical scene. As these collaborators are likely to be involved in the development of multiple products that are in different stages of the development process, they will have to switch between devices and degrees of virtuality frequently. This scenario does not only apply to the development of different physical items in the automotive or aerospace industry but also to factory layout planning, construction work, or interior design. Hence, to provide effective and efficient task performance in such XR settings, the technologies must provide high scalability such that the cognitive capacities required to switch between different XR systems can be kept as low as possible.

In this paper, we concentrate on the scalability of collaboration support features, more specifically awareness cues, with regard to different XR devices and increasing group sizes. To this end, we establish heuristics regarding the generation of awareness cues and outline scalability issues that are likely to arise when the group size increases and collaborators need to switch between devices. Based on these insights we design four collaboration support features that seek to address the identified scalability limitations and investigate how they can be implemented for nine different collaboration styles (i.e., distributed and co-located collaboration with head-mounted and handheld displays).

2   Background and Related Work

2.1   Extended Reality Devices and Degrees of Virtuality

The reality-virtuality continuum as introduced by Milgram et al. [15] distinguishes environments according to their degree of virtuality. It encompasses completely computer-generated, virtual environments (Virtual Reality, VR) as well as Mixed Reality (MR) environments that combine real and virtual components.

MR environments can be accessed either with head-mounted displays (HMDs) that directly place virtual augmentations in front of the users' eyes or handheld displays (HHDs) like tablets that virtually augment the real world as captured by the device camera on the screen. While the usage of HMDs leaves the user's hands free, they are expensive and prone to physical issues such as eye strain. Furthermore, HMDs are not yet qualified for many industrial settings. HHDs on the other hand are considered a rather cheap and ubiquitous tool as they are already being used in many industries for non-XR applications.

Ever since the introduction of the reality-virtuality continuum researchers have outlined the potential of XR technologies in various fields. However, to date, the application of XR technologies in real-world settings is still limited. In [13,14] we argue that the use of XR technologies in practical and profit-making settings can be increased by multidimensional scalability enhancements. To this end, we introduced so-called Scalable Extended Reality (XR^S) spaces which scale among different degrees of virtuality, among different XR devices, and from single to multiple possibly distributed users. In this way, XR^S seeks to reduce the users' cognitive efforts and to make it easier for them to combine and switch between different XR systems. As demonstrated by the framework for XR^S in [13], this concept can be applied in different use cases including for example collaborative prototyping, training, or teleoperation.

2.2   XR-Supported Collaboration Styles

In our paper, we follow the time and place based classification of collaboration presented by Johansen [9] and focus on synchronous collaboration where collaborators can be either at the same place or at different places.

While systems enabling distributed collaboration have been considered useful for saving time and business travel already prior to the Covid-19 pandemic, their adoption has been significantly accelerated by the pandemic and online meetings are nowadays well-established in many businesses. However, these systems are usually limited to 2D applications that support video-conferences and screen sharing. Widespread tools that allow remotely sharing 3D content are still missing.

XR technologies hold a lot of potential to support exactly these use cases [17]. For example, remote experts can be provided with virtual replications of a local worker's field of view during maintenance tasks. At the same time remote collaborators could benefit from XR applications that allow joining design review sessions for instance in the automotive industry (see for example [5]) or factory layout planning sessions such as presented in [4]. In addition to distributed collaboration, XR technologies also have great potential to support co-located collaborators who are working on fully or partially virtual 3D content. In this context, MR tools enable users to see their co-located collaborators and the virtual 3D content simultaneously. A detailed analysis of XR's potential to support use cases for co-located and distributed collaboration can be found in [13].

2.3 Awareness Cues

While XR technologies provide a lot of benefits for supporting collaboration, they also pose challenges regarding the visualization and perception of every collaborator's location and activities. These challenges do not only arise in distributed settings when collaborators are unable to see each other but also during co-located collaboration. While in co-located settings collaborators are usually aware of each other's location, it may still be difficult to follow the activities of their collaborators, for example when they reference or manipulate virtual components in the MR scene.

In the past, a lot of research has been conducted to improve communication and coordination in XR-supported collaborative settings. For example, different avatar representations to display each collaborator's spatial location during distributed collaboration have been proposed as well as different awareness cues that augment co-located collaborators or avatars of remote collaborators. These awareness cues include field of view frustums that give a basic idea of the collaborator's current orientation in space, sketches or hints that collaborators can add to the other collaborators' fields of view, or rays that indicate where someone is pointing or looking at. A detailed survey on communication cues for remote guidance is presented by Huang et al. [7] who distinguish between explicit and implicit communication cues. They group explicit communication cues into pointers, virtual annotations, hand gestures, or virtual models of known task objects. On the other hand, implicit communication cues include facial expressions, eye-tracking, or body posture. They conclude that adding these implicit cues to the explicit cues effectively supports communication between collaborators.

For instance, Piumsomboon et al. [18] compared three awareness cues (i.e., a field of view frustum, a field of view frustum combined with a ray originating from the head, and a field of view frustum with a ray originating from the eye) against a baseline (i.e., virtual head and hands without further cues) and found that the combination of view frustum and head-ray was most useful. Further research on gaze visualizations was conducted by Jing et al. [8] who compared uni-directional gaze (i.e., each user sees only the gaze visualizations of the other collaborator) and bi-directional gaze (i.e., each user sees their own and the other collaborator's gaze visualization) combined with different visualizations displaying the current gaze behavior state (i.e., browsing state, focus state, and joint state). They found that bi-directional gaze including gaze behavior was the preferred condition and note that participants appreciated the provided confirmation that their gaze visualization is successfully delivered. Kim et al. [10] compared different visualizations for conveying hand movements (i.e., a virtual hand, a virtual hand with pointer-ray, a virtual hand which can make virtual sketches in mid-air, and a virtual hand with both a pointer-ray and the sketching option) in a remote assistance task. They compared these cues using a dependent view setting (i.e., the remote user's viewpoint matches the viewpoint of the local worker) and an independent view setting (i.e., the remote user accesses the scene independently). The authors report that compared to the dependent view setting it was much more difficult for the local user to correctly interpret the hand gesture of the remote user with the independent view. Similarly, the sketching option was only useful with the dependent view. On the contrary, the pointer-ray was more useful with the independent view setting than with the dependent view. In a related study, they found that additional cues such as ray or sketch led to an increase of the perceived mental effort [11]. Bai et al. [1] compared virtual hand gesture cues, a ray displaying a remote collaborator's gaze direction, and the combination of gesture cues and gaze rays to support communication between a local worker in MR and a remote worker in VR. They report that both the local and the remote worker preferred the combination of hand gestures and gaze rays over either of them alone.

Further research has explored the use of advanced avatar representations that integrate awareness cues [19,20]. In [19] a remote user was represented by a miniature avatar which was equipped with a pointer and represented body movements of the remote collaborator such that the local worker knew at which part of the scene the remote user was looking or pointing. The location of the avatar was updated according to the local worker's current field of view and hence did not correspond to the actual location of the remote collaborator. Instead, an arrow at the miniature avatar's feet pointed to the actual location of the remote worker in space. In [20] the miniature avatar representing the remote user was not attached to the local user's field of view but to a 360° camera. By manipulating the camera, the local user was able to manipulate the position of the remote user's avatar as well as the remote worker's field of view. Furthermore, they provided the remote worker with a feature that allows to attract the local worker's attention using a virtual torch. The authors performed a detailed user study on different avatar representations, methods to manipulate the avatar, and methods to adapt the remote worker's viewpoint. Based on their findings, they recommend using avatars in combination with view frustums. In this context they highlight the importance of features that allow users to change the avatar representations individually. They also note that the local workers preferred to individually control the position of the avatar while the remote workers preferred to control their viewpoint by themselves.

3   Terminology and Research Focus

As stated in the previous section, the potential of MR and VR technologies to support different forms of collaboration is very broad. This also applies to the associated fields of research and the terms used in research papers. In the following, we describe the collaboration styles, technologies, and awareness cues that are considered in this paper along with the terminology being used.

In this paper, we focus on VR and MR technologies which we summarize by XR technologies. More specifically, we concentrate on XR-supported synchronous co-located and distributed collaboration (i.e., collaborators can be either at the same place or at different places) involving HMDs (i.e., MR-HMDs and VR-HMDs) and HHDs (i.e., MR-HHDs). As displayed in Fig. 1(a), this results in 9 different collaboration styles.

We build up on the XR^S framework as presented in [13] which seeks to foster XR's application in the real world through multidimensional scalability enhancements. While [13] also recommends providing collaborators with a subscription feature which allows to define the amount of visible awareness cues, the paper does not elaborate on the design and implementation of activation and deactivation methods. In this paper, we contribute to closing this gap in two steps. First, we investigate the scalability of two popular awareness cues: Head-rays (i.e., rays originating from a user's or avatar's head) and hand-rays (i.e., rays originating from a user's or avatar's hand). Based on the insights gained, we develop collaboration support features for collaborative sessions that scale with XR devices and group size.

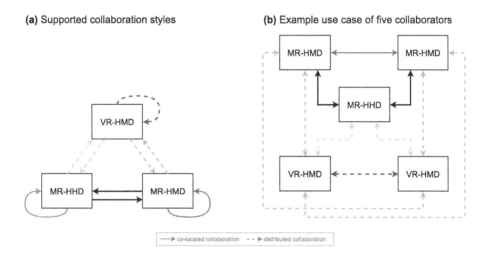

Fig. 1. (a) displays the nine collaboration styles that are supported by AWARE^{S}CUES. E.g., the arrow pointing from MR-HMD to VR-HMD describes how a MR-HMD user sees a VR-HMD user, the opposite arrow describes how a VR-HMD user sees a MR-HMD user, self-referencing arrows describe how a user sees users that are equipped with the same device; (b) shows an example of a collaborative session with five collaborators along with the types of collaboration styles included (for reasons of clarity, pairwise collaboration styles of the same color are summarized by double arrows).

4 Scalability of Available Awareness Cues

While the awareness cues presented above are deemed useful, the respective user studies are limited to two collaborators and only take into account HMDs (e.g., [1,8,10,18–20]). However, practical applications such as collaborative decision-making processes, often involve more than two collaborators from various fields that need to cooperate in cross-device settings. While some research papers (e.g., [2,12,16]) also consider the integration of HHDs, these papers are rather focused on providing technical solutions for collaborative cross-device settings than on evaluating the scalability of awareness cues. For instance, García-Pereira et al. [2] present a system that allows HMD users, HHD users, and a user of a Desktop-PC application to join a collaborative session whereby each collaborator is provided with a visual representation of the absent collaborators. Similarly, Pereira et al. [16] propose a system that enables collaboration between HMD and HHD users. Communication among the collaborators is supported through avatars consisting of virtual heads and hands. The orientation of the users in space is given through a face on the avatar's head. They also proposed different effects to guide a user to a specific location. Kostov and Wolfartsberger [12] present a system that can be accessed with HMDs, HHDs, and Desktop-PCs. They integrate laser pointers for all users but provide little information on the virtual representation of the collaborators and the system has not yet been evaluated in a collaborative user study. Hence, it remains to be examined how the previously proposed awareness cues scale with different devices and an increasing number of non-experienced users.

In this section, we contribute to closing this gap as we discuss the applicability of awareness cues in cross-device settings of large groups based on the heuristics listed below. More specifically, we outline potentially arising issues and violations of the heuristics when head- and hand-rays are enabled permanently.

- **H1.** Each collaborator can see the location and orientation of all other collaborators.
- **H2.** Each collaborator can see the activities of all other collaborators.
- **H3.** The awareness cues represent each collaborator's behavior correctly.
- **H4.** All collaborators are equipped with the same set of awareness cues.
- **H5.** All collaborators can intuitively control their own awareness cues.
- **H6.** All collaborators can match all visible awareness cues to the corresponding collaborator.
- **H7.** All visible awareness cues support the collaborative work process.

As the group size increases, collaborators are—theoretically—still able to derive each other's location in space from the position of the avatar and can follow the activities as displayed by the awareness cues. However, deriving the correct orientation of HHD users can become difficult. In contrast to HMD users whose orientation in space can be derived from the orientation of the HMD as long as it is worn on the head, a HHD's orientation does not necessarily display a user's orientation in space at all times. Hence, **H1** applies only partially in cross-device settings. The same holds for **H2** as the activities of HHD users that are derived from the visualization of the awareness cues may be misleading if the HHD user is not interacting with the HHD but awareness cues are still being generated. Hence, **H1** and **H2** partially apply as the collaborators can see the awareness cues but the awareness cues might not capture the user behavior correctly (**H3**).

While the correct representation of user behavior (**H3**) is not affected by an increasing group size, it is heavily affected in cross-device settings: The technical realization of head- and hand-rays for VR-HMDs, MR-HMDs, and MR-HHDs requires knowledge about the position and orientation of each collaborator's head and hand. As outlined above, the generation of head-rays for HHD users is more difficult than for HMD users and was not considered in [2,12,16]. Similarly, generating hand-rays for HHD users is much more complex as HHDs are used in a different style. In [2] the HHD user is represented by a basic avatar and a virtual tablet. A virtual hand appears on the virtual tablet on the position of the touchscreen that corresponds to the touched point. As the user touches the HHD's screen, a virtual ray originating from the tablet appears. However, holding HHDs in XR settings with one hand is deemed unfavorable in the context of interaction with MR-HHDs as the arm holding the HHD is likely to experience fatigue [3]. Hence, we favor approaches where laser pointers originate from the center of the HHD's camera like for example presented in [12], as this allows holding the HHD with two hands. On the contrary, the generation of hand-rays for HMD-users is more straightforward, especially when hands or controllers are tracked by an external tracking system such that they cannot move outside the tracked area. Hence, depending on the XR device being used, providing all collaborators with the same set of awareness cues (**H4**) can be related to minor or major challenges in cross-device settings.

The fact that user behavior is represented correctly (**H3**) does not necessarily imply that it is possible for users to intuitively control their own awareness cues (**H5**). Users need to know on the basis of which data the awareness cues are generated and how they are processed. Furthermore, their cognitive load required to control their awareness cues should be kept as low as possible. If users have to spend a lot of cognitive capacities to use the device in a way that generates data for correct behavioral representations, less cognitive capacities are available for performing the actual task. Thus, they should be able to intuitively switch between MR-HHDs, MR-HMDs, and VR-HMDs while their behavior is still represented correctly by the cues.

As the group size increases enabling all awareness cues for all collaborators is likely to produce visual clutter. In this case, matching the visible awareness cues to the correct collaborator (**H6**) is likely to evoke cognitive overload which may impede collaboration rather than support it (**H7**). This is also emphasized by the findings of Pereira et al. [16] who considered larger group sizes during their evaluation and note that the users had difficulties in identifying the source of highlight mechanisms. We think that especially hand- and head-rays are prone to this kind of visual clutter as they may take up a large part of the screen. Further occlusion issues may be evoked by the integration of avatars. In this context, Piumsomboon et al. [20] note that their miniature avatar provides the benefit of occupying less display space. Furthermore, avatars may become redundant in co-located settings when users can see each other. However, if co-located collaborators are pointing or looking at a virtual object, it may still be useful to display the corresponding ray.

5   Concept and Design of AWARE^{S}CUES

Addressing these scalability issues, we present AWARE^{S}CUES – the design of four scalable collaboration support features named GazeCollision, StareForCues, LookAtMe, and FreezeCues that are based on natural cooperation paradigms and can be used for individually activating awareness cues. As such, we follow the recommendation of other researchers (e.g., [6,8]) to avoid the continuous activation of all awareness cues.

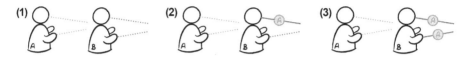

Fig. 2. (1) *UserA* and *UserB* only see their own head- and hand-rays; (2) *UserA* sees *UserB*'s head-ray; (3) *UserA* sees *UserB*'s head- and hand-ray.

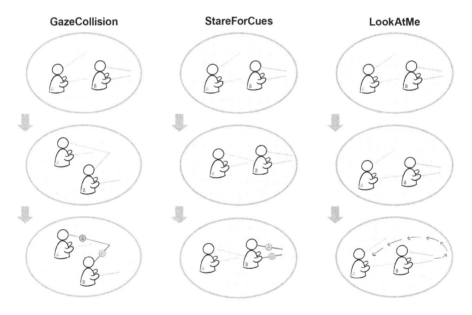

Fig. 3. Temporary visibility of awareness cues activated by GazeCollision, StareFor-Cues, and LookAtMe; see Fig. 2 for the representation of visible and invisible rays

The design of AWARE^{S}CUES considers co-located and distributed collaboration between users of three XR-devices: VR-HMDs, MR-HMDs, and MR-HHDs. This yields nine different collaboration styles as displayed in Fig. 1(a). These nine collaboration styles can be combined individually depending on the group size, the collaborators' locations, and the involved devices (see the exemplary collaborative session in Fig. 1(b)). For instance, remote collaborators can join with VR-HMDs whereas co-located collaborators can join through MR-HMDs or MR-HHDs that allow seeing each other. For each type of inter-device collaboration, two collaboration styles need to be considered. For instance, the two collaboration styles *MR-HHD user sees VR-HMD user* and *VR-HMD user sees MR-HHD user* need to be handled differently regarding the visualization of the corresponding collaborator. Regarding the awareness cues, we consider avatars equipped with view frustums, head-rays, and hand-rays as we agree with Jing et al. [8] who note that rays can facilitate tracing the cue back to its origin. Only distributed collaborators are provided with a visualization of each other's avatar since co-located collaborators can naturally see each other. However, we recommend integrating an invisible avatar in co-located settings as this allows the collaborators to interact with each other like with distributed collaborators (e.g., pointing at the body). Furthermore, we choose head-rays over eye-rays. While eye-rays originate from a user's eye and therefore provide more accurate information about the current viewing direction, they also change at a high frequency which we consider uncomfortable for the other collaborators.

As explained in the previous section, providing collaborators of all nine collaboration styles (see Fig. 1(a)) with hand- and head-rays that correctly represent their behavior is challenging. Since HHDs are held in the user's hand their orientation does not necessarily display the current spatial orientation of its user. An alternative approach for generating the head-rays of HHD users could be to equip them with additional hardware like eye-trackers that are worn on the head. However, this invalidates the main benefits of HHDs, i.e., its ubiquity and easy setup. Therefore, we propose to use the HHD's front-facing camera to track the HHD user's head orientation. If the user's head orientation deviates from the HHD's orientation in space, the head-ray can be visualized accordingly. While the front-facing camera's tracking area is limited, knowing that the face is outside the tracked area (i.e., the user is potentially not looking at the device) is still a relevant information which should be transmitted to the other collaborators. In this case, we recommend disabling both the head- and the hand-ray originating from the HHD as they are likely to provide incorrect representations of the HHD user's behavior. Similar issues can occur for the hand-rays of HMD users if the user's hands or controllers move outside the tracked area. In this context, a major hardware issue related to the limited hand tracking area of MR-HMDs such as the Microsoft HoloLens seems to have been solved by the Apple Vision Pro. Alternatively, this issue could also be handled through additional relatively non-obstructive hardware like wristbands that capture the position and orientation of the user's wrist.

In the following, we describe the design of GazeCollision, StareForCues, LookAtMe, and FreezeCues. Thereby, we refer to two exemplary collaborators *UserA* and *UserB* which serve as blueprints for all the nine collaboration styles shown in Fig. 1(a). For all of our scalable collaboration support features, head-

and hand-rays of all other collaborators are disabled by default while the collaborator's own cues remain visible. When *UserA* and *UserB* look towards the same area (i.e., the collision points of their head-rays are within a specified distance for a specified time), GazeCollision is triggered. This automatically activates the head-rays for *UserA* and *UserB*. If *UserA* wants to see the current activities of another *UserB*, StareForCues can be applied: By staring at *UserB* (i.e., *UserA*'s head-ray collides with *UserB*'s body or avatar for a specified time), the head- and hand-rays of *UserB* become visible for *UserA*. In this way, StareForCues takes up the face-to-face cooperation paradigm which also requires looking at someone to obtain information about this person's current activities. If *UserB* wishes to see *UserA*'s cues as well, *UserB* can apply StareForCues too. To get *UserB*'s attention, *UserA* can use LookAtMe by pointing and tapping at *UserB*'s body or avatar (i.e., *UserA* performs a single tapping gesture while the hand-ray collides with *UserB*'s body or avatar). This mechanism corresponds to the natural interaction paradigm of tapping on someone's shoulder. *UserB*'s field of view is then temporarily augmented with arrows pointing towards *UserA*. For example, *UserA* and *UserB* can then use StareForCues to activate each others' cues. The arrows, head- and hand-rays activated by GazeCollision, StareForCues, and LookAtMe (see Fig. 2 and Fig. 3) are disabled automatically after a specified time. For permanent activation of the hand- and head-rays FreezeCues can be applied at any time by double tapping while pointing at another user with the hand-ray. Tapping has to be implemented individually for the corresponding XR device which depends on the user's location and use case. For example, double-clicks can be performed with a controller that is paired with a HMD, air tap gestures, or touch events.

6   Implementing AWARE^{S}CUES

In the following we outline how AWARE^{S}CUES could be implemented to support collaborators in XR settings. Thereby, we distinguish between *users* and *collaborators*. We use the term *user* to describe this *user's* individual view of the XR scene including information about this *user's collaborators* represented by awareness cues. Each of these *collaborators* is considered an individual *user* too.

Each user has a list of collaborators. Each of these collaborators has a *<bool: co-located>* as well as three timers *<Timer: head_ray>*, *<Timer: hand_ray>*, and *<Timer: arrows>*. Each timer stores a *<bool: permanent>* and a *<int: seconds>*. In this way, different timers can be assigned to different cues. At the beginning of a collaborative session, a list of all other collaborators is set along with *<bool: co-located>*. Then, the initial scene is configured for each user. For each remote collaborator, the user's scene is augmented with a virtual avatar. While avatars of co-located collaborators are made invisible they should remain active such that the user can still interact with this collaborator (e.g., pointing at the collaborator's body while performing clicks).

The visibility of hand-rays, head-rays, and arrows is then handled as illustrated in Fig. 4: The flowchart displays when the awareness cues describing the

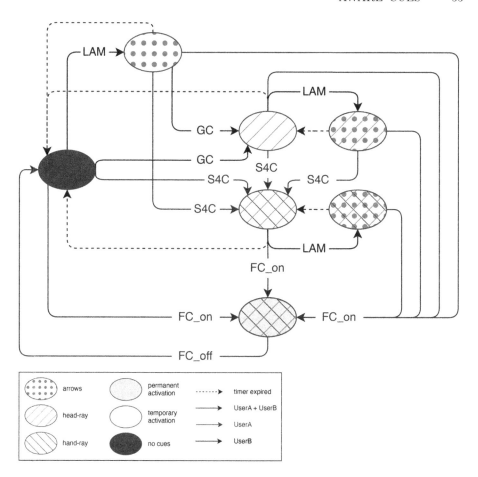

Fig. 4. Visibility of awareness cues describing *UserB*'s activities from the perspective of *UserA*. The visibility is adapted if a timer expires, if *UserA* applies StareForCues (S4C) or FreezeCues (FC_on/FC_off), if *UserB* applies LookAtMe (LAM), or if *UserA* and *UserB* meet through GazeCollision (GC).

activities of *UserB* become visible for *UserA*. Considering Fig. 1(a), the flowchart summarizes the visibility of awareness cues for a single collaboration style (i.e., *UserA* sees *UserB*). For instance, if *UserA* is a MR-HHD user and *UserB* is a MR-HMD user, this corresponds to the purple arrow pointing from MR-HHD to MR-HMD at the bottom of Fig. 1(a).

Initially, all rays and arrows are disabled ● . *UserA*'s field of view may then be adapted depending on the activities of *UserA* and *UserB*. Starting from the dark-gray ellipse on the left, three scenarios are possible: If *UserA* performs StareForCues, *UserB*'s head- and hand-ray become visible for *UserA* ⬭ . If instead, *UserB* performs LookAtMe, *UserA*'s view is augmented with arrows pointing towards *UserB* ⬭ . The third scenario describes the case in which the head-rays of *UserA* and *UserB* collide such that *UserB*'s head-ray becomes visible for *UserA* ◯ . This third scenario further activates *UserA*'s head-ray for *UserB*. However, this concerns *UserB*'s field of view which is handled outside the flowchart given in Fig. 4 and therefore will not be outlined further in this section. In any of these scenarios, *UserA*'s list of collaborators is searched for *UserB* and the respective timers of *UserB* are started. This also applies for the temporary cue activations described below.

In Fig. 4, ellipses with white background represent cues that are activated temporarily only. This means that cues are disabled automatically once the timer expired unless another event occurs prior to the expiration of the timer. At any time, *UserA* can permanently enable head- and hand-rays of *UserB* by applying FreezeCues (FC_on), i.e., performing a double-click which will set the corresponding boolean of the timers to true ⊗ . To disable the cues and set these values to false, another double-click (FC_off) has to be performed.

The arrows appearing upon LookAtMe cannot be enabled permanently and will disappear either automatically after the timer expired or after the occurrence of GazeCollision, StareForCues, or FreezeCues. For instance, the two ellipses on the right side of Fig. 4 show that *UserA*'s field of view is temporarily augmented with arrows if *UserB* performs LookAtMe after the occurrence of StareForCues ⊕ or after GazeCollision ⊕ . If *UserA* performs FC_on, the arrows disappear and *UserB*'s head- and hand-ray become permanently visible ⊗ . If *UserA* performs StareForCues when only the head-ray and arrows are visible ⊕ , the arrows disappear and *UserB*'s head- and hand-ray become temporarily visible ⊗ . If none of these actions is performed and the arrows' timer expired, the arrows disappear automatically. If *UserB* initially performs LookAtMe, *UserA*'s view is augmented with arrows pointing towards *UserB* ⊕ . Upon the occurrence of GazeCollision, the arrows disappear and *UserB*'s head-ray becomes temporarily visible for *UserA* ◯ . If *UserA* performs StareForCues or Freeze-Cues instead, the arrows disappear and both the head- and hand-rays become temporarily ⊗ or permanently ⊗ visible. If none of this happens prior to the expiration of the timer the arrows are disabled automatically ● . If *UserA* has already permanently enabled the cues of *UserB* ⊗ and hence has made an active decision to follow *UserB*'s activities, LookAtMe performed by *UserB* will have no effect on *UserA*'s view since these arrows are considered superfluous in most cases.

7   Conclusions

In this paper, we have identified scalability limitations of previously proposed awareness cues that become relevant in collaborative cross-device settings with an increasing group size. Based on a set of heuristics we highlighted that especially the integration of HHDs poses challenges in collaborative settings as the data obtained from the device cannot always represent its user's behavior correctly. To this end we proposed the integration of face tracking through the device's front-facing camera. Apart from this, we explained how existing awareness cues, especially hand- and head-rays, fail to scale with an increasing group size due to visual clutter. As the number of collaborators increases, adding rays for each collaborator is likely to result in information overload which will make it more difficult for the collaborators to separate necessary from superfluous information. Hence, the cognitive capacities demanded during the collaborative session are expected to increase which is likely to impede collaboration rather than support it.

Addressing these issues, we presented AWARE^{S}CUES which consists of four collaboration support features named LookAtMe, StareForCues, GazeCollision, and FreezeCues. These features allow collaborators to individually configure the awareness cues that are visible to them. At the same time, they can also draw attention to themselves and take influence on their collaborators' fields of view. To reduce the cognitive workload for activating and deactivating cues, the configuration of the cues is handled based on natural cooperation paradigms such as looking at someone or tapping on someone's shoulder.

We believe that these enhanced awareness cues can be applied in a variety of collaborative use cases like for example design reviews in different industries and hence contribute to the establishment of powerful remote collaboration platforms that enable sharing 3D content. In future work, we are planning to apply the proposed features for collaborative factory layout planning and conduct evaluations including cognitive load measurements.

Acknowledgments. This research was funded in parts by the Deutsche Forschungsgemeinschaft (DFG, German Research Foundation, #252408385 - IRTG 2057) and by the Innovative University Initiative (Bund-Länder-Initiative Innovative Hochschule, BMBF/GWK, 13IHS254B).

References

1. Bai, H., Sasikumar, P., Yang, J., Billinghurst, M.: A user study on mixed reality remote collaboration with eye gaze and hand gesture sharing. In: Proceedings of the 2020 CHI Conference on Human Factors in Computing Systems (CHI 2020), pp. 1–13. ACM, New York (2020). https://doi.org/10.1145/3313831.3376550
2. García-Pereira, I., Gimeno, J., Pérez, M., Portalés, C., Casas, S.: Mime: a mixed-space collaborative system with three immersion levels and multiple users. In: 2018 IEEE International Symposium on Mixed and Augmented Reality Adjunct (ISMAR-Adjunct), pp. 179–183 (2018). https://doi.org/10.1109/ISMAR-Adjunct.2018.00062
3. Goh, E.S., Sunar, M.S., Ismail, A.W.: 3D object manipulation techniques in handheld mobile augmented reality interface: a review. IEEE Access **7**, 40581–40601 (2019). https://doi.org/10.1109/ACCESS.2019.2906394
4. Gong, L., Berglund, J., Fast-Berglund, Å., Johansson, B., Wang, Z., Börjesson, T.: Development of virtual reality support to factory layout planning. Int. J. Interact. Design Manuf. **13**, 935–945 (2019). https://doi.org/10.1007/s12008-019-00538-x

5. Gong, L., et al.: Interaction design for multi-user virtual reality systems: an automotive case study. Procedia CIRP **93**, 1259–1264 (2020). https://doi.org/10.1016/j.procir.2020.04.036

6. Günther, S., Kratz, S., Avrahami, D., Mühlhäuser, M.: Exploring audio, visual, and tactile cues for synchronous remote assistance. In: Proceedings of the 11th PErvasive Technologies Related to Assistive Environments Conference (PETRA 2018), pp. 339–344. ACM, New York (2018). https://doi.org/10.1145/3197768.3201568

7. Huang, W., Wakefield, M., Rasmussen, T.A., Kim, S., Billinghurst, M.: A review on communication cues for augmented reality based remote guidance. J. Multimodal User Interfaces **16**, 239–256 (2022). https://doi.org/10.1007/s12193-022-00387-1

8. Jing, A., May, K., Matthews, B., Lee, G., Billinghurst, M.: The impact of sharing gaze behaviours in collaborative mixed reality. Proc. ACM Hum.-Comput. Interact. **6**(CSCW2) (2022). https://doi.org/10.1145/3555564

9. Johansen, R.: Teams for tomorrow (groupware). In: Proceedings of the Twenty-Fourth Annual Hawaii International Conference on System Sciences, vol. 3, pp. 521–534 (1991). https://doi.org/10.1109/HICSS.1991.184183

10. Kim, S., Lee, G., Billinghurst, M., Huang, W.: The combination of visual communication cues in mixed reality remote collaboration. J. Multimodal User Interfaces **14**, 321–335 (2020). https://doi.org/10.1007/s12193-020-00335-x

11. Kim, S., Lee, G., Huang, W., Kim, H., Woo, W., Billinghurst, M.: Evaluating the combination of visual communication cues for HMD-based mixed reality remote collaboration. In: Proceedings of the 2019 CHI Conference on Human Factors in Computing Systems (CHI 2019), pp. 1–13. ACM, New York (2019). https://doi.org/10.1145/3290605.3300403

12. Kostov, G., Wolfartsberger, J.: Designing a framework for collaborative mixed reality training. Procedia Comput. Sci. **200**, 896–903 (2022). https://doi.org/10.1016/j.procs.2022.01.287

13. Memmesheimer, V.M., Ebert, A.: A human-centered framework for scalable extended reality spaces. In: Aurich, J.C., Garth, C., Linke, B.S. (eds.) Proceedings of the 3rd Conference on Physical Modeling for Virtual Manufacturing Systems and Processes, pp. 111–128. Springer, Cham (2023). https://doi.org/10.1007/978-3-031-35779-4_7

14. Memmesheimer, V.M., Ebert, A.: Scalable extended reality: a future research agenda. Big Data Cognit. Comput. **6**(1) (2022). https://doi.org/10.3390/bdcc6010012

15. Milgram, P., Takemura, H., Utsumi, A., Kishino, F.: Augmented reality: a class of displays on the reality-virtuality continuum. In: Das, H. (ed.) Telemanipulator and Telepresence Technologies, vol. 2351, pp. 282–292. SPIE (1995). https://doi.org/10.1117/12.197321

16. Pereira, V., Matos, T., Rodrigues, R., Nóbrega, R., Jacob, J.: Extended reality framework for remote collaborative interactions in virtual environments. In: 2019 International Conference on Graphics and Interaction (ICGI), pp. 17–24 (2019). https://doi.org/10.1109/ICGI47575.2019.8955025

17. Pidel, C., Ackermann, P.: Collaboration in virtual and augmented reality: a systematic overview. In: De Paolis, L.T., Bourdot, P. (eds.) Augmented Reality, Virtual Reality, and Computer Graphics, pp. 141–156. Springer, Cham (2020). https://doi.org/10.1007/978-3-030-58465-8_10

18. Piumsomboon, T., Dey, A., Ens, B., Lee, G., Billinghurst, M.: The effects of sharing awareness cues in collaborative mixed reality. Front. Robotics AI **6** (2019). https://doi.org/10.3389/frobt.2019.00005

19. Piumsomboon, T., et al.: Mini-me: an adaptive avatar for mixed reality remote collaboration. In: Proceedings of the 2018 CHI Conference on Human Factors in Computing Systems (CHI 2018), pp. 1–13. ACM, New York (2018). https://doi.org/10.1145/3173574.3173620
20. Piumsomboon, T., Lee, G.A., Irlitti, A., Ens, B., Thomas, B.H., Billinghurst, M.: On the shoulder of the giant: a multi-scale mixed reality collaboration with 360 video sharing and tangible interaction. In: Proceedings of the 2019 CHI Conference on Human Factors in Computing Systems (CHI 2019), pp. 1–17. ACM, New York (2019). https://doi.org/10.1145/3290605.3300458

Factors of Haptic Feedback in a VR Experience Using Virtual Tools: Evaluating the Impact of Visual and Force Presentation

Kairyu Mori[(⊠)], Masayuki Ando, Kouyou Otsu, and Tomoko Izumi

Ritsumeikan University, Kusatsu 525-8557, Shiga, Japan
is0527rp@ed.ritsumei.ac.jp, {mandou,k-otsu,
izumi-t}@fc.ritsumei.ac.jp

Abstract. In this study, we explore the factors influencing the generation of haptic feedback during interactions with virtual objects using a rod-shaped tool within a virtual reality environment. Previously, we introduced a haptic feedback method involving a string-based haptic feedback device attached to a VR controller rather than utilizing a physical tool. In an experiment comparing a scenario where the device is attached to a real tool with our proposed method, it was confirmed that when the length of the tool is shorter than 50 cm, our method, without the physical tool, can provide haptic feedback which is equivalent to using the real tool. However, the interaction between force presentation from the device and visual information in the virtual reality environment in forming the haptic feedback remains unclear. Therefore, this study investigates the individual and combined effects of visual information and force feedback on the tactile experience of interacting with objects using tools in virtual reality. Our findings suggest that although visual information significantly influences the experience, integrating it with the restraint imposed by the haptic device can enhance the haptic feedback.

Keywords: Cross-modal Interaction · Haptic Feedback · Force Feedback · String-Based Haptic Feedback Device · Virtual Reality · Visual Feedback

1 Introduction

Virtual Reality (VR) has advanced significantly in its applications, aiming to replicate real-world sensations for an enhanced user experience. Specifically, haptic feedback from VR devices plays a central role in increasing immersion [1].

Many VR systems rely on vibrations generated by device motors to create haptic feedback [2, 3]. However, this method primarily targets haptic feedback to the hand. For instance, in scenarios such as attacking a monster with a sword in a VR game, this method is not suitable because haptic feedback should be directed to the arm, not the hand, to prevent unnecessary movement. Thus, providing a highly realistic sense of contact becomes challenging when interacting with objects using a tool, as it requires restricting arm movement.

© The Author(s), under exclusive license to Springer Nature Switzerland AG 2024
J. Y. C. Chen and G. Fragomeni (Eds.): HCII 2024, LNCS 14706, pp. 60–72, 2024.
https://doi.org/10.1007/978-3-031-61041-7_5

In this study, we explore methods for providing haptic feedback when a tool in a VR space interacts with a virtual object. Various feedback devices have been proposed to replicate a realistic touch experience with virtual objects [4]. One such device utilizes string tension to limit the user's arm movement, thereby offering force feedback. For example, Achberger et al. introduced the "STRIVE" device, which employs a string attached to real tools, providing haptic feedback when touching objects with tools in VR [5]. However, their approach is limited to cases where real tools correspond to virtual ones operated in VR. Therefore, if multiple tools need to be used and switched in the virtual world, preparing the corresponding real tool to receive continuous force feedback could be costly.

Our prior research explored the feasibility of simulating haptic feedback when a virtual rod-shaped tool interacts with a virtual object using a string-based haptic feedback device attached to the hand [6]. This method generates force feedback on a controller held in the hand, eliminating the need for an actual tool and facilitating the handling of various virtual objects. We examined how the sensation of touching virtual objects with a tool in VR varies depending on where the device generates force feedback (whether in the handheld controller or at the tip of a real tool). The experimental results demonstrated that for virtual tools shorter than 50 cm, a string-based haptic feedback device can deliver realistic haptic feedback without the need for real tools. Building upon our prior research [6] and existing studies [5], we contemplate the possibility that when using the device, haptic feedback may be influenced by both the force feedback provided by the device and the visual information depicting contact with an object. However, the interaction between force presentation and visual information in shaping the haptic feedback remains unclear.

Therefore, this research aims to elucidate the individual and combined impacts of visual information and force feedback on haptic feedback in VR utilizing our proposed haptic feedback device. This study investigates how the interplay of visual information and force feedback influences users' experiences when virtual tools interact with virtual objects in VR. We conducted experiments to ascertain whether a combined approach offers users more realistic haptic feedback by comparing different feedback types with and without visual information and force feedback.

2   Related Research

2.1   Using Devices to Enhance Haptic Feedback

Various haptic devices have been proposed to deliver more lifelike haptic feedback and enrich physical interaction with virtual objects. Haptic gloves, for instance, are hand-worn devices employing wires to control the user's hands and fingers, mimicking the sensation of grasping objects in VR [7, 8]. Furthermore, Achberger et al. introduced "STRIVE," a string-based haptic feedback device that delivers feedback to real tools held in hand via wires connected to a device worn on the shoulder [5]. The methods of imparting haptic feedback to the actual tools used by users in VR have been explored in diverse forms. Devices such as 'Extick Touch,' 'VR Grabbers,' and 'Strandholt' have been proposed for virtual tool experiences, replicating sensations like picking up with chopsticks, hammering nails, or screwing [9–11]. Moreover, Takahashi et al. developed a fishing game using a straightforward haptic feedback mechanism to mimic the pulling force experienced during fishing [12].

Although these methods necessitate the preparation of real tools, alternative approaches have been considered for providing haptic feedback to virtual tools in scenarios where real tools are not employed. One such device is 'Hap Tug,' which enhances user realism and immersion by simulating the sensation of a virtual tool being pulled, imposing constraints on wrist movement [13]. However, Hap Tug offers only partial haptic feedback to the wrist, failing to replicate the comprehensive haptic feedback experienced when using a tool that transmits feedback to the entire arm.

2.2 Enhancing VR User Experience with Visual and Tactile Feedback Interactivity

In VR, the visual information presented can significantly influence haptic feedback. Previous studies have demonstrated the possibility of creating illusions of sensations not physically felt in real space through innovative presentation of tactile information. For instance, Botvinick et al. reported that visual information could significantly affect the sense of touch by incorporating an illusion of a rubber hand as part of the participant's body [14]. Kilteni et al. explored how arm length affects touch sensation in VR, finding that visual illusions can extend up to three times the arm's length [15]. Feicket et al. proposed a method for experiencing VR music DJ by employing visual illusions when interacting with multiple virtual buttons using just one physical button [16]. Research has also investigated how disparities between visual and tactile feedback experiences in VR spaces influence haptic feedback, such as when holding a rod-shaped tool [17]. This study demonstrated that even in situations where there is a visual mismatch of the hand or tool in a stick tool holding scenario, users perceive the illusion of no mismatch if the disparity is minimal. These studies suggest that haptic-related sensations in VR experiences may be highly influenced by the force illusion induced by visual information.

2.3 Relationship Between Validation Content in This Study and Existing Research

In our previous research, we investigated replicating haptic feedback when interacting with objects using virtual tools in VR space through haptic feedback to the hand [6]. As highlighted in Sect. 2.1, many of the discussed haptic devices necessitate the player to wield a real tool matching the virtual one, which can pose challenges when various tools are required. However, our proposed method aims to validate the replication of haptic feedback with virtual tools without the necessity for real counterparts. In our earlier study, we found that if the tool's length is under 50 cm, it can provide the same sensation as using a real tool. However, it remains unclear which aspects of our proposed method contribute to generating this haptic feedback.

Studies in Sect. 2.2 explored how visual information in VR space can induce haptic illusions, potentially influencing haptic feedback. Consequently, it is unclear how the haptic feedback provided by string-based haptic feedback devices contributes to the haptic sensation of touching an object with a tool in VR. Therefore, our aim is to clarify through an experiment how the visual effects and the force generated by the device contribute to the tactile feedback experienced in a VR setting using a haptic feedback device with strings.

3   VR Environment and String-Based Haptic Feedback Device

We created an environment to assess whether combining visual and force feedback can enhance the realism of haptic feedback during interactions with objects using tools in a VR space. This assessment environment comprises a VR setup for detecting object interactions and a string-based haptic feedback device.

3.1   VR Environment

The VR environment utilized in this study was constructed using Unity and showcases a three-dimensional space populated with virtual tools and objects for user interaction (Fig. 1). The Meta Company's "Oculus Quest 2" serves as the VR device for this setup. Building upon previous research [6], this VR configuration centers on scenarios where users manipulate a red rod-shaped virtual tool from top to bottom, interacting with yellow virtual objects. Participants initiate tool manipulation by pressing a button on the Oculus controller. Upon contact between the virtual tool and the virtual object, the tool halts its movement upon reaching the object's surface, visually indicating to participants that contact has been made. A distinct signal is dispatched to a string-based haptic feedback device upon a contact decision between the virtual tool and the virtual object, while another signal is transmitted when there is no contact between the tool and any object. Consequently, force feedback is generated by dynamically reflecting the user's actions in the VR space to the device.

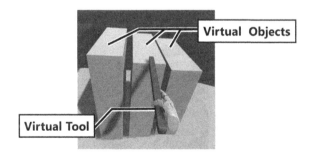

Fig. 1. Virtual tool and virtual objects in the VR environment

3.2 String-Based Haptic Feedback Device

When the virtual tool interacts with objects in the VR environment, haptic feedback is delivered through force feedback using a string-based haptic feedback device proposed in our prior research [6]. The device employed in this experiment draws inspiration from the STRIVE [5] device developed by Achberger et al. (Fig. 2). Our device distinguishes itself from these models by employing a servo motor to regulate string movement instead of a 5 V solenoid. This design enhancement aims for durability, particularly during prolonged usage. The device is affixed to the user's shoulder, with its string connected to the VR controller (Fig. 3). It incorporates a microcomputer (Arduino Uno) that receives signals from the VR space and manages string operation. The string is automatically wound up by the winding mechanism. Upon the virtual tool making a contact with a virtual object in VR, the servo motor rotates clockwise to halt string movement, creating a perceptible resistance for the user (Fig. 4). When the virtual tool is not in contact with virtual objects, the servo motor rotates counterclockwise, releasing the constraint. This mechanism offers haptic feedback simulating the sensation of the virtual tool interacting with virtual objects.

Fig. 2. Structure of the sting-based haptic feedback device

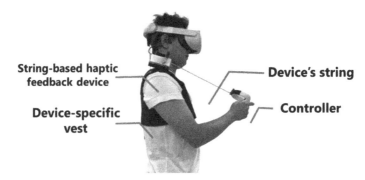

Fig. 3. User-side settings in the experiment. The haptic feedback device's wire is connected to the VR controller held by the user.

Fig. 4. The servo motor is activated, and the stopper stops the gear from rotating

4   Verification Experiment

4.1   Objective

Our previous research [6] discovered that when interacting with virtual objects using virtual tools, connecting the device's string to a controller can generate appropriate haptic feedback. However, it remains unclear whether this feedback stems from the device's force or visual cues in virtual reality. Therefore, in this study, we aim to elucidate how the perception of haptic feedback varies when altering the presence or absence of visual and force feedback during interactions with objects in a VR space.

In the experiment, utilizing the verification environment and the string-based haptic feedback device outlined in Sect. 3, participants were tasked with assessing the haptic feedback while holding a virtual tool and touching an object. The evaluation of haptic feedback encompassed three perspectives; "discomfort," "sense of resistance," and "realism." This experiment tests hypotheses in an experience where participants interact with virtual objects using a virtual rod-shaped tool in a VR space with the assistance of the string-based haptic feedback device.

- **H1:** Haptic feedback increases when either visual or force feedback is provided, compared to when neither is provided.
- **H2.1:** Providing visual feedback has a greater impact on reducing discomfort and increasing realism than force feedback.
- **H2.2:** Providing force feedback has a greater impact on increasing the sense of resistance than visual feedback.
- **H3:** Haptic feedback increases when both visual and force feedback are provided.

Hypothesis H1 suggests that reproducing either visual or haptic feedback enhances the user's tactile experience. This is grounded in the understanding that sensory inputs such as sight and touch are pivotal for recreating real-world interactions, and their absence may diminish the feeling of contact. In essence, replicating visual or haptic feedback makes the interaction between tools and objects in VR feel more authentic.

The sensation of "discomfort" during tool usage in VR is believed to be significantly influenced by visual factors, as opposed to force feedback. In real contact scenarios with tools, objects are perceived to halt at the surface upon contact. Thus, even if force feedback is present in a VR experience, deviating from this real-world scenario with visual scenes depicting contact is likely to heighten user discomfort and decrease the sense of realism (Hypothesis H2.1). Conversely, the "sense of resistance" is thought to be impacted by force feedback, rather than visual cues. Therefore, when force feedback accompanies a tool's physical contact with an object, the sense of resistance is expected to intensify (Hypothesis H2.2).

Hypothesis H3 suggests that the sense of contact is enhanced when visual and haptic feedbacks are combined. This stems from the belief that both visual and haptic feedbacks are pivotal in shaping the contact experience, and their combined reproduction enhances the realism of the contact experience.

4.2 Experiment Settings

This experiment established the following four conditions with or without visual feedback and force feedback in the VR space:

- **No Feedback:** This condition lacks both visual and force feedback. The tool visually traverses objects in the VR space without generating visual feedback, and the haptic feedback device remains inactive, thus not generating force feedback.
- **Visual Feedback:** In this condition, visual feedback is present, but force feedback is absent. The tool halts at the surface of objects visually in the VR space, generating visual feedback, while the haptic feedback device remains inactive, thus not generating force feedback.
- **Force Feedback:** This condition includes force feedback but lacks visual feedback. The tool visually passes through objects in the VR space without generating visual feedback, while the haptic feedback device operates, generating force feedback.
- **Combined:** This condition integrates both visual and force feedback. The tool halts at the surface of objects visually in the VR space, generating visual feedback, and the haptic feedback device operates, generating force feedback.

The objects placed in the VR space for verification remain consistent across the four experimental conditions. The variation lies solely in the feedback provided when the virtual tool interacts with the virtual objects. In the Visual Feedback and Combined conditions, virtual tools are prevented from visually passing through objects during interaction. Force feedback is provided during interaction in the Force Feedback and Combined conditions.

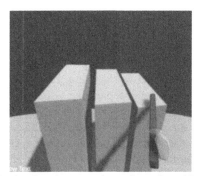 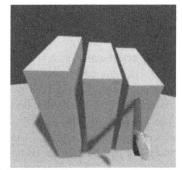

(a) A virtual tool stops at the surface of an object   (b) A virtual tool passes through an object

Fig. 5. Situations where a virtual tool touches virtual objects

We constructed an experimental VR environment, depicted in Fig. 5, which contains a 50 cm virtual stick and several boxes. We established two visualization modes regarding how the virtual tool behaves upon contact with the virtual objects. One mode visualizes the virtual tool's movement halting at the surface of objects upon contact (Fig. 5(a)), whereas the other allows the tool's movement to continue uninterrupted, passing through objects (Fig. 5(b)).

Table 1. Question items in the Questionnaire

	Questionnaire items	
Q1	I felt discomfort when touching the objects in the VR environment	Discomfort
Q2	I felt resistance when touching the objects in the VR environment	Sense of Resistance
Q3	When touching the objects in the VR environment, I felt like my arm couldn't move because the tool touched the objects	
Q4	The experience of touching the objects in the VR environment felt realistic	Reality
Q5	It felt as if I was actually touching objects in real space when touching the objects in the VR environment	

4.3 Evaluation Items

In this experiment, participants were tasked with completing a survey regarding their discomfort, sense of resistance, and perception of reality across each experimental condition. The survey consisted of five items, as outlined in Table 1, and participants were required to respond using a 7-point Likert scale (1: Strongly disagree to 7: Strongly agree). Specifically, Q1 assessed discomfort, whereas Q2 and Q3 addressed the sense of resistance; Q4 and Q5 focused on perceptions of realism.

4.4 Experiment Procedure

Participants were given a comprehensive overview of the experiment, and their consent was obtained through an informed consent form. They were provided with VR goggles, a VR controller, and the string-based haptic feedback device. Additionally, they were required to wear a special vest to securely attach the device to their shoulder during the experiment.

Before engaging in the VR space experiment, participants were instructed to touch a real object using a real rod-shaped tool. This exercise aimed to familiarize them with the process of interacting with objects using a virtual tool in a VR environment and to understand the tactile sensation of touching a real object with a physical tool. In this experiment, the tool length was set to 50 cm, based on the findings from previous research [6]. The real tool and objects were crafted using styrene board and Styrofoam.

Subsequently, participants underwent practice sessions using the VR goggles and controllers in a training environment featuring grabbable objects (Fig. 6). They were tasked with picking up wooden brick objects during this training phase, intended to enhance their proficiency in maneuvering and grasping objects within the VR space. Following the donning of the special vest and the string-based haptic feedback device, participants were provided instructions on specific tool movements, such as slow top-to-bottom swings and precise touching.

Participants were instructed to wear the VR goggles and hold the VR controller in their hands to commence the experiment. Within the VR space, participants were tasked with touching three yellow objects, as depicted in Fig. 5, approximately ten times in total using the virtual tool. Upon completing the task, participants were prompted to respond to the survey, including the items listed in Table 1. This process was repeated a total of four times, each time under different conditions. To mitigate order effects, the four conditions were presented to each participant in a randomized sequence.

Fig. 6. Training VR Environment

5 Experimental Results and Discussion

5.1 Results

Twenty undergraduate and graduate students (14 males and 6 females) participated in the experiment. In addition to the questionnaire items outlined in Table 1, participants were queried about their level of VR experience. One participant reported engaging in VR experiences every six months, two reported once a year, and ten reported experiencing VR several times. Among the remaining participants, thirteen had encountered controller-based VR experiences, albeit infrequently.

Figure 7 displays the results of the questionnaire items depicted in Table 1 using a box-and-whisker plot. In the analysis, the Friedman test and Holm's multiple comparison method were employed to scrutinize differences in mean values among conditions, and a comparison of the mean values for each question was undertaken.

First, the results for question Q1, which investigates discomfort, are discussed. Lower scores correspond to reduced discomfort experienced by participants. As illustrated in Fig. 1, the Combined condition exhibits the lowest mean value across all conditions.

The Friedman test conducted across the four conditions—No Feedback, Visual Feedback, Force Feedback, and Combined—indicates a significant difference ($p < 0.01$). Subsequently, Holm's multiple comparison tests reveal significant disparities between the Combined condition and the other three conditions.

Subsequently, Q2 and Q3 regarding the sense of resistance are examined. A higher score indicates a greater sense of force feedback perceived by participants. In both cases, the No Feedback condition yields lower scores compared to the others, while the Combined condition yields higher scores. The Friedman test for these questions indicates significant differences ($p < 0.01$), with Holm's multiple comparison tests revealing significant differences between all conditions except for between the Visual Feedback and Force Feedback conditions.

Finally, we elaborate on the results pertaining to questions Q4 and Q5 regarding perceptions of reality. The data depicted in Fig. 7 indicates a trend where the Visual Feedback and Combined conditions yield higher scores compared to the other two conditions. The Friedman test conducted for these questions reveals significance ($p < 0.01$). Moreover, Holm's multiple comparison tests indicate significant differences among all combinations of the conditions.

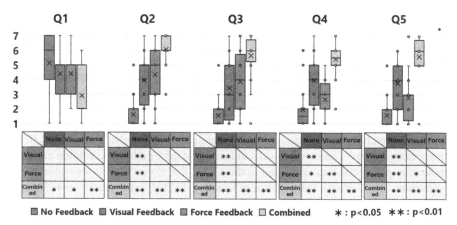

Fig. 7. Mean scores in each condition in questions Q1–Q5 of the questionnaire. (Box and whisker plot, *: $p < 0.05$, **$p < 0.01$) The tables below display the outcomes of multiple comparison tests (Holm's method) for the mean scores of each condition in the questions.

5.2 Discussion

Discussing Hypothesis H1, to validate this hypothesis, significant differences must exist between the No Feedback and the Visual Feedback conditions and between the No Feedback and Force Feedback conditions. In the case of question Q1, which pertains to discomfort, no significant differences are observed in these two comparisons. However, the mean values of the Visual and Force Feedback conditions are lower than those of the No Feedback condition. Additionally, the Visual and Force Feedback conditions yield significantly higher scores in questions Q2 to Q5, which address the sense of resistance and reality. Thus, these findings partially support H1.

For Hypothesis H2.1, we anticipated that the Visual Feedback condition would exhibit significantly lower discomfort in question Q1 and higher perceptions of reality in questions Q4 and Q5 compared to the No Feedback and the Force Feedback conditions. From the results of the survey questions, although there is no significant difference in discomfort for Q1 between the Visual Feedback and No Feedback conditions, the mean value in the Visual Feedback condition is slightly lower than that in the No Feedback condition. However, the mean values of the Visual and Force Feedback conditions are nearly identical. Thus, there was no observed effect of visual feedback on reducing discomfort compared to force feedback. In terms of reality perception, the Visual Feedback condition has significantly higher scores than the No Feedback and the Force Feedback conditions. This suggests that participants perceive haptic feedback as more realistic when visual feedback is provided, thereby partially supporting H2.1.

To substantiate Hypothesis H2.2, the Force Feedback condition must exhibit significantly higher scores in questions Q2 and Q3 regarding force feedback compared to the No Feedback and the Visual Feedback conditions. The survey results indicate that the Force Feedback condition yields significantly higher scores than the No Feedback condition in both of these questions, implying the impact of force feedback on the sense of resistance. However, there are no significant differences in the sense of resistance between the Force and Visual Feedback conditions, despite the Force Feedback condition displaying higher mean scores than the Visual Feedback condition. Therefore, although a significant advantage over visual feedback is not observed, Hypothesis H2.2 is partially supported by the fact that force feedback provides significantly higher sense of resistance compared to the experiment without any feedback.

Finally, to substantiate Hypothesis H3, the Combined condition must show significant differences compared to each of the Visual and Force Feedback conditions from all three perspectives. The survey results indicate that the Combined condition exhibits significantly positive scores compared to the Visual and Force Feedback conditions in all questions. This implies that when feedback is provided both visually and through force, participants perceive better haptic feedback, supporting H3.

Next, we discuss the impact of both visual and force feedback on haptic feedback derived from the experiment. In question Q1, related to 'discomfort,' there is no significant difference between the Visual and Force Feedback conditions. Their mean values are nearly identical, suggesting that the discomfort caused by the lack of feedback in each condition is similar. Questions Q2 and Q3 focus on the 'sense of resistance,' and the results do not significantly differ between the Visual and Force Feedback conditions. These findings suggest that both visual and force feedback generate similar haptic feedback.

However, regarding perceptions of reality, the results of questions Q4 and Q5 indicate that visual feedback has a more substantial effect than force feedback, whereas force feedback also significantly enhances reality compared to no feedback. From these results, it can be inferred that visual feedback plays an important role in providing an experience with high reality when interacting with objects using a tool. When only visual feedback is provided, however, suitable haptic feedback is not generated due to a lack of the sense of resistance. Similarly, when only force feedback is provided, a high sense of reality is not generated owing to a lack of consistent visual information with the sense of resistance provided by the device. However, incorporating the device's force into visual feedback can significantly improve haptic feedback by reducing discomfort and producing more realistic and resistant haptic feedback. This underscores the importance of combining both visual and force feedback for an immersive haptic experience when using tools in a VR space. The findings of this study suggest that integrating visual and force feedback can enhance the reality and suitability of haptic feedback in virtual reality.

6 Conclusions

This study aimed to elucidate which type of feedback (visual or force) exerts a more significant influence on haptic feedback in a VR experience where users handle a rod-shaped virtual tool touching objects. We assessed the impact of utilizing a string-based haptic feedback device to replicate the contact experience within a virtual environment. The experiment examined four scenarios: visual feedback only, force feedback only, combined visual and force feedback, and no feedback.

The findings reveal that both visual and force feedbacks influence haptic feedback when interacting with virtual objects using virtual tools. Although visual feedback is more effective than force feedback in enhancing the sense of reality, combining both types of feedback enhances the quality of haptic feedback compared to using either visual or force feedback alone. The study concludes that string-based haptic feedback devices, even without the use of real tools, can generate suitable haptic feedback, particularly when combining visual and force feedback, particularly in scenarios involving short virtual tools less than 50 cm.

However, it is important to note that this study's string-based haptic feedback device may only provide specific directions for touching objects. Consequently, if the touch direction in the VR space diverges from the direction of the haptic feedback provided by the device, unsuitable haptic feedback may occur owing to the discrepancy. Therefore, future research should delve into a detailed examination of the effects of touch direction when using tools on objects in VR spaces. Moreover, integrating auditory elements such as sound effects could further enhance the reality and immersion of the touch experience in virtual environments.

References

1. Ramsamy, P., Haffegee, A., Jamieson, R., Alexandrov, V.: Using haptics to improve immersion in virtual environments. In: Computational Science–ICCS 2006. LNCS, vol. 3992, pp. 603–609. Springer, Heidelberg (2006)
2. Meta Quest2. https://www.meta.com/jp/quest/. Accessed 06 Jan 2023
3. Vive. https://www.vive.com/jp/. Accessed 06 Jan 2023
4. Fang, C., Zhang, Y., Dworman, M., Harrison, C.: Wireality: Enabling complex tangible geometries in virtual reality with worn multi-string haptics. In: Proceedings of the 2020 CHI Conference on Human Factors in Computing Systems, pp. 1–10 (2020)

5. Achberger, A., Aust, F., Pohlandt, D., Vidackovic, K., Sedlmair, M.: STRIVE: string-based force feedback for automotive engineering. In: The 34th Annual ACM Symposium on User Interface Software and Technology, pp. 841–853 (2021)
6. Mori, K., Ando, M., Otsu, K., Izumi, T.: Effect of repulsive positions on haptic feed-back on using a string-based device virtual objects without a real tool. In: International Conference on Human-Computer Interaction, pp. 266–277. Springer, Cham (2023)
7. Blake, J., Gurocak, H.B.: Haptic glove with MR brakes for virtual reality. IEEE/ASME Trans. Mechatron. **14**(5), 606–615 (2009)
8. Caeiro-Rodríguez, M., Otero-González, I., Mikic-Fonte, F.A., Llamas-Nistal, M.: A systematic review of commercial smart gloves: current status and applications. Sensors **21**(8), 2667 (2021)
9. Kataoka, K., Otsuki, M., Shibata, F., Kimura, A.: Evaluation of ExtickTouch: an advanced extendable virtual object touching device. In: Computer Vision and Image Media (CVIM), vol. 2021, no. 20, pp. 1–6 (2021)
10. Yang, J., Horii, H., Thayer, A., Ballagas, R.: VR grabbers: ungrounded haptic retargeting for precision grabbing tools. In: Proceedings of the 31st Annual ACM Symposium on User Interface Software and Technology, pp. 889–899 (2018)
11. Strandholt, P.L., Dogaru, O.A., Nilsson, N.C., Nordahl, R., Serafin, S.: Knock on wood: combining redirected touching and physical props for tool-based interaction in virtual reality. In: Proceedings of the 2020 CHI Conference on Human Factors in Computing Systems, pp. 1–13 (2020)
12. Takamoto, S., Amamiya, T., Ito, S., Gomi, Y.: Expression and application of the traction illusion in VR fishing. Trans. Human Interface Soc. **18**(2), 87–94 (2016)
13. Lim, J., Choi, Y.: Force-feedback haptic device for representation of tugs in virtual reality. Electronics **11**(11), 1730 (2022)
14. Botvinick, M., Cohen, J.: Rubber hands 'feel' touch that eyes see. Nature **391**(6669), 756 (1998)
15. Kilteni, K., Normand, J.M., Sanchez-Vives, M.V., Slater, M.: Extending body space in immersive virtual reality: a very long arm illusion. PLoS ONE **7**(7), e40867 (2012)
16. Feick, M., Kleer, N., Zenner, A., Tang, A., Krüger, A.: Visuo-haptic illusions for linear translation and stretching using physical proxies in virtual reality. In: Proceedings of the 2021 CHI Conference on Human Factors in Computing Systems, pp. 1–13 (2021)
17. Zhou, Y., Popescu, V.: Tapping with a handheld stick in VR: redirection detection thresholds for passive haptic feedback. In: 2022 IEEE Conference on Virtual Reality and 3D User Interfaces, pp. 83–92 (2022)

Does It Look Real? Visual Realism Complexity Scale for 3D Objects in VR

Rahel Schmied-Kowarzik[✉][iD], Lina Kaschub[iD], Thore Keser[iD],
Rebecca Rodeck[iD], and Gerko Wende

German Aerospace Center (DLR), Hamburg, Germany
{rahel.schmied-kowarzik,lina.kaschub,thore.keser,rebecca.rodeck,
gerko.wende}@dlr.de

Abstract. The visual realism classification scale (VRCS) is a tool to help researchers judge, compare, and describe the visual realism of objects in virtual environments. In Human-Computer Interaction, visual realism is a much-investigated topic, as different tasks benefit from a particular level of detail. The subjective feeling of realism becomes more tangible by judging 3D objects based on the objective criteria: *lighting, reflection, texture, structure, form,* and *internal consistency*. This paper revises the original VRCS using statistical analysis and an expert focus group. The adopted changes are evaluated through a complementary user study of 34 participants, which resulted in high validity due to a significant correlation between the subjective measure and VRCS. Furthermore, the scale significantly predicts subjective realism and improves the inter-rater reliability on multiple questions. Using the focus group and user study results, this paper offers guidance on applying the VRCS in research.

Keywords: Human factors · Realism perception · Extended Reality · Visualization and image rendering

1 Introduction

The perception of visual realism in virtual environments has been investigated in research for many years. It focuses on the effects of varying levels of realism on tasks [14,16,23] or on the feeling of presence [15,31,34]. Studies compare multiple virtual environments with different levels of realism. The researchers choose the level of realism and the difference between environments based on objective and subjective criteria.

Current ratings of visual realism complexity range from simple binary distinction [9] to arbitrary rating scales [7,19,39,40]. Yu et al. [39], for example, asked the participants to rate the subjective realism of objects on a scale from 0 to 100. While these approaches are great for measuring the perceived realism of participants in the virtual environment, they are not applicable for designing a study that compares different visual realism. Researchers should avoid subjective biases, hence a more objective grounded scale is necessary. It allows researchers

© The Author(s), under exclusive license to Springer Nature Switzerland AG 2024
J. Y. C. Chen and G. Fragomeni (Eds.): HCII 2024, LNCS 14706, pp. 73–92, 2024.
https://doi.org/10.1007/978-3-031-61041-7_6

to distinguish different levels of realism and compare environments with each other. In 2023, Schmied-Kowarzik et al. [30] proposed a novel method to classify the visual realism of 3D models. The Visual Realism Complexity Scale (VRCS) helps researchers define the visual realism of objects in virtual environments and opens up opportunities to conduct comparable research in this field.

The paper shows a significant correlation between a subjective realism rating and the developed VRCS. It further shows good inter-rater reliability for the 3D models. However, it still leaves room for improvement: the authors discussed that some items in the scale might refer to the same underlying concept and that improved phrasing could reach a higher consensus among the raters. In consequence, this paper aims to review the data and further analyze the individual items and their weight towards the VRCS score. The revised VRCS allows for better and more consistent ratings of the VRCS, as investigated in this study.

With a score for visual realism of 3D objects, developers can tailor the environment to the task. Knowing the level of visual realism complexity required, resources can be allocated more efficiently. The score further allows for a comparison between studies, which is currently challenging to the inherent personal bias of the authors when classifying objects as "realistic".

This paper aims to take the original study by Schmied-Kowarzik et al. [30] and improve it by conducting more research in the VRCS questions. Revision of the original VRCS is done on two different levels. First, the data from the first study is analyzed quantitatively, going beyond the analysis of the original publication. Combining the results with a qualitative analysis by experts in the field leads an adaption of the VRCS and more applicable, as well as better results. This change is tested using a validation study, followed by another statistical analysis and in-depth discussion in the later sections.

2   Background

The amount of Virtual Reality (VR) research on different realism levels raises the question if it would not be best to always strive for the highest level of realism. Lugrin et al. [17] found that the level of realism had no impact on the effectiveness of their simulation. They pointed out that knowing when lower fidelity is sufficient could be a significant economic factor. Less realistic avatars and environments are often faster and cheaper to produce and need fewer computational resources [17].

Next to the monetary benefits, effects like the "Uncanny Valley" make an argument for less realistic models. The Uncanny Valley describes the effect that a certain level of resemblance to human beings leads to a high dislike of people towards these avatars [20].

Skulmowski et al. [33] explored the idea of cognitive load combined with the level of visual realism and found that cognitive load heightens with higher realism. These findings underline that it is crucial to see if high realism is needed to avoid unnecessary cognitive load.

Rogers et al. also show the multiple benefits of lower realism [27]. They refer to the distractive qualities of highly realistic applications, hindering learning and training effects. Others even found evidence of aesthetic preferences towards less realistic visuals [32]. It is further suggested that reduced realism might be needed for player engagement in gaming [4].

The task and its inherent requirements are critical for those considerations. Some applications might need a higher sense of presence without a high need for realism [2]. Sometimes, the less realistic objects are better suited for the task. Instructive illustrations benefit from a simplified perspective, conveying the message focused on the most relevant points [10]. Wijaynto et al. supported this idea by concluding that developers should keep relevant information in mind when designing virtual environments for specific tasks [36].

2.1 Defining Realism

The ability to perform effective research in this field relies on a shared understanding of the term *realism*. Gonçalves et al. [11] found that research in virtual realism uses the terms *fidelity* and *realism* with varying definitions. The authors were able to discriminate two fundamental concepts: *subjective realism* and *objective realism*. Subjective realism encompasses the individual experience in the virtual environment and whether users feel it is "real" [11]. It is not always dependent on whether the scenario is possible in the real world but depends on peoples' perceptions. The perception is based on various influences and differs between people perceiving the same virtual environment [11]. Objective realism describes how well the virtual environment can capture the real world. Depending on the system and its objects, the virtual environment can depict environments less or more accurately [11]. In realism research, the main focus lies on subjective realism, as the success of an application is mainly determined by how it feels for the user.

Pöschl and Döring [21] introduce the VR Simulation Realism Scale, aggregating multiple factors to get a realism score. This self-report, partly adapted from Witmer and Singer [37], is one way of capturing the participants' feeling of realism.

Other methods of measuring subjective realism investigate the level of presence that the participants experience. Slater et al. and Schwind et al. show that people experience higher presence in high-realism environments [32,34], which is why it has been used as a proxy indicator of realism. However, other papers [1,31] discuss that perceived realism, in specific applications, may not directly correlate to presence. This idea is underlined by Banos et al. [2], who define perceived realism and presence as different concepts. Bowman and McMahan [3] state that in some industry applications, a high visual realism is needed to understand complex structures correctly, but a high feeling of presence is not. Thus, presence as a measure of subjective realism is controversial and dependent on the circumstances.

This paper does not focus on the ways to capture subjective realism but objective realism. Objective realism is a helpful tool for judging objects and virtual environments since it disregards personal opinions. The focus is not on the final user but a researcher building a virtual environment.

Prior research about capturing objective realism introduces different ways to describe it. Schäffer et al. define different Levels of Detail (LoD) for objects [29] to better structure VR applications. They define seven steps from a cylinder to a fully functional 3D object with physics and animation. Looking at the international LoD definition for virtual houses [18], the method works well for some 3D buildings but is limited to that area. Thus, a good definition for every type of object is needed for LoD to be a valuable method for measuring realism. Further, the levels are often insufficient to describe the nuanced degrees of visual realism. Automated approaches, for example, with image processing [35], do not capture the full range of visual realism at this time, especially for the more complex 3D objects. The VRCS [30] intents to support researchers in their work. Influential factors of realism are captured with the VRCS and allow for a less biased score. It further enables objective comparison between different virtual environments and objects. The aim is to close the research gap in the objective realism measurement of objects in VR. Thus, unless otherwise indicated, realism in this paper is defined as objective realism.

2.2   Visual Realism Complexity

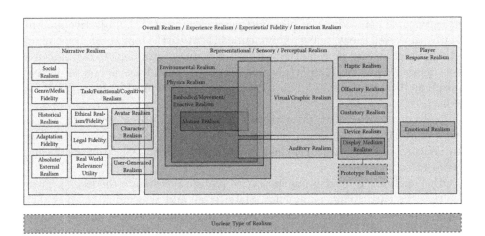

Fig. 1. Hierachical taxonomy of realism dimensions and how they relate by Rogers et al. [27]

Realism is a complex construct composed of many aspects. Rogers et al. [27] systematically studied realism in games and developed a framework to differentiate between concepts. It is crucial to make these distinctions as the categories are considered differently, and it allows future research to put it into context. Rogers et al. distinguished multiple aspects of realism, like *historical, haptic,* and *emotional realism,* as seen in Fig. 1. Exploring 3D objects is part of *visual/graphic realism*, a sub-category of *perceptual realism*. While the movement of objects is part of the overall perceptual realism, it belongs more to *environmental/physics realism*, which will not be explored here as it goes beyond the scope of this paper. The focus on visual realism is further supported by the immense impact of the visual system on perception [22], one of the reasons why visual realism is one of the most investigated topics in realism research for gaming [27].

Slater et al. [34] define two components of visual realism - geometric realism and illumination realism. Geometric realism describes whether 3D objects look like real objects, while illumination realism describes the lighting of the 3D object. These terms served as a starting point during the development of the VRCS. In the work of Huang & Klippel [14], Pouke et al. [23], Hvass et al. [15], and Lugrin et al. [17], the visual realism complexity is changed through the number of polygons or a lower texture fidelity; both are part of geometric realism. An isolated change in the number of polygons does not account for high or low visual realism, but it can influence the fidelity of a 3D model. Ramanarayanan et al. [26] describe how to save computing power, by calculating fewer polygons for an object, while retaining the visual look. In the VRCS, the number of polygons is not considered but rather the overall detail of the form, which may or may not be due to the number of polygons. The second factor, the object's texture, was used by Cover et al. [6] and Wang and Doube [35]. This is supported by the work of Fan et al. [8], who describe the essential factors for the realism of composite images as resolution, color, saturation, and illumination.

The VRCS combines resolution, color, and saturation into a broader texture category as part of geometric realism. Another geometric factor that influences visual realism is the surface structure, as explored by Rademacher et al. [25]. Moreover, they also explore illumination realism as a key point for realism [25], as in their study, it was shown that the look of the shadow shows a significant difference in how real an image is perceived. This was also used to define realism in the work of Wang and Doube [35]. Elhelw et al. [7] furthermore discovered that realistic reflections of an image can lead to higher perceived visual realism. Thus, in the original VRCS, the lighting (ambient, directional), the shadows, and the reflections are considered factors.

The original VRCS consists of four components: *shadow*, *light* (including *reflection*), *texture* (including *structure*), and *form*. Each factor contributes a score of 0 to 3, yielding a potential cumulative score of 0 to 10. This corresponds to a subjective realism score from "not looking like a real object at all" (0) to being "very realistic" (10).

3   Analysis

Improving the original VRCS includes looking at the factors both qualitatively and quantitatively. Schmied-Kowarzik et al. [30] hypothesized that some factors might have an overly large influence on the overall score. The results of the original VRCS showed that the questions correlate to subjective realism. To achieve improvement, the authors discussed possible problems with the categories, looked at whether the statistics supported their hypothesis, and then gave this input to a focus group. The qualitative analysis by experts in the field will allow for additional insights based on their experience. This combined analysis aims to find the items most influential on the overall score and impression of realism and combine or rephrase the items of the original VRCS.

Especially the components *shadow* and *light* are closely interdependent. Without directional lighting, no shadows are visible. A hypothesis would be that *light* does not give additional realism information that is not already given by the shadows, as the distinction between directional light and general light is usually made based on the absence or presence of shadows. To inspect the influence of every factor, a weighted least square regression analysis with the original dataset was done after removing two outliers and correcting for heteroscedasticity. The overall regression was statistically significant ($R^2 = 0.617$, adjusted $R^2 = 0.607$, $F(9, 356) = 63.689, p < .01$). All predictors except *light* were significant. While shadows influences the score, directional light does not improve the score compared to general light (coefficient $= -0.046, p = .873$). This would support the hypothesis that light is less relevant and acts more through other factors like shadows and reflections.

3.1   Focus Group

The qualitative expert analysis was undertaken to enhance the robustness and clarity of the questionnaire. Four experienced professionals in Extended Reality (XR) and human-computer interaction were invited to participate in a two-hour online focus group. The focus group was led in german by two moderators, with $M1$ leading the group through the process and $M2$ being an additional note-taker and observer to reduce observer bias.

The primary objective of the focus group was to inspect questions that exhibited variances in responses during the initial study, where many interpretations emerged. As discussed in Schmied-Kowarzik et al. [30], these ambiguities were attributed mainly to the phrasing of questions.

The focus group started with an initial explanation of visual realism complexity and an introduction to the original VRCS. The collaborative process of question revision revolved around looking at the essence of each question and eliminating potential sources of confusion. With the insights gained from each question, the answers became iteratively more refined. The findings were collected on a Miro Board[1] to allow everyone to keep track of the discussion and build on the collected ideas. The outcome of this expert-driven revision was a refined questionnaire. The main findings included 1) a refined definition of the reflections, as the definition is not solely about the presence of the reflections, but also their physical realism in that context; 2) phrasing like "intentional" was changed to more objective wording, as even very intentional objects can look unrealistic (especially looking at art pieces); 3) the removal of the directional light as a factor and 4) the need for a further question about the overall consistency of the objects. The linguistic clarity achieved through this process

---

[1] Miro (2023). *Miro Board.* www.miro.com.

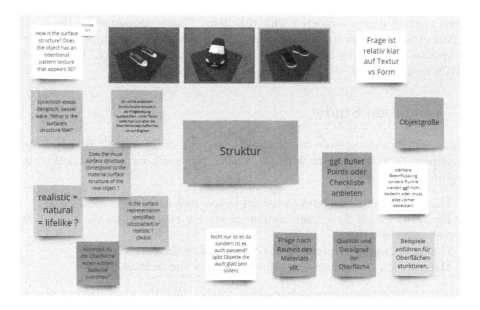

Fig. 2. Focus group results of the discussion about the *structure* question

is anticipated to contribute significantly to the validity and reliability of the results of this revision study. The revised questions should yield more consistent responses by aligning the questionnaire with a consensus-driven understanding of visual realism complexity.

3.2   Revision of the VRCS Items

Based on the output of the expert focus group and the statistical analysis, the questions from the original VRCS were revised.

The former categories *light* and *shadows* were merged as one *lighting* category. Reflections are not a part of that category but are seen as a separate concept. The experts identified that it was unclear whether the questions referred to the mere presence of any light reflection or a physically correct reflective behavior. The wording of *texture* and *form* was changed slightly to make it more precise. Additionally, the objects are now displaying their type (e.g., Cake, Plant, Car), allowing for an appropriate assessment even when there is a dissimilarity between an object's appearance and its designated type. For example a not very realistic banana could look like a very realistic plastic banana. *Structure* was formerly only part of *texture*. However, after revision, it was found that any 3D indications are interpreted as a detailed structure. Limiting the item *structure* to only the texture would require raters to inspect the objects closely, which is unrealistic in practice. Lastly, *internal consistency* was added as a new category. After the prior study, the author received feedback that some objects appeared "odd". Objects that score highly in all categories but still seem off or have mismatched levels of realism are considered with this item. This is supported by the work of Xue et al. [38], who stated consistency as important for realism perception in composite images. The new questionnaire is presented in Table 1. The revised VRCS ranges from $0 - 9$ points summed over all the factors.

4   Validation Study

This study provides a more comprehensive analysis of the VRCS. To assess the perception of visual realism with the VRCS, this work inspects the following hypotheses:

1. The VRCS score correlates to the subjective realism of participants. (H1)
2. The VRCS leads to a more consistent scoring compared to the subjective realism score. (H2)
3. The questionnaire improves quantitatively after the revision. (H3)
4. The questionnaire improves qualitatively after the revision. (H4)

To answer those questions and to delve further into the evaluation of visual realism within virtual environments the following experimental setup is used.

4.1   Stimuli

In both studies, the selection process was as random as possible. However, the object selection remained a subjective choice of the researcher. The objects were downloaded from the online source Turbosquid[2] and are downloadable free of charge. The selection was made by choosing categories and then picking the first two objects from the site that differed in their visual appearance and could be imported into the Unity3D Game Engine. The following categories were picked due to their common nature: *shoes, bananas, house plants, cake,* and *cars*. These categories were the same for both studies, except the *cake* category, which was newly added for the second study. The objects were selected to create a diverse dataset, with varying degrees of realism.

As seen in Fig. 3, the objects are not using the full capacity of modern object generation. This is due to the limiting nature of the Head Mounted Display (HMD) processors.

4.2   Procedure

Participants were presented with the 10 distinct virtual objects rendered in a VR environment. The environment was built with Unity3D Game Engine[3] and was focused on the objects presented on a grey cube in an otherwise empty world, ensuring that the context would not change the perception of the objects. Each participant was required to assess the visual realism of the presented objects

---

[2] Shutterstock (2023). *TurboSquid.* www.turbosquid.com.
[3] Unity Technologies (2023). *Unity3D.* Version 2021.3.7f1.

Table 1. Revised Visual Realism Classification Scale

Element	Item		Explanation
Lighting	No Shadow	0	The object has: (e.g. hard shadows have sharp edges, soft shadows have diffused edges)
	Hard Shadows	1	
	Soft Shadows	2	
Reflection	False	0	Does the light behave in a natural way? Does the material show reflections as you would expect? (e.g. see the light reflections in shiny material or see no reflections in matte objects)
	True	1	
Texture	Not fitting for the object	0	The texture here refers to the appearance of the surface of an object and its color.
	visibly simplified (plain colors)	1	
	has a detailed texture (can be one color if it fits the object)	2	
Structure	False	0	Does the object have a form or pattern structure that has depth indications? (e.g. bumps and dents that you would expect on this specific object)
	True	1	
Form	not/barely recognizable	0	The form is: [item]
	visibly simplified	1	
	detailed form/shape	2	
Internal Consistency	Yes, something stands out	0	Does one or more of the elements (texture, lighting, form) stand out compared to the rest of the object? (e.g. a very detailed object does not throw a shadow on itself or an object has a texture that is so unfitting that the object as a whole feels less realistic)
	No, the object is consistent	1	

using the modified version of the VRCS, which comprised six distinct questions, as described in Table 1. Participants were encouraged to examine the objects from different angles and distances, and there was no restriction on the duration of their observations. Subsequently, participants were tasked with providing an overall subjective realism rating (from $0 - 10$) for the objects, facilitating a comparison between their VRCS assessment and overall impressions.

Fig. 3. Objects rated with the VRCS (Objects from Shutterstock (2023) *TurboSquid*)

All experimental sessions were conducted on a laptop with the questionnaires and a second laptop with a VR HMD[4], ensuring consistent and controlled presentation of virtual objects. To mitigate order effects, the sequence in which participants encountered the virtual objects was randomized for each participant. In total, experimental sessions took $30 - 45$ minutes for each participant.

4.3   Subjective Workload and Immersion Tendency

After evaluating all the objects, participants were directed to complete two additional questionnaires. The first tool employed was the NASA Task Load Index (NASA-TLX) [13], a widely recognized tool for quantifying perceived workload [12]. This questionnaire gauged the cognitive demands posed by the task, encompassing dimensions such as mental, physical, and temporal workload.

The second supplementary questionnaire, the Immersive Tendency Questionnaire (ITQ) [37], investigated participants' predisposition to engage with immersive situations. This instrument aims to capture individual tendencies to embrace or avoid immersive experiences. The NASA-TLX and ITQ responses provided insights into participants' cognitive engagement and comfort within the VR environment.

5   Results

The statistical analysis was performed with the software SPSS[5] and the predetermined α level was .05.

A total of 34 participants were recruited for this study, all working in aerospace research. Out of the 34 participants, the majority identified as male (73.5%), the rest being female (23.5%) or diverse. Their ages ranged from early twenties to early sixties, with 41.2% being between 25 and 29 years old. Due to the selection process, the participants consisted mainly (73.5%) of research associates, the rest being students and technical or administrative employees. 58.8% had normal eyesight, with the rest (except one person) using correction aids like glasses or contacts. There were no participants with color blindness, and only 5.9% had a red/green deficiency. More than half of the participants

---

[4] HTC Corp. *HTC Vive Pro.*
[5] IBM Corp (2019). *IBM SPSS Statistics for Windows*, Version 26.0.

(58.8%) stated that it was their first time participating in the study, so they had never seen the objects or the prior questions.

All, except 2 people, had worn a VR HMD before, most of them more than once (70.6%). Of all the participants, 38.2% use 3D Models at least monthly or more often. Their gaming experience varied largely, with the majority gaming "a couple of times a year" (44.1%). The others split almost evenly into groups more or less than that.

On average, the ITQ score was 72.21, ranging from a minimum of 47 points to a maximum of 98, with a standard deviation of 13.14. A higher score in the ITQ indicates a higher level of immersive tendencies. The average ITQ score of participants in this study is just below the average value for people in general, which is 73.14, according to Rózsa et al. [28].

The perceived workload given by the NASA-TLX was, on average, across all categories, at 29.60 out of 100 possible points (min = 8.33, max= 59.50, SD = 11.91). Inspecting the factors individually mental was highest with a mean of 50.74 points (min = 10, max = 92, SD = 23.24), followed by effort with 36.32 (min = 1, max = 68, SD = 19.19), performance (mean = 35.09, min = 1, max = 84, SD = 21.23) and physical (mean = 23.94, min = 1, max = 94, SD = 22.40). The lowest two factors were temporal (mean = 16.26, min = 1, max = 68, SD = 15.68) and frustration (mean = 15.24, min = 1, max = 61, SD = 16.10). In prior works by Prabaswari et al. [24], the workload was categorized as *very high, high, somewhat high, medium,* and *low.* The average workload, as well as temporal and frustration, fall into the *medium* (10 − 29) category, while everything else, except mental, which is *high* (50 − 79), is of *somewhat high* (30 − 49) workload.

5.1 Predicting Subjective Realism

The first goal of this questionnaire is to provide a more comparable, objective measurement of visual realism while still capturing the individual feeling of realism. The VRCS Score needs to be linked with subjective realism to achieve that intent. If the VRCS Score does not mirror the perceived realism score, it can not measure visual realism. A Kendall-Tau-b correlation was calculated for each object individually and across all objects. The results can be seen in Table 2. All correlations except for one object (*object* 6) are significant with medium (> .3) to large (> .5) effect sizes according to Cohen [5].

Further, a regression analysis was done to analyze which questions were most influential for perceived visual realism. The subjective realism is the dependent variable, while each question is a predictor and thus an independent variable. For each question that is not dichotomous, dummy coding was used.

Table 2. Correlation between the VRCS Scores and the subjective realism (* significant with the $\alpha < .05$)

Object	Correlation Coefficient	p-Value
1	0.467	.001*
2	0.531	.000*
3	0.451	.002*
4	0.426	.002*
5	0.427	.002*
6	0.174	.216
7	0.611	.000*
8	0.563	.000*
9	0.414	.004*
10	0.386	.006*
Across all objects	0.652	.000*

In contrast to the correlation the model was generated for all objects. After initial analysis, there are no outliers with standardized residuals larger than 3, and a linear relationship between the variables was found. The model has no autocorrelation, and there is no multi-collinearity. Upon visual inspection, the residuals are normally distributed. However, homoscedasticity is not given. For that reason, a weighted least square regression is done. The Durbin-Watson statistic is 1.376. The R^2 for the overall model was 0.719 (adjusted $R^2 = 0.711$), indicative of a high goodness of fit [5]. The model is statistically significant with $F(9, 330) = 93.606, p < .01$. Table 3 shows the regression coefficients for each predictor.

All predictors are significant, except *structure*. Compared to the other predictors, the influence on subjective realism seems lower.

Table 3. Coefficients for each predictor (across all objects; * significant with $\alpha < .05$)

Model	Regression Coefficient	p-Value
Lighting 1	0.493	.025*
Lighting 2	0.993	.000*
Reflections	1.156	.000*
Texture 1	0.720	.013*
Texture 2	1.866	.000*
Structure	0.366	.105
Form 1	0.834	.015*
Form 2	2.941	.000*
Consistency 1	0.539	.003*

5.2   VRCS Compared to Subjective Realism

The second hypothesis can be tested by looking at the distribution of both subjective realism and VRCS score for each object. Upon visual inspection (see Fig. 4), the VRCS leads to more consistent scoring for most objects compared to subjective realism.

Doing a paired t-test on the subjective realism standard deviation and the VRCS standard deviation shows a significant difference. There are no outliers, and the data is normally distributed (Shapiro Wilk $p = .740$). The standard deviation of the subjective realism is significantly higher than the standard deviation of the VRCS with $t(9) = 3.187, p < .05$

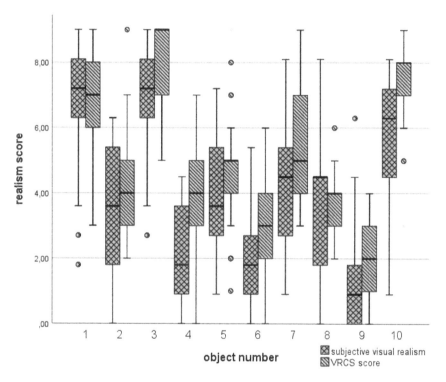

Fig. 4. Distribution of the VRCS Scores for each object compared to the subjective realism

5.3   Original VRCS Compared to the Revised VRCS

The third hypothesis compared the original VRCS to the revision. A good consensus between the participants indicates a better understanding of the questions. While it does not show anything about the validity of the answers, it indicates that the participants have a shared understanding of the matter, and the reliability of the questionnaire is high. The standard deviations for each question are compared to test if the revised questions lead to a better distribution. The eight objects which were shown to the participants in the original and the present study were considered. A paired t-test is used to show if there are any significant differences in the answer distribution before and after revising the VRCS. The data had no outliers, and the differences between the pre- and post-scores were normally distributed, as assessed by the Shapiro-Wilk test. There is no significant difference running the paired t-test on the subjective realism of study one compared to two ($t(7) = 0.444, p = .670$) or on the VRCS Scores overall ($t(7) = 1.623, p = .14$). However, there were significant differences between pre- and post-scores for *shadow*, *texture*, and *form*. The detailed results are shown in Table 4. While for *texture* and *form*, the answers had lower variance than before, *lighting* had a higher distribution. For the other two questions, there was no significant difference.

Table 4. T-test of standard deviations of the questions for study 1 and study 2 (* significant with the $\alpha < .05$)

Question	t	df	p-Value
Lighting	2.993	7	.020*
Reflections	1.930	7	.095
Texture	-3.264	7	.014*
Structure	1.277	7	.242
Form	-4.351	7	.003*

5.4   Qualitative Feedback

As one of the main aims was not only to improve the VRCS quantitatively but also to make the use of the VRCS more user-friendly, qualitative feedback was crucial. The participants could anonymously write comments after finishing the study, and additionally, any verbal feedback given to the experimenter was recorded. The people who took part in both iterations of the study voiced a general mood of improvement. Most people recognized a noticeable change between the iterations of the study. Five people noted that the new questionnaire was easier to understand and more enjoyable to use. One participant commented that: *"The explanations of the questions are very good"*. Others mentioned the shorter questions, which had an impact on the usability, as it leads to better readability.

6   Discussion

The validation study explored the relationship between subjective and objective realism and how objective realism can be measured.

First, a correlation explored H1, diving into the relationship between subjective realism and the VRCS score. The strong correlation implies the validity of the questionnaire and its usefulness in predicting subjective realism. *Object 6* had no significant correlation, which is underlined by problems on this object found in the first study. The object shows different levels of details in texture and form and thus appears inconsistent. While including *internal consistency* counters some of those effects, it is still crucial to consider consistency when choosing objects for the virtual environment.

The regression analysis shows that the questions significantly model subjective realism. This analysis expands the already found correlation between VRCS and subjective realism and explores H1 from a different perspective. While conclusive statements cannot be made from a sample size with as few objects, some trends are apparent. The *form* seems crucial to the impression of realism, as a detailed form increases the subjective feeling the most. In comparison, the *lighting* factor did not have an extensive impact.

While *structure* is not significant, looking at the actual values, it has a low p-value and a small effect on the subjective score. Additionally, the original VRCS, where *structure* had a positive impact, leads to the impression that it should be addressed. This discrepancy opens the room for future work, where each factor could be explored individually in more detail or larger sample sizes utilized.

Knowing that VRCS relates to subjective realism, the second hypothesis (H2), if the VRCS has less variance than the subjective realism, is investigated. Exploring the variance of the VRCS and the subjective realism was initially done with a visual inspection. The inspection showed that the deviation in the answers given is smaller for the VRCS. This was confirmed with a t-test comparing the standard deviations of each object, where a significant difference was found. As the VRCS has less variance, its reliability is thus higher than that of a simple 10-point scale.

This paper not only validates but improves the VRSC score. After an investigation of the data from the prior study and the input of an expert focus group, the revised VRCS was constructed. The revision had multiple goals. First, it should improve the reliability of each question. If participants answer questions the same it can be assumed that they have a shared understanding of what is asked (see H3). Second, the questionnaire should be more user-friendly and easier to understand (see H4).

The first goal was examined by using a paired t-test on the standard deviation of each question to see if the revision's textual changes improved the questions' clarity. While a change in standard deviation does not confirm an improved clarity of the question, however, it shows more uniform participant answers.

There was no difference for *reflection* and *structure* between the two studies. Those items are more complex concepts that might require a more comprehensive visual assessment. Both require some 3D movement (of object or viewer) to assess them accurately. It could be that they are more challenging to get a consensus on or need more expert knowledge for straightforward assessment. While the participants are primarily from technical backgrounds, and some have worked with 3D objects before, the user of the VRCS would likely be someone with even more in-depth knowledge of the topic. A deeper understanding of 3D Objects and visualization would help classify objects faster and more accurately.

The standard deviation for *texture* and *form* for the revision was significantly smaller than the original. As *texture* and *form* are not directly dependent on any settings but only on the objects themselves, it can be assumed that the revision of the questions is responsible for the changes in standard deviation in the two studies.

For *lighting*, the standard deviation was larger after the revision. As the question stayed close to the original phrasing, the recorded difference between the two studies is most likely due to a change in the lighting settings in the virtual environment. It demonstrates that it is crucial to be mindful of the settings (such as lighting) to ensure an accurate assessment of the objects. Further, it must be kept in mind that scoring only applies to the rendered image and not the object itself. Thus, if, for example, the lighting changes, the VRCS score will subsequently shift.

The second goal, to improve user experience, was examined by collecting qualitative feedback. About 40% of the participants had seen the original questionnaire, so they could state their opinion on the changes. While this feedback could be biased and shifted into a desirable answer by participants, the general notion indicated that the revision was easier to understand and the shortening of the text much appreciated.

The study was done in a controlled environment, which makes it crucial to remember that objects are rarely looked at individually but as part of a larger environment. Complex surroundings are expected to vary the subjective realism and, thus, the overall feel of the scene - for example, the impact of *lighting* changes when inspecting whole environments instead of objects. Moreover, the movement of objects is an additional influencing factor that could be considered for the subjective experience of the environment, as shown by Rogers et al. [27] and in the Witmer & Singer [37] presence questionnaire.

In future work, pursuing studies with virtual environments instead of objects would be valuable to further understanding visual realism perception. Moreover, the perception of a realistic virtual object can change over the years due to historical circumstances, technical advancements and ethnographic settings. For this study, the object selection was highly intertwined with the processing capabilities of the HMD. With technological advancements and the potential ability to include more photo-realistic objects, the VRCS could be revisited.

7 Conclusion

The primary use of the Visual Realism Classification Scale is to compare realism in research. It can classify different levels of realism within a study or establish comparability with other research. One could further use this scale to find threshold values of realism for tasks or conduct a meta-analysis of visual realism studies. Compared to other visual realism classifications the VRCS is not made for end users to rate the visual realism complexity but for researchers to establish the realism levels when planning and implementing their work. The VRCS enables researchers to have an objective tool and not depend on building their own classification of visual realism.

This paper provides an in-depth analysis of the VRCS. It shows the reliability and validity of the revised VRCS. The VRCS significantly correlates with subjective realism and shows lower variation in answer behavior. Through a user study, an expert focus group, and detailed statistical analysis, the VRCS is introduced as an effective way to measure visual realism.

References

1. Ang, S., Fernandez, A., Rushforth, M., Quarles, J.: You make me sick! the effect of stairs on presence, cybersickness, and perception of embodied conversational agents. In: 2023 IEEE Conference Virtual Reality and 3D User Interfaces (VR), pp. 561–570. IEEE (2023). https://doi.org/10.1109/VR55154.2023.00071
2. Baños, R.M., Botella, C., Garcia-Palacios, A., Villa, H., Perpiña, C., Alcañiz, M.: Presence and reality judgment in virtual environments: a unitary construct? Cyberpsychol. Behav. Impact Internet Multim. Virt. Real. Behav. Soc. 3(3), 327–335 (2000). https://doi.org/10.1089/10949310050078760
3. Bowman, D.A., McMahan, R.P.: Virtual reality: how much immersion is enough? Computer 40(7), 36–43 (2007). https://doi.org/10.1109/MC.2007.257
4. Chambilla, R., Tomiuk, D., Marcotte, S., Plaisent, M., Bernard, P.: Factors affecting satisfaction with serious games - direct, mediated and higher-order constructs. In: 2020 11th IEEE Annual Information Technology, Electronics and Mobile Communication Conference (IEMCON), pp. 0845–0853 (2020).https://doi.org/10.1109/IEMCON51383.2020.9284862
5. Cohen, J.: Statistical Power Analysis for the Behavioral Sciences, 2nd edn. Routledge (1988)
6. Cover, S.A., Ezquerra, N.F., O'Brien, J.F., Rowe, R., Gadacz, T., Palm, E.: Interactively deformable models for surgery simulation. IEEE Comput. Graph. Appl. 13(6), 68–75 (1993). https://doi.org/10.1109/38.252559
7. Elhelw, M., Nicolaou, M., Chung, A., Yang, G.Z., Atkins, M.S.: A gaze-based study for investigating the perception of visual realism in simulated scenes. ACM Trans. Appl. Percept. 5(1), 1–20 (2008). https://doi.org/10.1145/1279640.1279643
8. Fan, S., et al.: Image visual realism: from human perception to machine computation. IEEE Trans. Pattern Anal. Mach. Intell. 40(9), 2180–2193 (2018). https://doi.org/10.1109/tpami.2017.2747150
9. Fan, S., Wang, R., Ng, T.T., Tan, C.Y.C., Herberg, J.S., Koenig, B.L.: Human perception of visual realism for photo and computer-generated face images. ACM Trans. Appl. Percept. 11(2), 1–21 (2014). https://doi.org/10.1145/2620030

10. Ferwerda, J.A.: Three varieties of realism in computer graphics. In: Rogowitz, B.E., Pappas, T.N. (eds.) Human Vision and Electronic Imaging VIII, p. 290. SPIE Proceedings, SPIE (2003). https://doi.org/10.1117/12.473899
11. Gonçalves, G., Coelho, H., Monteiro, P., Melo, M., Bessa, M.: Systematic review of comparative studies of the impact of realism in immersive virtual experiences. ACM Comput. Surv. **55**(6), 1–36 (2023). https://doi.org/10.1145/3533377
12. Hart, S.G.: Nasa-task load index (nasa-tlx); 20 years later. Proc. Hum. Fact. Ergon. Soc. Annu. Meet. **50**(9), 904–908 (2006). https://doi.org/10.1177/154193120605000909
13. Hart, S.G., Staveland, L.E.: Development of nasa-tlx (task load index): results of empirical and theoretical research. In: Hancock, P.A., Meshkati, N. (eds.) Human Mental Workload, Advances in Psychology, vol. 52, pp. 139–183. North-Holland (1988). https://doi.org/10.1016/S0166-4115(08)62386-9
14. Huang, J., Klippel, A.: The effects of visual realism on spatial memory and exploration patterns in virtual reality. In: Teather, R.J., et al. (eds.) 26th ACM Symposium on Virtual Reality Software and Technology, pp. 1–11. ACM, New York (2020). https://doi.org/10.1145/3385956.3418945
15. Hvass, J., Larsen, O., Vendelbo, K., Nilsson, N., Nordahl, R., Serafin, S.: Visual realism and presence in a virtual reality game. In: 2017 3DTV Conference: The True Vision - Capture, Transmission and Display of 3D Video (3DTV-CON), pp. 1–4. IEEE (2017). https://doi.org/10.1109/3DTV.2017.8280421
16. Lee, C., Rincon, G.A., Meyer, G., Höllerer, T., Bowman, D.A.: The effects of visual realism on search tasks in mixed reality simulation. IEEE Trans. Visual Comput. Graphics **19**(4), 547–556 (2013). https://doi.org/10.1109/TVCG.2013.41
17. Lugrin, J.L., Wiedemann, M., Bieberstein, D., Latoschik, M.E.: Influence of avatar realism on stressful situation in VR. In: 2015 IEEE Virtual Reality (VR), pp. 227–228. IEEE (2015). https://doi.org/10.1109/VR.2015.7223378
18. Löwner, M.-O., Benner, J., Gröger, G., Gruber, U., Häfele, K.-H., Schlüter, S.: Citygml 2.0 – ein internationaler standard für 3d-stadtmodelle. teil 1: Datenmodell. ZFV - Zeitschrift fur Geodasie, Geoinformation und Landmanagement **137**(6), 340–349 (2012). https://geodaesie.info/zfv/heftbeitrag/1035
19. McDonnell, R., Breidt, M., Bülthoff, H.H.: Render me real? ACM Trans. Graph. **31**(4), 1–11 (2012). https://doi.org/10.1145/2185520.2185587
20. Mori, M., MacDorman, K., Kageki, N.: The uncanny valley [from the field]. IEEE Robot. Automat. Magaz. **19**(2), 98–100 (2012). https://doi.org/10.1109/MRA.2012.2192811
21. Poeschl-Guenther, S., Döring, N.: The German VR simulation realism scale - psychometric construction for virtual reality applications with virtual humans. Stud. Health Technol. Inform. **191**, 33–37 (2013). https://doi.org/10.3233/978-1-61499-282-0-33
22. Posner, M.I., Nissen, M.J., Klein, R.M.: Visual dominance: an information-processing account of its origins and significance. Psychol. Rev. **83**(2), 157–171 (1976). https://doi.org/10.1037/0033-295X.83.2.157
23. Pouke, M., Tiiro, A., LaValle, S.M., Ojala, T.: Effects of visual realism and moving detail on cybersickness. In: 2018 IEEE Conference on Virtual Reality and 3D User Interfaces (VR), pp. 665–666. IEEE (2018).https://doi.org/10.1109/VR.2018.8446078
24. Prabaswari, A.D., Basumerda, C., Utomo, B.W.: The mental workload analysis of staff in study program of private educational organization. IOP Conf. Ser.: Mater. Sci. Eng. **528**(1), 012018 (2019). https://doi.org/10.1088/1757-899x/528/1/012018

25. Rademacher, P., Lengyel, J., Cutrell, E., Whitted, T.: Measuring the perception of visual realism in images. In: Gortler, S.J., Myszkowski, K. (eds.) Rendering Techniques 2001, pp. 235–247. Eurographics, Springer Vienna, Vienna (2001). https://doi.org/10.1007/978-3-7091-6242-2_22

26. Ramanarayanan, G., Bala, K., Ferwerda, J.A.: Perception of complex aggregates. ACM Trans. Graph. **27**(3), 1–10 (2008). https://doi.org/10.1145/1360612.1360659

27. Rogers, K., Karaosmanoglu, S., Altmeyer, M., Suarez, A., Nacke, L.E.: Much realistic, such wow! a systematic literature review of realism in digital games. In: Barbosa, S., et al. (eds.) CHI Conference on Human Factors in Computing Systems, pp. 1–21. ACM, New York (2022). https://doi.org/10.1145/3491102.3501875

28. Rózsa, S., et al.: Measuring immersion, involvement, and attention focusing tendencies in the mediated environment: the applicability of the immersive tendencies questionnaire. Front. Psychol. **13** (2022). https://doi.org/10.3389/fpsyg.2022.931955

29. Schäffer, E., Metzner, M., Pawlowskij, D., Franke, J.: Seven levels of detail to structure use cases and interaction mechanism for the development of industrial virtual reality applications within the context of planning and configuration of robot-based automation solutions. Procedia CIRP **96**, 284–289 (2021). https://doi.org/10.1016/j.procir.2021.01.088

30. Schmied-Kowarzik, R., Reisewitz, P., Kaschub, L., Rodeck, R., Wende, G.: An approach for visual realism complexity classification of 3d models in virtual and augmented reality. In: Chen, J.Y.C., Fragomeni, G. (eds.) Virtual, Augmented and Mixed Reality, pp. 192–202. Springer, Cham (2023). https://doi.org/10.1007/978-3-031-35634-6_14

31. Schmied-Kowarzik, R.L., Paelke, V.: Examining the importance of realism in virtual reality therapy environments for people with specific phobias. In: Weier, M., Bues, M., Wechner, R. (eds.) GI VR/AR Workshop. Gesellschaft für Informatik e.V. (2021). https://doi.org/10.18420/vrar2021_16

32. Schwind, V., Leicht, K., Jäger, S., Wolf, K., Henze, N.: Is there an uncanny valley of virtual animals? a quantitative and qualitative investigation. Int. J. Hum.-Comput. Stud. **111**, 49–61 (2018). https://doi.org/10.1016/j.ijhcs.2017.11.003

33. Skulmowski, A., Rey, G.D.: The realism paradox: realism can act as a form of signaling despite being associated with cognitive load. Hum. Behav. Emerg. Technol. **2**(3), 251–258 (2020). https://doi.org/10.1002/hbe2.190

34. Slater, M., Khanna, P., Mortensen, J., Yu, I.: Visual realism enhances realistic response in an immersive virtual environment. IEEE Comput. Graphics Appl. **29**(3), 76–84 (2009). https://doi.org/10.1109/MCG.2009.55

35. Wang, N., Doube, W.: How real is reality? a perceptually motivated system for quantifying visual realism in digital images. In: 2011 International Conference on Multimedia and Signal Processing, pp. 141–149. IEEE (2011). https://doi.org/10.1109/CMSP.2011.172

36. Wijayanto, I.A., Babu, S.V., Pagano, C.C., Chuang, J.H.: Comparing the effects of visual realism on size perception in VR versus real world viewing through physical and verbal judgments. IEEE Trans. Visualiz. Comput. Graph. **29**(5), 2721–2731 (2023). https://doi.org/10.1109/TVCG.2023.3247109

37. Witmer, B.G., Singer, M.J.: Measuring presence in virtual environments: a presence questionnaire. Presence: Teleoper. Virt. Environ. **7**(3), 225–240 (1998). https://doi.org/10.1162/105474698565686

38. Xue, S., Agarwala, A., Dorsey, J., Rushmeier, H.: Understanding and improving the realism of image composites. ACM Trans. Graph. **31**(4), 1–10 (2012). https://doi.org/10.1145/2185520.2185580

39. Yu, I., Mortensen, J., Khanna, P., Spanlang, B., Slater, M.: Visual realism enhances realistic response in an immersive virtual environment-part 2. IEEE Comput. Graphics Appl. **32**(6), 36–45 (2012). https://doi.org/10.1109/MCG.2012.121
40. Zhu, J.Y., Krähenbühl, P., Shechtman, E., Efros, A.A.: Learning a discriminative model for the perception of realism in composite images. In: 2015 IEEE International Conference on Computer Vision (ICCV), pp. 3943–3951 (2015). https://doi.org/10.1109/ICCV.2015.449

Augmenting Self-presentation: Augmented Reality (AR) Filters Use Among Young Adults

Pitch Sinlapanuntakul[(✉)] and Mark Zachry

Department of Human Centered Design and Engineering, University of Washington, Seattle, WA 98105, USA
{wspitch,zachry}@uw.edu

Abstract. The rise of real-time camera enhancements, particularly on social media platforms like Instagram, Snapchat, and TikTok, has reshaped self-presentation within youth culture. While previous research has explored avatars and technology-mediated identity, a knowledge gap exists regarding the motivations, perceptions, and implications of augmented reality (AR) filters. This study investigates the impact of AR filters on self-presentation among young adults on Instagram. The study engages 12 young adults, aged 18 to 25, through semi-structured interviews, revealing strategies of online persona curation for targeted groups of followers, a growing societal acceptance of augmented online appearances, and a delicate balance between presenting an authentic and ideal self. Participants use AR filters to enhance creative expression for their own sake as well as mediated appearance for meaningful connections and social engagement. The findings indicate the dynamic role of AR filters in shaping online self-image, emphasizing the need for a nuanced understanding of users' intentional curation and the evolving social norms surrounding AR filter usage on social media.

Keywords: Augmented reality · AR filters · Self-presentation · Social media · Young adults

1 Introduction

AR filters, real-time camera enhancements, have increasingly gained substantial popularity across social media platforms, notably Instagram, Snapchat, and TikTok, particularly within youth culture [1]. While AR filters offer a lower sense of self and embodiment compared to avatars, they hold the potential to enhance self-image satisfaction [2,3] and foster creativity for self-expression [4]. Previous research efforts have explored the relationship between avatars and technology-mediated identity [5–9], yet a knowledge gap persists concerning the influence of AR filters on self-presentation among young adults, including motivations, perceptions of mediated self and others, and their implications [10].

Even within the domain of AR, AR face filters are notably different than other types of AR technologies. AR headset devices, such as Microsoft HoloLens,

© The Author(s), under exclusive license to Springer Nature Switzerland AG 2024
J. Y. C. Chen and G. Fragomeni (Eds.): HCII 2024, LNCS 14706, pp. 93–105, 2024.
https://doi.org/10.1007/978-3-031-61041-7_7

and mobile-based AR games, such as Pokémon Go, predominantly focus on augmenting the external environment [11]. This augmentation involves overlaying virtual objects, like a Pokémon, into the user's surroundings through AR-enabled devices. In contrast, AR filters primarily enhance the appearance of the users, modifying facial features or adding virtual elements to the face, which create visual effects augmented on the device's screen [12].

While research has contributed insights into, for example, the use of social media, user experience of AR technologies, AR filters for health and well-being, and avatars' mediation of self-presentation, a significant gap remains in understanding the multifaceted influence of AR filters on young adults' perceptions of self. This study bridges this gap by exploring current AR filter practices among young adults aged 18 to 25, specifically within the context of the Instagram platform, given its emphasis on the concept of self. Through qualitative exploration, the study uncovers young adults' perceptions when using AR filters, particularly self-concept and expression on social media. Therefore, this study explores the following research questions:

RQ1. How do young adults use and perceive AR filters on Instagram?

RQ2. What are the underlying motivations of young adults in their utilization of AR filters for self-presentation?

1.1 The Use of AR Technologies and Filters

The adoption and usability of AR headsets has been extensively investigated in the current literature, reflecting the growing interest in and exploration of AR. AR headsets have showcased the potential to revolutionize various industries, including gaming, education, and healthcare, by overlaying interactive 3D information in the real-world environment. For instance, in gaming, AR headsets offer immersive experiences that blend the virtual and physical worlds together, enhancing satisfaction, engrossment, and gratification [13]. In education and workspaces, these headsets provide interactive learning environments and a creative space to augment the physical surroundings, enabling users to visualize complex concepts and productively engage in their tasks [14]. Additionally, in healthcare, AR headsets have been explored for applications like visualizing medical data and patient-specific anatomy to support surgeons and medical students [15,16]. Despite these areas of use cases, AR headset technology is still very much under development. Challenges related to device size, field of view, simulator sickness, and usability are actively being addressed by researchers in both social sciences and computer science.

In contrast, AR filters are easily accessed through AR-enabled devices, such as mobile devices and, at times, laptop devices. In addition to their accessibility, AR filters can be designed using platforms like Meta Spark Studio, owned by Meta, and launched on Instagram and Facebook for public usage. These real-time filters serve multiple specific purposes related to social interaction on technology-mediated platforms, including drawing attention, content engagement, and initiating social interactions [17,18].

1.2 AR Filters and Mental Well-Being

AR filters have the potential to influence mental well-being in diverse directions, depending on their use and users' understanding toward social media. On one hand, virtual modification of one's appearance through AR filters may introduce negative consequences related to unrealistic body image expectations conveyed by social media and perpetual social comparison [10,19]. The real-time and realistic nature of AR filter modifications can exacerbate negative self-esteem and perceived body distortion, with extreme cases even leading individuals, especially women, toward cosmetic surgery [20].

On the other hand, AR filter modifications can act as social lubricants, attracting forms of online social interactions, such as additional comments and likes, that increase a sense of social acceptance and connectedness. This aligns with prior literature establishing a strong link between social activities and personal well-being [21] as using these filters on social media can provide users such benefits. In addition, a similar study [18] indicated that using AR filters for social media engagement purposes can have positive effects on mood. As AR filters are mainly used on social media for content-sharing purposes, the process of using them can positively influence mental well-being by allowing individuals to present hidden aspects of themselves or explore their identity [22].

1.3 Technological Mediation of Self-presentation

Within the literature of technology-mediated self-presentation, researchers have spent years researching the use and effects of avatars for their mediation of users' digital personas, behaviors, and interactions, commonly within virtual environments such as virtual reality (VR) [5–7,9,23]. The affordances of avatars provide users the possibility to shape their self-presentation, prompting inquiries into the alignment between these constructed digital representations and users' authentic identities [8,24].

While avatars mediate interactions and identities within virtual environments, AR filters introduce an overlay of digital elements onto users' lived experiences. The differences between these two forms of mediation lies in their primary spatial contexts: avatars operate within the virtual space, whereas AR filters augment real-world visuals. In the case of AR filters, the interplay between digital augmentation and real-world identity introduces unique considerations, such as the perceived coexistence of virtual and tangible self-perceptions [25]. Although this body of avatar research has initiated the understanding of virtual self-presentation, the emergence of AR filters as a distinct mode of technological mediation introduces new dynamics that need empirical investigations into their effects on perceptions of self and interactions with others.

2 Methods

2.1 Participants

A total of 12 participants with ages ranging between 18 to 25 years ($M = 20.75$, $SD = 2.38$) participated in this study. Among the 12 participants, six self-identified as Cis Woman and the other six as Cis Man. Four participants reported that they used AR filters on Instagram approximately four to five times per week, while the remaining eight reported using AR filters more frequently, exceeding five times per week. It is noteworthy that all participants had set their Instagram accounts set as public. Table 1 provides a summary of the demographic characteristics of the participants.

Participants were recruited using a snowball sampling method, starting with the first author posting on a personal Instagram Story. Only a few participants ($n = 4$) mutually followed the first author's Instagram account but had no direct interactions with the author prior to the study, ensuring that there were no preexisting personal relationships to minimize biases.

Table 1. Demographic information of participants.

ID	Gender Identity	Ethnicity	Age (years)	Account Setting	Usage Frequency (per week)
P1	Cis Man	Asian	22	Public	More than 5 times
P2	Cis Man	White	19	Public	More than 5 times
P3	Cis Man	Asian	23	Public	4 to 5 times
P4	Cis Woman	Asian	24	Public	4 to 5 times
P5	Cis Man	Asian	19	Public	More than 5 times
P6	Cis Man	White	20	Public	4 to 5 times
P7	Cis Man	Asian	25	Public	More than 5 times
P8	Cis Woman	White	19	Public	More than 5 times
P9	Cis Woman	White	20	Public	More than 5 times
P10	Cis Woman	Black	22	Public	More than 5 times
P11	Cis Woman	Asian	18	Public	More than 5 times
P12	Cis Woman	White	18	Public	4 to 5 times

2.2   Interviews

We conducted in-depth, semi-structured interviews with the participants, in which most of the interview questions asked them to reflect on their past experience and usual behaviors. Interviews were conducted via Zoom with either audio or video chat, depending on participants' preferences. All the sessions were transcribed using Zoom automatic audio transcription feature for cloud recordings. The average interview duration was 45 min. This study was approved by the University's Institutional Review Board (IRB).

We acknowledged the inherent complexity and sensitivity surrounding the infrequently discussed topic of self-presentation and self-concept. Engaging with interviewees in an ethical and thoughtful manner was our paramount intention, given the potential for this research to investigate the interplay between AR filter and digital self-perception. Therefore, we encouraged participants to freely share as much detail as they felt appropriate and comfortable regarding their personal experiences and perceptions with the use of AR filters.

2.3 Data Analysis

We conducted reflexive thematic analysis [26] with an inductive coding approach to analyze the interview data. Given the single-researcher process, we employed triangulation reviews involving both authors and memoing techniques [27] in lieu of inter-rater reliability (IRR) and agreement [28]. This approach followed established best practices in HCI to ensure the systematic analysis of meaningful qualitative insights [29].

We used the following analytical procedures. First, the first author closely read through the interview data to acquire the sense of the whole picture. Second, the first author coded the data line by line, reflecting single ideas, and assigned codes to capture shared ideas [30]. Third, the initial codes were then used to develop the code book, which was refined based on initial themes derived from the codes. Fourth, the first author re-coded interview data using the final set of codes from the code book, while writing analytical memos during the process. Fifth, the first author read through and iteratively refined the memos to develop key findings from the observed themes. Last, both authors engaged in a triangulation review to examine and refine themes, along with our description and interpretation regarding young adults' motivations to use AR filters, thus enhancing the validity and robustness of the analysis.

3 Findings

In this section, we identify four main themes to report participants' perception and underlying motivation in using AR filters on Instagram.

3.1 Strategic Online Persona Curation for Targeted Audience

Participants described the multifaceted nature of their Instagram usage, involving both self-promotion and relationship maintenance with their followers. They intentionally employed various engagement strategies to enhance their social media presence and capture a large follower base, which includes both personal acquaintances and unfamiliar individuals. As mentioned by a participant, *"right now, I have just over 2,000 followers. They mostly [started following my Instagram account] from my previously Reel videos. Some are my friends, though"* (P1). Another participant highlighted, *"my followers are both my friends and people whom I don't know personally. I believe they follow me because of my lifestyle and content"* (P11). This belief that their followers are interested in their lifestyles and content served as a motivating factor of their commitment to maintain and strengthen these online relationships.

To maintain their follower base, participants tried to engage with them through various types of content, such as selecting positive and visually appealing images for their posts, sharing glimpses of their daily lifestyle in Stories (i.e., posts that only last 24 h), and showcasing their talents and emotionally-evoking content through Reels (i.e., short-form videos). This engagement calculation aimed to capture and maintain the interest of their followers as well as encourage a sense of connection. P4 explained the specific approach they used to increase followers' interactions.

"For posts, I post pictures that have a positive presence like pictures [of myself] at festivals or at a beach. For stories, I post my daily lifestyle [content], like me getting a cup of coffee or asking my followers to participate in a Q&A game. For reels, I post videos to promote myself, like singing and dancing videos from my classes." (P4)

Participants recognized the impact of their reputation on Instagram and the potential benefits it could bring. They *"valued having endorsements from influencers in elevating their credibility and reputation"* (P7). Additionally, participants with a significant number of followers were able to attract *"business opportunities, such as product reviews"* (P7).

To increase their chances of connecting with like-minded individuals, especially in the same age group, they intentionally targeted specific interest groups or demographics: *"I think I want to reach the same type of audience, potentially around the ages of 18 to 25, so that we can easily connect through the same lifestyle, content, and vibes since we're in the same generation"* (P2). Additionally, some participants expressed a desire to boost their popularity and increase their reach, stating that *"it would be ideal to reach a wider audience, including a younger audience, (...) just for the sake of popularity"* (P11).

3.2 Social Acceptance of Augmented Online Appearances

Participants recognized a shift in societal norms and the increasing use and acceptance of augmented appearances facilitated by AR filters on social media platforms where it is expected that AR filters are used or to be used. This acceptance is perceived as a new shifted reality where technology leaves positive impressions, while exerting influence on social engagement and interactions. As P8 pointed out,

"Using AR filters leaves good impressions on my followers. I don't think that [my followers] care who has or does not have AR filters on because most of our pictures posted are either augmented with AR filters or edited in some way, if not baked with makeup. It's a new reality now that people accept others visually even with AR filters on. I think using it doesn't damage your branding or others' impressions." (P8)

P10 also added that *"[using] filters could make my selfies more playful and authentic, and people may (...) decide to start a conversation with me. It's like showing another side of myself that makes me seem less serious as a personal brand."* Participants are aware of the evolving perceptions and expectations surrounding augmented appearances on social media. This shift represents a *"new reality"* (P8) where augmented technology is no longer perceived as deceptive but rather as a means to showcase different aspects of their personality.

However, participants strongly preferred using AR filters for their Instagram Stories, primarily due to the its ephemeral nature in which the content posted disappears after 24 h. This preference stems from the perception that "*AR filters used in posts make it less authentic*" (P2). Notably, while participants readily embraced apparent AR filters when used in others' posts, they viewed AR filters in their own permanent posts as diminishing authenticity, demonstrating their desire for an authentic presence while maintaining a non-judgmental stance toward others.

3.3   Balancing the Presentation of Authentic and Ideal Self

Engagement of participants with AR filters encompasses their desire for self-presentation and social connection. By using filters that make them appear cute, playful, or resemble animals, participants sought positive emotional responses and affection from others (see Fig. 1), as noted by P3:

> "Personally, I love dogs; they are very cute. I really like Golden Retrievers and I am also a bit of a needy person. So, I think if I use a dog filter, people will see me as cute and playful, just like a dog." (P3)

These filters serve as a form of self-expression, allowing participants to convey their desired image and evoke specific reactions. The desire to be seen as adorable reflects participants' need for validation and acceptance, as well as their expectations of positive interactions. Furthermore, the use of AR filters to "*conceal pimples and smoothen my skin*" (P1) can cover these, so-called, imperfections and "increase confidence in [own] appearance" (P12) as participants believed that "*viewers would be more likely to approach [someone] if that person looks good in their pictures or videos*" (P5). They perceived and used AR filters as a means

Fig. 1. Examples of the AR filters used by participants, including a sample portrait with no AR filter (left), dalmatian dog filter (left-center), smooth skin filter (right-center), and dynamic glitter filter (right). Each filter type is applied to the same image for illustrative purposes.

to construct their ideal self-image, which includes attributes such as enhanced attractiveness and improved physical features.

For some, their real-world insecurities can be addressed through the use of AR filters for positive mediated self-perceptions, like the following statement: "*I like using dog filters because they make my face look slimmer. I wish my face was this slim in real life. Make me look less ugly, which is honestly a life goal*" (P3). However, the long-term use to attain a certain desired look that aligns with their personal standards of attractiveness may negatively affects their perceived real-life appearance. For others, they used these AR filters to maximize their satisfaction of self, for example, P5 mentioned:

> "Applying this [smooth skin filter] represents a version of me that I want to look like when I hold up a phone camera to check on my face. With this on, I am more confident with how I look and believe that others like me more this way as well. With it on, I am the better version of myself, appearance-wise." (P5)

By using filters that enhance their appearance or convey specific traits, participants believed they are more likely to attract attention and be approached by others. The perception that good-looking individuals are more likely to be approached highlighted participants' understanding of the social dynamics at play on social media platforms. They recognized the role of filters in influencing others' perceptions and strategically used them to create a favorable impression and encourage interaction. In addition, participants showed intention to shape their perceived persona on social media through the use of AR filters. They used filters to project specific qualities, evoke positive reactions, and control the overall tone of their posts.

In addition to appearance enhancement, participants also pointed out that using AR filters make them "*look more approachable as the selection of these filters reflects [the user's] interests and personality*" (P9). By aligning filters with their unique characteristics, participants aimed to attract like-minded individuals and foster connections based on shared traits or interests. The use of filters as a reflection of personality and interests signified participants' desire to establish a sense of identity and to connect with others who appreciate and resonate with those aspects of themselves. For instance, P3 showed that they were self-aware of their traits and wanted to highlight those sides by communicating through an AR dog filter:

> "I really like using that dog filter. I feel like I'm starting to become identified as a person who is also mischievous because of my own kind of playful tendencies. It's like using that particular filter emphasizes this aspect of myself, and now when other people look at me, they just see someone who is mischievous and playful. It's become a symbol that's associated with me." (P3)

They also showed intention to shape their social media persona and create a favorable impression. To illustrate, P2 mentioned that they usually went for an AR dog filter because "*I want people to see me as a dog sometimes because it is adorable. I want my head to be patted. I want to be loved.*" As mentioned, participants tended to use filters in projecting specific qualities and controlling emotional perception of their content while intentionally balancing their authentic and ideal self-presentation.

3.4 Creative Expression for Own Sake

Participants expressed a preference for AR filters that surpass static visuals. They valued filters with interactive-like effects and moving components as these additions imbued their Instagram Stories with a sense of liveliness. For example, a participant described their preferred AR filter as "*it just has the glitter effect. I think when it comes to stories, I appreciate things that are more dynamic like it's moving*" (P9). However, it is not for the purpose of capturing their followers' interests, building personal brand, or increasing social interactions but rather for creative expression of their own preference and satisfaction. This choice reflects their aspiration to not only actively posting content for others but also passively "*enjoying the creative process of both selecting which AR filter to use and seeing different visual elements layered on top of the picture*" (P8). Additionally, adding these dynamic elements is more than just aesthetic enhancements; it emphasizes the desire for augmented elements that bring pictures to life, as P6 stated:

> "I appreciate AR filters that move-you know, those that don't simply put stickers on my face but rather include visual elements that give my picture life. [For example], there's this filter projecting heartbeams from your cheeks. The heart illustrations on my cheeks have a continuously resizing loop where they start off small, become bigger and bigger, and then go back to being small again. That filter makes my selfies less boring; it's more fun, so I just personally enjoy it more. I guess it's my way of making my selfies uniquely mine." (P6)

This specific example of a filter projecting infinite-heartbeams-loop shows that the enjoyment derived from using AR filters is inherently individualistic. Importantly, P6 sees a deeper purpose beyond mere visual appeal-these dynamic elements are seen as a way of injecting personality into photos, making them more than just static images. Additionally, the act of making selfies "*uniquely mine*" (P6) when the selfies are of yourself suggests a strong desire for a self-expression and individuality. The inclusion of playful and creative features in AR filters contributes to a sense of uniqueness and personalization in social media content.

4 Discussion

In youth culture, social media presentation is important and relates to the users' psychological well-being [31]. In order to meet social expectations, young adults turn to the use of AR filters to visually augment their social media content, including pictures and videos [1]. However, to our knowledge, the underlying motivations behind this behavior has not been formally researched with young adults. In this study, we offer exploratory qualitative insights into the influence of AR filters on social media self-presentation among young adults, aged 18 to 25. The findings reveal the multifaceted role of AR filters in enhancing creative expression as well as fashioning an online self-image, which, in turn, encourages social engagement. Despite evolving social norms increasingly valuing AR filters for positive self-presentation, users balance their ideal self-presentation with an awareness of the potential perception of inauthenticity by others as they seek meaningful online connections.

4.1   How Do Young Adults Use and View AR Filters?

As AR filters serve as a versatile tool for projecting chosen qualities, participants use them for self-expression, addressing insecurities, enhancing attractiveness, and shaping their perceived online personas. The selection of filters mainly reflects their intention to connect with others and, to a certain extent, control the overall emotional perception of their content. These goals can be achieved while delicately balancing between authentic and ideal self-presentations [23].

Acknowledging a shift in societal norms toward the acceptance and usage of AR filters on social media, participants indicated a preference for using these filters on Instagram Stories due to its ephemeral nature. This choice suggests a temporal pattern in the usage of AR-filtered content. They readily embraced apparent AR filters when used in others' posts, which demonstrates a positive reception of AR-filtered content in the broader social media space. However, they exhibited caution of using AR filters in their own permanent posts and expressed concerns about potential impacts on perceived authenticity.

4.2   Why Do Young Adults Use AR Filters?

Young adults use AR filters as a means of projecting a specific image while upholding authentic connections with their followers. They engage with AR filters to create a positive online persona that mirrors their ideal self. Despite the growing acceptance of AR filters, the reluctance to use these filters in their own permanent posts suggests that maintaining an authentic online presence remains a significant social expectation for young adults. The use of AR filters for shaping versions of a mediated self, enhancing appearance, and addressing perceived flaws aligns with the motivation to boost self-confidence and positive self-perception, all of which aligns with previous research [2,3,10,18,20,25]. In this context, authenticity does not necessarily imply revealing a bare face; instead, it refers to presenting the best version (i.e., ideal self) of one's true self while ensuring it does not diminish the genuine aspects (i.e., real self) of the individual.

4.3   Limitations and Future Research

This study has a few limitations. We focused only on the use of AR filters on the social media platform Instagram due to its self-centered nature. Future research could consider other platforms, like Snapchat or TikTok, as different contexts of use may produce unexplored findings. In addition, this experience-based interview study demonstrates an initial exploration of the motivation to use AR filters in the context of social media self-presentation. Building upon this work, experimental and longitudinal studies could be conducted to quantify the findings and investigate the long-term use and potential changes in user perceptions. For example, future work could employ netnography to observe performative behaviors involving the use of AR filters on social media as well as archetype creation based on types of AR filters used.

References

1. Kriegel, E.R., et al.: Youth and Augmented Reality. In: Springer Handbook of Augmented Reality, pp. 709–741. Springer, Cham (2023). https://doi.org/10.1007/978-3-030-67822-7_29
2. Alsaggaf, R.M.: The impact of snapchat beautifying filters on beauty standards and self-image: a self-discrepancy approach. In: The European Conference on Arts and Humanities (2021)
3. Fribourg, R., Peillard, E., Mcdonnell, R.: Mirror, mirror on my phone: investigating dimensions of self-face perception induced by augmented reality filters. In: 2021 IEEE International Symposium on Mixed and Augmented Reality (ISMAR), pp. 470–478. IEEE (2021). https://doi.org/10.1109/ISMAR52148.2021.00064
4. Leong, J., et al.: Exploring the use of real-time camera filters on embodiment and creativity. In: Extended Abstracts of the 2021 CHI Conference on Human Factors in Computing Systems. ACM (2021). https://doi.org/10.1145/3411763.3451696
5. Nowak, K.L., Fox, J.: Avatars and computer-mediated communication: a review of the definitions, uses, and effects of digital representations. Rev. Commun. Res. **6**, 30–53 (2018). https://doi.org/10.12840/issn.2255-4165.2018.06.01.015
6. Sibilla, F., Mancini, T.: I am (not) my avatar: a review of the user-avatar relationships in massively multiplayer online worlds. Cyberpsychol. J. Psychos. Res. Cybersp. **12**(3) (2018). https://doi.org/10.5817/CP2018-3-4
7. Vasalou, A., Joinson, A., Bänziger, T., Goldie, P., Pitt, J.: Avatars in social media: balancing accuracy, playfulness and embodied messages. Int. J. Hum.-Comput. Stud. **66**(11), 801–811 (2008). https://doi.org/10.1016/j.ijhcs.2008.08.002
8. Waggoner, Z.: My Avatar, My Self: Identity in Video Role-Playing Games. McFarland (2009)
9. Zimmermann, D., Wehler, A., Kaspar, K.: Self-representation through avatars in digital environments. Curr. Psychol. **42**(25), 21775–21789 (2023). https://doi.org/10.1007/s12144-022-03232-6
10. Javornik, A., Marder, B., Pizzetti, M., Warlop, L.: Augmented self-the effects of virtual face augmentation on consumers' self-concept. J. Bus. Res. **130**, 170–187 (2021). https://doi.org/10.1016/j.jbusres.2021.03.026
11. Dargan, S., Bansal, S., Kumar, M., Mittal, A., Kumar, K.: Augmented reality: a comprehensive review. Archiv. Comput. Methods Eng.**30**(2), 1057–1080 (2023). https://doi.org/10.1007/s11831-022-09831-7
12. Eugeni, R.: Augmented reality flters and the faces as brands: personal identities and marketing strategies in the age of algorithmic images. In: Meiselwitz G. (ed.) Social Computing and Social Media: Applications in Education and Commerce

(HCII 2022). LNCS, 13316, pp. 223–234. Springer, Cham (2022). https://doi.org/10.1007/978-3-031-05064-0_17

13. Sinlapanuntakul, W.P., Derby, J.L., Chaparro, B.S.: Understanding the effects of mixed reality on video game satisfaction, enjoyment, and performance. Simulat. Gaming **53**(3), 237–252 (2022). https://doi.org/10.1177/10468781221094473

14. Sinlapanuntakul, P., Korentsides, J., Chaparro, B.S.: Exploring the user experience (UX) of a multi-window augmented reality environment. Front. Virtual Reality **4** (2023). https://doi.org/10.3389/frvir.2023.1194019

15. Sinlapanuntakul, P., Skilton, K.S., Mathew, J.N., Chaparro, B.S.: The effects of background noise on user experience and performance of mixed reality voice dictation. In: Proceedings of the Human Factors and Ergonomics Society Annual Meeting, vol. 66, pp. 1028–1032. SAGE Publications (2022). https://doi.org/10.1177/1071181322661376

16. Park, S., Bokijonov, S., Choi, Y.: Review of microsoft hololens applications over the past five years. Appl. Sci. **11**(16), 7259 (2021). https://doi.org/10.3390/app11167259

17. Sheldon, P., Rauschnabel, P.A., Antony, M.G., Car, S.: A cross-cultural comparison of croatian and american social network sites: exploring cultural differences in motives for instagram use. Comput. Hum. Behav. **75**, 643–651 (2017). https://doi.org/10.1016/j.chb.2017.06.009

18. Javornik, A., et al.: 'What lies behind the filter?' uncovering the motivations for using augmented reality (AR) face filters on social media and their effect on well-being. Comput. Hum. Behav. **128**, 10712 (2022). https://doi.org/10.1016/j.chb.2021.107126

19. Chae, J.: Virtual makeover: selfie-taking and social media use increase selfie-editing frequency through social comparison. Comput. Hum. Behav. **66**, 370–376 (2017). https://doi.org/10.1016/j.chb.2016.10.007

20. Miller, L., McIntyre, J.: From surgery to cyborgs: a thematic analysis of popular media commentary on instagram filters. Feminist Media Stud. **23**(7), 3615–3631 (2023). https://doi.org/10.1080/14680777.2022.2129414

21. Hoffman, D.L., Novak, T.P., Kang, H.: Let's get closer: feelings of connectedness from using social media, with implications for brand outcomes. J. Assoc. Consum. Res. **2**(2), 216–228 (2017). https://doi.org/10.1086/690938

22. Yau, A., Marder, B., O'Donohoe, S.: The role of social media in negotiating identity during the process of acculturation. Inf. Technol. People **33**(2), 554–575 (2020). https://doi.org/10.1108/ITP-09-2017-0305

23. Higgins, E.T.: Self-discrepancy: a theory relating self and affect. Psychol. Rev. **94**(3), 319–340 (1987). https://doi.org/10.1037/0033-295X.94.3.319

24. Clark, A., Chalmers, D.: The extended mind. Analysis **58**(1), 7–19 (1998). https://www.jstor.org/stable/3328150

25. Isakowitsch, C.: How augmented reality beauty filters can affect self-perception. In: Irish Conference on Artificial Intelligence and Cognitive Science, pp. 239–250. Springer, Charm (2022). https://doi.org/10.1007/978-3-031-26438-2_19

26. Braun, V., Clarke, V.: Using thematic analysis in psychology. Qualitat. Res. Psychol. **3**(2), 77–101 (2006). https://doi.org/10.1191/1478088706qp063oa

27. Birks, M., Chapman, Y., Francis, K.: Memoing in qualitative research: probing data and processes. J. Res. Nurs. **13**(1), 68–75 (2008). https://doi.org/10.1177/1744987107081254

28. Cohen, J.: A coefficient of agreement for nominal scales. Educ. Psychol. Measur. **20**(1), 37–46 (1960). https://doi.org/10.1177/001316446002000104

29. McDonald, N., Schoenebeck, S., Forte, A.: Reliability and inter-rater reliability in qualitative research: norms and guidelines for CSCW and HCI practice. Proc. ACM Hum.-Comput. Interact. **3**(CSCW) (2019). https://doi.org/10.1145/3359174

30. Sarker, S., Lau, F., Sahay, S.: Building an inductive theory of collaboration in virtual teams: an adapted grounded theory approach. In: Proceedings of the 33rd Annual Hawaii International Conference on System Sciences, p. 10. IEEE (2000). https://doi.org/10.1109/HICSS.2000.926934

31. Yang, C.C., Holden, S.M., Ariati, J.: Social media and psychological well-being among youth: the multidimensional model of social media use. Clin. Child Family Psycholo. Rev. **24**(3), 631–650 (2021). https://doi.org/10.1007/s10567-021-00359-z

Motion-Sensing Interactive Game Design of Wuqinxi for Hearing-Impaired People

Xiaowen Yu[✉] and Rongrong Fu

College of Art Design and Media, East China University of Science and Technology, Shanghai,
China
1275088968@qq.com

Abstract. People with hearing impairment cannot perceive information and usually rely on their eyes to perceive society and the present situation. In the process of practicing fitness qigong, the hearing impaired can only imitate the basic movements of fitness qigong, but they cannot feel the health benefits of fitness qigong through music and guidance at a deeper level. Fitness qigong Wuqinxi can combine breathing, guidance, consciousness, and music to work on the human body to produce good fitness and health effects. Therefore, this study takes the Wuqinxi as an example, and aims to design a Wuqinxi interactive game with VR as the carrier for the whole interactive experience of the game; using Kinect sensor to assist in recognizing the standard of the user's movements; and enhance the effectiveness of practicing fitness qigong for the hearing impaired people through the immersive visual experience, so as to make up for the obstacles of the hearing impaired people due to the lack of music guidance during the process of practicing.

Keywords: Wuqinxi · Motion-sensing game · VR · Kinect · hearing-impaired people

1 Introduction

Research has found that hearing-impaired people usually rely only on their eyes when observing society and the current situation because they lack an ability to perceive information; they also show a sense of loneliness psychologically [1]. Based on the characteristics of hearing-impaired patients, we found that hearing-impaired patients can only learn fitness qigong through visual perception because they are unable to perceive music and instructions, and the effect of their practice is greatly reduced. Therefore, to improve the effectiveness of the practice of hearing-impaired patients through the enhancement of visual perception, so as to make up for the obstacles of hearing-impaired patients due to the lack of music guidance in the process of practicing is the key problem to be solved in this study.

As a traditional Chinese medicine fitness qigong at the same time, Wuqinxi is also China's outstanding intangible cultural heritage, its movements imitate the animal form, has very typical fitness qigong characteristics and therapeutic effects, and has its own

© The Author(s), under exclusive license to Springer Nature Switzerland AG 2024
J. Y. C. Chen and G. Fragomeni (Eds.): HCII 2024, LNCS 14706, pp. 106–127, 2024.
https://doi.org/10.1007/978-3-031-61041-7_8

characteristics to match the music and the oral command, so in this paper, the author chooses t Wuqinxi as the research carrier.

Therefore, the purpose of this paper is to design an immersive VR somatosensory interactive game based on Wuqinxi as an example, to create a soothing atmosphere brought by music through immersive gaming experience, and to make up for the auditory deficiencies through visual-verbal cues, to enhance the experience and effectiveness of practicing fitness qigong in hearing impaired patients, and to provide a new way and method for hearing impaired patients to enhance the effectiveness of the practice of fitness qigong.

2 Related Works

Music therapy is an activity in which music is used to promote positive cognitive, physical, psychological, and social changes in individuals with health or behavioral disorders [2]. Rehabilitation is achieved primarily through improvisation, music composition, sound reproduction, and other techniques that use rhythm, harmony, and melody to enhance an individual's ability to express, learn, and organize [3]. Zhang et al. (2024) pointed out that music sound waves can stimulate human auditory organs, and through the brain response can directly trigger human emotional transformation [4]. Zhang et al. (2022) noted that music with different melodies and rhythms stimulates human meridians, which in turn promotes changes in qi and blood near the meridians [5].

Music therapy has been found to have a positive impact on a wide range of disorders, and many different moods. Kailimi Li et al. (2022) found in an experimental study that a combination of music intervention and physical activity was beneficial in improving cognition, functioning, and health in patients with attention deficit disorder [6]. Franceli L. Cibrian et al. (2020) demonstrated that neuromusic therapy is an effective treatment for improving coordination in children with autism through a controlled trial of an elastic touch screen and a tambourine [7]. Tereza Raquel Alcântara-Silva et al. (2018) demonstrated through an experiment with female patients with breast or other gynecological cancers that music therapy was effective in reducing cancer-related fatigue and depressive symptoms and improving patients' quality of life [8].

In traditional Chinese medicine fitness qigong, the role of music is mainly reflected in the three aspects of physiology, psychology, and environment, and the lack of music not only affects the coordination of movements but also affects human emotions, thus weakening the effect of the exercise. Garry Kuan et al. (2021) pointed out through literature analysis that the use of music in exercise can enhance positive emotions and reduce negative emotions [9]. Zhou (2016) pointed out that in different Chinese fitness qigonges, music not only standardizes the movements but also improves the effect of physical and mental exercise for the practitioners [10]. Zhou et al. (2018) pointed out that the use of music in the Five Animal Circus can enhance the health benefits of the Five Animal Circus from three aspects: physiological, psychological, and environmental [11].

Somatosensory interaction technology can make up for the lack of hearing perception of hearing-impaired patients through immersive visual experience and enhance the ability of hearing-impaired patients to perceive information [12]. Yang et al. (2021)

designed an immersive articulation rehabilitation training system for hearing-impaired children based on virtual reality VR technology, which effectively improved the articulation ability of hearing-impaired children [13]. Qin (2017) showed that somatosensory interaction technology can fill the invisible service needs of people with disabilities, reduce the user cognitive load of people with disabilities, satisfy the diverse contexts of people with disabilities, as well as improve the participation and emotional experience of activities for people with disabilities [14]. Xiao et al. (2018) pointed out that virtual reality technology "immerses" hearing-impaired children with realistic images, and its advantages of immersion, interactivity, and imagination play a greater role in enhancing the level of oral narratives of hearing-impaired children [15].

In the practice of fitness qigong, hearing-impaired patients are unable to complete the practice through the music guidance due to the lack of hearing perception, and the VR somatosensory interactive game can create a soothing atmosphere brought by the music, enhance the effectiveness of the hearing-impaired patients' practice of fitness qigong through immersive visual experience, and make up for the obstacles of the hearing-impaired patients who are unable to practice the practice of fitness qigong through the guidance of the music due to the lack of hearing perception.

3   Methodology

This study proposes a game design method based on somatosensory interaction technology to construct a game system that enhances the effectiveness of fitness qigong practice for hearing-impaired users. It consists of four main stages: in the first stage, the

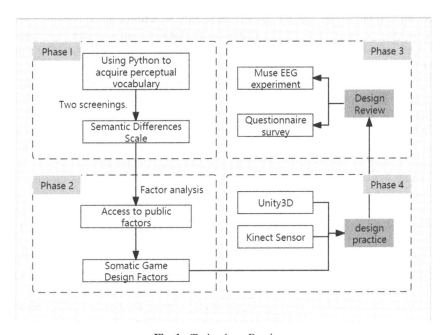

Fig. 1. Technology Roadmap

perceptual vocabulary of exercise-based somatosensory games is collected and screened, and the semantic difference scale is constructed. In the second stage, the results of the semantic difference scale are analyzed using factor analysis, and the common factors are extracted to construct the design dimensions of the somatosensory interactive game. In the third stage, Unity3D is used to build the game scene, and the Kinect sensor is used to recognize human skeletal movements to complete the design practice. In the fourth stage, combined with the previous results, use Muse EEG experiment supplemented with a questionnaire to verify the validity of the design practice, the technical route is shown in Fig. 1.

3.1 Acquisition of Perceptual Vocabulary to Construct a Semantic Differential Scale

The Semantic Difference Method is a quantitative evaluation method for measuring human perception created by C.E. Osgood [16]. The salient feature of the semantic difference method is the use of adjective pairs to determine the intuitive feelings of people, first determine the appropriate adjectives and evaluation scales, and then according to the study select the interview subjects to score the experimental subjects, and finally the data of the survey is statistically analyzed, which is a common method of quantitative analysis of demand.

In this study, the Semantic Difference Scale was used to obtain the needs of hearing-impaired users for motion-based somatosensory interactive games. In the acquisition of the evaluation dimensions of the semantic difference scale, firstly, Python was used to obtain users' perceptual evaluations of sport-based somatosensory games on the game website and carry out word frequency statistics; secondly, students and designers with industrial design backgrounds were recruited to carry out a round of screening of high-frequency vocabulary; and finally, experts carried out a second round of screening and summarized the results of the first round of screening, obtained the evaluation dimensions of the semantic difference scale, and carried out the final semantic difference scale design. Final semantic differential scale design.

3.2 Factor Analysis to Obtain Game Design Factors

To obtain the needs of hearing-impaired users for sport-based somatosensory games, this study used factor analysis to downgrade and categorize the data obtained from the Semantic Difference Scale and extracted the public factors as the design factors for the design of somatosensory interactive games.

Before factor analysis, the data obtained from the semantic differential scale needs to be tested for reliability and validity. Firstly, the imported data will be analyzed for reliability, in general, Cronbach $\alpha \geq 0.8$ indicates high reliability and reliable data for further analysis. Second, the imported data were subjected to KMO and Bartlett tests. In general, a KMO value greater than 0.6 indicates that the data can be factor analyzed; greater than 0.7 indicates that it is more suitable for factor analysis.

The tested data were analyzed using factor analysis to extract the number of factors with eigenvalues greater than 1, to generate the ANOVA table and to extract the common factors; then the factors were rotated by Kaiser's Normalized Maximum Variance method to obtain the rotated factor loading coefficients table, and each common factor was ranked by the absolute size of the factor loading values, and the components of the factor composition were analyzed and named to serve as a design factor for guiding the game.

3.3 Build the Game System

Based on the above experiments and analysis, the factors extracted from the factor analysis are used as the main design factors for the design of the somatic interaction game in this study and guide the generation of the corresponding design principles. This study combines with combining the above-generated design principles, using VR as the game carrier; building the game scene in the Unity environment; combining with Kinect sensors, recognizing the movement of the human skeleton, recording and analyzing the skeletal information in the movement, and completing the design of somatosensory interactive health assistance game.

At present, the common supporting devices for somatosensory games are Kinect, Wii, CyWEE, Leap Motion, and so on. The Kinect sensor can obtain data from the outside world to form a data source to provide depth image information and color image information at the same time; the depth image information can identify the joints of various parts of the human body to form skeletal information; the color image information can identify the user's movements to get the position information of the hand and the whole body. Among them, Kinect V2 can recognize 25 skeletal nodes, as shown in Fig. 2. After the recognition is completed, Kinect will further recognize the 3D coordinates of the joint points of the human body to realize the 3D modeling of the human skeleton, which will provide the basis for the subsequent action recognition [17, 18]. Therefore, in this study, the Kinect sensor is used to recognize the skeletal movements of the character.

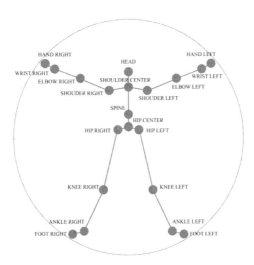

Fig. 2. Kinect Skeleton Node Graph

Unity 3D is the mainstream game engine technology, this paper adopts Unity 3D to build the game scene of the somatosensory interactive game and carry out the character bone binding. Firstly, we collect and render the materials of the scene and the characters, and secondly, we set the skeleton of the characters so that the data captured by Kinect can drive the movement of the character's skeleton.

3.4   Game Effectiveness Review

After the practice, the validity of the game design was verified using the Muse EEG experiment paired with a questionnaire, i.e., user experience research and perceptual evaluation of the design practice output. Firstly, users were invited to watch the game samples in the previous section and the game video of the somatosensory interactive game designed in this study from the visual and interactive dimensions, and the EEG data were recorded using Muse; secondly, the five dimensions for evaluating the somatosensory interactive game obtained from the Semantic Difference Scale designed in the previous section were combined with the experimental samples, and questionnaires were designed to support the study. Objective data analysis paired with users' subjective perceptions proved that the game design of this study can effectively improve the effectiveness of fitness qigong practice for hearing-impaired users compared with existing market solutions.

The EEG devices used in this study are Muse 2 and Muse: Meditation& Sleep App analysis software. Muse 2 is a head-mounted EEG sensor, as shown in Fig. 3, which can output real-time EEG information after filtering and algorithmic processing, and it contains seven sensors, as shown in Fig. 4, of which FP1 and FP2 are the prefrontal sensors corresponding to the frontal lobe area of the brain, and Muse app uses Active, Neutral, and Calm as the evaluation indexes of the activity of frontal lobe area of the subject. In this paper, the frontal lobe area feedback is chosen as the main reference data, and the Muse app uses Active, Neutral, and Calm as the evaluation indexes of the activity of the frontal lobe area of the subject [19]. The main data observed in this study were Active values, with higher Active values reflecting higher arousal, stronger stimuli, and more triggering of the subject's interest.

Fig. 3. Muse equipment

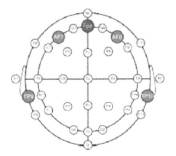

Fig. 4. Sensor position distribution

4 Motion-Sensing Interactive Game Design of Wuqinxi

4.1 Constructing the Semantic Differences Scale

To further acquire the needs of hearing-impaired users for sports-type somatosensory games, which can be used to guide the design practice. This experiment is based on the Semantic Difference Scale (SDS), which allows target users to experience and score the selected samples, and analyze the scoring data to extract the common factors, which can be used as a design strategy to guide the design practice. Firstly, 50 hearing-impaired users were invited to experience and score the game; secondly, 150 online users were invited to simulate hearing-impaired patients to watch the video of the silent game and score the game through an online questionnaire.

Experimental Sample. The author initially selected 10 VR game samples for experimentation from the dimensions of game type, game rating, and game heat. After further screening by 5 experts, 6 VR game samples were determined to be the final ones used for experimentation in this paper. These 6 VR games all belong to sports VR games, with high game ratings and high heat among VR game users, which match the research theme of this paper. The 6 VR games are shown in Table 1.

Acquisition of Perceptual Vocabulary Design Semantic Differential Scales. After determining the evaluation samples of the six sports VR games, the collection of perceptual evaluation vocabulary was carried out, and these vocabularies were eventually used in the design of the semantic difference scale. To obtain the perceptual evaluation vocabulary of VR games, the author used Python to obtain 6,579 related reviews of the above six VR games on the Steam gaming website and carried out word frequency statistics, to dig out the user's concerns about VR games in a data-driven way.

After initial screening 100 high-frequency and meaningful adjectives and nouns were obtained as shown in Table 2.

Next, a total of ten students and designers with industrial design backgrounds were recruited to conduct the first round of screening of the 100 high-frequency perceptual words mentioned above, leaving 20 perceptual words, as shown in Table 3.

The remaining 20 perceptual words were screened and summarized in a second round following the experts' suggestions, and summarized into five dimensions, which were used to design the final semantic differential scale, as shown in Table 4.

Table 1. Sample of six VR games

name of game	photograph
Box VR	
OhShape	
Pistol Whip	
PowerBeatsVR	
VR Ping Pong Paradise	
Racket:Nx	

Table 4 summarizes the five dimensions of designing the semantic difference scale, according to which the author selected the corresponding five groups of adjectives and designed the semantic difference scale as shown in Table 5.

Experimental Subject. First, the experiment invited 50 young groups of 20–30-year-old simulated hearing-impaired patients as subjects, the subjects were autonomous to

Table 2. 100 high-frequency perceptual words after preliminary screening

word	word frequency	word	word frequency	word	word frequency	word	word frequency
game	6043	exercise	357	bad	242	headset	174
VR	1801	few	354	enough	240	enjoy	172
fun	1567	content	345	nice	239	come	168
music	1318	Whip	342	hours	238	each	166
good	1195	right	335	aim	236	ball	161
songs	984	far	320	fitness	235	awesome	161
great	973	bit	317	enemies	226	vr	159
games	932	Great	312	same	217	gun	154
time	733	mode	310	day	214	start	150
Saber	702	pretty	309	update	212	maps	150
rhythm	678	different	290	move	210	campaign	150
well	501	saber	288	high	209	take	149
better	489	gameplay	287	down	206	dodge	148
new	455	people	282	quite	206	boxing	147
work	451	experience	279	body	205	BoxVR	141
best	449	worth	278	devs	202	style	141
Wick	444	sweat	272	things	201	favorite	140
song	431	doesn	260	score	199	legs	139
love	423	difficulty	260	review	196	punch	138
hit	414	little	257	put	191	hour	138
custom	384	many	250	bullets	189	calories	135
level	371	easy	247	long	188	guns	134
Pistol	371	amazing	247	price	188	free	131
hard	370	minutes	245	tracks	186	real	126
levels	358	thing	244	游戏	178	issues	125

Table 3. Remaining 20 sensory words from the first round of screening

fun	music	time	rhythm	level
hard	easy	content	mode	worth
sweat	fitness	price	headset	style
calorie	free	experience	difficulty	song

Table 4. Dimensions used to design the semantic differential scale

Difficulty level	interestingness	rhythmic sense	(art) composition	coloration

Table 5. Semantic Differences Scale

Evaluation Glossary	5	4	3	2	1	Evaluation Glossary
Hard						Easy
Fun						Boring
Rhythmic						Unrhythmic
Aesthetic						Unsightly
Colorful						Flat

participate in this experiment, their mental condition before the experiment was good, and do not have a priori knowledge of the experimental materials.

Secondly, 150 online young user groups aged 20–30 years old were invited and had gaming experience of sports VR games, and did not have a priori knowledge of the material of this experiment.

Experimental Procedure. After the scale was designed, 50 users were first invited to score the sample. The subjects were asked to simulate hearing-impaired patients, firstly, the experiment was conducted in a quiet environment, and secondly, the game music was turned off and noise-canceling earplugs were worn for the subjects. The subjects were asked to observe and experience the samples from both the visual and interactive dimensions, and to rate each sample based on the sensory experience obtained from the visual and interactive dimensions (5 for complete agreement, 4 for agreement, 3 for neutral, 2 for disagreement, and 1 for complete disagreement). Before the start of the experiment, the subjects were informed about the use of the VR device with the rules of using the game, and each subject was given 10 min to familiarize themselves with the use of the VR device. During the experiment, each subject was given 10 min to review each game for a total duration of approximately 1 h.

Second, 150 online users were invited to watch silent videos of six game samples in a quiet environment and to score the game samples, each of which was two minutes long, for a total duration of 12 min.

4.2 Factor Analysis to Obtain the Design Factors of the Wuqinxi Physical Game

The 200 valid questionnaires collected by the semantic differential method were standardized for data, and the data were entered into SPSSAU for reliability analysis, Cronbach α was 0.922, which can be used for further analysis. The specific results are shown in Table 6.

Table 6. Reliability Statistics (Cronbach Alpha)

Item count	Cronbach α	Standardized Cronbach alpha
5	0.922	0.950

The imported data was then subjected to the KMO and Bartlett test of sphericity. From Table 7, it can be seen that the KMO value is 0.705 and the significance of the Bartlett test is 0.004, indicating that the data is suitable for factor analysis.

Table 7. KMO and Bartlett test

KMO		0.705
Bartlett test	Approx. Chi-Square	22.682
	df	10
	p value	0.004

SPSSAU was used to conduct factor analysis, and factor analysis with dimensionality reduction was used to extract the number of factors with eigenvalues greater than 1, generating an ANOVA table as shown in Table 8. From Table 8, it can be seen that the characteristics of sports VR games are mainly analyzed based on five evaluation factors, and 91.143% of the internal relationships in the characteristics of sports VR games are explained by two public factors, indicating that these two factors reflect most of the information of the characteristics of sports VR games, and the effect of the factor analysis is also ideal. Factor 1 explained 50.142% of the features of sport VR games and factor 2 explained 41.001% of the features of sport VR games. It is also verified by the gravel plot (shown in Fig. 5) - the scatter plot of the evaluation factors output from the factor analysis - that component 3 is the turning point, and the slope of the folded segment before component 3 is relatively large, while the folded segment after it becomes gradually flat, so component 1 and component 2 contribute more to explaining the features of the sport VR game, and are overall 5 factor is very important and is the main factor in the evaluation and analysis. Meanwhile, from the side, it can be seen that the factor analysis of this is meaningful and credible, and can continue to carry out the research of data analysis.

The public factors were extracted by factor analysis, and then the factors were rotated by the Kaiser normalized maximum variance method to obtain a table of the rotated factor loading coefficients (see Table 9). Each public factor was ranked according to the size of the absolute value of the factor loading values, and the components of the factor composition were analyzed and named, as shown in Table 10.

Among the evaluation items of Factor 1, there are three groups with absolute values of factor loadings exceeding 0.6, which are fun, difficulty, and sense of rhythm, among them, fun reaches the highest value of 0.896, and all of the above evaluation indexes are related to interactivity, so Factor 1 is named interactivity.

Table 8. Table of Explanation of Variance for Factor Analysis

Factor	Eigen values			% of variance (Initial)			% of variance (Rotated)		
	Eigen	% of Variance	Cum. % of Variance	Eigen	% of Variance	Cum. % of Variance	Eigen	% of Variance	Cum. % of Variance
1	2.507	50.142	50.142	2.507	50.142	50.142	2.471	49.429	49.429
2	2.050	41.001	91.143	2.050	41.001	91.143	2.086	41.715	91.143
3	0.379	7.584	98.727	–	–	–	–	–	–
4	0.063	1.266	99.993	–	–	–	–	–	–
5	0.000	0.007	100.000	–	–	–	–	–	–

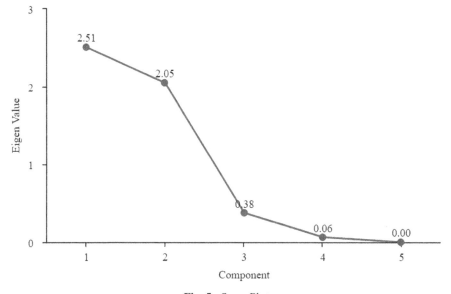

Fig. 5. Scree Plot

Among the evaluation items of Factor 2, there are two groups with factor loadings exceeding 0.6 in absolute value, namely, composition and color, in which the evaluation index of color reaches 0.981 at the highest level, and all of the above evaluation indexes require human subjective visual feelings, so Factor 2 is named visual effect.

Therefore, a total of 2 factors were extracted from this factor analysis, named interactivity and visual effect, which in turn were used as the main basis for the design of sports VR games.

4.3 The Practice of Designing the Wuqinxi Body Interactive Game

Design Principles. Based on the above experiments and research, the author summa-

Table 9. Factor loading (Rotated)

Items	Factor loading		Communalities
	Factor 1	Factor 2	
Difficulty level	0.883	0.128	0.796
Interestingness	0.896	0.141	0.823
rhythmic sense	0.789	-0.594	0.976
(art) composition	0.508	0.857	0.993
coloration	−0.085	0.981	0.969

Rotation method: maximum variance method Varimax

Table 10. Factor analysis results

Interactivity (Factor 1)	Visual effects (factor 2)
interestingness	(art) composition
Difficulty level	coloration
rhythmic sense	

rizes that the influencing factors of the design of the Wuqinxi physical interactive game are interactivity and visual effect, and the corresponding design principles, respectively, are shown in Fig. 6.

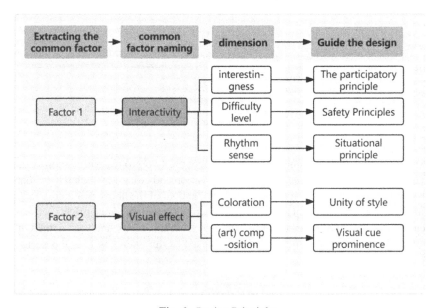

Fig. 6. Design Principles

Interactivity Principle

1. Participation Principle

The participatory principle emphasizes the human-centered design concept. The main purpose of the interaction design study of the Wuqian Opera interactive game is to let users experience the fun of the Chinese traditional intangible cultural heritage of Wuqian Opera through the way of somatosensory movement. In the whole interactive process, the users need to participate in the game wholeheartedly, and the visual interaction is strengthened to enhance the sense of participation of the hearing-impaired users. Based on the concept of customization, users can choose the game difficulty, game mode, and so on to improve the satisfaction of users.

2. The situational principle

According to Cooper's Experiential Learning, the four contextual learning models mentioned are the context of experience, the context of reflection, the context of concept formation, and the context of application [20]. In the Motion-sensing interactive game of Wuqinxi, the experience context is expressed in the game to provide users with real environmental space, so that users are immersed in the context of the Wuqinxi picture. The reflective context is mainly manifested in the process of the game through the visual prompting of the user's movement standardization, so that the user is clear about the wrong posture, corrects the wrong posture, and changes to the correct movement. The concept formation context is mainly manifested in the process of reflecting on one's own movement to help users subconsciously form experience summarization and movement summary and form abstract concepts. The application context is to verify the correctness of the abstract concept by playing the game again.

3. Security principles

The interactive movement of the Wuqinxi Games needs to be centered on the principle of safety, especially for hearing-impaired users, and the principle of safety needs to be taken into account. Ensure that the medical movement and interactive movement can meet the requirements of medical movement, but also meet the requirements of interactive ergonomics, to ensure that the user in the use of somatosensory games generated by the action is a guarantee of safety.

Visual Effect

1. Uniform game interface style.

As a traditional Chinese intangible cultural heritage, the game style should conform to the traditional Chinese cultural style as a whole, and the color, font, and icon should be consistent.

2. Visual cues are prominent.

From the perspectives of visual perception and language prompts, we can bring users closer to the somatosensory game, attract their attention, and improve the user stickiness of the product. For hearing-impaired users, it is necessary to highlight the correct and incorrect prompts of user actions during the game at the visual level through graphic supplementation, etc., so as to improve the participation of hearing-impaired users in the somatosensory game by means of visual enhancement.

Game Interaction Design

Introduction to the Wuqinxi Process. Wuqinxi is a guiding technique that imitates the movements of five kinds of animals - tiger, deer, bear, ape, and bird - and is based on physical movement, supplemented by breathing and exhaling with the idea of cooperation [21]. Wuqinxi is divided into five plays, the first play tiger play, mainly exercises and regulates the function of the liver, the requirements of the tiger's posture, and daily life through the imagination of the tiger's movements and simulation to reflect the tiger's ferocious and robust. The second play of deer, mainly exercises and regulates the function of the kidneys, the requirements of the posture of the deer through the imagination of the movements and daily life, simulation of the deer's gentle and elegant. The third play is Bear, which mainly exercises and regulates the function of the spleen, and requires that through imagining the posture and movement of the bear and daily life, it simulates and embodies the robustness of the bear. The fourth play is Ape, which mainly exercises and regulates the function of the heart, and requires simulating the alertness and agility of the ape by imagining the ape's gestures and movements and daily life. The fifth play, Bird Play, mainly exercises and regulates the function of the lungs, and requires simulating the lightness of the bird through imagining the bird's postural movements and daily life.

The five different scenes of Wuqinxi physical interactive game are designed according to the five acts of Wuqinxi, which are also divided into five different game scenes of tiger, deer, bear, ape, and bird. Different game scenes are unlocked by accumulating gold coins, and this reward mechanism is applied to improve the fun of users' game experience.

Interaction Design System. Users based on VR equipment, in the game scene constructed by Unity 3D, carry out Wuqinxi movement practice; through the Kinect sensor on the human skeleton movement recognition, in line with Wuqinxi movement norms, then appear the corresponding correct visual prompts and get the corresponding gold rewards; does not meet the norms of the visual graphic to the user for the error warning, and the system records the user's wrong posture, to provide users with optional targeted exercises. The system will record the user's wrong postures and provide the user with optional targeted exercises. The accumulated gold coins can unlock different game scenes and different difficulty modes of Wuqinxi, which can enhance the user experience of Wuqinxi interactive game for the hearing impaired users through the immersive visual experience, and the specific information architecture diagram and interaction flowchart of the game are shown in Fig. 7 and Fig. 8.

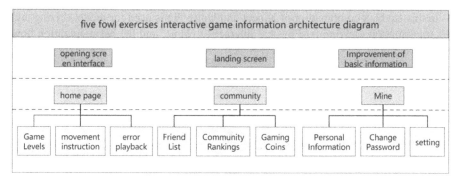

Fig. 7. Wuqinxi interactive game information architecture diagram

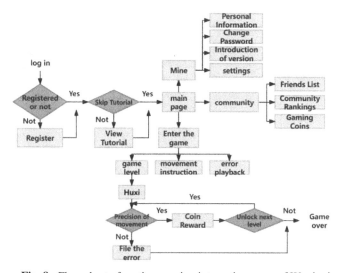

Fig. 8. Flow chart of motion-sensing interactive game of Wuqinxi

Device Architecture and Technology Development. The design of Wuqinxi Interactive Game uses Unity 3D to build the game scene and the skeleton binding of the game characters; Kinect SDK 2.0 and Kinect middleware Kinect V2 with MS-SDK to process the Kinect data flow; and Pico4 pro device as the game carrier, to enhance the user's immersion and participation in the somatosensory game.

In this paper, the video recording of action samples is carried out by Kinect device and Kinect studio, Visual Gesture Builder software and Adaboos algorithm are used to train machine learning on the recorded sample actions, to define the interaction logic of the actions, and to establish the pose database file of Wuqinxi.

Unity 3D is used to build the game scene of the Wuqinxi interactive game and to bind the character bones. Firstly, the scene and characters are materialized and rendered, and secondly, the characters are skeletonized so that the data captured by Kinect can drive the movement of the characters' skeletons.

In this study, a combination of Kinect and Unity 3D is used for model driving and data transmission of Wuqinxi Physical Interactive Game, and the basic operation flow is shown in Fig. 9.

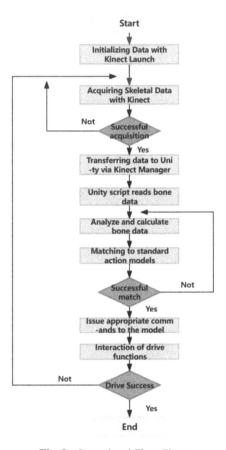

Fig. 9. Operational Flow Chart

Game Visual Design. The game uses Unity to build the three-dimensional game scene of Wuqinxi Sensory Interactive Game, and the design of the scene is in line with the theme of the Chinese traditional intangible cultural heritage of Wuqinxi Sensory Interactive Game. The whole game scene takes the Chinese traditional landscape elements as the background of the game, and the screen and character style adopts the ink and watercolor style that is preferred by the users, and the overall hue adopts a low-saturation color scheme. Each scene of the game is enriched with animal elements consistent with the theme of Wuqinxi Games, and the game interface is shown in Fig. 10.

Fig. 10. Game Interface Diagram

5   Design Validity Assessment

5.1   Experimental Design

To verify whether the design of the Wuqinxi Somatic Interactive Game in this paper can improve the gaming experience of hearing-impaired users, the game design of this paper was evaluated by using Muse EEG experiments together with questionnaires in the design validity evaluation section. Firstly, users were invited to watch the game videos of the six game samples in the previous paper and the Wuqinxi interactive game designed in this study from the visual and interactive dimensions, each video was 1 min and 30 s long, and Muse was used to record the EEG data of the users; secondly, a questionnaire was designed to assist the study by combining the five dimensions of evaluating the physical interactive game obtained by designing the Semantic Difference Scale in the previous paper with the experimental samples.

5.2   Experimental Subjects

A total of 15 young user groups aged 20–30 years old were invited to simulate hearing-impaired users, of which 6 were male and 9 were female; all of them had participated in the previous game reviews and had experience in using VR somatosensory interactive games. The experiment was conducted in a quiet environment, with silent video and users wearing noise-canceling earplugs.

5.3   Experimental Procedure

First, the subjects were told to perceive the game videos to be shown from both visual and interactive dimensions, the users were shown the silent videos of the six game samples in the previous section as well as the game designed in this study, each video was 1 min and 30 s, and the users watched it autonomously wearing earbuds in a quiet environment, and the Active value of the users was recorded by using Muse, and the results of the experiments are shown in Table 11.

At the end of the experiment, a questionnaire was distributed asking users to subjectively evaluate the games designed in this study in five aspects: difficulty, fun, rhythm, composition, and color.

Table 11. Summary of Active data statistics for Muse

	Wuqinxi Interactive Game	Box VR	OhShape	Pistol Whip	PowerBeatsVR	VR Ping Pong Paradise	Racket: Nx
Subject 1	6	1	0	3	1	0	2
Subject 2	3	0	1	0	1	1	2
Subject 3	1	1	0	1	0	0	1
Subject 4	7	2	1	2	3	2	3
Subject 5	15	6	1	3	6	3	4
Subject 6	6	3	0	1	2	2	3
Subject 7	15	3	2	2	7	2	7
Subject 8	16	6	1	2	6	3	3
Subject 9	11	7	0	3	4	3	2
Subject 10	3	1	0	0	2	1	2
Subject 11	2	1	0	1	1	0	1
Subject 12	14	3	3	6	3	0	6
Subject 13	11	2	3	3	4	1	3
Subject 14	10	6	2	4	2	0	5
Subject 15	3	2	0	2	2	0	3
total	123	44	14	33	44	18	47

In the results of the Muse EEG experiment, the Active value of the Wuqinxi Physical Interactive Game designed in this study is significantly higher than that of the six experimental samples in the previous paper, indicating that the user experience of this game for hearing-impaired users is higher than that of several existing motion-based VR physical games on the market. At the same time, the five dimensions for evaluating sports VR somatosensory games summarized in the previous section were used to question the subjects in the form of a questionnaire. The questionnaire adopts a 5-level evaluation scale $(-2, -1, 0, 1, 2)$, which represents from left to right "very dissatisfied -2" "dissatisfied -1" "general 0" "satisfied 1" "very satisfied 2". The results of the questionnaire show that the users' overall evaluation of the Wuqinxi Sensory Interactive Game is high (Table 12).

Table 12. Statistical results of post-test questionnaire data

	Difficulty level	interestingness	rhythmic sense	(art) composition	coloration
average	1.61	1.82	1.67	1.68	1.62

6 Discussion

This study found through practical validation that the Wuqinxi somatosensory interactive game designed in this study is better than the existing samples in the dimensions of interactivity as well as a visual effect, which solves the problem of reduced effectiveness of hearing-impaired patients due to their inability to practice fitness qigong through the guidance of music, and provides a new method and way for hearing-impaired patients to practice fitness qigong.

Firstly, Python is used to obtain the user evaluation on the game website, and after two layers of screening, the perceptual evaluation vocabulary of sports physical games is obtained and the semantic difference scale is constructed, which is used to construct the evaluation dimensions of the semantic difference scale in a data-driven way, which provides a more objective and rational method for the analysis of demand.

Second, factor analysis is used to analyze the data obtained by the semantic differential method, to extract the public factors and derive strategies to guide the design, to provide sufficient data support for the perceptual design, and to make the perceptual design become data visualized.

Finally, based on the VR device, using Kinect as the sensor, the game scene of Wuqinxi physical interactive game was constructed in Unity3D, which enhances the information perception ability of the hearing impaired with an immersive visual experience and improves the effectiveness of the fitness qigong practice for the hearing impaired users.

However, due to the limitations of the experimental conditions, the experimental population in this paper is a group of healthy young people aged 20 to 30 years old, and the simulation of hearing-impaired patients by means of silent video and wearing noise-canceling earplugs in a quiet experimental environment may have certain deviations from the actual hearing-impaired patients, and further experimental validation studies are needed.

7 Conclusion

This study focuses on the problem of reduced effectiveness of practice due to the inability of hearing-impaired users to practice fitness qigong through musical guidance and selects the Chinese intangible cultural heritage of Wuqiu Opera as a case study. The data of the semantic difference method was analyzed using factor analysis to obtain the design principles of the physical interactive game; according to the design principles, the design practice of the Wuqinxi interactive game was carried out, and the effectiveness of the design practice was evaluated by using Muse EEG experiments with questionnaires, and the validation found that the design solution of the present study has obvious improvement in visual effect and interactivity compared with the existing market solutions. The research case applied in this study is also applicable to other exercises supplemented with music, which provides more effective methods and approaches for exercise practice for hearing-impaired patients.

References

1. Yu, Y.: "Xiaoyu"-Service Application Design for the Hearing Impaired. Tsinghua University (2013)
2. Vinolo-Gil, M.J., Casado-Fernández, E., Perez-Cabezas, V., et al.: Effects of the combination of music therapy and physiotherapy in the improvement of motor function in cerebral palsy: a challenge for research. Children **8**(10), 868 (2021)
3. Jones, J.D.: Songs composed for use in music therapy: a survey of original songwriting practices of music therapists. J. Music Ther. **43**(2), 94–110 (2006)
4. Wang, K., Liang, Y., Hu, K.: Innovative design of Tang Dynasty Baoxiang flower patterns in Guochao clothing. J. Fashion **8**(01), 64–73 (2023)
5. Zhang, Y., Li, L., Chen, J., et al.: Exploration of the origin of the idea of five-sound therapy in the Yellow Emperor's Internal Canon. J. Liaoning Univ. Tradition. Chin. Med. **26**(01), 1–4 (2024). https://doi.org/10.13194/j.issn.1673-842x.2024.01.001
6. Li, K., Cui, C.C., Zhang, H., et al.: Exploration of combined physical activity and music for patients with Alzheimer's disease: a systematic review. Front. Aging Neurosci. **14**, 962475 (2022)
7. Cibrian, F.L., Madrigal, M., Avelais, M., et al.: Supporting coordination of children with ASD using neurological music therapy: a pilot randomized control trial comparing an elastic touch-display with tambourines. Res. Dev. Disabil. **106**, 103741 (2020)
8. Alcântara-Silva, T.R., de Freitas-Junior, R., Freitas, N.M.A., et al.: Music therapy reduces radiotherapy-induced fatigue in patients with breast or gynecological cancer: a randomized trial. Integr. Cancer Ther. **17**(3), 628–635 (2018)
9. Karageorghis, C., Kuan, G., Schiphof-Godart, L.: Music in sport: From conceptual underpinnings to applications. In: Essentials of Exercise and Sport Psychology: An Open Access Textbook, pp. 530–564 (2021)
10. Zhou, Y.-Q.: The important role and significance of music in fitness qigong exercise. J. Chengdu Univ. (Soc. Sci. Edn.) **04**, 102–105 (2016)

11. Zhou, F.-C., Li, J.-Y.: Exploring the mechanism of health maintenance of fitness qigong five bird play based on traditional music therapy. Martial Arts Res. **3**(11), 109–111 (2018). https://doi.org/10.13293/j.cnki.wskx.007497
12. Yang, Q., Zhong, S.: Research on the development of virtual reality technology in China: review and outlook. Sci. Manag. Res. **38**(05), 20–26 (2020). https://doi.org/10.19445/j.cnki.15-1103/g3.2020.05.003
13. Yang, Y., Zhao, J., Shi, L., et al.: An immersive pronunciation rehabilitation training system for hearing impaired children based on VR technology. J. Jilin Univ. (Inf. Sci. Edn.) **39**(06), 700–705 (2021). https://doi.org/10.19292/j.cnki.jdxxp.2021.06.010
14. Qin, Y.: Research on the Design of Product Service System for People with Disabilities Based on Somatosensory Interaction Technology. Donghua University (2017)
15. Xiao, R., Lei, J.: Progress in the application of computer-assisted technology in language intervention for children with hearing impairment. Mod. Spec. Educ. **14**, 8–14 (2018)
16. Osgood, C.E., Suci, G.J., Tannenbaum, P.H.: The Measurement of Meaning. University of Illinois Press (1957)
17. Zhang, J.: Design and Realization of Kinect-Based Fitness Game. Huazhong Normal University (2017)
18. Jian, W.: Gesture Recognition and Human-Computer Interaction Based on Kinect. Nanjing University of Posts and Telecommunications (2018)
19. Lu, Y.: Research on Parametric Design of Lacquer Jewelry. East China University of Science and Technology (2021). https://doi.org/10.27148/d.cnki.ghagu.2021.000569
20. Wang, Z.: Research on the Interaction Design of Cervical Spine Health Care Somatosensory Game for College Student Groups. Wuhan University of Technology (2018)
21. Zhou, Y., Zhang, W., Liu, Q., et al.: An analysis of the fitness mechanism of five bird play based on the view of form, qi and spirit as a trinity of life. Jiangxi Trad. Chin. Med. **54**(06), 7–9+12 (2023)

Perceived Playfulness: Factors Affecting the VR Display Experience in Museums

Zehui Zhao[1], Ruisi Liu[2], and Junjie Chu[1(✉)]

[1] Ocean University of China, Qingdao 266100, China
chujunjie@ouc.edu.cn
[2] Northwestern Polytechnical University, Xi'an 710072, China

Abstract. At present, virtual reality is an important technology for digitizing museums. The application of VR in museums can not only better protect cultural relics, but also create an immersive visiting experience for tourists. Therefore, it is necessary to explore what factors affect users' acceptance of VR in museum. Through literature review, we rated the VR displays of 204 National First-Class Museums in China, and conducted a follow-up investigation on the VR display of "Xun Jing Dun Huang" with the highest score. This study proposes an extended TAM to explore which factors affect users' intention to use VR display in museum. A total of 296 questionnaires were collected, and 208 questionnaires were used. The research results indicate that perceived playfulness has a significant impact on perceived usefulness, and perceived usefulness has a significant impact on behavioral intention. This means that VR in museum not only needs to have gaming attributes and enhanced gamification features, but it also needs to promote the integration of education and entertainment, which called "edutainment". In addition, interactivity has a significant impact on perceived usefulness and perceived ease of use. Therefore, in the construction of museum VR, smooth interactive design is crucial for attracting users.

Keywords: Technology Acceptance Model (TAM) · VR · Museum

1 Introduction

As a kind of public cultural institution, museums play an important role in disseminating culture. Through the establishment of exhibitions, museums provide the public with cultural knowledge including art, history, science, etc. [1]. China has a profound culture and tangible cultural heritage, with a large number of museums and a wide variety of exhibits, attracting many tourists to visit them. In 2022, China added 382 new museums for the record, bringing the total number of official museums for the record to 6,565 nationwide. Throughout the year, 34,000 offline exhibitions and nearly 230,000 educational activities were held, receiving 5.78 million visitors [2]. However, the capacity of museums is limited after all, and many famous museums are gradually experiencing the problem of overcrowding and under-ticketing. Although a number of large museums, such as the Palace Museum, have already started the reservation system, the flow of

© The Author(s), under exclusive license to Springer Nature Switzerland AG 2024
J. Y. C. Chen and G. Fragomeni (Eds.): HCII 2024, LNCS 14706, pp. 128–141, 2024.
https://doi.org/10.1007/978-3-031-61041-7_9

people in the museums is still very heavy. This not only makes it impossible for visitors to observe the details of cultural relics, but also jeopardizes the conservation of cultural relics. At the same time, the static presentation of cultural relics makes the visit less interactive, which affects the authenticity and immersion of the exhibition [3]. In addition, some cultural relics cannot be displayed as exhibits in museums due to their material limitations. In addition, due to time and space limitations, as well as physical reasons of tourists (such as the disabled), some tourists cannot go to the museum to visit the artifacts in the field. In view of the above problems, it is very necessary to adopt the virtual display of museums.

Virtual reality (VR) has been gradually applied to museum displays to provide tourists with sensory experiences in a variety of ways, such as visual, auditory, and tactile [4]. As a complement to the traditional exhibition, virtual reality applied to the museum environment not only improves the availability of the exhibition, but also increases people's interest in the exhibition, providing visitors with an immersive experience [5, 6]. VR also increases museum participation including students and disabled groups, as well as provides engaging and informative ways for visitors to access and interact with geographically dispersed artifacts [7]. In addition, VR displays can provide interesting learning experiences, and a study on museum learning found that VR and AR technologies are primarily used in science, art, and history museums to support learning about scientific and artistic concepts [1]. However, most of the current research on VR in museums focuses on design practices, and few studies have investigated what factors influence user acceptance of VR displays in museums in China. Therefore, this paper focuses on VR displays in existing museums in China, and explores the factors that influence user acceptance by constructing an extended technology acceptance model, as well as provides design recommendations for future museum VR displays.

2   Literature Review

2.1   Virtual Reality (VR)

Virtual Reality (VR) technology is the use of computer technology, simulation technology, system integration technology, real-time three-dimensional graphics generation technology and other advanced means to simulate the real environment, so as to provide people with a sense of immersion in the technology means [8, 9], including computers, electronic information, simulation technology and other high-tech achievements of the latest developments, which provides realistic three-dimensional visual, tactile, olfactory and other sensory experiences for the virtual world [10]. By wearing specific VR equipment (e.g., helmets or glasses), users can interact as if they were in the real world, while experiencing deep immersion, presence, and interactivity even in the virtual world [1]. In a study on the application of VR in the tourism, VR was broadly defined as "the use of a computer-generated 3D environment – called a 'virtual environment' (VE) – that one can navigate and possibly interact with, resulting in real-time simulation of one or more of the user's five senses" [10]. Over the years, virtual reality technology has been widely used in a variety of fields such as entertainment, education, healthcare, military, business, cultural heritage and tourism, providing users with immersive, interactive and innovative experiences [11].

2.2 The Application of Virtual Reality to Museum

According to the definition of a museum in the ICOM Statutes adopted by the International Council of Museums (ICOM) in Vienna, Austria, museums, as non-profit permanent institutions, serve the community by engaging in the research, collection, preservation, interpretation, and exhibition of both tangible and intangible forms of heritage.

With the transformation of traditional museums into digital museums, museums are gradually completing a paradigm shift from "object-centered" to "experience-centered" in nature [12]. In this context, museum experts pay more attention to how to improve visitors' edutainment (education + entertainment) experience [13]. Many museums around the world have introduced many cutting-edge technologies to overcome these two problems, and the development of VR technology breaks through the limitations of space and time, and is adopted by more and more museums.

Virtual museum is a product of modern science and technology development, which is based on computer network, digitizes the museum itself and its collections, realizes grid storage, and then provides diversified museum services such as collection exhibition, research and teaching with the help of computers, smartphones and other terminals, which is characterized by strong interactivity, immersiveness, and spatial and temporal nondifferentiation, and so on [14]. The virtual museum utilizes VR technology to change the traditional visual display, promote the interaction between visitors and exhibits, and enhance the sense of participation of visitors.

2.3 Technology Acceptance Model (TAM)

Technology acceptance model (TAM) is a theoretical framework proposed by Davis [15, 16] to explain the acceptance of information technology based on theories of rational behavior (TRA). The initial model was later refined and adapted into various extensions of the TAM to explore user acceptance of new technologies.

TAM has been widely used to test user acceptance of information technology. The rationality of TAM has been validated in multiple fields including education, health, sports, retail, as well as leisure and tourism through literature review [17]. In the museum field, TAM also has a wide range of applications, for example, Shi et al. used the Sanxingdui Museum as an example to explore the key drivers of users' continued intention to use digital museums [18], Cheng et al. explored the effect of augmented reality quality on the dimensions of immersion using Wuhan Nature Museum as an example [19], Wu et al. explored the key factors that influence the environment in which users embrace the digital museum experience [20].

3 Research Object and Research Hypotheses

3.1 Research Object

In order to further explore the development of virtual exhibition technology in the field of museums, three expert users rated 144 museums with virtual exhibition halls among 204 National First-Class Museums in China based on indicators such as visiting experience, interactive experience, immersive experience, and emotional experience, from three dimensions: sensory level, interactive level, and reflection level [21, 22]. Finally, the highest scoring VR display *"Xun Jing Dun Huang"* from the Dunhuang Research Institute was selected as the representative research object.

Table 1. Museum VR Display Evaluation Criteria

Dimension	First-rank evaluation index	Second-rank evaluation index	Score (1–5)
Sensory level	Visiting experience	Explanation: The description of cultural relics should be as comprehensive as possible, including basic information such as age, specifications, background, etc.	5
		Voice: In addition to textual explanations, it should also have a voice explanation function	5
		Details: Provide detailed displays of cultural relics in various ways	4.3
		Images: The pictures and models of cultural relics should have high resolution and realistic sense	4.6
		Text: The font, size, and spacing of the text should be designed to be easy to read, or personalized settings should be provided	4.6
		Icon: With texture and connotation, the guiding symbols are easy to understand	4.6
		Layout: Reasonable layout, simple and elegant	4.6
Interaction level	Interactive experience	Realtime: Provide timely feedback and guidance on user operations	3.6
		Smoothness: unobstructed interaction, less interface lag, and fast information loading	4
		Animation: Entering and jumping to the page should be set with opening and transition animations	4.3
		Cleanliness: The overall interface has fresh colors, neat layout, moderate content, clear functional modules, and flat information presentation	4.3
		Guide: The function navigation bar is clear at a glance, making it easy for users to fully grasp the museum's functions	4.6

(continued)

Table 1. (*continued*)

Dimension	First-rank evaluation index	Second-rank evaluation index	Score (1–5)
	Immerse experience	Action immersion: simulating real behavior through interactive behavior	4.3
		Motion relationship: Scene switching is continuous and smooth, connecting naturally, with a sense of roaming	4.3
		Light and shadow matching: Light and shadow matching user behavior changes	3.6
		Sound coordination: The sound effect changes with user behavior	5
Reflection level	Emotional experience	Novelty: As if immersive, with diverse operating methods	4
		Sense of exploration: presenting museum related knowledge through gameplay	4
		Personalization: Able to make personal preference choices	3

3.2 Research Hypotheses

In this study, based on previous research, Technology Acceptance Model (TAM) was extended according to the actual situation. The perceived usefulness, perceived ease of use, and behavioral intention in TAM are retained, and two external variables are added: interactivity and perceived playfulness. Finally, the research model is constructed and hypotheses are formulated to explore the key factors affecting the user experience and behavioral intention of *"Xun Jing Dun Huang"*. The proposed research model in this study is shown in Fig. 1.

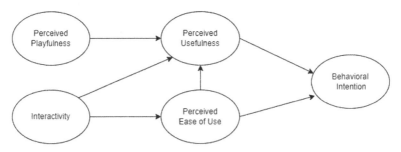

Fig. 1. Proposed research model.

Perceived Usefulness (PU) and Perceived Ease of Use (PEU). Perceived usefulness (PU) is defined as "the degree to which a person believes that using a particular system would enhance his or her job performance". Perceived ease of use (PEU), in contrast, refers to "the degree to which a person believes that using a particular system would be free of effort" [15]. In the revised TAM, PU and PEU have a positive impact on user behavioral intention [23]. Zhang et al. [24] found that users' perception that a VR-based safety training system is useful has a significant effect on users' intention to use it in their study. Fussell et al. [25] further found that students will be more willing to use VR for training if it is easy to use and improves performance. In addition, empirical studies have found that perceived ease of use has a positive impact on perceived usefulness and this finding has been validated in many other areas of research [26, 27]. Therefore, the following hypotheses were formulated for this study:

H1. Perceived usefulness (PU) has a positive impact on behavioral intention (BI).
H2. Perceived ease of use (PEU) has a positive impact on behavioral intention (BI).
H3. Perceived ease of use (PEU) has a positive impact on perceived usefulness (PU).

Perceived Playfulness (PP). Perceived playfulness (PP) refers to the intrinsic beliefs or motivations formed by an individual's experience of the environment [28]. Numerous studies have demonstrated that perceived playfulness plays a key role in influencing users' behavioral intentions [29] and is related to perceived ease of use and perceived usefulness [30]. Lin et al. [31] found that perceived playfulness contributed significantly to the users' intention to use a web site. Huang et al. [29] found that perceived playfulness as an intrinsic motivator would influence users' intention to use VR-based training methods in their study. Hence, this study hypothesizes:

H4. Perceived playfulness (PP) has a positive impact on perceived usefulness (PU).

Interactivity (IN). Steuer et al. [32] define interactivity(IN) as "the extent to which users are able to participate in modifying the form and content of the mediated environment in real time" and suggest three important factors affecting interactivity in their study: speed, which refers to the rate at which inputs are absorbed by the mediated environment; range, which refers to the number of possibilities for action at any given time; and mapping, which refers to the ability of the system to map its control to changes in the mediated environment in a natural and predictable way. There have been many previous studies on the effect of interactivity on user behavioral intentions. Dalgarno et al. [33] found that learning using three-dimensional (3D) virtual learning environments (VLEs) enhances interactivity and increases user intrinsic motivation and engagement through experiential and situational learning, which strengthens the perceived usefulness of VR. Huang et al. [34] found that interactivity had a positive effect on PEU when analyzing the factors that may influence medical students' acceptance of 3D VR learning. Similar findings were reported by Makransky et al. [35] who suggested that increased immersion led to a significant increase in interactivity, which in turn increased PU and PEU. Based on the above research, this study proposes the hypothesis:

H5. Interactivity (IN) has a positive impact on perceived usefulness (PU).
H6. Interactivity (IN) has a positive impact on perceived ease of use (PEU).

4 Research Methodology

4.1 Data Collection

The survey was conducted through a questionnaire distributed online. The questionnaire consisted of two main sections: the basic information of the respondents and variable measurement using the 7-point Likert scale. The statistical results show that the largest number of respondents are aged 19–30, accounting for 71.62% of the total. 8.45%, 9.12%, 7.09%, and 3.72% of the respondents are aged 18 and below, 31–50, and 51 and above. 79.05% of the respondents are with bachelor's degree or above. In addition, women accounted for 73.31% of the total number of respondents, while men accounted for 26.69%. The questionnaire sample includes groups of different ages, genders, and educational backgrounds, which is highly representative. The basic information of the respondents is shown in Table 2.

Prior to the formal distribution of the questionnaire, a pre-distribution was first carried out to pilot test the questionnaire with 30 respondents. The results of the pretest showed that the respondents were able to understand the questions well and complete the questionnaire independently. A total of 296 questionnaires were collected. Through screening, we removed questionnaires that (1) Questionnaires with respondents that have not experienced the VR display from Dunhuang Research Institute - "*Xun Jing Dun Huang*"; (2) Questionnaires that took less than 90s; (3) All but two (or fewer) answers are the same. Finally, 208 valid questionnaires were used. The scales used in the questionnaire were taken from previously used scales in the existing literature to measure interactivity, perceived playfulness, perceived ease of use, perceived usefulness, and behavioral intention. The items of each factors and sources are presented in Table 3.

Table 2. The basic information of the respondents

Information		Number	Percentage
Gender	Male	79	26.69%
	Female	217	73.31%
Age	0–18	25	8.45%
	19–30	212	71.62%
	31–40	27	9.12%
	41–50	21	7.09%
	51–70	11	3.72%
education attainment	Junior high school and below	25	8.45%
	High school (or junior college)	37	12.5%
	Bachelor's degree (or college) and above	234	79.05%

Table 3. The items of each factors

Factor	Items	References
PP1	Using 'Xun Jing Dun Huang' to visit Dunhuang Grottoes online is exciting	[17]
PP2	The online tour experience of 'Xun Jing Dun Huang' is fun for me	[17]
PP3	Using 'Xun Jing Dun Huang' to visit Dunhuang Grottoes online can stimulate my interest	[24]
IN1	'Xun Jing Dun Huang' provided me with a high standard of interaction	[18]
IN2	In the process of using 'Xun Jing Dun Huang', my interaction feedback with the system is in line with my habits	[36]
IN3	Overall, I feel that the interactive experience provided by 'Xun Jing Dun Huang' is very good	[18]
PU1	I find 'Xun Jing Dun Huang' can help me learn about Dunhuang grottoes more quickly	[23]
PU2	Using 'Xun Jing Dun Huang' enabled me to learn about Dunhuang grottoes efficiently	[17]
PU3	'Xun Jing Dun Huang' make it easier for me to learn about Dunhuang grottoes more quickly	[23]
PEU1	It is easy for me to learn how to operate the 'Xun Jing Dun Huang'	[16, 23]
PEU2	It is easy for me to become skillful at using the 'Xun Jing Dun Huang'	[16, 23]
PEU3	I found that my interaction with the 'Xun Jing Dun Huang' is clear and understandable	[16, 23]
PEU4	Overall, I find the 'Xun Jing Dun Huang' is easy to use for me	[18]
BI1	I am willing to recommend 'Xun Jing Dun Huang' to my friends	[18]
BI2	If given the opportunity, I would be willing to use 'Xun Jing Dun Huang' again	[25]
BI3	If I need to learn about Dunhuang Grottoes in the future, I will be willing to choose 'Xun Jing Dun Huang' to learn	[18]

4.2 Data Analysis

Structural equation modeling (SEM) was used to analyze the data in this study. The data analysis includes two parts: analysis of measurement model and structural model.

Measurement Model. Confirmatory factor analysis (CFA) was used to obtain a better measurement model in this study. Table 4 shows the parameters of significant test and item reliability. The standardized factor loadings of more than 0.6 is acceptable for an item in a dimension, and more than 0.7 is ideal. As the table shows, all the standardized factor loadings are greater than 0.6, and most of them are greater than 0.7, proving that the recommended standards have been met. Significance Estimation Divided by Standard Error (S.E.) yields a significant Z-value (Est./S.E.), greater than 1.96 indicates a significant presence, and P-value < 0.05 indicates a significant presence. The Z-value of each topic in Table 4 is greater than 1.96, and the P-value are all less than 0.001, which means that all measures are significant. Item reliability is the ability of the dimension to interpret the items. Its rating index is the square of the standardized estimate (R-square). In this study, all the R-square values are greater than 0.36, most of them are greater than 0.5, indicating that the item reliability is up to standard.

Table 5 shows the results of composite reliability, convergent validity, and discriminate validity. The Composite Reliability of all constructs are greater than 0.7, indicating that the component reliability is ideal [37]. The average variance extracted (AVE) values were analyzed to assess convergent validity (CV). AVE is the Average Variance Extraction quantity that refers to the average explanatory power of the dimension for the topic. The higher AVE, the stronger the average explanatory power of the dimension to the topic. All AVE values in Table 5 exceeded the recommended minimum threshold of 0.5 which indicated that all dimensions have good explanatory power [38].

Table 4. Parameters of significant test and item reliability.

Factor	Items	Estimate	S.E	Est./S.E	P-value	R-square
PP	PP1	0.773	0.067	11.479	***	0.598
	PP2	0.922	0.041	22.401	***	0.850
	PP3	0.753	0.066	11.382	***	0.567
IN	IN1	0.826	0.037	22.196	***	0.682
	IN2	0.813	0.042	19.265	***	0.661
	IN3	0.797	0.040	19.923	***	0.635
PU	PU1	0.782	0.054	14.611	***	0.612
	PU2	0.783	0.053	14.878	***	0.613
	PU3	0.890	0.037	24.08	***	0.792
PEU	PEU1	0.709	0.05	14.247	***	0.503
	PEU2	0.851	0.035	24.206	***	0.724
	PEU3	0.661	0.050	13.245	***	0.437
	PEU4	0.761	0.041	18.358	***	0.579
BI	BI1	0.792	0.045	17.634	***	0.627
	BI2	0.875	0.036	24.356	***	0.766
	BI3	0.763	0.043	17.736	***	0.582

Constructs' discriminant validity was analyzed by using the Fornell-Larcker's (1981) [38] method that compares the AVE and squared correlation coefficients of the constructs in this study. The difference validity AVE has a diagonal root sign value and the lower triangle is the Pearson correlation coefficient between dimensions. If the AVE root sign value is larger than the Pearson correlation coefficient of the corresponding dimension rows and columns, the difference validity between dimensions is good. The square root value of each AVE is greater than the other figures (the Pearson correlation coefficients with other constructs) in its row and column, which means that there is a certain degree of discriminate validity between each dimension.

Table 5. Composite reliability, convergent validity, and discriminate validity

	CR	AVE	PP	IN	PU	PEU	BI
PP	0.859	0.672	**0.820**				
IN	0.853	0.659	0.716	**0.812**			
PU	0.860	0.672	0.736	0.811	**0.820**		
PEU	0.835	0.561	0.494	0.737	0.599	**0.749**	
BI	0.852	0.658	0.632	0.787	0.616	0.620	**0.811**

Structural Model. Table 6 shows the model fitting indices and each index meets the recommended value, indicating that the structural model fits well. Table 7 shows the results of the hypotheses. P-value < 0.05 indicates that the influence between dimensions is significant which means the hypothesis is valid. As shown in Table 7, there are 6 hypotheses in the model, H1, H2, H4, H5, H6 are valid. The research results are shown in Fig. 2.

Table 6. Model fitting degree.

	Recommended value	Index	
$\chi 2/df$	$1 < \chi 2/df < 3$	2.195	Matched
CFI	>0.9	0.926	Matched
TLI .	>0.9	0.909	Matched
RMSEA	<0.08	0.076	Matched
SRMR	<0.08	0.054	Matched

Table 7. Hypothesis analysis.

DV	IV	Estimate	S.E.	Est./S.E.	P-value	R^2	Hypothesis
PU	PP	0.332	0.127	2.616	0.009	0.742	Support
	PEU	−0.052	0.105	−0.498	0.619		Not Support
	IN	0.633	0.117	5.403	***		Support
PEU	IN	0.757	0.053	14.240	***	0.573	Support
BI	PU	0.430	0.096	4.477	***	0.549	Support
	PEU	0.397	0.095	4.187	***		Support

5 Discussion and Conclusion

5.1 Discussion

As institutions that propagate culture and facilitate cultural exchange, museums have been increasingly popular among visitors in recent years. As technology advances, major museums are keeping pace by using a variety of innovative technological methods to

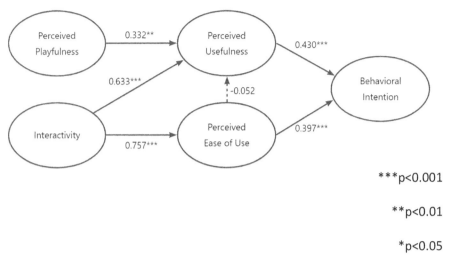

***p<0.001

**p<0.01

*p<0.05

Fig. 2. Results of the research model.

deliver online exhibitions that engage visitors while alleviating issues such as crowding and artifact preservation associated with offline visits. VR displays offer visitors a variety of sensory experiences, enhancing visitor engagement, and are being adopted by an increasing number of museums. This paper scores 144 National First-Class Museums in China with VR displays, resulting in the highest average score for the VR display "Xun Jing Dun Huang". By establishing an extended TAM (Technology Acceptance Model), the study explores factors influencing user acceptance of the "Xun Jing Dun Huang" VR display.

In line with the findings of the previous article [24], perceived playfulness has a significant impact on perceived usefulness, implying that the stronger the interactive pleasure experienced by users during the museum VR display, the more significant their perception of the usefulness of the VR display, thus promoting the intention to use. Enhancing interactive experiences and incorporating gaming elements can effectively enhance users' intention to use VR displays.

Interactivity has a significant impact on both perceived usefulness and perceived ease of use, consistent with previous research [39]. High interactive quality increases users' perception of the usefulness and ease of use of VR in the museum, resulting in positive user feedback. By enhancing the interactive quality in VR digital services, museums can not only respond to users' needs through multiple channels but also provide users with more opportunities and experiences to interact with exhibits. Museums can optimize the interactive experience of VR displays by providing interactive guidance and establishing interactive logic that aligns with users' daily habits, thereby increasing user satisfaction and attracting more users.

Additionally, perceived usefulness significantly influences behavioral intention. Therefore, museums should fully consider the concept of "edutainment" when designing VR displays, focusing not only on enhancing entertainment attributes but also on improving educational attributes, allowing users to learn relevant cultural knowledge while experiencing VR, thus enhancing user acceptance.

5.2 Conclusion

By establishing an extended Technology Acceptance Model (TAM), this study investigates the factors influencing user acceptance of VR displays in museum and provides recommendations for the design direction of VR in the museum. The results indicate that perceived playfulness significantly impacts perceived usefulness. This suggests that when designing VR exhibits, designers should consider appropriately enhancing the entertainment value and optimizing the gaming experience to make VR in museum more appealing to users. Additionally, interactivity has a significant impact on both perceived usefulness and perceived ease of use. Enhancing interactive experiences and improving interaction quality are crucial aspects that VR in museums should focus on. Furthermore, perceived usefulness significantly influences users' behavioral intention. This implies that educational aspects should remain a priority in the design of VR exhibits in the museum field. In the construction of museum VR, it is crucial to engage users by introducing gameplay and providing a smooth interactive design. However, the ultimate goal of museum VR exhibitions is to disseminate historical knowledge and promote the development of historical civilization. Therefore, the ability of museum VR to help users achieve specific learning objectives and acquire new knowledge is a key criterion for increasing users' intention to use it. Additionally, the limitations of this study include the concentration of our participant sample primarily on students, teachers, etc., with limited coverage of older adults, children, and individuals with disabilities. We aim to broaden the research population in future studies and establish theoretical models with broader applicability.

References

1. Zhou, Y., Chen, J., Wang, M.: A meta-analytic review on incorporating virtual and augmented reality in museum learning. Educ. Res. Rev. **36**, 100454 (2022). https://doi.org/10.1016/j.edu rev.2022.100454
2. https://www.gov.cn/govweb/lianbo/bumen/202307/content_6895343.htm. Accessed 30 Jan 2024
3. Cai, Y., Cao, Y.: Research on the display of VR animation art in historical relics–take the example of the eastern Han dynasty silver copper bull lamp. In: Proceedings of the 6th International Conference on Digital Signal Processing, pp. 98–103. ACM, Chengdu (2022). https://doi.org/10.1145/3529570.3529587
4. Bekele, M.K., Pierdicca, R., Frontoni, E., Malinverni, E.S., Gain, J.: A survey of augmented, virtual, and mixed reality for cultural heritage. J. Comput. Cult. Herit. **11**, 1–36 (2018). https://doi.org/10.1145/3145534
5. Żyła, K., Montusiewicz, J., Skulimowski, S., Kayumov, R.: VR technologies as an extension to the museum exhibition: a case study of the Silk Road museums in Samarkand. Muzeol. Kultúrne Dedičstvo. **8**, 73–93 (2020). https://doi.org/10.46284/mkd.2020.8.4.6
6. Schofield, G., et al.: Viking VR: designing a virtual reality experience for a museum. In: Proceedings of the 2018 Designing Interactive Systems Conference, pp. 805–815. ACM, Hong Kong (2018). https://doi.org/10.1145/3196709.3196714

7. Walczak, K., Cellary, W., White, M.: Virtual museum exhibitions. Computer **39**, 93–95 (2006). https://doi.org/10.1109/MC.2006.108
8. Burdea, G.C., Coiffet, P.: Virtual Reality Technology. Wiley (2003)
9. Vince, J.: Introduction to Virtual Reality. Springer (2004)
10. Guttentag, D.A.: Virtual reality: applications and implications for tourism. Tour. Manag. **31**, 637–651 (2010). https://doi.org/10.1016/j.tourman.2009.07.003
11. Jerald, J.: The VR Book: Human-Centered Design for Virtual Reality. Morgan & Claypool (2015)
12. Hein, H.S.: The Museum in Transition: A Philosophical Perspective. Smithsonian Institution (2000)
13. Pallud, J., Straub, D.W.: Effective website design for experience-influenced environments: the case of high culture museums. Inf. Manage. **51**, 359–373 (2014). https://doi.org/10.1016/j.im.2014.02.010
14. Luo, F.C.: Discussion on the application of VR and AR in virtual museum exhibitions. China Natl. Exhibit. 198–201 (2022)
15. Davis, F.D.: Perceived usefulness, perceived ease of use, and user acceptance of information technology. MIS Q. **13**, 319–340 (1989). https://doi.org/10.2307/249008
16. Venkatesh, V., Morris, M.G., Davis, G.B., Davis, F.D.: User acceptance of information technology: toward a unified view. MIS Q. **27**, 425–478 (2003). https://doi.org/10.2307/30036540
17. Huang, Y.-C., Li, L.-N., Lee, H.-Y., Browning, M.H.E.M., Yu, C.-P.: Surfing in virtual reality: an application of extended technology acceptance model with flow theory. Comput. Hum. Behav. Rep. **9**, 100252 (2023). https://doi.org/10.1016/j.chbr.2022.100252
18. Shi, M., Wang, Q., Long, Y.: Exploring the key drivers of user continuance intention to use digital museums: evidence from China's Sanxingdui Museum. IEEE Access. **11**, 81511–81526 (2023). https://doi.org/10.1109/ACCESS.2023.3297501
19. Cheng, A., Ma, D., Pan, Y., Qian, H.: Enhancing museum visiting experience: investigating the relationships between augmented reality quality, immersion, and TAM using PLS-SEM. Int. J. Hum.–Comput. Interact. 1–12 (2023). https://doi.org/10.1080/10447318.2023.2227832
20. Wu, Y., Jiang, Q., Ni, S., Liang, H.: Critical factors for predicting users' acceptance of digital museums for experience-influenced environments. Information **12**, 426 (2021). https://doi.org/10.3390/info12100426
21. Chen, Q.M.: Research on User Experience Evaluation and Quantitative Model of Virtual Exhibition Hall of Intangible Cultural Heritage. Chongqing University (2019)
22. Tie, Z., Jiang, C., Yan, Y., Lei, T.: Research on the evaluation method of digital museum service design based on user satisfaction. Relics Museol. 105–112 (2022)
23. Davis, F.D., Bagozzi, R.P., Warshaw, P.R.: User acceptance of computer technology: a comparison of two theoretical models. Manag. Sci. **35**, 982–1003 (1989). https://doi.org/10.1287/mnsc.35.8.982
24. Zhang, M., Shu, L., Luo, X., Yuan, M., Zheng, X.: Virtual reality technology in construction safety training: extended technology acceptance model. Autom. Constr. **135**, 104113 (2022). https://doi.org/10.1016/j.autcon.2021.104113
25. Fussell, S.G., Truong, D.: Using virtual reality for dynamic learning: an extended technology acceptance model. Virtual Real. **26**, 249–267 (2022). https://doi.org/10.1007/s10055-021-00554-x
26. Lu, J.-L., Chou, H.-Y., Ling, P.-C.: Investigating passengers' intentions to use technology-based self-check-in services. Transp. Res. Part E Logist. Transp. Rev. **45**, 345–356 (2009). https://doi.org/10.1016/j.tre.2008.09.006
27. Gong, M., Yan, X., Yuecheng, Y.: An enhanced technology acceptance model for web-based learning. J. Inf. Syst. Educ. **15**, 365–374 (2004)

28. Lee, B.-C., Yoon, J.-O., Lee, I.: Learners' acceptance of e-learning in South Korea: theories and results. Comput. Educ. **53**, 1320–1329 (2009). https://doi.org/10.1016/j.compedu.2009.06.014

29. Hung, S.-Y., Tsai, J.C.-A., Chou, S.-T.: Decomposing perceived playfulness: a contextual examination of two social networking sites. Inf. Manage. **53**, 698–716 (2016). https://doi.org/10.1016/j.im.2016.02.005

30. Hong, J.-C., Hwang, M.-Y., Hsu, H.-F., Wong, W.-T., Chen, M.-Y.: Applying the technology acceptance model in a study of the factors affecting usage of the Taiwan digital archives system. Comput. Educ. **57**, 2086–2094 (2011). https://doi.org/10.1016/j.compedu.2011.04.011

31. Lin, C.S., Wu, S., Tsai, R.J.: Integrating perceived playfulness into expectation-confirmation model for web portal context. Inf. Manage. **42**, 683–693 (2005)

32. Steuer, J., Biocca, F., Levy, M.R.: Defining virtual reality: dimensions determining telepresence. Commun. Age Virtual Real. **33**, 37–39 (1995)

33. Dalgarno, B., Lee, M.J.W.: What are the learning affordances of 3-D virtual environments? Br. J. Educ. Technol. **41**, 10–32 (2010). https://doi.org/10.1111/j.1467-8535.2009.01038.x

34. Huang, H.-M., Liaw, S.-S., Lai, C.-M.: Exploring learner acceptance of the use of virtual reality in medical education: a case study of desktop and projection-based display systems. Interact. Learn. Environ. **24**, 3–19 (2016). https://doi.org/10.1080/10494820.2013.817436

35. Makransky, G., Lilleholt, L.: A structural equation modeling investigation of the emotional value of immersive virtual reality in education. Educ. Technol. Res. Dev. **66**, 1141–1164 (2018). https://doi.org/10.1007/s11423-018-9581-2

36. Guo, X., Qiao, J., Yan, R., Wang, Z., Chu, J.: The Smaller the Better? A Study on Acceptance of 3D Display of Exhibits of Museum's Mobile Media. In: Kurosu, M. (ed.) Human-Computer Interaction. Design and User Experience Case Studies, pp. 303–324. Springer, Cham (2021). https://doi.org/10.1007/978-3-030-78468-3_21

37. Hairs, J.F., Anderson, R.E., Tatham, R.L., Black, W.C. Multivariate data analysis. Prentice Hall, Englewood Cliffs (1998)

38. Fornell, C., Larcker, D.F.: Evaluating structural equation models with unobservable variables and measurement error. J. Mark. Res. **18**, 39–50 (1981). https://doi.org/10.1177/002224378101800104

39. McLean, G., Wilson, A.: Shopping in the digital world: examining customer engagement through augmented reality mobile applications. Comput. Hum. Behav. **101**, 210–224 (2019). https://doi.org/10.1016/j.chb.2019.07.002

User Experience and Evaluation

HoloLens 2 Technical Evaluation as Mixed Reality Guide

Prabhakaran Balakrishnan◉ and Hung-Jui Guo$^{(\boxtimes)}$◉

The University of Texas at Dallas, Richardson, TX 75252, USA
{bprabhakaran,hxg190003}@utdallas.edu

Abstract. Mixed Reality (MR) [19,20] has developed rapidly in recent years and is used to potentially improve human living environments (such as life-related and entertainment applications) and work efficiency. Microsoft HoloLens [17] has played an essential role in the progress of MR as a state-of-the-art head-mounted device (HMD) from the first generation to the second generation. By incorporating multiple sensors, such as depth and RGB cameras, along with the Inertial Measurement Unit (IMU), the tracking and sensing accuracy has significantly improved from the previous generation. However, currently, there are no studies evaluating the accuracy of HoloLens 2 sensors, which makes it difficult for researchers to compare the device with others and improve it. In this paper, we systematically evaluate the sensors utilized in the HoloLens 2, including RGB, eye, depth cameras, and microphone array to show the progress compared to the previous HoloLens generation HMD. Based on the evaluation results for most of the available features in the HoloLens 2, we provide discussion and suggestions for future researchers to design applications (such as entertainment [5,7], education [12,25,27] and training [23]) or research works with existing capabilities.

Keywords: Mixed Reality · HoloLens · Sensor Evaluation · Hologram · Inertial Measurement Unit (IMU)

1 Introduction

Mixed Reality (MR) [19,20], a well-known concept that is generally known as a combination of Augmented Reality (AR) [1] and Virtual Reality (VR) [3], normally render virtual objects in real-world through a monitor-like device. Such devices are usually built as helmet-like instruments and are called Head-mounted devices (HMDs), and one of the most known HMDs equipped MR environment is "Microsoft HoloLens" [17]. Microsoft released two versions: HoloLens 1 in 2016 and HoloLens 2 in 2019. HoloLens 1 was unique as it offered a complete MR experience, unlike other VR devices. The HoloLens device has the remarkable capability to scan its surrounding environment automatically, creating a virtual world for the user. Furthermore, users can create their own virtual objects and place them wherever they want, and interact with them directly by moving, scaling, or rotating them in the real world using their own hands.

© The Author(s), under exclusive license to Springer Nature Switzerland AG 2024
J. Y. C. Chen and G. Fragomeni (Eds.): HCII 2024, LNCS 14706, pp. 145–165, 2024.
https://doi.org/10.1007/978-3-031-61041-7_10

Compared to HoloLens 1, HoloLens 2 significantly improves, especially in the display resolution, accuracy of hand-tracking, and width of field of view. Also, several new functions and sensors have been implemented, such as biometric security system and two hands tracking. The software updates, including the newer version of research mode, offer significant improvements for HoloLens 2 users, enabling access to multiple sensors (including Visible Light cameras, IR (Infra-Red), Depth cameras, and Inertial Measurement Unit (IMU) sensors) via C++ Application Programming Interfaces and research mode tools [26]. Researchers who need to develop sensor-based applications in the future will find these significantly helpful.

In this paper, we introduce a series of performance evaluation tests on most available sensors and features in HoloLens 2, including RGB cameras, eye tracking, depth cameras, microphone array, Azure Spatial Anchor, and research mode IMU sensor (Accelerometer and Gyroscope) data. Part of the tests in this paper refers to a HoloLens 1 paper [15] to evaluate the performance improvements by comparing HoloLens 2 with HoloLens 1. The experimental results and the subsequent discussions can assist readers in understanding the development of HoloLens 2 and also introduce the abilities and potential constraints of the device's sensors. This is the first and comprehensive assessment of the MR device based on the functionality of its sensors, which has the potential to be used as a baseline for future research and applications.

2   Related Work

2.1   Mixed Reality

The concept of MR involves the use of hybrid rendering techniques to create virtual objects in real-world settings, which can be interacted with directly using the user's hands, providing new avenues for researchers to explore and develop new experiments. To address the cognitive differences that arise from the development of MR, [24] conducted interviews with experts and referred to various documents to identify MR-related concepts. Some other researchers used this technology in aesthetic design [10], education [12,22,25], and entertainment [5,7]. In [4], the authors utilized MR technology to develop an indoor positioning system to provide a benchmark for future related research. Lastly, in [2,6], the authors made a detailed survey on MR to provide additional information on this field.

2.2   HoloLens 2

HoloLens 2 [17] was first released in 2019 by Microsoft, an HMD running the Windows Mixed Reality platform. According to paper [21], the authors discuss the new features and upgrades of HoloLens 2, including the Holographic Processing Unit. Meanwhile, [26] announced a new version of research mode for HoloLens 2, allowing users to access individual sensors in the device, which is helpful for researchers who need more sensor data for their studies. Researchers have been exploring the use of HoloLens 2 in different fields to create useful applications. For example, in education, [27] used HoloLens 2 to improve interaction between teachers and students. In the medical field, [23] applied HoloLens 2 to increase the success rate of operations and reduce operation time. Due to COVID-19, many works have focused on remote collaboration applications, [14,16] proposed using HoloLens 2 for remote patient care to minimize contact between doctors and patients.

2.3   HMD Technical Evaluation

In recent years, numerous AR/VR/MR-based HMDs have been released, and many related papers have evaluated these devices in many different aspects to provide other researchers with references to develop further applications. For example, [8,15] conducted evaluation tests to evaluate the performance, advantages, and disadvantages of HoloLens 1. Similarly, [13] evaluates the sensors of HoloLens 1, including depth-sensing and indoor mapping effects. In addition, several papers also provide systematic overviews of the capacities and limitations of HMDs over a period of time. For example, [9] summarized underlying technical in HMD, such as visualization, tracking, and context awareness. [11] surveyed multiple HMD-based measurement papers with different HMDs based on environmental factors and the presence of user feedback.

At present, there is no comprehensive performance evaluation available to assess the features of HoloLens 2 based on its device and sensors, as was done for HoloLens 1 [8,15]. Due to the extensive data availability of HoloLens 2 sensors, we conducted several experiments to evaluate various device functionalities. The findings outlined in this paper can be used as both benchmarks and design criteria for future MR applications.

3   Materials and Methods

To assess HoloLens 2's functionality, we conducted several experiments to test its features. All test applications were developed in Unity 3D or using C++ APIs and then deployed to the HoloLens 2 device with software version 20H2. To evaluate device's capability, we used 6 environmental conditions including: **Daylight Indoor** (*DI*, 247 lux), **Daylight Outdoor** (*DO*, 1460 lux), **Night time indoor with headlight and lamp** (*NIHL*, 33 lux), **Night time indoor with headlight only** (*NIH*, 4 lux), **Night time indoor with lamp only** (*NIL*, 21 lux), and **Night time outdoor with lamp only** (*NOL*, 3 lux). The same environmental condition names in each section have the same parameters.

3.1   Hand Tracking

Using the Articulated Hand Tracking depth camera [26], the HoloLens 2 can capture hand movements for tracking data. To evaluate this feature, we measure the error distance between hand joints hologram and real-world human hand

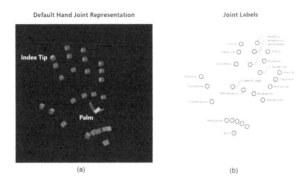

Fig. 1. Examples of human hand joint (a) Hand joint representation in HoloLens 2 (b) Real-world hand joint labels (Picture taken from Microsoft website)

joints. Figure 1(a) shows the default hand joint hologram generated in HoloLens 2, and Fig. 1(b) shows the corresponding joint name of the human hand.

In this experiment, we evaluate the hand tracking feature under various conditions, including *DI*, *DO*, *NIHL*, *NIH*, *NIL*, and *NOL*. Hand moving speed is also considered, with velocities of $0.2/0.5/1$ m per second. However, when projecting hand joints from HoloLens 2 world space to 2D image space, a slight error is observed between the hand hologram and real-world hand (shown in Fig. 2), even though there is no discrepancy between these two in users' eyes. Therefore, we utilized the projection of experimenters' non-moving hands as a baseline to eliminate this error.

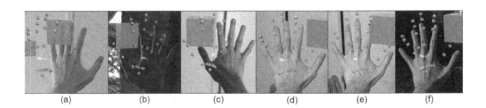

Fig. 2. Steady hand tracking, including virtual joints and real hands in 2D image space, under varying environmental conditions (a) *DI* (b) *DO* (c) *NIHL* (d) *NIH* (e) *NIL* (f) *NOL*

As part of our testing procedure, we built a virtual box (0.1 m $\times$ 0.1 m $\times$ 0.1 m) in HoloLens 2. We made it move left and right like a pendulum at a fixed speed with a moving distance of 1 m to allow us, as the experimenters, to wave hands back and forth at the moving cube's speed to record the generated hand joints, taking out five frames as test results to calculate the errors.

3.2 Eye Tracking

HoloLens 2 Eye Tracking API provides a tool for developers to access eye-tracking data, which is newly introduced compared to HoloLens 1. In this experiment, we assess the functionality of eye-tracking in various environmental conditions and apply it to real-world and virtual-world objects. During the eye-tracking procedure, we, as the experimenters, fixate on each target object for two seconds and repeat the process three times to calculate the average error distance, the Euclidean distance between the eye-gaze ray and target points.

Virtual Objects Eye Gaze Tracking. In this experiment, we create five gray virtual cubes with a size of 0.01 m × 0.01 m × 0.01 m as target objects and generate a virtual black platform behind the boxes to visualize the eye gaze point, as shown in Fig. 3(a) and (b). We, as the experimenters, stand at a selected location and gaze at each point for two seconds. The error distance is then calculated as the experiment results.

Fig. 3. Virtual and real eye-tracking experiments, (a) and (b) are virtual ones under *DI* and *DO* environmental conditions, where the white dot represents the experimenter's eye-gaze point, and gray boxes indicate the target virtual cubs. (c) and (d) are real ones with the same environmental conditions *DI*, where the blue dot represents the experimenter's eye-gaze point, and black dots indicate the target points.

Real-World Objects Eye Gaze Tracking. In this experiment, we place five black dots with a 0.01 m diameter onto a box (Fig. 3(c) and (d)), then, we, as the experimenters, stand at the selected location, gaze at each point for two seconds, and record the test process to extract the experiment results. We only selected two environmental variables, *DI* and *NIL*, for the experiment since the target is difficult to discern in insufficient lighting conditions.

3.3 Hologram Stability

Hologram creation stability is crucial in HoloLens 2, which utilizes the long-throw depth camera to achieve this functionality. This experiment evaluates the reality of holograms. To compare with previous work, we use the same accuracy deviation to evaluate the result.

Hologram Visualization. In this experiment, we refer to a HoloLens 2 product box (0.38 m × 0.25 m × 0.27 m) to create a red hologram box in the MR world, as shown in Fig. 4. In addition, we constrain the hologram box to disable rotation or size changes to prevent us, as the experimenters, from accidentally changing their shape. We will precisely align the hologram box with the real-world box and take three pictures of the front, side, and top views as the evaluation result, as shown in Fig. 4.

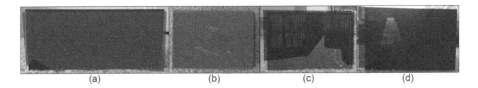

Fig. 4. Hologram box (red) overlaps with a real-world HoloLens 2 product box (black) by experimenters (a) Front view (b) Top view (c) Left side view (d) Right side view (Color figure online)

Virtual and Real-World Environment Overlapping Ratio. This experiment demonstrates the accuracy of the hologram surface generated by the device and its attachment to the corresponding real-world surface. First, we, as the experimenters, create a virtual cube (0.1 m × 0.1 m × 0.1 m) and put it onto the hologram surface (Fig. 5(a)). Then, we take a side-view photograph to calculate the error distance between the virtual object and the real-world surface (Fig. 5(b, c)).

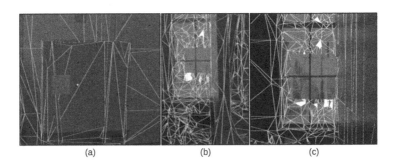

Fig. 5. Sample virtual and real-world environments overlapping ratio (a) Experimenters attached a red virtual cube onto the hologram surface observed and created by HoloLens 2 (b) Side view of the flat surface with minor gap between the red cube and the surface (c) Closer side view and gap (marked by a red circle) (Color figure online)

3.4   Real Environment Reconstruction

HoloLens 2 can reconstruct a real-world item into a hologram. To evaluate the reconstruction accuracy, we generate holograms of real-world objects and indoor rooms as evaluation results.

Real-World Objects Reconstruction. To evaluate the construction speed and complete percentage of HoloLens 2's object reconstruction functionality, we select four different size real-world boxes as target objects, which are large tall box (0.50 m × 0.33 m × 0.76 m), regular size box (0.56 m X 0.47 m × 0.47 m), thin box (0.41 m × 0.21 m × 0.29 m), and small box (0.16 m × 0.14 m × 0.23 m).

We, as the experimenters, walk around the target box to aid HoloLens 2 in constructing the box's hologram. Then, we moved around the target box again and recorded a video of the completed construction. Here, we set the construction time limit to 60 s (Our experiment shows that a stable box-like hologram can be established within 60 s); whenever the hologram becomes stable, stop counting construction time.

Real-World Indoor Room Reconstruction. In this case study, we choose four rooms: living room (7 m × 3.92 m × 2.97m), personal room (3.81 m × 3.02 m × 2.40 m), restroom (2.50 m × 2.48 m × 2.40 m), and walk-in closet (0.79 m × 0.54 m × 2.40 m) as the reconstruction target. Initially, we, as the experimenters, stand at a designated corner of the room and face the wall, then walk along the wall while exploring the surrounding environment by looking around to reconstruct the wall in front until it is completely constructed. After returning to the original position, stop recording and save it as the evaluation result.

3.5   Speech Recognition

This experiment evaluates the effectiveness of speech commands in HoloLens 2. To compare the speech recognition improvement from HoloLens 1 to HoloLens 2, we refer to the paper [15] to select speech commands and add some additional commands, including system-defined commands ("select," "Move this...there," "face me," "bigger/smaller," "What's my IP address," "hide and show hand ray," "shut down device," "close," "Open the Start menu," "Follow me," and "take a picture") and user-defined commands selected from Wobbrock's paper [28] ("move," "rotate," "delete," "zoom in/out," "open," "duplicate," "previous," and "help").

The number of recognized commands will be counted as the evaluation result to evaluate the capability of HoloLens 2's speech recognition feature. All participants lived in an English-speaking environment for over a year and could speak English fluently. The native language proportion is shown in Table 1 (middle). We also recruited some non-student participants to balance the education status ratio, the proportion is shown in Table 1 (bottom). Furthermore, to compare different voice lines, we recruited people of varying age groups as participants and a balance in the ratio of men and women to make the experiment more accurate, as shown in Table 1 (top).

Table 1. Recruited participants' age range, gender, native language, and current education status in speech recognition experiment.

Participants' age range and gender						
	19-22	23-26	27-30	31-34	35 up	Total
Man	1	3	5	1	1	11
Woman	2	1	2	1	1	7

Participants' native language					
	English	Chinese	Vietnamese	Korean	Japanese
Native language	3	11	2	1	1

Participants' current education status		
	Student	Non student
Education status	10	8

3.6   Azure Spatial Anchor

Microsoft Azure provides a spatial anchors feature [18] to create persistent, accurate digital anchors that could be operated at real-world scale, which can be utilized in HoloLens 2 to share world anchors with others or locate objects in real-world. As such, we conduct an evaluation to determine if the position has changed from upload to download. After connecting to the Azure Spatial Anchor server, we create and move an anchor cube to a fixed position (uploaded to Azure Spatial Anchor server) on the real-world table and take a picture as a test benchmark, as shown in Fig. 6(a). Then, remove the local cube and download the anchor cube from the server, as shown in Fig. 6 (b). Lastly, take a picture of the Anchor and calculate the error distance between the benchmark and the downloaded cube.

(a)   (b)

Fig. 6. Created Azure Spatial Anchor (yellow cube) put on a real-world table (a) User-created benchmark on the local end (b) User-created anchor download from the server with a blue line and a red line indicating the length of the table in the image (Color figure online)

3.7   Research Mode – IMU Sensors

In HoloLens 2's research mode, accessing Inertial Measurement Unit (IMU) sensors - Accelerometer, Gyroscope, and Magnetometer - is possible, which was not available in HoloLens 1. Due to external magnetic field interference from the earth, Magnetometer-related experiments are not feasible.

Accelerometer. HoloLens 2 Accelerometer detects linear acceleration along the X, Y, and Z axes as well as gravity. The Accelerometer output data includes the projection of force on X, Y, and Z axes of the acceleration, combined acceleration, and time, which can be used to calculate the user's movement direction, distance, and tilt angle. In this experiment, we, as the experimenters, move a fixed distance along the x, y, or z-axis or tilt their bodies in a specified direction to evaluate accuracy. Since the Accelerometer provides the linear acceleration along the X, Y, and Z axes, we can use double integrals to obtain the current position. According to the output data from the IMU sensors, we know that the HoloLens 2 uses a three-dimensional space setting like Fig. 7 (b). Let r_x, r_y, r_z represent the projection of the force on X, Y, and Z axes of the acceleration, which represent the instantaneous acceleration at the current point. Since the time interval between each acceleration point is a brief 0.083 s, we can assume that the instantaneous acceleration is equal to the average acceleration between each point. Let one of the average acceleration $a_1 = (a_1x, a_1y, a_1z)$, and another average acceleration $a_2 = (a_2x, a_2y, a_2z)$ right after a_1. Then, we may assume a linear equation $\mathbf{a}(t)$ to represent points between a_1 and a_2 as

$$\mathbf{a}(t) = (a_1x + (a_2x - a_1x) * 12t, a_1y + (a_2y - a_1y) * 12t, a_1z + (a_2z - a_1z) * 12t). \quad (1)$$

Since we assume that the instantaneous acceleration is the same as average acceleration, we can integrate $\mathbf{a}(t)$ to yield velocity $\mathbf{v}(t)$

$$\mathbf{v}(t) = (a_1xt + (a_2x - a_1x) * 6t^2 + C_x, a_1yt + (a_2y - a_1y) * 6t^2 + C_y,$$
$$a_1zt + (a_2z - a_1z) * 6t^2 + C_z). \quad (2)$$

Here C_x, C_y, and C_z are the constants that represent the velocity calculated previously at the point a_1 and we assume first point's velocity is $(0, 0, 0)$. Then, we can integrate $\mathbf{v}(t)$ to produce position $\mathbf{s}(t)$

$$\mathbf{s}(t) = (\frac{1}{2}a_1xt^2 + (a_2x - a_1x) * 2t^3 + C_xt + K_x,$$
$$\frac{1}{2}a_1yt^2 + (a_2y - a_1y) * 2t^3 + C_yt + K_y, \quad (3)$$
$$\frac{1}{2}a_1zt^2 + (a_2z - a_1z) * 2t^3 + C_zt + K_z).$$

Here K_x, K_y, and K_z are the constants representing the position calculated previously at the point a_1, and we also assume first point's position is $(0, 0, 0)$. Lastly, we can use $\mathbf{s}(t)$ calculated on every two points a_1 and a_2 to calculate the current position of HoloLens 2 and compute the moving distance accordingly to compare with the actual moving distance.

We also tilt our heads at a fixed angle when wearing the HoloLens 2 device to evaluate the tilting angle accuracy, as shown in Fig. 7(d). According to the output r_x, r_y, r_z, we can use the following equation to calculate the tilt angle along each axis

$$A_{xr} = arccos(\frac{R_x}{R}) * (\frac{180}{\pi}) \quad (4)$$

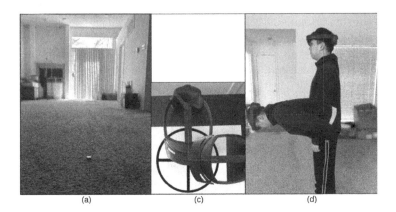

Fig. 7. (a) Two marks on the ground indicating the walking start point and end point in the Accelerometer walking distance measurement experiment (b) Three-dimensional space used in HoloLens 2 (c) Example of Gyroscope rotating 90°C along x-axis (d) Example of Accelerometer tilt 90°C along x-axis and z-axis

where $R = \sqrt{R_x^2 + R_y^2 + R_z^2}$ express the combined force on the current location. Since the data output from the device is in the form of radian by default, we need to multiply $\frac{180}{\pi}$ to transform it into degree form.

Gyroscope. By utilizing the Gyroscope, we can extract angular velocity on the X, Y, and Z axes and the corresponding time, which can be used to determine the rotation angle made by the users. To achieve accurate measurements, we draw and print a circle with a vertical cross as 90-degree intervals ground truth to assist us in rotating the device, as shown in Fig. 7(c).

According to the output data, there are three angular velocities per unit of time, G_x, G_y, and G_z, and each unit of time is 0.048 s. Therefore, we can transform the three angular velocities to actual angle change per unit time by substituting the following formula.

$$Accuracy = ((G_x * \frac{180}{\pi}) * 0.048, (G_y * \frac{180}{\pi}) * 0.048, (G_z * \frac{180}{\pi}) * 0.048) \quad (5)$$

Similarly, the data output from the device is in the form of radian by default, so we need to multiply $\frac{180}{\pi}$ to transform it into degree form. By calculating angle changes for every unit of time, we can compare the output of the Gyroscope with the actual rotation angle.

4   Results and Discussion

Based on the experiment design and procedure, this section contains the outcome of experimental results and discussions.

4.1 Hand Tracking

In this experiment, we calculated the error distance between each hologram hand joint point and real-world hand joint point with the error distance ER, which is calculated as follows:

$$ER = \frac{1}{N} \sum_{i \in N} d\left(r_i, g_i\right) \tag{6}$$

where N represents the number of hand joints, d is the Euclidean distance of two points, and r_i, g_i are the corresponding hand joint point in real-world hand and HoloLens 2 generated hand. ER is greater than or equal to 0, indicating the accuracy of HoloLens 2 generated points; higher ER means a larger error. We split the experiment result into four speeds: steady, $0.2\,\mathrm{m/sec}$, $0.5\,\mathrm{m/sec}$, and $1\,\mathrm{m/sec}$; the results are shown in Table 2.

Table 2. Hand tracking experiment result including error distance, average error, and standard error (SE) under each speed and environmental conditions

Steady hand tracking (Error distance (m))

	DI	DO	NIHL	NIH	NIL	NOL	Average	SE
Right Hand	0.052	0.063	0.068	0.068	0.063	0.058	0.062	0.003
Left Hand	0.048	0.052	0.047	0.058	0.050	0.047	0.050	0.001

0.2 m / second (Error distance (m))

	DI	DO	NIHL	NIH	NIL	NOL	Average	SE
Right Hand	0.082	0.068	0.063	0.055	0.058	0.065	0.065	0.003
Left Hand	0.067	0.055	0.050	0.042	0.045	0.053	0.052	0.003

0.5 m / second (Error distance (m))

	DI	DO	NIHL	NIH	NIL	NOL	Average	SE
Right Hand	0.108	0.090	0.072	0.080	0.097	0.098	0.091	0.005
Left Hand	0.113	0.125	0.080	0.085	0.062	0.100	0.094	0.008

1.0 m / second (Error distance (m))

	DI	DO	NIHL	NIH	NIL	NOL	Average	SE
Right Hand	0.152	0.185	0.140	0.118	0.115	0.135	0.140	0.010
Left Hand	0.123	0.102	0.135	0.128	0.108	0.155	0.125	0.008

As stated previously, minor errors will occur during the process of converting hand tracking results from world space to 2D image space. Therefore, it is necessary to subtract the steady hand tracking error to calculate the actual error distance for each speed condition. According to the experiment, there is no direct correlation between hand tracking and environmental conditions, but the error distances increase as the moving speed increases. When the hand moving speed is up to $1\,\mathrm{m/sec}$, the average error distance is still lower than $0.05\,\mathrm{m}$ after subtracting steady error, indicating that the hand tracking feature accurately follows the user's real hands. However, if the hand moving speed exceeds $1\,\mathrm{m/sec}$, the average error distance will likely exceed $0.05\,\mathrm{m}$ after subtracting steady error in most environments, which may lead to a delay in hand interaction.

4.2   Eye Tracking

Virtual Objects Eye Gaze Tracking. In this experiment, we calculate *ER* between five virtual cubes and corresponding eye gaze points under each position and environmental conditions, as shown in Fig. 8 (top).

Real-World Objects Eye Gaze Tracking. In this experiment, we calculate *ER* between five virtual cubes and corresponding eye gaze points under two environmental conditions, results shown in Fig. 8(bottom).

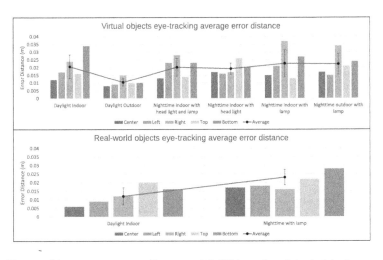

Fig. 8. Eye-tracking average error distance with SE bars for virtual objects experiment (top) and real-world objects experiment (bottom)

According to the experiment results, both virtual and real-world objects' eye-tracking error distances are sub-0.05 m, which indicates a high accuracy eye-tracking feature in the HoloLens 2. It has been observed that both in virtual and real-world environments, when there is high illuminance (referred to as *DO* in virtual experiments and *DI* in real experiments), the accuracy of eye-tracking feature increases, which is due to high clarity of objects allows users to aim their line of sight more accurately towards the intended target. In the *NIL* condition, the lamplight is behind the user and to the top center, which causes smaller error distances in the top and center compared to the other side. Similarly, in the *NOL* condition, the lamplight is from the user's left side, resulting in a smaller error distance on the left side than in other environmental conditions. In conclusion, HoloLens 2 exhibits excellent eye-tracking accuracy on both virtual and real-world objects, and higher illuminance can improve accuracy.

4.3 Hologram Stability

Based on the experimental design of the main comparison paper [15], we choose to use the same accuracy deviation σ_A^R to compare the difference between real-world environment and reconstructed model

$$\sigma_A^R = \sum_{i \in N} \left(\frac{|L - l_i|}{L \cdot N} \right) \tag{7}$$

where N represents the number of measurements, L refers to the real-world object's edge length, and l_i is the corresponding edge length measured in the ith measurement by HoloLens 2. Range of σ_A^R is greater than or equal to 0, where 0 indicates when real-world objects and their holographic models match, and higher values represent significant differences.

Hologram Visualization. We calculate the difference between each edge of the real-world box and hologram box using σ_A^R. As we cannot calculate one edge of each view, we calculate the deviation accuracy of only two edges on each view. This situation can be seen in Fig. 4.

Table 3. Hologram visualization accuracy deviation for each edge and view, and the average values for each view

	Length	Width	Height	Average
		Hologram visualization accuracy deviation		
Front view	3.66%	N/A	0.84%	2.25%
Side view	N/A	7.41%	2.30%	4.86%
Top view	0.63%	7.91%	N/A	4.27%
Average	2.15%	7.66%	1.57%	N/A

According to Table 3, HoloLens 2 has a sub-ten percent accuracy deviation, especially the length and height of each view. Results demonstrate the high accuracy of device-generated holograms in human eyes and the correct positioning between real-world objects and their corresponding virtual objects. In the previous work, the average accuracy deviation of HoloLens 1's hologram visualization result was 6.64%, which is two times higher than HoloLens 2's average accuracy deviation of 3.79% evaluated in this paper. This shows a significant improvement that HoloLens 2 can show holograms more accurately than HoloLens 1.

Virtual and Real-World Environment Overlapping Ratio. Accuracy deviation σ_A^R under this experiment, L refers to the real-world length of virtual cube's one edge, and l_i is the distance between the distance from the farthest edge to the target surface. Different from the previous work, we use different environmental settings as environmental variables.

Table 4. Virtual and real-world environment overlapping ratio accuracy deviation

Virtual & real-world environment overlapping ratio						
	DI	DO	NIHL	NIH	NIL	NOL
Accuracy Deviation	29.02%	12.72%	53.69%	34.45%	30.80%	23.58%

Based on the findings presented in Table 4, it appears that high illuminance can improve the accuracy of creating virtual environments. Conversely, a low illuminance environment can lead to a decrease in accuracy, but it can still maintain a certain level of accuracy until a specific illuminance threshold is reached. Based on the results, the lowest accuracy deviation is 12.72%, and the average accuracy deviation is 30.71%, which is much better than the previous generation (lowest 70% and average 73.85%), which shows notable improvement in reconstructing the real-world environment.

4.4   Real Environment Reconstruction

We estimate the reconstruction result using two metrics: construction time and complete percentage. The complete percentage CP is calculated as follows

$$CP = \frac{\sum_{i \in N} H_i}{\sum_{i \in N} R_i} \qquad (8)$$

where N represents the number of measurements, H_i is the hologram area generated by HoloLens 2, which is estimated by using the square method, and R_i is the real environment area.

Real-World Objects Reconstruction. This experiment aims to explore how object size will affect object reconstruction outcomes in HoloLens 2. In this experiment, H_i in CP means the hologram area on each side of the box, and R_i is the area of the real-world box.

Based on the findings presented in Table 5, it can be concluded that both object size and illumination have a significant impact on the construction completeness and the construction time. It was observed that larger real-world objects took longer for HoloLens 2 to construct the corresponding hologram. However, if the real-world box is smaller than the small box or has insufficient illumination, the HoloLens 2 will see this object as an environmental obstruction or ignore it and fail to construct a complete hologram. For example, a small box under high illuminance DI shows an excellent result, but under other low illuminance conditions, CP drops, and construction time exceeds 60 s.

Real-World Indoor Room Reconstruction. In this experiment, we evaluated the results of constructing real-world environments in different room sizes

Table 5. Real-world objects reconstruction time and complete percentages

Objects construction result – Large tall box				
	DI	NIHL	NIH	NIL
Construction time	49 seconds	Over 60 seconds	Over 60 seconds	Over 60 seconds
Complete percentage	83%	91%	81%	76%

Objects construction result – Regular box				
	DI	NIHL	NIH	NIL
Construction time	20 seconds	41 seconds	53 seconds	55 seconds
Complete percentage	95%	98%	93%	89%

Objects construction result – Thin box				
	DI	NIHL	NIH	NIL
Construction time	35 seconds	40 seconds	50 seconds	56 seconds
Complete percentage	97%	83%	85%	76%

Objects construction result – Small box				
	DI	NIHL	NIH	NIL
Construction time	17 seconds	Over 60 seconds	Over 60 seconds	Over 60 seconds
Complete percentage	97%	43%	47%	41%

and illumination. Based on Table 6, we found that generating a holographic room takes longer in larger rooms. Also, higher illumination can decrease construction time and increase CP. For example, in Table 6, daylight results in lower construction time and higher CP than night time living room.

Table 6. Real-world rooms reconstruction time and complete percentages

Real-world room construction results						
	Daylight living room	Daylight personal room	Night time living room	Night time personal room	Restroom with lamp only	Walk-in closet with lamp only
Construction time	45 seconds	33 seconds	55 seconds	40 seconds	30 seconds	15 seconds
Construction complete percentage	50%	85%	38%	77%	61%	97%

It is important to note that the construction complete percentage of the largest living room is less than 50%, which is due to the HoloLens 2 app can only support about 50% of the living room hologram (approximately 40 cubic meters) at one time. Once the experimenters walk from one side to the other side, the device will automatically drop some hologram to reduce the load on the system, as shown in Fig. 9(a). On the other hand, irregular real-world corners could be challenging for HoloLens 2 to identify and generate holograms if the user stands far away. Therefore, an app may request that the user move in front of a corner to help the app observe an object if it requires a detailed reconstruction of a room, an example shown in Fig. 9(b).

Fig. 9. (a) An example of HoloLens 2's maximum hologram in the living room in our experiment environment, (b) On the left side, there is a red circle indicating that a part of the construction in the corner is incomplete. On the right side, the same corner is shown with a red circle, which indicates that it has been completed after the user captured it with HoloLens 2 while walking in front of the corner. (Color figure online)

4.5 Speech Recognition

In this experiment, agreement rate A_r, the same evaluation matrix as previous work [15], is used to indicate the level of consensus among the participants for a specific referent r and is defined as

$$A_r = \sum_{P_i \in P_r} \left(\frac{|P_i|}{|P_r|} \right)^2 \qquad (9)$$

where P_r is the set of operation commands for referent r and P_i is a subset of P_r. The speech recognition agreement rate result of HoloLens 2 is shown in Fig. 10, yellow and blue bars represent the agreement rates A_r for the system-defined commands and user-defined commands respectively.

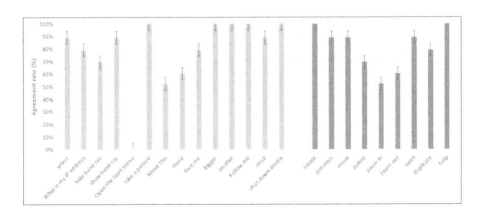

Fig. 10. Speech recognition agreement rate of the eighteen participants for the user-defined commands (yellow bars) and system-defined commands (blue bars) (Color figure online)

The average agreement rates A_r for system-defined commands and user-defined commands are 79.12% and 80.97%. This result indicates that the

HoloLens 2 maintains high agreement rates in the speech recognition function despite the use of voices of different genders, native languages, and ages. However, none of our participants were able to successfully issue the voice command "Open the start menu," as stated in the HoloLens 2 document. Compared to the HoloLens 1 speech recognition result, there is a major improvement in both the system-defined commands and the user-defined commands from 66.87% and 74.47% to 79.12% and 80.97%.

4.6 Azure Spatial Anchor

To calculate the average error distance percentage between the length and width of the created and the server-downloaded spatial anchor, we use the blue and red lines depicted in Fig. 6(b) as a benchmark to calculate the ratio. Since the length and width of the white table in each picture will be identical, we can compute the error distance by the following equation

$$\text{ErrorPercentage}(\%) = \left(\frac{\left| \frac{L_c^s}{L_c^l} - \frac{L_d^s}{L_d^l} \right|}{\frac{L_c^s}{L_c^l}} + \frac{\left| \frac{W_c^s}{W_c^l} - \frac{W_d^s}{W_d^l} \right|}{\frac{W_c^s}{W_c^l}} \right) /2 * 100 \qquad (10)$$

where L and W indicate length and width, s and l present short line segments and long line segments, c and d indicate the created and downloaded anchors and the whole equation is divided by 2 to calculate the average error ratio. Experimenters performed this test three times in each of the six different environments. The result is shown in Table 7.

Table 7. The Azure Spatial Anchor error distance percentage in six different environments based on the created anchor and downloaded anchor.

Azure Spatial Anchor error distance percentage						
	DI	DO	NIHL	NIH	NIL	NOL
Virtual Cube	5.42%	2.89%	2.96%	3.22%	2.87%	3.36%

After conducting the analysis, we found that all the error percentages were below 6%, and environmental illuminance will not affect the error distance, indicating the accuracy and consistency of creating and retrieving the Azure Spatial Anchor in HoloLens 2 from the Azure server.

4.7 Research Mode – IMU Sensors

In this experiment, we use an error percentage to calculate the difference between the IMU sensor's output result and the actual movement:

$$\text{IMUError}(\%) = \frac{1}{N} \sum_{i=1}^{N} \frac{|T_i - P_i|}{T_i} \qquad (11)$$

where N is the number of total tests, T_i indicates the true movement result of the test N and P_i expresses the device predicted result of the test N.

Accelerometer. In this experiment, experimenters walk in four different directions (straight, right, backward, and left) and different distances (4 m and 3 m) to help the Accelerometer observe device movement; the testing environment setting is shown in Fig. 7(a). Then, we compare the device's moving distance with the actual moving distance using *IMU Error*. The result is shown in Table 8(top).

In the tilt angle experiment, the participants tilt their bodies three times in two different directions. This includes tilting 90°C, altering their bodies along the X-axis and Y-axis, and tilting 90°C to the right, moving their bodies along the X-axis and Z-axis (Fig. 7(d)). This helps calculate the average error. The result is shown in Table 8 (Center).

Based on the experimental results, it was observed that the moving distance experiment produced unstable and high error percentage results, which might be due to the gravity acceleration that affects the Accelerometer result. As time progresses, the error becomes more extensive, which is why three parts of IMU sensors need to be used complementary to achieve the best accuracy. On the other hand, the tilt experiment shows much better error percentage performances; since the experimenters are not physically walking, the gravity effect will not have a significant impact. Therefore, researchers can still use the HoloLens 2 built-in Accelerometer to calculate tilt angle for application usage.

Gyroscope. In this experiment, we rotate the HoloLens 2 device along the X, Y, and Z axes in three directions to calculate the error percentage by using *IMU Error*. Based on the experimental result shown in Table 8 (bottom), the error percentages are low when rotating clockwise or counterclockwise on different axes. One notable difference between x-axis and the other two axes is the ease of operation. We can rotate the device on a table with ease while maintaining

Table 8. The evaluation result of IMU sensors experiment, including Accelerometer moving distance error percentage (top), Accelerometer tilt angle error percentage (middle), and Gyroscope rotate error percentage (bottom)

Accelerometer moving distance error percentage			
	Walk straight 4 meters	Walk right 4 meters	Walk backward 3 meters	Walk left 3 meters
Error percentage	33.57%	23.18%	47.95%	72.53%

Accelerometer tilt angle error percentage	
	Tilt forward 90 degree (x-axis and y-axis)	Tilt right 90 degree (x-axis and z-axis)
Error percentage	16.95%	4.32%

Gyroscope rotate error percentage		
	x-axis Clockwise 180 degree	y-axis Clockwise 90 degree	z-axis Counterclockwise 90 degree
Error percentage	0.19%	4.37%	4.35%

stability, whereas performing operations on y and z-axes can be more challenging. Consequently, the error percentage on y and z-axes can be attributed to operation errors.

5 Conclusions

In this paper, we evaluated most of the available features in the HoloLens 2, including hand tracking, eye tracking, hologram stability, real environment reconstruction, speech recognition, Azure Spatial Anchor, and research mode IMU sensors, by building multiple applications to show their capacities and limitations. Then, we compared the results with the HoloLens 1 evaluation paper [15] with similar experiments to show the evolution between the two versions of HoloLens. Having these results as objective standards can benefit future testing, improvement, and changes, whether software or hardware. Currently, except for the speech recognition experiment, most experiments lack sufficient participants. Therefore, we can recruit more participants to enrich our experiment results and build additional evaluation applications based on the updated HoloLens 2 software in the future.

Acknowledgments. This research was sponsored by the DEVCOM U.S. Army Research Laboratory under Cooperative Agreement Number W911NF-21-2-0145 to B.P. The views and conclusions contained in this document are those of the authors and should not be interpreted as representing the official policies, either expressed or implied, of the DEVCOM Army Research Laboratory or the U.S. Government. The U.S. Government is authorized to reproduce and distribute reprints for Government purposes notwithstanding any copyright notation.

References

1. Azuma, R.T.: A survey of augmented reality. Presence: Teleoper. Virtual Environ. **6**(4), 355-385 (1997). https://doi.org/10.1162/pres.1997.6.4.355
2. Bekele, M.K., Pierdicca, R., Frontoni, E., Malinverni, E.S., Gain, J.: A survey of augmented, virtual, and mixed reality for cultural heritage. J. Comput. Cult. Herit. **11**(2), March 2018. https://doi.org/10.1145/3145534
3. Burdea, G.C., Coiffet, P.: Virtual reality technology. John Wiley & Sons (2003)
4. Carotenuto, R., Merenda, M., Iero, D., Della Corte, F.G.: An indoor ultrasonic system for autonomous 3-d positioning. IEEE Trans. Instrum. Meas. **68**(7), 2507–2518 (2019). https://doi.org/10.1109/TIM.2018.2866358
5. Cheok, A.D., Haller, M., Fernando, O.N.N., Wijesena, J.P.: Mixed reality entertainment and art. Int. J. Virtual Reality **8**(2), 83–90 (2009). https://doi.org/10.20870/IJVR.2009.8.2.2729. https://ijvr.eu/article/view/2729
6. Costanza, E., Kunz, A., Fjeld, M.: Mixed Reality: A Survey, pp. 47–68. Springer, Heidelberg (2009). https://doi.org/10.1007/978-3-642-00437-7_3
7. Coutrix, C., Nigay, L.: Mixed reality: a model of mixed interaction, pp. 43–50, May 2006. https://doi.org/10.1145/1133265.1133274

8. Evans, G., Miller, J., Pena, M.I., MacAllister, A., Winer, E.: Evaluating the Microsoft HoloLens through an augmented reality assembly application. In: Sanders-Reed, J.J.N., III, J.T.J.A. (eds.) Degraded Environments: Sensing, Processing, and Display 2017. vol. 10197, pp. 282 – 297. International Society for Optics and Photonics, SPIE (2017). https://doi.org/10.1117/12.2262626

9. Fang, W., Chen, L., Zhang, T., Chen, C., Teng, Z., Wang, L.: Head-mounted display augmented reality in manufacturing: a systematic review. Robot. Comput.-Integrated Manuf. **83**, 102567 (2023). https://doi.org/10.1016/j.rcim.2023.102567. https://www.sciencedirect.com/science/article/pii/S0736584523000431

10. Fiorentino, M., de Amicis, R., Monno, G., Stork, A.: Spacedesign: a mixed reality workspace for aesthetic industrial design. In: Proceedings. International Symposium on Mixed and Augmented Reality, pp. 86–318 (2002). https://doi.org/10.1109/ISMAR.2002.1115077

11. Guo, H.J., Bakdash, J.Z., Marusich, L.R., Prabhakaran, B.: Augmented reality and mixed reality measurement under different environments: a survey on head-mounted devices. IEEE Trans. Instrum. Measur. **71**, 1–15 (2022). https://doi.org/10.1109/TIM.2022.3218303

12. Hughes, C., Stapleton, C., Hughes, D., Smith, E.: Mixed reality in education, entertainment, and training. IEEE Comput. Graph. Appl. **25**(6), 24–30 (2005). https://doi.org/10.1109/MCG.2005.139

13. Hübner, P., Clintworth, K., Liu, Q., Weinmann, M., Wursthorn, S.: Evaluation of hololens tracking and depth sensing for indoor mapping applications. Sensors **20**(4) (2020). https://doi.org/10.3390/s20041021. https://www.mdpi.com/1424-8220/20/4/1021

14. Levy, J.B., et al.: The mixed reality medical ward round with the MS hololens 2: innovation in reducing covid-19 transmission and PPE usage. Future Healthc J. (2021). https://doi.org/10.7861/fhj.2020-0146

15. Liu, Y., Dong, H., Zhang, L., El Saddik, A.: Technical evaluation of HoloLens for multimedia: a first look. IEEE Multimed. **25**(4), 8–18 (2018). https://doi.org/10.1109/MMUL.2018.2873473

16. Martin, G., et al.: Use of the HoloLens2 mixed reality headset for protecting health care workers during the COVID-19 pandemic: prospective, observational evaluation. J. Med. Internet Res. **22**(8) (2020). https://doi.org/10.2196/21486

17. Microsoft: Hololens (2015). https://www.microsoft.com/en-us/hololens

18. Microsoft: Azure spatial anchor (2019). https://azure.microsoft.com/en-us/products/spatial-anchors

19. Milgram, P., Kishino, F.: A taxonomy of mixed reality visual displays. IEICE Trans. Inf. Syst. **vol. E77-D, no. 12**, 1321–1329 (1994)

20. Milgram, P., Takemura, H., Utsumi, A., Kishino, F.: Augmented reality: a class of displays on the reality-virtuality continuum. In: Das, H. (ed.) Telemanipulator and Telepresence Technologies. vol. 2351, pp. 282 – 292. International Society for Optics and Photonics, SPIE (1995). https://doi.org/10.1117/12.197321

21. O'Connor, P., et al.: Custom silicon and sensors developed for a 2nd generation mixed reality user interface. In: 2019 Symposium on VLSI Circuits, pp. C186–C187 (2019). https://doi.org/10.23919/VLSIC.2019.8778092

22. Pan, Z., Cheok, A.D., Yang, H., Zhu, J., Shi, J.: Virtual reality and mixed reality for virtual learning environments. Comput. Graph. **30**(1), 20–28 (2006). https://doi.org/10.1016/j.cag.2005.10.004. https://www.sciencedirect.com/science/article/pii/S0097849305002025

23. Park, B.J., Hunt, S.J., Nadolski, G.J., Gade, T.P.: Augmented reality improves procedural efficiency and reduces radiation dose for CT-guided lesion targeting: a phantom study using HoloLens 2. Sci. Rep. **10**(1), 1–8 (2020). https://doi.org/10.1038/s41598-020-75676-4

24. Speicher, M., Hall, B.D., Nebeling, M.: What is mixed reality? In: Proceedings of the 2019 CHI Conference on Human Factors in Computing Systems, CHI 2019, pp. 1–15. Association for Computing Machinery, New York (2019). https://doi.org/10.1145/3290605.3300767

25. Tang, Y.M., Au, K., Lau, H.C., Ho, G.T., Wu, C.: Evaluating the effectiveness of learning design with mixed reality (MR) in higher education. Virtual Reality **24**(4), 797–807 (2020). https://doi.org/10.1007/s10055-020-00427-9

26. Ungureanu, D., et al.: Hololens 2 research mode as a tool for computer vision research. arXiv preprint arXiv:2008.11239 (2020)

27. Vidal-Balea, A., et al.: Analysis, design and practical validation of an augmented reality teaching system based on Microsoft hololens 2 and edge computing. Eng. Proc. **2**(1) (2020). https://doi.org/10.3390/ecsa-7-08210. https://www.mdpi.com/2673-4591/2/1/52

28. Wobbrock, J.O., Morris, M.R., Wilson, A.D.: User-defined gestures for surface computing. In: Proceedings of the SIGCHI Conference on Human Factors in Computing Systems, CHI 2009, pp. 1083–1092. Association for Computing Machinery, New York (2009). https://doi.org/10.1145/1518701.1518866

Games that Move You: A Cinematic User Experience Evaluation of VR Games

Andrew Bedard, Kevin Bedard, and Qiping Zhang[✉]

Long Island University, 720 Northern Blvd, Brookville, NY 11548, USA
{andrew.bedard,kevin.bedard}@my.liu.edu, qiping.zhang@liu.edu

Abstract. As the entertainment landscape continues to evolve, researchers have concentrated their efforts on the potentiality of digital technologies to promote more immersive experiences, especially the relevance of virtual reality and gaming technologies for their unique approaches to maintaining the attention of viewers while also eliciting both meaningful and immersive experiences. The objective of this paper is to examine the immersion and continuity of cinematic virtual reality (CVR) through interactive media such as gaming. We developed a heuristic checklist to evaluate core aspects of the gameplay and cinematic experience of an adventure VR game. It features four aspects: *general usability, mobility, playability, and cinematic engagement.* For playability, this research focuses on heuristic elements of gameplay, game mechanics, game story, and *onboarding.* For cinematic engagement, we highlighted four factors that are influential to the continuity of cinematic experiences: captivation, real-world dissociation, comprehension, and transformation. Our results revealed the usability problems in three areas: (1) General Usability, (2) Gameplay Heuristics, and (3) Dynamic Gameplay in Cinematic Context (DGCC). Captivation was found to be the least affected by gameplay experience, as graphical fidelity maintained its consistency throughout play sessions, while real-world dissociation was limited by a lack of continuity with the game controls. In summary, our results suggested that even when players' cinematic and graphical impressions of Red Matter 2 were primarily positive, the lack of diegetic referencing such as text-based instruction and help with in-game activities, led to a negative experience with the game and considerable frustration.

Keywords: cinematic virtual reality · user experience · narrative games · video games · virtual reality · augmented reality

1   Introduction

Narrative storytelling in Virtual Reality (VR) video games has the potential to offer even more immersive experiences than those found in traditional digital gaming contexts. Head-mounted display (HMD) technologies have created an avenue for gaming and cinematic experiences to empower professionals to deliver more meaningful experiences. Scholarly research endeavors have focused on developing a scale that could measure the influence of qualitative experiential factors on the representation of a satisfactory

© The Author(s), under exclusive license to Springer Nature Switzerland AG 2024
J. Y. C. Chen and G. Fragomeni (Eds.): HCII 2024, LNCS 14706, pp. 166–181, 2024.
https://doi.org/10.1007/978-3-031-61041-7_11

play experience in video gaming contexts. The goal of these studies is to assess common usability and heuristic problems associated with control, navigation, and feedback provided by the system. These general concerns have been broadened to include emphatically interactive experiences such as gaming. Players can encounter various challenges with the efficiency, mechanics, and overall gameplay impression, which can positively or negatively influence their perception of its quality.

2   Literature Review

2.1   Cinematic Virtual Reality and Gaming

As emerging technologies such as virtual reality (VR) and gaming continue to persist as fields that are reshaping the landscape of digital entertainment, scholarly intrigue, and exploration of the domain of Cinematic VR, which involves the use of 360-degree videos to create immersive experiences. Cinematic VR leaves much to be desired in terms of its interactivity. "Although users have a certain level of autonomy within the cinematic virtual environment (cVE), there are no mechanisms that provide them a greater level of interaction with the narrative text. The interaction with the environment is limited to the sensation of immersion and to the possibility of visually exploring the cVE, without any real power over the development of the story" [1]. Much like traditional cinema and film viewing activities, users are still confined to a more passive experience, with no direct influence on characters, events, or the environment. VR gaming experiences are fundamentally different from traditional gaming in that virtual, mixed, and augmented reality can use precise tracking tools and devices to record the gestures and movements of various parts of the body, in ways that mimic the coordination of the human body. Products such as the Meta Quest 3 and PSVR 2 have allowed auxiliary industries to develop more immersive entertainment experiences through other digital media such as gaming.

2.2   Diegetic and Non-diegetic Cues in Virtual Reality

Nielson et al. [2] studied the influence of three forms of guidance on immersion and presentation of narrative content. They purported that the representation of diegetic and non-diegetic cues is fundamentally implicit or explicit. Diegetic cues are those that are indicative of the world that the user is experiencing, while explicit cues offer additional context or information that users need to navigate in the virtual world. "… explicit diegetic cues that do not limit interaction could be virtual characters that through dialogue or gestures point to relevant elements in the VE or diegetic signs that serve the same purpose." [2] Video games are more reliant on these types of signifiers, as they are meant to provide referential information to players while maintaining their agency in the interaction. They suggested that players were more receptive to guidance offered by third-party objects such as a butterfly to guide them through the environment, while the freedom presented with no referential guidance was more immersive in these regards.

One of the biggest challenges in maintaining a desirable immersive experience is the use of diegetic and non-diegetic cues to ensure that users are progressing through the story interactively, while also adhering to the intentions of the developers of the narrative as intended [3]. Rothe et al. [4] developed a taxonomy of guidance cues that could be used to attract and maintain the attention of virtual reality users. More specifically, they emphasize the importance of using diegetic and non-diegetic cues, which they suggest can be (1) visual, (2) auditive, and (3) haptic. Visual cues, while easy to integrate into a narrative, may not always be visible or could be missed by participants. Auditive cues can be used to guide the viewers' attention to important content off-screen. However, it may be difficult for users to discern whether the sounds produced are diegetic or non-diegetic, with respect to their position in the virtual world. Lastly, haptic cues are implemented discretionarily and might require the use of supplementary or auxiliary equipment to enhance the experience through sensory feedback such as haptic interactions. The use of these techniques can depend on whether certain cues are forced by the system, reflexively, or entirely voluntary. While effective in some scenes, forced guidance could potentially disrupt the feeling of presence or immersion within the environment.

2.3 Video Games and Narrative

Like other forms of digital media, video games often rely on different storytelling approaches, designed to keep consumers engaged. "In the classic narrative construction practiced in traditional media such as films or novels, the careful design of this art is a powerful tool for channeling and guiding the reader's experience of the story." [5]. In the traditional sense of narrative expression, the goal of the author(s) of a particular text is to guide and transport the users through the world, or thoughtful design of the distinct features of the world. While Story worlds, Characters, and Narrative Interface are individual aspects of the world's construction, they each help to immerse its interpreters into the world. Gaming media offers a unique blend of narrative structure and play experience, while still adhering to the aspects of enjoyment and entertainment that players are often seeking. The premise of indulging in gaming has been primarily about the enjoyment of the play experience. Game developers have concentrated on keeping the player(s) engaged with their game by infusing the narrative and cinematic content in their game worlds. Elson et al. [5] argued that games should be considered "more than just stories with buttons".

Game environments often rely upon narrative structure to deliver a dualistic game experience. However, if a game is not able to strike a unique balance between its gameplay and narrative continuity, it can result in a disconnection from the game's story, world, and characters [6]. "The combination of narrativity and interactivity oscillates between two forms: the narrative game, in which narrative meaning is subordinated to the player's actions, and the playable story, in which the player's actions are subordinated to narrative meaning [7]". In these regards, there are inherent synergies between attempting to convey a narrative from a given perspective, such as a single author. However, in gaming environments, the narrative capabilities of the player can change according to the type of game being played. In some games, the player's actions have the potential to redefine the entire story, by choosing to take a particular course of actions [8].

2.4 Usability in VR Games

Playability. Usability and Playability are two unique heuristic evaluation concepts that are frequently used to evaluate the performance of user-driven systems [9]. "Usability is your perception of how consistent, efficient, productive, organized, easy to use, intuitive, and straightforward it is to accomplish tasks within a system" [10]. In this context, satisfaction with the system's interactivity is determined by how quickly users can learn the system's intricacy to complete tasks efficiently and effectively. However, researchers have suggested the use of usability parameters to evaluate video games as a form of "entertainment system" as opposed to other general-use systems such as desktop computers, which are typically used to complete common or daily activities [11]. Common desktop systems are primarily concerned with the effectiveness, efficiency, and satisfaction of completing tasks or objectives, while video games are concerned with broader applications of immersion, motivation, and emotional attachment to the system, which inherently promotes continuous use. This suggests that "A Video Game can be considered a 'special' interactive system, in that it is used for leisure purposes by users seeking fun and entertainment." [11]. Therein, they imply that these systems ought to be evaluated using the same set of heuristic principles, akin to those deployed for Usability. There are many different facets of Playability, but the intricacies of 'fun' indicative of overall satisfaction with one or more aspects of the system that encourages its continuous use. For example, one player may enjoy the artistic or visual presentation of the game, while another simply focuses on the mechanics of the game, as a sense of control in the game world [12–14].

Motion Sickness and Comfortability Ratings. Motion Sickness in VR (also commonly referred to as Cybersickness) is a condition that stems from extended or continuous exposure to artifacts represented through virtual environments [15]. More specifically, users will often experience discomfort such as eye strain, headaches, vertigo, and vomiting [16], which can have compound effects on players' performance and enjoyment, when compared to gaming on traditional gaming platforms, such as Desktop PCs [17].

Comfortability ratings indicate the degrees of feasibility players are expected to have during play sessions. Different head-mounted display makers provide their own ratings. For example, Steam's VR Curator ratings range from Comfortable to Extreme [18], while Meta range from Comfortable to Intense [19]. Meta's ratings are specified as follows:

- *Comfortable*: avoid camera movement, player motion, or disorienting content and effects.
- *Moderate*: incorporate some camera movement, player motion, or occasionally disorienting content and effects.
- *Intense*: incorporate significant camera movement, player motion, or disorienting content and effects, and not appropriate for most people, especially those who are new to VR.

Interpreting the impact of comfortability ratings is contextually relevant to our study in that games that fail to meet a satisfactory rating could potentially impact users' attachment to the game, its story, or its characters. Weech et al. [20] identified two significant correlations regarding motion sickness and narrative virtual reality games. Firstly, they observed that prolonged gameplay of such games led to users experiencing symptoms of cybersickness. Additionally, they found that users had difficulty recalling the game's storyline or significant events that occurred during their play sessions.

3 Method

3.1 Objectives

The primary goal of this research is to evaluate cinematic user experience in video games, and particularly the effects of narrative storytelling on user VR game experiences. We developed a heuristic checklist to evaluate Dynamic Gameplay in Cinematic Context (DGCC), focusing on cinematic engagement and gameplay experiences. Among eight heuristic categories identified through our examination of the literature on game heuristic and cinematic continuity, four of them are related to game experience and dynamics, while the other four concentrate on the engagement and retention of the experience through graphical, cinematic or narrative immersion.

3.2 VR Game

Game Selection Criteria. The game *Red Matter 2* was chosen for this study based on the following four criteria:

- *Comfortability*: only games with a "Comfortable" score was chosen to eliminate the effect of motion sickness and other disorienting effects.
- *Overall review score:* only games with a greater potential of a desirable experience was chosen. Red Matter 2 currently maintains a 4-star review rating on the Meta Quest Store with over 4,000 unique user reviews.
- *Genre*: The selected game falls within the genre of adventure, most of which require narrative elements, key to our study.
- *Orientation*: To eliminate the effect of body movement on player experience, we only selected games that could be played in both a seated or standing orientation.

Game Descriptions of Red Matter 2. According to Meta [19], Red Matter 2, is an Adventure/Puzzle game that has received D.I.C.E Awards for "Immersive Reality GOTY" and "Immersive Reality Technical Achievement". The story of Red Matter 2, is a dystopian Space Fantasy set during the Cold War Period wherein, players take control of the protagonist, Sasha. Throughout the main story, players encounter challenging interactive puzzles to uncover the whereabouts of their missing crewmates.

Facility. The Meta Quest 3 Virtual Reality Headset was used for inspectors to get familiarized with the gameplay and capture recordings, along with the Arctis 7P Headset for spatial audio. Before inspecting the game, inspection experts check the play boundaries to ensure there would be adequate space to maneuver effectively through the environment.

3.3 Inspection Experts

Two experts conducted the heuristic evaluation. Both have HCI experience. In addition, Expert 1 has rich knowledge and experience in alpha and beta testing console games before their official release and has several hours of experience with virtual reality games. Expert 2 has professional experience in New Media and Cybersecurity, with knowledge and experience in several game genres, such as RPGs and Adventure, across PC, Mobile, and VR Platforms.

3.4 Checklist for Dynamic Gameplay in Cinematic Context (DGCC)

Reyes et al. [21] developed a measurable scale to assess the immersion of Interactive Fiction in Cinematic Virtual Reality (IFcVR.). While this scale proposed unique intersections between gaming and literary or digitally mediated content, the scope of their research does not feature any player engagement heuristics, but rather impressions of the passive viewership elements, which have limited applicability to dynamic interactions with game or controls. Our investigation on the cinematic immersion is more concerned with the continuity and enjoyment of the dynamic gameplay and consistency of mechanics. We were particularly interested in whether some of these factors would positively or negatively influence the fluidity of the game experience caused by inconsistencies with play, which could be further attributed to the perception of the game's cinematic or graphical quality. However, we also expect that minimal disruption could have an inverse relationship, leading to greater investment in the characters, world, and story. In the following tables shown below, we identify relevant scholarly works related to gameplay experience and cinematic engagement. We examine each of these constructs later to discuss their contextual relevance to virtual reality environments.

Table 1 lists the definitions of four heuristic principles used in our study: General Usability, Mobility, Playability, and Cinematic Engagement based on previous related literature.

Heuristic evaluation aspects were adapted from previous related work and are listed according to four heuristic categories.

Table 2 lists heuristic evaluation questions for general usability & mobility [22]. Table 3 lists heuristic evaluation questions for Playability [22] compassing four subcategories: *Gameplay, Game Mechanics, Game Story* [23] *and Onboarding* [24]. Table 4 lists heuristic evaluation questions for Cinematic Engagement including four subcategories: *Captivation, Real-world Dissociation, Comprehension, and Transportation* [25].

3.5 Procedure

Step 1: Individual Inspection. Two experts first conducted individual inspections, where they played the game until they felt familiar with it and conducted a heuristic evaluation using the principles defined in Table 1, and questions in Tables 2, 3 and 4. These questions were used to allow experts to familiarize themselves with the game's story, onboarding, and gameplay mechanics.

Table 1. Definition of Heuristic Principles

Category	Definition
General Usability	Covers the game controls and interface through which the player interacts with the game
Mobility	How easily the game allows a player to enter the game world and how it behaves in diverse and unexpected environments
Playability	• **Game Play:** The set of problems and challenges a user must face to win the game or complete activities • **Game Story:** Narrative context of the game such as Game Environment, Characters, Story Progression • **Game Mechanics:** Features such as controls and game structure that dictate when and how players should expected to operate in the game environment • **Onboarding:** Game systems used to introduce the world to the player, while also facilitating progression through the virtual environment
Cinematic Engagement	• **Captivation:** How interested the viewer was and their motivation to continue playing • **Real-word Disassociation:** Awareness of the viewer to the game's environment and surroundings, as opposed to the real world • **Comprehension:** How well the viewers were able to understand in-game tasks events and their importance to the overall game story • **Transportation:** The degree to which the user felt like they were experiencing events for themselves, and how much they felt they were existing in the game world, instead of the physical world

Step 2: Group Inspection. Following their evaluations, the two experts conducted a group inspection, where they discussed their evaluation results and agreed upon the severity of the problems they identified.

The severity of the problems was reported on a scale of 0–3:

1. **no problem:** no evident heuristic problems.
2. **cosmetic problem**: suggested minor inconvenience during the in-game experience, or slightly disturbed the continuity of the interaction.
3. **minor problem**: implied challenges with the playability and game heuristics that directly affected the player's resonance with audio-visual or narrative impressions of the game.
4. **major problem**: suggested dissatisfaction with the game dynamics, which reflects core frustration with the game dynamics, and could not be resolved via guidance from the system or continuous play.

4   Results

In the following we report our findings corresponding to four heuristic categories: general usability, mobility, playability, and cinematic engagement.

Table 2. Heuristic Evaluation Questions for General Usability and Mobility

Category	Principles	Source
General Usability	GU1 Audio-visual representation supports the game GU2 **Audio**: Music in the game can help support the game genre and environment but usage of sound depends on the surrounding context, GU3 **Layout:** Screen layout is efficient and visually pleasing GU4 **Help:** Provide context-sensitive help while playing without relying on a manual GU5 **Feedback:** Sounds from the game provide meaningful feedback or stir a particular emotion GU6 **Menu:** Make the menu layers well-organized and minimalist to the extent the menu options are intuitive GU7 **Learnability**: this factor emphasizes how easily users can accomplish a task on the first attempt and how quickly users can improve GU8 **Efficiency:** Concerns the time users take to accomplish a task. The difference between efficiency and learnability is that before efficiency is measured, users should have already experienced using the game GU9 **Comprehensibility**: It measures how easily users can understand the game. This encompasses the presentation of visual and textual information used. to progress the game's story or activities	[22]
Mobility	MO1 the game and play sessions can be started quickly MO2 the game accommodates with the surroundings MO3 interruptions are handled reasonably	[22]

4.1 Results of Heuristic Evaluation on General Usability and Mobility

Table 5 lists heuristic problems related to general usability and mobility. Overall the game demonstrated a good general usability and mobility. Only 6 heuristic problems were identified out of the total of 12 heuristic questions. Three major problems were related to help, learnability, and comprehensibility. One minor problem is related to the efficiency, and two cosmetic problems were on layout and mobility.

4.2 Results of Heuristic Evaluation on Playability

Table 6 lists the heuristic problems related to playability. Twenty heuristic problems out of the total of 21 heuristic questions were identified. Onboarding showed major problems (1 major problem, 3 minor problems, 1 cosmetic problem), followed by gameplay (2 minor problems). Game mechanics and Game story showed few problems (1 minor problem, 1 cosmetic problem). Our evaluation revealed that onboarding is very important for complicated game like Red Matter 2.

Table 3. Heuristic Evaluation Questions for Playability

Category	Principles	Source
Gameplay	GP1 the first-time experience is encouraging GP2 players discover the story as part of the play GP3 players should not experience being penalized repetitively for the same failure GP4 Challenges are positive game experiences, rather than negative experiences (results in their wanting to play more, rather than quitting GP5 Players' fatigue is minimized by varying activities and pacing during gameplay	[22] [23]
Game Mechanics	GM1 Game should react in a consistent, challenging, and exciting way to the player's actions (e.g., appropriate music with the action GM2 A player should always be able to identify their score/status and goal in the game GM3 Controls should be intuitive and mapped naturally; they should be customizable and default to industry standard settings GM4 Player should be given controls that are basic enough to learn quickly yet expandable for advanced options	[23]
Game Story	GS1 The game story supports the gameplay and is meaningful GS2 The Player spends time thinking about possible story outcomes GS3 The game transports the player into a level of personal involvement emotionally (e.g., scare, threat, thrill, reward, punishment) and viscerally (e.g., sounds of the environment) GS4 Player is interested in the characters because (1) they are like me; (2) they are interesting to me, (3) the characters develop as action occurs GS5 I would replay the game for its interesting characters, story, and environment	[23]
Onboarding	OB1 Game Difficulty diminished my immersion and interest in the game OB2 The game narrative structures help maintain feelings of immersion during the game's first moments OB3 Players should be able to learn core game mechanics quickly during the onboarding phase, to ensure that they know how to play the game. Players should also be able to quit the game during the learning phase OB4 Immersion can be the outcome of a well-designed onboarding phase. The game needs to challenge the player but not be stressful, it needs to provide a clear goal whiteout inhibiting the feeling of autonomy OB5 Players should receive information about how well they are during and when succeeding in a goal. Too much information can overwhelm players while to little can confuse them OB6 There is an interesting and absorbing tutorial that mimics gameplay systems OB7 player is taught skills early that you expect the players to use later, or right before the new skill is needed	[24]

4.3 Results of Heuristic Evaluation on Dynamic

Table 7 lists the heuristic problems identified related to cinematic engagement. Only 5 heuristic problems were identified out of the total of 21 heuristic questions. Captivation and Transportation showed one major problem each, while Real-world Disassociation

Table 4. Heuristic Evaluation Questions for Dynamic Gameplay in Cinematic Context (DGCC)

Category	Principles	Source
Captivation	CAP1 Audio cues and sound design were necessary to maintain attention CAP2 Visual presentation of the game was able to hold my attention CAP3 Little effort is needed in watching the movie, TV show, or clip CAP4 I tried my best to follow the story of the game, most of the time CAP5 Characters, world, story, and events motivated me to keep playing CAP6 To what extent were you interested in seeing how the events in the game, would progress? CAP7 How much did you want the events in the game, to unfold successfully for the main characters involved? CAP8 Were you in suspense about how the events would unfold? CAP9 Overall impressions of game visuals and imagery were positive	[25]
Real-world Dissociation	RWD1 Overall impression of game's cinematic presentation and visual aesthetics were positive RWD2 Presence in the virtual world was stronger than the real world RWD3 Story and game activities kept my attention rather than real-world responsibilities	[25]
Comprehension	COMP1 Players found the concepts and themes of the game, TV show, or clip challenging COMP2 To what extent did you find the concepts and themes easy to understand? COMP3 Gameplay actions allowed me to understand the story more clearly COMP4 How well do you think you understood what happened	[25]
Transportation	TRAN1 I could picture myself in the game's scene or environment TRAN2 The game allowed me to forget about the real world TRAN3 Interactions and storytelling felt more like an experience than a game being played on a system TRAN4 To what extent was your sense of being in the environment shown in the game, stronger than your sense of being in the real world? TRAN5 Game elicited palpable responses (talking aloud, frustration, etc.)	[25]

Table 5. Results of Heuristic Evaluation on General Usability and Mobility

Heuristics	Principle	Problems	Severity
GU4	**Help:** Provide context-sensitive help while playing without relying on a manual	Very limited help was provided, when help was provided, it was primarily through voice-over, with no textual references that could be referred to later	3
GU7	**Learnability**: this factor emphasizes how easily users can accomplish a task on the first attempt and how quickly users can improve	Puzzles were rarely completed quickly and did not provide help that could be used for future puzzles in the game	3
GU9	**Comprehensibility**: It measures how easily users can understand the game. This encompasses the presentation of visual and textual information used. to progress the game's story or activities	When puzzles take too long to complete, it would sometimes be hard to remember their relevance to the game's story	3
GU8	**Efficiency:** Concerns the time users take to accomplish a task. The difference between efficiency and learnability is that before efficiency is measured	Game's puzzles were sometimes too challenging and could not be skipped to continue with the game's story	2
GU3	**Layout:** Screen layout is efficient and visually pleasing	Occasional interference from the HUD and Menus	1
MO3	Interruptions are handled reasonably	Experienced few game crashes; rebooting resulted in minimal loss of progress	1

showed three minor problems. No heuristic problems were identified for Comprehension. This suggested an overall good cinematic engagement for the game of Red Matter 2.

5 Discussion

5.1 Gameplay and Mechanics

In choosing Red Matter 2 for evaluation in this study, we were particularly interested in whether the Puzzle aspects of the game would add to our impressions of the game's cinematic impressiveness. Through the inspection of the game, experts encountered several different overarching issues with the gameplay experience that were believed to impact cinematic content with the virtual environment. we noted issues with the difficulty of the game's interactive puzzles and the game's inability to offer additional tips or provide the option to skip puzzles after repetitive failure. There were also some cases wherein input error led to unintentional falling when traversing through the game's environment, forcing the player to repeat the movement, which could only be accomplished one way.

Table 6. Results of Heuristic Evaluation on Playability

Heuristics	Principle	Problems	Severity
OB1	Game Difficulty diminished my immersion and interest in the game	Beginning puzzles were easy, while hard puzzles took too much time to complete which hindered the overall game experience	3
GP3	players should not experience being penalized repetitively for the same failure	Sometimes platform puzzles seemed too challenging and could not be skipped	2
GP4	Challenges are positive game experiences, rather than negative experiences (results in their wanting to play more, rather than quitting	Overcomplicated puzzles were sometimes frustrating and detracted from the play experience	2
GM1	Game should react in a consistent, challenging, and exciting way to the player's actions (e.g., appropriate music with the action	Games controls could be changed to suit the users, but accidental input was not entirely avoided. Input errors sometimes forced game activities to be repeated	2
GS5	I would replay the game for its interesting characters, story, and environment	Based on our visual presentation of the game, I would play this game again, despite having several issues with the game help and feedback systems	2
OB3	Players should be able to learn core game mechanics quickly during the onboarding phase, to ensure that they know how to play the game. Players should also be able to quit the game during the learning phase	Players introduced to the core mechanics only a few times and never reminded of their importance or how they function	2
OB4	Immersion can be the outcome of a well-designed onboarding phase. The game needs to challenge the player but not be stressful, it needs to provide a clear goal whiteout inhibiting the feeling of autonomy	Audio-visual representation of the game story was very positive, but puzzles became too challenging	2
OB7	player is taught skills early that you expect the players to use later, or right before the new skill is needed	Players were introduced to tools and puzzles that repeated throughout the game but offered no additional help in completing them	2
GM3	Controls should be intuitive and mapped naturally; they should be customizable and default to industry standard settings	The game offered control adjustments such as handedness, and seating/ standing orientation; input error was not entirely avoidable	1
GS4	Player is interested in the characters because (1) they are like me; (2) they are interesting to me, (3) the characters develop as action occurs	Although the game had limited characters, the story and game environment encouraged continuous play	1
OB6	There is an interesting and absorbing tutorial that mimics gameplay systems	Initial tutorials offered textual and voice-over guidance but were infrequent and inconsistent later in the game	1

Table 7. Dynamic Gameplay in Cinematic Context (DGCC)

Heuristics	Principle	Problems	Severity
CAP 3	Enough effort is needed to play and enjoy the game. I was not frustrated when having to use too much effort to complete game activities	Puzzles were necessary but also considerably challenging, and the game's story and required keen attention from the player to complete them Prolonged exposure led to cybersickness	3
TRAN 5	Game elicited palpable responses (talking aloud, frustration, etc.)	Frustration with game puzzles; positive impressions of the game's environment	3
RWD 1	Overall impression of game's cinematic presentation and visual aesthetics were positive	The game leaned heavily into the space-themed environment, reinforced the space adventure aesthetic	2
RWD 2	Presence in the virtual world was stronger than the real world	Game puzzles require too much attention without help or guidance. Once completed, players were able to re-engage with the game's narrative	2
RWD 3	Story and game activities kept my attention rather than real-world responsibilities	Gameworld was interesting and mysterious; however. Lack of guidance made players want to disconnect from the virtual experiences	2
COMP 2	To what extent did you find the concepts and themes easy to understand?	Themes and concepts were mostly easy to understand; players forgot how certain puzzles were related to the story	2
COMP 3	Gameplay actions allowed me to understand the story more clearly	Each scenic environment had its puzzle. The puzzles had key information (door and keypad codes, items needed for secondary puzzles)	2
TRAN 1	I could picture myself in the game's scene or environment	The game did not have any direct cut scenes; space themes remained consist throughout	2
TRAN 4	To what extent was your sense of being in the environment shown in the game, stronger than your sense of being in the real world?	Visual aesthetics of the game were pleasing; traversal was enjoyable; players became frustrated with difficult puzzles	2

(continued)

Table 7. (*continued*)

Heuristics	Principle	Problems	Severity
CAP 4	I tried my best to focus on and follow the story and characters in the game	It was easy to follow the game's story but there was not supporting text for spoken dialogue, by default	1
COMP 1	Players found the concepts and themes of the game challenging to understand. The complexity of themes was not interesting after long periods of play	The themes of space exploration were apparent and helped to reinforce the potential of story events and outcomes	1
TRAN 2	The game allowed me to forget about the real world	The game required a lot of concentration and made me forget about the real world	1

5.2 Dynamic Gameplay in Cinematic Context (DGCC)

Despite overall negative impressions of the game's core mechanics, experts also noted several positive impressions of graphics and audiovisual representations with a narrative storytelling component. Notably, diegetic features such as narrative voice-over, and music soundtracks, motivated the players to continue their game sessions. However, the limited usage of text-based guidance or instruction made it difficult to progress through the story and failed to reinforce the learnability of in-game tools needed to traverse the environment or complete puzzles. Throughout the individual and group inspection sessions, experts noted that the dynamic aspects of diegetic cues and user experience not only grabbed and maintained the user attention, but also provided suggestive navigation prompts for players to advance the narrative proposed by the developers. In these regards, the player was placed into an environment where an interactable object was presented to them to progress along the game's linear narrative trajectory.

5.3 Limitations of Research

While the checklist's composition offers an extensive evaluation of the qualitative charac-teristics of cinematic and video game heuristics, this research only evaluates one game with narrative constructs. Secondly, the variance between the crucial elements of the game suggests that gameplay experiences can vary between observations or inspections. Lastly, virtual reality experiences are niche in the gaming communities and therefore require more refinement and technological acceptance to improve upon the limitations of gameplay functionality and the limitations of the games analyzed. Our expert inspections suggest that while the environments offer unique and aesthetically pleasing represen-tations of the virtual against the real world, limitations in the continuity were most associated with the game's controls and mechanics rather than the graphical fidelity of the game assets.

5.4 Areas for Future Research

The results of this research suggest that virtual reality games can be quite immersive with regards to their graphical and aesthetic presentation. The playability, and overall enjoyability of the games on these platforms is hindered by barriers common barriers with controls and efficiency. These problems were noted to have directly negative effects on the performance of the game, despite the use of engaging narrative strategy using character voiceovers, which can in some respects, lead to the transformation of the digital immersion to the physical world. Future studies in this area would benefit from the development or refine platform-specific standardization, to enhance the equality of the experience for expert and novice VR users.

References

1. Reyes, M.., Dettori, G.: Developing a Media Hybridization based on Interactive Narrative and Cinematic Virtual Reality. Ekphrasis (2067–631X), 22(2) (2019)
2. Nielsen, L.T., et al.: Missing the point: an exploration of how to guide users' attention during cinematic virtual reality. In: Proceedings of the 22nd ACM Conference on Virtual Reality Software and Technology, pp. 229–232, November 2016
3. Tong, L., Lindeman, R.W., Regenbrecht, H.: Viewer's role and viewer interaction in cinematic virtual reality. Computers 10(5), 66 (2021)
4. Rothe, S., Buschek, D., Hußmann, H.: Guidance in cinematic virtual reality-taxonomy, research status, and challenges. Multimodal Technol. Interact. 3(1), 19 (2019)
5. Elson, M., Breuer, J., Ivory, J.D., Quandt, T.: More than stories with buttons: narrative, mechanics, and context as determinants of player experience in digital games. J. Commun. 64(3), 521–542 (2014)
6. Bizzocchi, J.: Games and narrative: an analytical framework. Loading-The J. Canadian Games Stud. Assoc. 1(1), 5–10 (2007)
7. Ryan, M.L.: From narrative games to playable stories: toward the poetics of interactive narrative. Story Worlds J. Narrative Stud. 1, 43–59 (2009)
8. Tancred, N., Vickery, N., Wyeth, P., Turkay, S.: Player choices, game endings and the design of moral dilemmas in games. In: Proceedings of the 2018 Annual Symposium on Computer-Human Interaction in Play Companion Extended Abstracts, pp. 627–636, October 2018
9. Nielsen, J.: Usability engineering. Morgan Kaufmann (1994)
10. McGee, M., Rich, A., Dumas, J.: Understanding the usability construct: User-perceived usability. In: Proceedings of the Human Factors and Ergonomics Society Annual Meeting, vol. 48, No. 5, pp. 907–911. SAGE Publications, Sage CA, September 2004
11. González Sánchez, J.L., Padilla Zea, N., Gutiérrez, F.L.: From usability to playability: Introduction to player-centred video game development process. In: Human Centered Design: First International Conference, HCD 2009, Held as Part of HCI International 2009, San Diego, CA, USA, July 19-24, 2009 Proceedings 1, pp. 65–74. Springer, Heidelberg (2009)
12. Bostan, B.: Player motivations: a psychological perspective. Comput. Entertainment (CIE) 7(2), 1–26 (2009)
13. Shafer, D.M., Carbonara, C.P., Korpi, M.F.: Factors affecting enjoyment of virtual reality games: a comparison involving consumer-grade virtual reality technology. Games Health J. 8(1), 15–23 (2019)
14. Sánchez, J.L.G., Simarro, F.M., Zea, N.P., Vela, F.L.G.: Playability as extension of quality in use in video games. In: I-USED, August 2009

15. LaViola, J.J., Jr.: A discussion of cybersickness in virtual environments. ACM Sigchi Bull. **32**(1), 47–56 (2000)
16. Chang, E., Kim, H.T., Yoo, B.: Virtual reality sickness: a review of causes and measurements. Int. J. Hum.-Comput. Interact. **36**(17), 1658–1682 (2020)
17. Yildirim, C.: Cybersickness during VR gaming undermines game enjoyment: a mediation model. Displays **59**, 35–43 (2019)
18. Steam Curator (2024). VR Comfort Rating. https://store.steampowered.com/curator/339 61168-VR-Comfort-Rating/
19. Meta Quest Store (2024). Shop Meta Quest VR Games. https://www.meta.com/experiences/ search/?q=red%20matter%202
20. Weech, S., Kenny, S., Lenizky, M., Barnett-Cowan, M.: Narrative and gaming experience interact to affect presence and cybersickness in virtual reality. Int. J. Hum. Comput. Stud. **138**, 102398 (2020)
21. Reyes, M.C.: Measuring user experience on interactive fiction in cinematic virtual reality. In: Interactive Storytelling: 11th International Conference on Interactive Digital Storytelling, ICIDS 2018, Dublin, Ireland, December 5–8, 2018, Proceedings 11, pp. 295–307. Springer International Publishing (2018)
22. Korhonen, H., Koivisto, E.M.: Playability heuristics for mobile games. In: Proceedings of the 8th Conference on Human-Computer Interaction with Mobile Devices and Services, pp. 9–16, September 2006
23. Desurvire, H., Caplan, M., Toth, J.A.: Using heuristics to evaluate the playability of games. In: CHI'04 Extended Abstracts on Human Factors in Computing Systems, pp. 1509–1512, April 2004
24. Thomsen, L.E., Petersen, F.W., Drachen, A., Mirza-Babaei, P.: Identifying onboarding heuristics for free-to-play mobile games: a mixed methods approach. In: Entertainment Computing-ICEC 2016: 15th IFIP TC 14 International Conference, Vienna, Austria, September 28–30, 2016, Proceedings 15, pp. 241–246. Springer (2016)
25. Rigby, J.M., Brumby, D.P., Gould, S.J., Cox, A.L.: Development of a questionnaire to measure immersion in video media: the Film IEQ. In: Proceedings of the 2019 ACM International Conference on Interactive Experiences for TV and Online Video, pp. 35–46, June 2019

Scientific Knowledge Database to Support Cybersickness Detection and Prevention

Milton França[1], Ângelo Amaral[1] , Ferrucio de Franco Rosa[1,2] ,
and Rodrigo Bonacin[1,2(✉)]

[1] University of Campo Limpo Paulista (UNIFACCAMP), Campo Limpo Paulista,
SP, Brazil
miltondsw@gmail.com
[2] Renato Archer Information Technology Center (CTI), Campinas, SP, Brazil
{ferrucio.rosa,rodrigo.bonacin}@cti.gov.br

Abstract. Exploring new data pre-processing features and techniques
to improve the accuracy and generalizability of machine learning (ML)
models is a concern, especially in the context of disease prevention and
detection. We develop and make available a scientific knowledge base on
ML methods and techniques applied to cybersickness detection and prevention. The proposed knowledge base is intended to support researchers
and developers working on ML and cybersickness.

Keywords: Cybersickness · Motion Sickness · Detection ·
Prevention · Knowledge Database · Virtual Reality · Augmented
Reality · Machine Learning · Healthcare

1 Introduction

Cybersickness is a disease that affects users of Virtual Reality (VR) or Augmented Reality (AR) devices (e.g., glasses, headphones, helmets), among other
wearable devices. Studies have explored the use of Machine Learning (ML) techniques to detect and predict cybersickness (e.g., based on physiological and eye
movement data) [6,19].

To propose and maintain knowledge databases to support ML methods and
techniques aimed at detecting and preventing cybersickness is essential [19]. ML
research aimed at cybersickness should consider collecting good quality data
and exploring new features and data preprocessing techniques to improve the
accuracy and generalization of ML models [4,13].

We present a scientific knowledge database on ML methods and techniques
for detecting and preventing cybersickness. Our knowledge database is made
available through a dashboard to support healthcare researchers and developers,
making this a valuable contribution to the scientific community that strives to
detect and predict cybersickness.

The remainder of this paper is presented as follows: Sect. 2 presents the
literature review and related work; Sect. 3 introduces the proposed knowledge

© The Author(s), under exclusive license to Springer Nature Switzerland AG 2024
J. Y. C. Chen and G. Fragomeni (Eds.): HCII 2024, LNCS 14706, pp. 182–199, 2024.
https://doi.org/10.1007/978-3-031-61041-7_12

database to support cybersickness detection and prevention; Sect. 4 presents an application of the knowledge database in an implementation of a dashboard, along with a discussion on the results; Sect. 5 presents the final remarks.

2   Literature Review and Related Works

Based on the guiding questions *"What characteristics of individuals (e.g., gender, age) impact the propensity for cybersickness diagnosis?"* and *"Which biological signals (e.g., heart rate, blood pressure, physical movements) have a higher efficacy percentage in detecting or preventing cybersickness?"*, a literature review was carried out using the approach proposed by Kitchenham (2004) [14]. The goal was to identify the necessary inputs for research and define its parameters, coverage period, scientific databases, and keywords.

The search period for publications was defined between 2015 and 2022, reflecting the recent nature of these inquiries and aiming to report the current state of the art. The search string used was adapted to the syntax of each research database and can be summarized as: (*"virtual reality" OR "VR" OR "augmented reality" OR "virtual world" OR "metaverse" OR "immersion"*) AND (*"education" OR "educational" OR "school" OR "learning" OR "training" OR "class"*) OR *"cybersickness"* AND (*"API" OR "dashboard" OR "Knowledge base" OR "machine learning" OR "detection" OR "prevention" OR "physiological data"*).

The search yielded a total of 180 articles, with 56 obtained from Springer Link, 28 from IEEE Xplore, 66 from the ACM Digital Library, and 30 from the Google Scholar platform. The following inclusion and exclusion criteria were then applied: (i) *Inclusion Criteria*: (I1) Articles from journals or proceedings of scientific events with full text available for consultation; (I2) Publications from 2015 to 2022; (I3) Works presenting methods and techniques related to the VR or AR context; (I4) Works published in English; and (ii) *Exclusion Criteria*: (E1) Research area other than Computer Science; (E2) Works not related to the guiding questions; (E3) Short papers and abstracts.

From applying the filter, we analyzed 21 articles that cover a wide range of virtual or augmented reality applications, often supported by artificial intelligence and AR, where cybersickness cases originate. The results reflect the state of the art in research on VR applications, enabling discussion on cybersickness symptoms and their tabulation and analysis.

We analyzed and classified the works based on the following *Objectives*: (i) Presentation of a tool for building a VR environment, (ii) Discussion of a method for classifying techniques for implementing VR solutions, (iii) Systematization and correlation between different technologies, and (iv) approach to other topics related to the use of VR. They were also classified according to their *Application Domains*: (i) AR and VR environments or (ii) AI applied to the generation of VR applications.

We identified five related works through the snowballing process. and we classified them founded on the following objectives: (i) Tool for building one of the related application domains, (ii) Method for classifying techniques for implementation in one of the application domains, (iii) Systematization and correlation between different technologies, and (iv) approach to other topics related to the use of application domains. We considered the following application domains: (i) Development and maintenance of Knowledge Databases, (ii) Cybersickness, and (iii) Dashboard development using APIs.

2.1   Analyzed Works

Yang et al. (2022) [30] address methods and machine learning (ML) systems for studying cybersickness induced by VR. They discuss the main symptoms and how to employ ML for identifying cybersickness cases through optimized data collection from devices and appropriate algorithms. Fatahi et al. (2016) [8] present challenges for modeling human behavior in e-learning virtual environments. The authors review psychological models of personality used in computer science and explore their applications in ML for supporting cybersickness diagnosis due to their simplicity and comprehensive coverage of human behavior characteristics.

Rechy-Ramirez et al. (2018) [18] discuss application areas of sensors related to emotion and reaction identification through electroencephalographic signals, vision techniques, electromyography, and VR immersion tools. The authors aim to systematize ways to reduce the communication gap between humans and computers through multimodal sensors. Sarker (2022) [21] presents principles and resources of AI techniques applied to intelligent systems in different application areas such as business, finance, health, agriculture, smart cities, and cybersecurity. Guarnera et al. (2017) [10] study material rendering in VR processes, discussing the observer's perception of objects based on different aspects of material lighting, which can impact the user experience and limit its use in VR.

Altaheri et al. (2021) [1] address deep learning (DL) algorithms for classifying motor imagery (MI) signals based on electroencephalogram (EEG) and brain-computer interface (BCI). The authors systematically review research from the last ten years, analyzing preprocessing techniques, input formulation, DL architecture, and performance evaluation, exploring available public datasets, and discussing current challenges and future directions. Rautaray et al. (2015) [17] present a study on established manual gestures as an interface, representations, recognition techniques, and structures from the perspective of human-computer interaction (HCI). The taxonomic investigation of gestures focuses on three main phases of hand gesture recognition (detection, tracking, and recognition), identifying areas where more research is needed.

Dwivedi et al. (2018) [7] present a VR environment design tool for supporting the planning of complex system assembly, addressing user performance during assembly in immersive (VR) and non-immersive (desktop) environments. A genetic algorithm calculates a collision-free optimized path sequence between elements. Ramos et al. (2015) [16] present a tool capable of training people in response to natural phenomena, such as earthquakes, fires, and other weather phenomena, adopting virtual entities with autonomous behavior derived from human behavior through a Learning Classifier Systems (LCS) adjusted with a genetic algorithm to promote autonomy and adaptability of entities.

González Izard et al. (2019) [12] present a visualization system for radiological images using VR and AR to improve surgery planning and monitoring, adopting three-dimensional models that users can visualize and manipulate. Zhang et al. (2017) [32] present a method to improve the design of 3D scenes, simulating user behavior and assessing individual reactions. The goal is to avoid errors caused by fatigue during manual design evaluation. Steshina et al. (2021) [23] present a technique for training people in a VR environment, adopting a mechanism to change dynamic parameters in VR based on a fuzzy model with a set of rules and membership functions based on a genetic algorithm. This approach was applied to a simulator for training forestry cutting machine operators.

Zhang et al. (2022) [33] present a 3D layout optimization method that combines visualization information in the VR environment through an interactive genetic algorithm to optimize the layout of virtual environments, focusing on architectural projects, urban planning, and landscaping. Kán et al. (2017) [15] present a system that automatically populates indoor virtual scenes with furniture objects, optimizing their positions and orientations according to interior design guidelines represented as mathematical expressions. Sra et al. (2016) [22] present a system to automatically generate immersive and interactive VR environments using a real-world model. The aim is to allow users to create diverse virtual worlds without specialized equipment or training, capturing indoor scenes in 3D, detecting obstacles, and mapping walkable areas in the generated environment.

Batras et al. (2016) [2] address VR agents to explore the interactive gestural dialogue between real and virtual actors through computer-mediated interactions. Takacs et al. (2020) [26] present a framework based on a genetic algorithm to create and optimize modular and extensible descriptors for specific outdoor environments. This involves defining elements widely adopted in VR environments, such as travel speed, light conditions, image resolution, scale, transformation, rotation, and classification. Henshall et al. (2017) [11] present an approach for behavioral assessment in a procedural animation system, where users interactively classified two sets of dolphins, one using a regular monitor and the other using a VR device (Oculus Rift).

Wang et al. (2022) [29] present an approach that adopts the Metaverse concept in the field of civil engineering. Although they do not directly address VR elements, they discuss application fields that could be addressed. Borck et al. (2017) [5] address genetic algorithms for case creation, using individuals to represent the initial parameters of a low-fidelity simulator and a target task that must be simulated through VR. Zahabi et al. (2020) [31] use adaptive VR training techniques, considering user capabilities and needs. They also present a systematic literature review, identifying adaptive VR-based training approaches in different domains.

We present a synthesis of the analyzed works in Table 1, where *Objectives* are (To) Tool for building VR environments, (Mt) Method for classifying techniques for implementing VR solutions, (S) Systematization and correlation between different technologies, (A) Approach to other topics related to VR; and *Application*

Domains (AppDo) are: (AVR) Augmented and Virtual Reality environments, (AI) Artificial Intelligence applied to the generation of VR applications.

Table 1. Analyzed Work

Authors	Objective				AppDo	
	To	Mt	S	A	VR	AI
Yang et al. (2022) [30]		X			X	
Fatahi et al. (2016) [8]			X			X
Rechy-Ramirez et al. (2018) [18]			X		X	
Sarker (2022) [21]			X			X
Guarnera et al. (2017) [10]				X	X	
Altaheri et al. (2021) [1]				X		X
Rautaray et al. (2015) [17]	X					X
Dwivedi et al. (2018) [7]	X				X	
Ramos et al. (2015) [16]	X				X	
González Izard et al. (2019) [12]	X				X	
Zhang et al. (2017) [32]		X			X	
Steshina et al. (2021) [23]		X			X	
Zhang et al. (2022) [33]		X			X	
Kán et al. (2017) [15]			X		X	
Sra et al. (2016) [22]			X		X	X
Batras et al. (2016) [2]			X		X	X
Takacs et al. (2020) [26]			X		X	
Henshall et al. (2017) [11]				X	X	
Wang et al. (2022) [29]				X		
Borck et al. (2017) [5]				X	X	
Zahabi et al. (2020) [31]				X	X	

2.2   Related Work

As related work, we considered articles that address knowledge base construction, API usage, and dashboard development. We summarize the related work in Table 2, where **Objectives** are (To) Tool for building one of the related application domains, (Mt) Method for classification of techniques for implementing one of the application domains, (S) Systematization and correlation among different technologies, (A) Approach to other topics related to the application domains; and **Application Domains** (AppDo) are (Kb) Construction and maintenance of Knowledge Bases, (Cs) Cybersickness, (Db) construction of Dashboards and APIs.

Table 2. Related Work

Authors	Objective				AppDo		
	To	Mt	S	A	Kb	Cs	Db
Bello López et al. (2021) [3]	X				X		
Su et al. (2019) [24]		X		X	X		
Valluripally et al. (2022) [28]	X					X	
Sarikaya et al. (2019) [20]				X			X
Sun et al. (2019) [25]				X			X

Bello López et al. (2021) [3] deal with the belief revision process and its challenges by presenting a knowledge base that allows adding new information even if contradictory. An algorithm that can determine when the base becomes inconsistent is proposed.

Su et al. (2019) [24] address the relationship between AI and IoT with Deep Learning-based question-answering systems, contrasting with traditional methods of structured querying. They present a response acquisition method for building knowledge bases using dynamic memory networks and representation learning to interpret natural language questions and subgraphs.

Valluripally et al. (2022) [28] discuss the concept of Social Virtual Reality for Learning Environments (VRLE), with an emphasis on user safety in domains such as education, flight simulations, and military training. The authors present a framework to quantify security and privacy issues triggered by immersion attacks and other types of attacks and failures in VRLE. They discuss how such attacks can induce certain levels of cybersickness.

Sarikaya et al. (2019) [20] present dashboard elements whose design and context of use significantly differ from exploratory visualization tools. The authors analyze the practical employment and classify the design objectives, interaction levels, associated practices, implementation, and utilization.

Sun et al. (2019) [25] present aspects related to third-party libraries and APIs to support software and dashboard evolution and integration. The authors propose a technique for recommending API methods from analyzing software repositories.

3   Scientific Knowledge Database to Support Cybersickness Detection and Prevention

We present the Cybersickness Scientific Knowledge Database (CSKD) (Fig. 1), which is composed of an Entity-Relationship Model (ERM) and a populated database. The main entities of the knowledge base were defined for systematizing knowledge about concepts related to ML methods and techniques that are useful and applicable in the context (e.g., diagnosis, treatment, etc.) of cybersickness.

CSKD provides, for example, implementation artifacts (e.g., source codes and models), medical treatment protocols, recommended medications, and VR

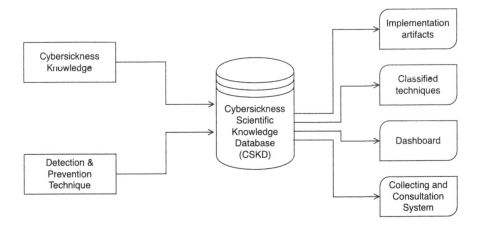

Fig. 1. Overview of CSKD: inputs and outputs.

and AR devices capable of causing cybersickness, among other information that can support experts from computing (for the development of ML techniques) and healthcare (for diagnosis and treatment). The knowledge base engineering documentation (e.g., ERM and class diagram) and the implementation artifacts (e.g., JSON, API's source code, and software prototype graphical interface - dashboard) are publicly available in the GitHub repository [9]. In Fig. 2, we present the ERM (Version 1.2) of CSKD, containing the main database entities.

The database entity *Cybersickness* is characterized by motion sickness that occurs when a person is exposed to VR or AR environments or other forms of computer simulation. *DetectionPreventionTechnique* represents information regarding techniques used to detect or predict Cybersickness, including the identification of technique, description, algorithm, and other essential information for developers. *Immersion* represents aspects related to the users' immersion in the VR or AR experience, including, for example, the stimulus used, whether users were immobile or moving, and the type of VR or AR content experimented.

Biosignal represents information on biological signals used in evaluations. Examples of Biosignal include ECG (electrocardiogram), EOG (electrooculogram), blink rate, breathing rate, GSR (Galvanic Skin Response), skin temperature, and the type of classification performed (e.g., detection). Algorithms (e.g., Fine Gaussian SVM, linear SVM, and KNN) can be used for classification, resulting in varying accuracies for different classes, such as "sc" (soft comfort), "minor" (moderate discomfort) and "severe" (severe discomfort) [7].

Questionnaire represents information on the styles of questionnaires that can be used in cybersickness research. The "labeled" attribute represents complete VR or AR immersion, while the "unlabeled" attribute is comprised of a specific SSQ (Simulator Sickness Questionnaire) score.

Device represents detailed information on the user devices (both in VR or AR usage) and on collecting data for diagnosis, e.g., brand and model, year of

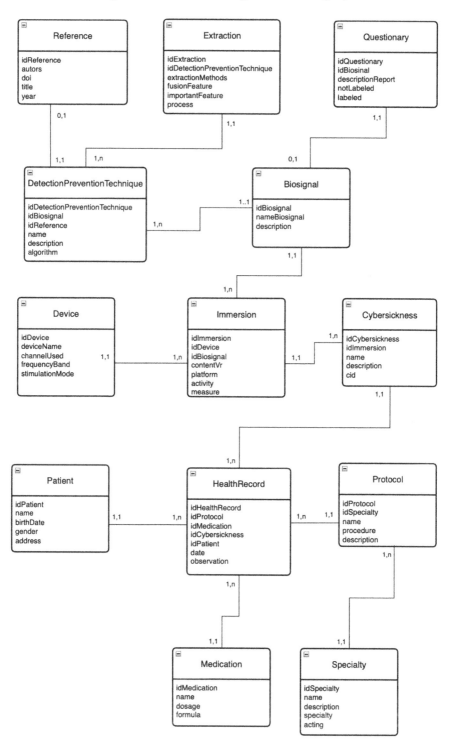

Fig. 2. ERM (Version 1.2) of CSKD: main database entities.

manufacture, specific channels from which signals were obtained, and frequency ranges considered, among other information critical to the detection process.

Reference represents detailed information concerning the scientific source, i.e., technical-scientific articles, technical reports, books, etc., which originated the information used in the study. *Extraction* represents detailed information on the methods applied to biosignals, among other critical resources used to choose the most relevant characteristics. *Medication* represents detailed information about the different medications used in the clinical context, including data such as medicine name, dosage, and formula, among other details necessary to ensure adequate prescription, prevent unwanted interactions, and assure effective treatment of patients.

Protocol represents information on medical protocols and treatments employed in the clinical context, e.g., protocol title and description, among other details for standardizing and defining the effectiveness of medical procedures. *Specialty* represents information on areas of specialization in the medical field of research, e.g., specialty titles and descriptions, among other data for classifying healthcare professionals.

HealthRecord represents information about patient health records, including patient data, medical history, and medications. Medical record information is essential for providing personalized and quality care, allowing healthcare professionals a comprehensive view of patient health status. *Patient* represents information on VR or AR users affected by symptoms who receive medical care, including critical and sensitive data, such as full name, date of birth, gender, and address, among other personal characteristics.

Describing a Data Dictionary is aimed at facilitating the organized and centralized management of data resources [27]. Data represents a valuable resource in both its physical and descriptive aspects. Therefore, its dimensions should be managed like any other essential organizational resource, implying that data needs to be available throughout the organization and, consequently, requires centralized control. We developed a complete Data Dictionary of CSKD, available in [9]. In Appendix 1 (Table 3), we provide an excerpt of the data dictionary to illustrate elements in the proposed CSKD model, highlighting essential entities, attributes, and relationships for the detection and prevention of cybersickness. It also establishes a clear foundation for implementing the proposed knowledge base.

4   Applying CSKD Through a Dashboard

We present an implementation of CSKD through a dashboard. The implementation framework encompasses the creation of artifacts, data classification techniques, a proposed interactive dashboard, and devising features for data insertion and querying.

We have considered an application scenario where multidisciplinary researchers teams from the computing and healthcare fields of research request information on, e.g., how to apply ML to detect cybersickness. These researchers can consult the CSKD dashboard and obtain relevant information on the detection of cybersickness that until now was available in an unstructured manner and formats not appropriate for treatment, e.g., in multiple PDF format tables, scientific articles, technical reports, etc.

With structured, centralized, streamlined, easy-to-visualize, and freely available knowledge, we can use the techniques and information provided to perform various analyses and summaries. The proposed dashboard provides answers (textual or graphical) to essential questions, such as: *Which VR/AR devices can cause or intensify cybersickness symptoms? What biosignal collecting devices can be used to identify cybersickness? What characteristics of individuals (e.g., gender, age) impact the propensity to be diagnosed with cybersickness? Which biological signals (e.g., heart rate, blood pressure, physical movements) are most effective in detecting or preventing cybersickness?*

In Fig. 3, we present a screenshot of the CSKD dashboard, designed for researchers in the health field, and that shows critical information in a friendly and summarized perspective, e.g., graphics and information necessary for a fast and clear understanding of cybersickness.

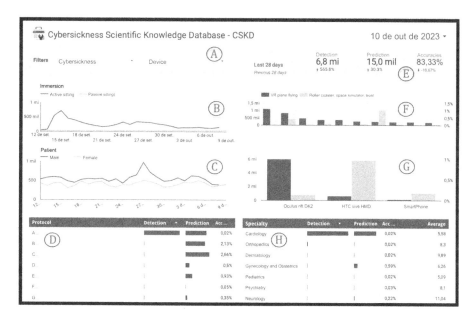

Fig. 3. Dashboard of CSKD

From Fig. 3, the proposed dashboard offers an intuitive interface for classifying data with the following options: i) filter cybersickness information (Fig. 4(A)); ii) monitor the immersion (Fig. 5(B)); iii) visualize the patient's gender (Fig. 6(C)); iv) specific visualizations, such as to provide medical protocols (Fig. 7(D)); v) provide a comprehensive view that contains cybersickness detection and prevention indicators in VR environments (Fig. 8(E)); vi) identify platform types (Fig. 9(F)); vii) enable the viewer to identify with updated metrics charts of device types (Fig. 10(G)); and viii) provide medical specialty (Fig. 11(H)).

Fig. 4. Dashboard: filter

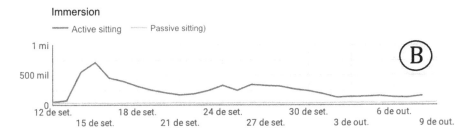

Fig. 5. Dashboard: immersion

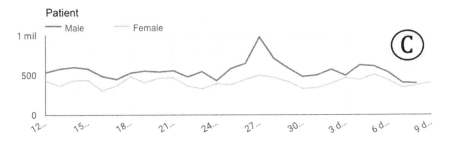

Fig. 6. Dashboard: gender

Using the dashboard, we can obtain data classification from CSKD to train models with the necessary information set to achieve essential accuracy and enhance the analysis. With the dashboard proposal, CSKD becomes more collaborative for technical and scientific professionals.

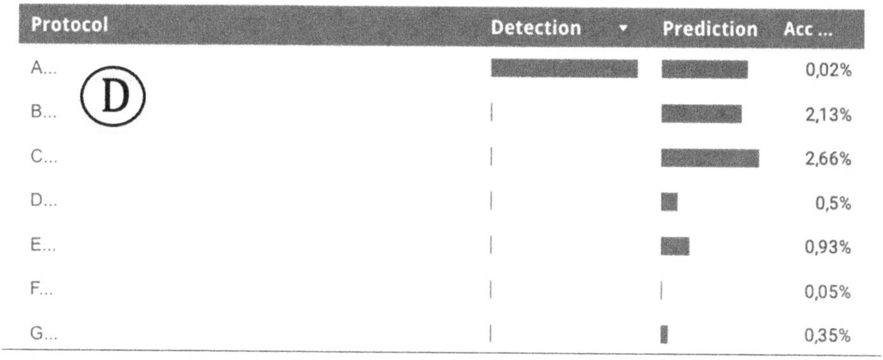

Protocol	Detection ▾	Prediction	Acc ...
A...			0,02%
B...			2,13%
C...			2,66%
D...			0,5%
E...			0,93%
F...			0,05%
G...			0,35%

Fig. 7. Dashboard: medical protocol

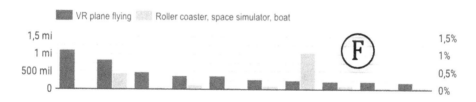

Last 28 days — Detection **6,8 mi** ↑ 565.8% — Prediction **15,0 mil** ↑ 30.3% — Accuracies **83,33%** ↓ -16,67%
Previous 28 days

Fig. 8. Dashboard: detection and prevention

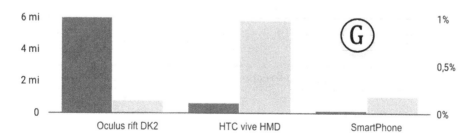

VR plane flying   Roller coaster, space simulator, boat

Fig. 9. Dashboard: platforms

Fig. 10. Dashboard: devices

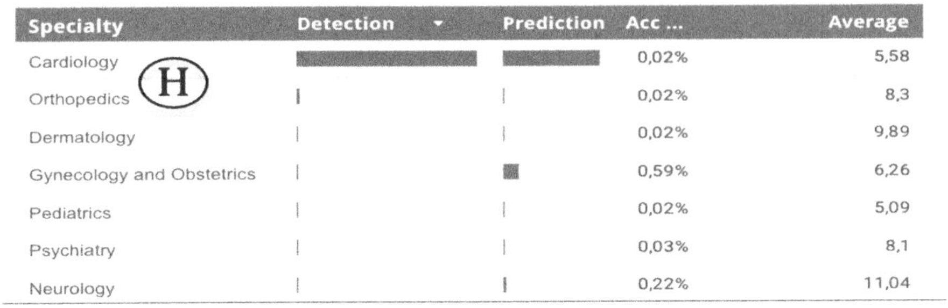

Specialty	Detection ▾	Prediction	Acc ...	Average
Cardiology ⒣	▬▬▬▬▬▬	▬▬▬▬	0,02%	5,58
Orthopedics				0,02%	8,3
Dermatology				0,02%	9,89
Gynecology and Obstetrics		▮	0,59%	6,26
Pediatrics				0,02%	5,09
Psychiatry				0,03%	8,1
Neurology				0,22%	11,04

Fig. 11. Dashboard: medical specialties

4.1 Artifact Implementation

CSKD artifacts represent a crucial step as they make the source-code available in the GitHub repository [9] and provide an open, accessible, and collaborative environment for the scientific community. Artifacts such as design, model, JSON[1], and source-code enables a clear understanding of the CSKD structure.

Figure 12 presents a part of an implementation artifact with the attributes of the Biosignal entity. The complete JSON file is available in GitHub [9] to computing developers and researchers, providing a structured representation of the information for a more in-depth technical analysis.

The public repository facilitates knowledge dissemination and applicability. Furthermore, the artifacts in CSKD extend beyond documentation and the dashboard, encompassing fundamental resources (e.g., API as an integration tool). This element provides users with a better experience, enabling higher efficiency in the data and results presented by the CSKD with other systems. This integrated approach reinforces the commitment of CSKD to be an accessible tool.

```
[ ⊟
  { ⊟
    "biosignal":{ ⊟
      "accuracies":"Binary: fine Gaussian SVM: no cs: 57.6%, minor: 74.2%, severe: 81.8%",
      "algorithm":"Fine Gaussian SVM, linear SVM, KNN",
      "binaryMulticlass":"Binary and Multiclass",
      "biosignal":"ECG, EOG, blink rate, breathing rate, GSR",
      "classificationType":"Detection"
    },
```

Fig. 12. Part of the JSON file presenting the attributes of the Biosignal entity.

---

[1] JavaScript Object Notation (JSON) is an open-standard format for exchanging data between systems.

4.2 Data Classification Techniques

In defining the data classification implemented in the context of CSKD for cybersickness detection and prevention, data was collected from advanced machine learning and signal processing approaches related to user experience in VR environments.

Algorithms allowed for a thorough analysis of biosignals, providing a deeper understanding of patterns associated with cybersickness occurrence. Within the scope of classification techniques, the integration of feature fusion methods stands out, aiming to optimize the combination of multiple biometric signals for a more comprehensive assessment.

The continuous evolution of classification techniques in CSKD is driven by the constant insertion of information and the incorporation of technology in simulated AR/VR environments. This ensures that the model remains up-to-date regarding cybersickness detection and prevention strategies, adapting to emerging complexities and offering a contribution to research advancement.

4.3 Data Insertion and Query

Implementing methods for data insertion and querying in CSKD ensures continuous collection. Researchers can perform queries, exploring relevant information to address this challenge in AR and VR environments. Data insertion and querying are critical in the CSKD's dynamics.

Data insertion is carefully designed to allow researchers to contribute with new findings and relevant information, enriching CSKD. The insertion process promotes active researcher contribution, ensuring constant updates.

Regarding queries, CSKD offers a robust and efficient user interface to extract specific information quickly and accurately. The flexible query functionality, through API and dashboard, allows researchers to perform customized searches, exploring the knowledge base in a way adaptable to their objectives. This not only simplifies the retrieval of relevant data but also promotes critical analysis and understanding of trends and patterns associated with cybersickness.

5 Discussion on the Results

The CSKD model enables improvements in the efficiency of cybersickness detection and prevention due to the ability to centralize and structure knowledge, enabling researchers to conduct more detailed analyses. CSKD has become a valuable source of information, providing quick access to previously scattered knowledge. Researchers, both in the field of computing and in the medical field, can now explore systematized knowledge on detection and prevention techniques and other actions related to cybersickness.

The availability of source-code and engineering documentation on the GitHub repository has increased result reproducibility and contributed to transparency. Researchers can review and validate the methods used, promoting a culture of collaboration in the scientific community. CSKD is aimed at sharing knowledge in the cybersickness domain, being made publicly available, facilitating applicability, and encouraging collaboration between researchers from the computing and healthcare fields.

We are committed to continuously enhancing these features, ensuring an adequate user experience, and consolidating CSKD as an essential tool. We are aimed at contributing to and benefiting the following profiles:

- *Cybersickness Researchers* - CSKD provides a centralized and systematized source of information, enabling detailed analyses and faster advancements in cybersickness research. Its structure promotes a comprehensive understanding of detection and prevention techniques.
- *VR Developers and Engineers* - Through the source-code and database design (freely available), CSKD offers practical insights to enhance the user experience in VR environments. It provides tangible resources for the development community, promoting advances in the design of virtual environments.
- *Healthcare Professionals and Therapists* - Improved cybersickness detection and prevention benefit healthcare professionals, promoting more effective strategies in the therapeutic use of VR technologies.
- *Students and Academics* - With the availability of a comprehensive review, CSKD serves as a practical example and a valuable knowledge source for students and academics interested in cybersickness research.

6   Conclusion

Cybersickness is a new disease with high growth potential due to the intensive use of VR and AR technologies. By making scientific knowledge available in an accessible format, through a dashboard, quickly and free of charge, researchers will have access to valuable information that was previously unstructured and dispersed in different formats, allowing the execution of more detailed and efficient analyses. CSKD engineering documentation and source-code are made publicly available, enabling the replication and implementation of computational techniques for cybersickness study.

As a future work, we plan to evolve the knowledge base, including, for example, cybersickness prevention strategies and new CSKD development artifacts, and enhance the dashboard with new features and more developed visual elements. Our goal is always to maintain a user-friendly interface with detailed graphics and an intuitive user experience, providing a clearer data view in response to information requests. This ongoing expansion reflects our commitment to continuously update CSKD, keeping it relevant and comprehensive in the cybersickness landscape.

Acknowledgments. This study was financed in part by The Brazilian National Council for Scientific and Technological Development (CNPq) grant 405352/2021-2 and São Paulo Research Foundation (FAPESP) grant 2021/11905-0.

Appendix I

Table 3. Part of the data dictionary

Entity	Attributes	Type	Relationships
Reference	idReference	Int	
	autors	Text	
	doi	Text	
	title	Text	
	year	Int	
Extraction	idExtraction	Int	
	idDetectionPreventionTechnique	Int	
	extractionMethods	Text	
	fusionFeature	Text	
	importantFeature	Text	
	process	Text	
Questionary	idQuestionary	Int	
	idBiosinal	Int	
	descriptionReport	Text	
	notLabeled	Text	
	labeled	Text	
DetectionPrevention Technique	idDetectionPreventionTechnique	Int	Reference (idReference)
	idBiosignal	Int	Biosignal (idBiosignal)
	idReference	Int	
	name	Text	
	description	Text	
	algorithm	Text	
Biosignal	idBiosignal	Int	
	nameBiosignal	Text	
	description	Text	
Device	idDevice	Int	
	deviceName	Text	
	channelUsed	Text	
	frequencyBand	Text	
	stimulationMode	Text	
Immersion	idImmersion	Int	Device (idDevice)
	idDevice	Int	Biosignal (idBiosignal)
	idBiosignal	Int	
	contentVr	Text	
	platform	Text	
	activity	Text	
	measure	Text	

References

1. Altaheri, H., et al.: Deep learning techniques for classification of electroencephalogram (eeg) motor imagery (mi) signals: a review. Neural Comput. Appl. (2021). https://doi.org/10.1007/s00521-021-06352-5
2. Batras, D., Guez, J., Jégo, J.F., Tramus, M.H.: A virtual reality agent-based platform for improvisation between real and virtual actors using gestures. Association for Computing Machinery (2016). https://doi.org/10.1145/2927929.2927947
3. Bello López, P., De Ita Luna, G.: An algorithm to belief revision and to verify consistency of a knowledge base. IEEE Lat. Am. Trans. **19**(11), 1867–1874 (2021). https://doi.org/10.1109/TLA.2021.9475620

4. Boeldt, D., McMahon, E., McFaul, M., Greenleaf, W.: Using virtual reality exposure therapy to enhance treatment of anxiety disorders: identifying areas of clinical adoption and potential obstacles. Front. Psychiatry **10** (2019). https://doi.org/10.3389/fpsyt.2019.00773. https://www.frontiersin.org/articles/10.3389/fpsyt.2019.00773

5. Borck, H., Boddy, M.: Automated case generation using a genetic algorithm, pp. 187–188. Association for Computing Machinery (2017). https://doi.org/10.1145/3067695.3075603

6. Davis, S., Nesbitt, K., Nalivaiko, E.: A systematic review of cybersickness, pp. 1–9. Association for Computing Machinery (2014). https://doi.org/10.1145/2677758.2677780

7. Dwivedi, P., Cline, D., Joe, C., Etemadpour, R.: Manual assembly training in virtual environments, pp. 395–399 (2018). https://doi.org/10.1109/ICALT.2018.00100

8. Fatahi, S., Moradi, H., Kashani-Vahid, L.: A survey of personality and learning styles models applied in virtual environments with emphasis on e-learning environments. Artif. Intell. Rev. **46**, 413–429 (2016). https://doi.org/10.1007/s10462-016-9469-7

9. França, M., Rosa, F., Amaral, A.: Cskd repository (2024). https://github.com/FrancaFilho/cybersickness. Accessed 20 Jan 2024

10. Guarnera, G.C., Ghosh, A., Hall, I., Glencross, M., Guarnera, D.: Material capture and representation with applications in virtual reality. Association for Computing Machinery (2017). https://doi.org/10.1145/3084873.3084918

11. Henshall, G.I., Teahan, W.J., Cenydd, L.A.: Crowd-sourced procedural animation optimisation: comparing desktop and vr behaviour, pp. 48–55 (2017). https://doi.org/10.1109/CW.2017.52

12. Izard, S.G., Méndez, J.A.J., Palomera, P.R., García-Peñalvo, F.J.: Applications of virtual and augmented reality in biomedical imaging. J. Med. Syst. **43**, 102 (2019). https://doi.org/10.1007/s10916-019-1239-z

13. Kim, H., et al.: Effect of virtual reality on stress reduction and change of physiological parameters including heart rate variability in people with high stress: an open randomized crossover trial. Front. Psychiatry **12** (2021). https://doi.org/10.3389/fpsyt.2021.614539, https://www.frontiersin.org/articles/10.3389/fpsyt.2021.614539

14. Kitchenham, B.A.: Systematic reviews, pp. xii–xii (2004). https://doi.org/10.1109/METRIC.2004.1357885

15. Kán, P., Kaufmann, H.: Automated interior design using a genetic algorithm. Association for Computing Machinery (2017). https://doi.org/10.1145/3139131.3139135

16. Ramos, M.A., Muñoz-Jiménez, V., Ramos, F.F., Romero, J.R.M., López, A., G, B.E.O.: Evolutive autonomous behaviors for agents system in serious games, pp. 226–231 (2015). https://doi.org/10.1109/CSCI.2015.175

17. Rautaray, S.S., Agrawal, A.: Vision based hand gesture recognition for human computer interaction: a survey. Artif. Intell. Rev. **43**, 1–54 (2015). https://doi.org/10.1007/s10462-012-9356-9

18. Rechy-Ramirez, E.J., Marin-Hernandez, A., Rios-Figueroa, H.V.: Impact of commercial sensors in human computer interaction: a review. J. Ambient. Intell. Humaniz. Comput. **9**, 1479–1496 (2018). https://doi.org/10.1007/s12652-017-0568-3

19. kumar Renganayagalu, S., Mallam, S.C., Nazir, S.: Effectiveness of vr head mounted displays in professional training: a systematic review. Technol. Knowl. Learn. **26**, 999–1041 (2021). https://doi.org/10.1007/s10758-020-09489-9

20. Sarikaya, A., Correll, M., Bartram, L., Tory, M., Fisher, D.: What do we talk about when we talk about dashboards? IEEE Trans. Visual Comput. Graphics **25**(1), 682–692 (2019). https://doi.org/10.1109/TVCG.2018.2864903

21. Sarker, I.H.: Ai-based modeling: techniques, applications and research issues towards automation, intelligent and smart systems. SN Comput. Sci. **3**, 158 (2022). https://doi.org/10.1007/s42979-022-01043-x

22. Sra, M., Garrido-Jurado, S., Schmandt, C., Maes, P.: Procedurally generated virtual reality from 3d reconstructed physical space, pp. 191–200. Association for Computing Machinery (2016). https://doi.org/10.1145/2993369.2993372

23. Steshina, L., Petukhov, I., Glazyrin, A., Zlateva, P., Velev, D.: An intelligent virtual environment for training with dynamic parameters, pp. 79–84. Association for Computing Machinery (2021). https://doi.org/10.1145/3442705.3442718

24. Su, L., He, T., Fan, Z., Zhang, Y., Guizani, M.: Answer acquisition for knowledge base question answering systems based on dynamic memory network. IEEE Access **7**, 161329–161339 (2019). https://doi.org/10.1109/ACCESS.2019.2949993

25. Sun, X., Xu, C., Li, B., Duan, Y., Lu, X.: Enabling feature location for api method recommendation and usage location. IEEE Access **7**, 49872–49881 (2019). https://doi.org/10.1109/ACCESS.2019.2910732

26. Takacs, A., et al.: Descriptor generation and optimization for a specific outdoor environment. IEEE Access **8**, 52550–52565 (2020). https://doi.org/10.1109/ACCESS.2020.2975474

27. Uhrowczik, P.P.: Data dictionary/directories. IBM Syst. J. **12**(4), 332–350 (1973). https://doi.org/10.1147/sj.124.0332

28. Valluripally, S., Gulhane, A., Hoque, K.A., Calyam, P.: Modeling and defense of social virtual reality attacks inducing cybersickness. IEEE Trans. Dependable Secure Comput. **19**(6), 4127–4144 (2022). https://doi.org/10.1109/TDSC.2021.3121216

29. Wang, X., Wang, J., Wu, C., Xu, S., Ma, W.: Engineering brain: metaverse for future engineering. AI Civil Eng. **1**, 2 (2022). https://doi.org/10.1007/s43503-022-00001-z

30. Yang, A.H.X., Kasabov, N., Cakmak, Y.O.: Machine learning methods for the study of cybersickness: a systematic review. Brain Inform. **9**, 24 (2022). https://doi.org/10.1186/s40708-022-00172-6

31. Zahabi, M., Razak, A.M.A.: Adaptive virtual reality-based training: a systematic literature review and framework. Virtual Reality **24**, 725–752 (2020). https://doi.org/10.1007/s10055-020-00434-w

32. Zhang, Y., Fei, G., Shang, W.: 3d architecture facade optimization based on genetic algorithm and neural network, pp. 693–698 (2017). https://doi.org/10.1109/ICIS.2017.7960082

33. Zhang, Y., Yang, G.: Optimization of the virtual scene layout based on the optimal 3d viewpoint. IEEE Access **10**, 110426–110443 (2022). https://doi.org/10.1109/ACCESS.2022.3214206

Evaluation of Large Language Model Generated Dialogues for an AI Based VR Nurse Training Simulator

Nimit Kapadia[1], Shreekant Gokhale[1], Anthony Nepomuceno[1],
Wanning Cheng[1], Samantha Bothwell[2], Maureen Mathews[3],
John S. Shallat[3], Celeste Schultz[4], and Avinash Gupta[1(✉)]

[1] University of Illinois Urbana-Champaign, Champaign, IL 61820, USA
`avinashg@illinois.edu`
[2] Carle Foundation Hospital, Urbana, IL 61801, USA
[3] OSF HealthCare, Peoria, IL 61603, USA
[4] University of Illinois Chicago, Chicago, IL 60607, USA

Abstract. This paper explores the efficacy of Large Language Models (LLMs) in generating dialogues for patient avatars in Virtual Reality (VR) nurse training simulators. With the integration of technology in healthcare education evolving rapidly, the potential of NLP to enhance nurse training through realistic patient interactions presents a significant opportunity. Our study introduces a novel LLM-based dialogue generation system, leveraging models such as ChatGPT, GoogleBard, and ClaudeAI. We detail the development of our script generation system, which was a collaborative endeavor involving nurses, technical artists, and developers. The system, tested on the Meta Quest 2 VR headset, integrates complex dialogues created through a synthesis of clinical expertise and advanced NLP, aimed at simulating real-world nursing scenarios. Through a comprehensive evaluation involving lexical and semantic similarity tests compared to clinical expert-generated scripts, we assess the potential of LLMs as suitable alternatives for script generation. The findings aim to contribute to the development of a more interactive and effective VR nurse training simulator, enhancing communication skills among nursing students for improved patient care outcomes. This research underscores the importance of advanced NLP applications in healthcare education, offering insights into the practicality and limitations of employing LLMs in clinical training environments.

Keywords: Large Language Models · Nurse Training Simulation · Natural Language Processing · Healthcare Education · Patient Avatars · Dialogue Generation · ChatGPT · Bard · ClaudeAI · Virtual Reality · Extended Reality

1 Introduction

The integration of virtual reality (VR) in healthcare education represents a notable innovation, particularly in the context of nurse training. This paper

© The Author(s), under exclusive license to Springer Nature Switzerland AG 2024
J. Y. C. Chen and G. Fragomeni (Eds.): HCII 2024, LNCS 14706, pp. 200–212, 2024.
https://doi.org/10.1007/978-3-031-61041-7_13

positions itself at the confluence of human-computer interaction and nursing education, exploring the potential of advanced technology to address a critical gap in nurse training simulations: the lack of realistic, interactive patient communication. The pursuit of realism in these simulations is more than a technical challenge; it is a fundamental requisite for preparing nursing students for the complexities and nuances of real-world patient care.

Our approach is rooted in the application of Large Language Models (LLMs) within VR environments to simulate patient-nurse dialogues. The integration of NLP techniques, particularly sophisticated models like ChatGPT, Google-Bard, and ClaudeAI, proposes a paradigm shift in how we perceive and construct patient avatars in educational simulations. These AI-driven models offer an unprecedented level of dialogue generation, closely mimicking human conversation patterns and responses.

The objective of our study transcends technological innovation; it aims to critically evaluate the impact of LLM-generated dialogues on the training and development of nursing students. By comparing these AI-generated dialogues with traditional, expert-generated scripts, we seek to understand whether LLMs can significantly enhance the learning experience in nurse training simulations. This research focuses on the intersection of human-AI interaction, technology-driven education, and practical healthcare training.

Moreover, this study is instrumental in identifying the potential role of Human-Computer Interaction (HCI) in transforming nursing education. By integrating advanced computational models into VR simulations, we explore new realms of interactive learning. The potential outcomes of this research are manifold, including enhanced communication skills among nursing students, more effective training methodologies, and a broader understanding of the role of AI in healthcare education.

The subsequent sections of this paper will delve into related works that lay the groundwork for our study, the design and implementation of our LLM-based script generation system, a comprehensive assessment of the generated dialogues through various methodologies, and a discussion on the results obtained. We will conclude with insights into the implications of our findings for future research directions, aiming to enhance communication skills among nursing students, develop more effective training methodologies, and broaden our understanding of the role of AI in healthcare education.

2 Related Work

The advancement of nurse training simulations in the context of human computer interaction has been a focal point of academic research, particularly concerning the authenticity and interactivity of these educational tools. While traditional simulations provide a foundational framework for skill development, they often lack the ability to replicate the intricate dynamics of patient-nurse interactions. This limitation is not just a pedagogical concern but a critical gap in preparing nursing students for the complex realities of patient care [1].

Our literature review begins with an exploration of the current state of nurse training simulations. We delve into the methodologies and technologies that have shaped these simulations, highlighting their strengths and identifying their limitations in simulating realistic patient interactions. This review underscores the necessity for more sophisticated and interactive tools in nursing education, aligning with the ongoing discourse in HCI research [2–4].

The role of NLP in healthcare education, especially in the context of HCI, is a burgeoning area of interest. The emergence of LLMs as a transformative force in NLP has opened new avenues for enhancing the interactivity and realism of patient avatars in educational simulations. This paper provides a comprehensive overview of the application of NLP in healthcare, focusing on the evolution, capabilities, and limitations of LLMs in simulating patient dialogues [5–7].

We also explore the integration of VR in medical and nursing education, highlighting its potential to offer immersive learning experiences that closely mimic clinical settings. The use of VR in conjunction with AI and LLMs represents a significant step forward in creating realistic simulations that can improve learning outcomes and better prepare students for real-world healthcare scenarios [8–10].

Furthermore, the paper examines the challenges and ethical considerations involved in integrating AI into healthcare simulations. This includes an analysis of the complexities in natural language understanding, the adaptation of these models to healthcare-specific contexts, and the ethical implications of using AI in patient care scenarios. Lastly, the exploration of dialogue systems in educational settings, as reviewed in [11], provides valuable insights into the effectiveness of conversational agents in simulating human-like interactions. This research is particularly relevant to our study as it evaluates different methods for assessing the quality of dialogues generated by AI, offering a framework for evaluating the LLM-generated dialogues in our VR nurse training simulations. However, the comparative analysis of LLM-generated dialogues and expert-crafted scripts in nurse training simulations is a relatively unexplored area. Our research aims to fill this gap by providing a detailed evaluation of the effectiveness and practicality of using LLMs in nurse training, thus contributing to the broader conversation on the role of HCI in healthcare education, particularly in the development and application of interactive AI-driven learning tools [12,13,16,17].

3   Design of the LLM Based Script Generation System

3.1   Expert Script Generation

In efforts to evaluate LLM generated scripts, human generated scripts were authored as a baseline. The scripts were centered around established rubrics from nursing curriculum. Such rubrics were made in accordance with the guidelines set by the American Association of Colleges of Nursing (AACN) and other governing and acrediting institutional bodies [15]. In particular, two clinical nursing scenarios were presented: health history intake and ordinary conversation with a patient at the bedside. These two scenarios are distinct in their goals and key learning objectives as noted withing the referenced nursing course rubrics. From such rubrics, nursing faculty (n = 2) from the College of Nursing at the University of Illinois at Chicago authored and reviewed the reference human generated scripts used for this study. The following tables illustrate excerpts from such rubrics and human generated scripts [Tables 1–2].

Table 1. Health History Scenario Rubric and Expert Script Excerpt

Scenario	Health History		
	Allergies/Drug Reactions	Performance	Documentation
Assessment Rubric Excerpt	Allergies - seasonal and other environmental factors, medications, and food. Specifically address allergy to penicillin and latex. If a patient reports an allergy, note the allergen and the nature of the reaction	2 1 0	2 1 0
Expert Script Excerpt	Nurse: Do you have any allergies to medicine, food, latex, pets, or environment? Patient avatar: Yes. I am allergic to wheat, oats, and barley.		

Table 2. Ordinary Conversation Scenario Rubric and Expert Script Excerpt

Scenario	Ordinary Conversation	
		Performance
Assessment Rubric Excerpt	1. The student inquires how the patient is feeling	2 1 0
	2. The student appropriately responds to the patient's reply	2 1 0
Expert Script Excerpt	Nurse: How are you feeling? Patient: I am not feeling well. Nurse: Could you tell me more about that? Patient: Well, I ache all over; I am not interested in eating, and I am really sad that I am here.	

3.2 Generating Scripts Using LLMs

The generation of scripts was facilitated through the utilization of Language Models (LLMs) such as Bard, Claude AI, and GPT3.5. These scripts were produced by providing a single prompt that elucidated the scenario and outlined the characters participating in the script. Additionally, the prompt encapsulated a framework comprising 7-8 key points, derived from the rubric employed by medical experts during script generation. An illustrative example of a prompt employed for one of the scenarios is presented in the appendix of this paper.

3.3   Overall System Architecture

The creation of our LLM based Script Generation System was a collaborative effort, bringing together the expertise of nurses, technical artists, and developers [Fig. 1]. The development process involved utilizing Unity for creating the hospital environment, with nursing instructors contributing by crafting clinical nursing scenario scripts that guided the developers in constructing the dialogue logic and scenarios. Wit.ai was employed for Text-to-Speech processing of user inputs and provided inference for dialogue control logic. Meanwhile, character and animation artists played a crucial role in shaping the visual and interactive aspects, employing Reallusion's Character Creator and iClone software for designing 3D avatars and animations, respectively. The selected animations and audio clips were then integrated into the simulator through the developed Dialogue Controller [Fig. 2]. The final software iteration was deployed onto the Meta Quest 2 head-mounted display, culminating in a comprehensive and innovative nurse training simulation experience. However, limitations were found with the Wit.ai solution in developing dynamic patient dialogues. Recognizing the need for a more advanced solution, we later began to explore the utilization of LLMs for generative patient dialogues.

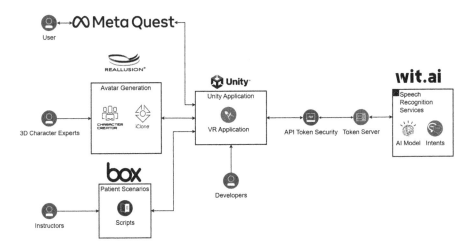

Fig. 1. Design of the Nurse Training Simulator

To assess LLMs for patient avatars in the nurse training simulation, we employed a comprehensive methodology, comparing GPT models with expert responses qualitatively and quantitatively [11]. We curated medical scripts covering diverse scenarios and utilized ChatGPT, Bard and ClaudeAI to generate coherent and contextually appropriate dialogue. The models, trained on large-scale corpora, employed a probabilistic approach and underwent post-processing to ensure clinical accuracy and ethical adherence. A mixed-methods approach assessed dialogue quality, empathy, and communication effectiveness [11,13,14]. Quantitative measures included perplexity and word overlap with expert responses [13,14]. Comparative analyses identified the strengths and limitations of GPT models, guiding focus group discussions with nursing educators for usability feedback. Our methodology offers a comprehensive evaluation of GPT-generated dialogue, emphasizing potential in nursing education. Advanced NLP techniques enable dynamic patient avatars, fostering meaningful dialogue and immersive training for nursing professionals.

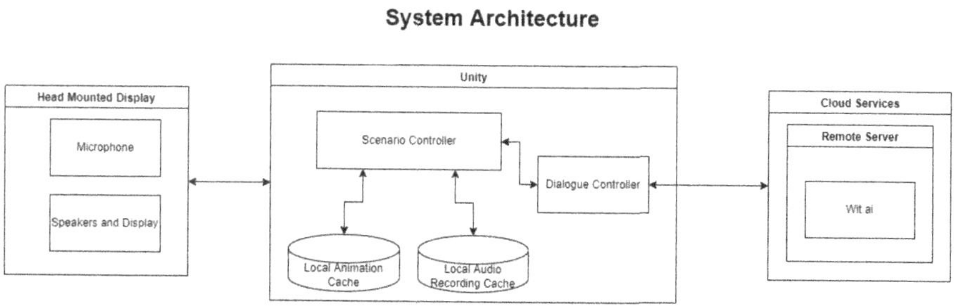

System Architecture

Fig. 2. Natural Language based VR-Interaction System Architecture

4   Assessment

For the scripts generated using LLMs to be used as the final product for the simulation, they need to be as indistinguishable from the scripts that the medical expert would write as possible. The entire flowchart from script generation to assessment can be seen in [Fig. 3]. To assess the performance of LLMs for achieving indistinguishability different aspects were identified. These aspects were as follows:

4.1   Lexical Matching

The Lexical matching approach is based on the tokens (words) in the script. The basic concept is that, more common words between the two scripts, more is the similarity within these scripts. This approach can be converted into various quantitative metrics. The prompt for the script generation is refined to ensure that the base of the generated scripts will be the same as the expert-written script. As these scripts have same situations and characters, number of common tokens can give us the idea of the similarity within those scripts. In this study, Recall one of such metric is used to measure the token overlap between the scripts. The recall is the ratio of the number of common tokens between the script and the reference to the total number of tokens in the script. To refine the recall metric, words carrying the information are identified in each of the scripts including the expert script. The expert script is used as the reference while calculating the recall for all LLM generated script.

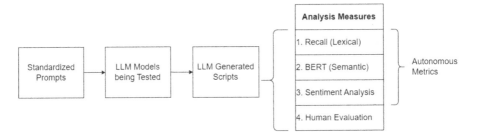

Fig. 3. Script-Evaluation Flowchart

4.2 Semantics Similarity

A notable limitation of the lexical matching approach lies in its exclusive dependence on tokens, neglecting the meaning of sentences. This limitation is addressed by incorporating the contextualized embeddings corresponding to the script text, as provided by a trained model. In this study, we evaluate the F1 similarity of LLM-based scripts using the Bert model. This method firstly converts the script text into corresponding textual embeddings using techniques such as tokenization, and vector conversion. The cosine similarity between the reference script embeddings and LLM-generated script is found for every token present in the script. The cosine similarity score is near 1 if the tokens are highly similar in their meaning. The similarity matrix for these embeddings is further used to find the F1 similarity score between the scripts. Evaluating the BertS is more complex than lexical matching as there are multiple steps involved in the process. Moreover, the process is memory extensive as fine-tuning needs to be carried out on top of the pre-trained BERT model to find the contextual embeddings. This metric is certainly more efficient than lexical matching as it not only finds out the proportion of common tokens but also matches the words with similar meanings. However, Bert embeddings cannot find factual errors in the text. It only indicates how similar are the scripts in terms of the context.

4.3 Sentiment Analysis

This aspect involves evaluating the subjectivity and polarity of individual dialogues within the script. Subjectivity is measured on a scale from 0 to 1, where a score of 0 indicates complete objectivity, and 1 signifies maximum subjectivity. Polarity measures range from -1 to 1, with -1 indicating the most negative connotation and 1 indicating the most positive. The mean subjectivity and polarity of individual characters are determined through sentiment analysis of their dialogues. This provides insights into each character's approach to the given situation.

4.4   Human Evaluation

It has been seen in the literature where autonomous metrics evaluate a very low similarity score, but the actual text is highly similar to the reference. This occurs because of the limitations of these autonomous metrics. Following discrepancies in the context of the medical scenario are identified after studying such cases in the LLM-generated scripts [Table 3].

Table 3. Discrepancies in LLM-generated scripts

Discrepancy	Example from the script
Inappropriate Follow-up	Nurse: Nice to meet you, Sam. I heard you had a bit of a fall. How are you feeling right now? Sam: Yeah, not too great. My leg and arm are killing me, and my shoulder is stinging Nurse: Great, thanks. Now, **what brought you into the hospital today?**
Lack of Detail	Doctor: (**Explains treatment plan and answers Sam's questions**) OR Sam: (**Answers honestly, expressing worries about potential long-term complications.**)
Lack of Specificity	Nurse: Hi there, I'm **Nurse (Nurse's name).**
Incomplete Information about Dosage	Nurse: Are there any medications you're currently taking for your anxiety and depression and their dosages? John: **I'm on Zoloft and Ativan,** but they haven't been very effective lately.
Lack of Personalization	Nurse Sarah: Thanks for sharing, John. Lastly, let's go through a review of systems. **Have you noticed any changes or issues with your eyes, ears, nose, throat, cardiovascular system, respiratory system, gastrointestinal system, or any other part of your body?**
Unrealistic Verbalization of a Clinical Technique	Nurse: I appreciate you sharing that, John. It helps us understand your situation better. If you don't mind, **let's take a moment of therapeutic silence,** and then we can continue our discussion or address any concerns you may have

To deal with these discrepancies, it was necessary to find out if the LLM-generated scripts satisfied all the requirements in the rubric that is used to create an expert script. Hence, a questionnaire specific to the scenario is made for human evaluation. Each question is designed such that the answer will be in a yes or no format. Furthermore, all these questions are independently answered by the 3 evaluators after going through the scripts in detail. The final human evaluation score for each script is calculated based on the majority of voting for the questions answered yes or no by each evaluator for the LLM-based script and the reference script.

5   Results

The assessment of recall values for individual scripts involves the conversion of each script into a tokenized list after eliminating stopwords and punctuation marks. The ratio of common tokens to the total number of tokens is then determined for each script. Additionally, BertScore F1 values (BertS) are computed by evaluating script embeddings using a pre-trained BERT model. The reproducibility of scripts is evaluated using a standardized prompt framework, where outcomes from generating scripts across three iterations with the same prompt are analyzed [Tables 4–5]. Minimal variation in results across subsequent iterations is observed. Averaged outcomes are compared to assess consistency among autonomous metrics, including recall, BertS, and human evaluation. In the Health History scenario, both autonomous and human evaluations indicate that the GPT3.5 model outperforms other language models (LLMs), with Claude AI surpassing the Bard model. A correlation of 0.799 is found between Recall and Human evaluation, and 0.848 between BertS and Human Evaluation, suggesting strong agreement between autonomous metrics and human evaluation scores. This alignment indicates the potential for using autonomous metrics to compare scripts generated by different LLMs, streamlining the evaluation process.

In the context of Ordinary Bedside Conversation, results over three iterations remain consistent, but recall and BertS metrics identify scripts generated by Bard and GPT3.5 as the best, respectively. Notably, there is no correlation between autonomous metrics and human evaluation in Ordinary Conversation scenarios. The nuanced nature of this scenario, depicting a day in a hospital, where characters must adhere to procedural behavior, leads to more discrepancies in generated scripts. Therefore, script evaluation is non-uniform, emphasizing the need for refining prompts to minimize observed discrepancies.

Sentiment analysis reveals that in both scenarios, the nurse exhibits greater subjectivity than the patient, attributed to the nurse asking open questions while the patient provides factual statements about how they are feeling. The polarity comparison between nurse and patient consistently shows the nurse's positivity and the patient's neutrality across all LLM-generated and expert scripts. However, in the Ordinary Conversation scenario, a discrepancy is observed in sentiment analysis for the doctor's character. Expert scripts portray the doctor as factual and neutral, while LLM-generated scripts consistently depict the doctor as more subjective and positive. This suggests a need for improvement in generating doctor-character dialogues to align with expert expectations.

Table 4. Recall metric results for different scenarios

(a) Health History

LLM model	Recall1	Recall2	Recall3
Bard	0.303	0.293	0.338
Claude AI	0.318	0.386	0.313
GPT 3.5	0.385	0.395	0.338

(b) Ordinary Bedside Conversation

LLM model	Recall1	Recall2	Recall3
Bard	0.344	0.340	0.323
ClaudeAI	0.366	0.326	0.315
GPT 3.5	0.349	0.331	0.306

Table 5. Bert Score for different scenarios

(a) Health History

LLM model	BertS1	BertS2	BertS3
Bard	0.839	0.840	0.841
ClaudeAI	0.840	0.839	0.840
GPT 3.5	0.855	0.845	0.846

(b) Ordinary Bedside Conversation

LLM model	BertS1	BertS2	BertS3
Bard	0.852	0.848	0.847
ClaudeAI	0.846	0.849	0.847
GPT 3.5	0.853	0.850	0.849

6 Discussions and Future Work

This research highlights the significant potential of integrating Large Language Models (LLMs) like ChatGPT, GoogleBard, and ClaudeAI into VR-based nurse training programs. Our findings suggest that LLM-generated dialogues offer a realistic and dynamic method of simulating patient-nurse interactions, potentially bridging the gap in current training methodologies that lack interactive communication elements. The use of advanced NLP techniques has enabled the creation of patient avatars capable of engaging in meaningful dialogues, mimicking the unpredictability and complexity of real-life patient interactions.

The comparison of LLM-generated scripts with expert-generated dialogues revealed a high degree of lexical and semantic similarity, indicating that LLMs can indeed serve as a suitable alternative or complement to traditional scriptwriting methods. This is particularly relevant in the context of preparing nursing students for the nuances of patient care, where effective communication is crucial. However, challenges such as ensuring the clinical accuracy of dialogues and the ethical considerations surrounding the use of patient data for training purposes were also identified.

Looking ahead, several avenues for future research have emerged from this study. First, there is a need to further refine the LLM-based dialogue generation system to ensure even greater clinical accuracy and relevance. This could involve the development of specialized LLMs trained on domain-specific datasets or the incorporation of feedback mechanisms allowing nursing professionals to tailor dialogues to specific learning objectives.

Moreover, exploring the impact of these advanced training tools on actual patient care outcomes remains a critical area of research. Longitudinal studies could assess how skills acquired through LLM-enhanced VR simulations translate into the clinical environment, potentially influencing nursing practice and patient satisfaction. Additionally, considering the diverse linguistic and cultural contexts in which nursing care is delivered, future work could also explore the adaptability of LLM-generated dialogues to various cultural settings, enhancing the global applicability of VR nurse training simulators.

While our research has laid the groundwork for the integration of LLMs into nurse training simulations, the journey towards fully realizing the potential of these technologies in healthcare education is just beginning. Ongoing collaboration between technologists, educators, and healthcare professionals will be key to navigating the challenges and unlocking the vast possibilities of AI in enhancing nursing education and patient care.

7   Conclusion

Our investigation into the use of LLMs for generating dialogues in VR nurse training simulators has revealed substantial promise for enhancing nursing education. The application of ChatGPT, Bard, and ClaudeAI within this context signifies a notable advancement in simulating realistic patient-nurse interactions, a crucial component often missing in traditional training methodologies. Our findings underscore the potential of these models to create immersive, interactive learning environments that can significantly improve communication skills, a fundamental aspect of nursing that directly impacts patient care outcomes.

This research contributes to the evolving dialogue on the integration of human-computer interaction (HCI) technologies in healthcare education, demonstrating the practical benefits and challenges of implementing advanced NLP solutions in training simulations. By bridging the gap between theoretical knowledge and practical skills, the study aligns with the broader objective of preparing nursing students for the complexities of real-world healthcare settings.

As we look forward, it is clear that the journey of integrating AI and VR into nursing education is only beginning. The potential for these technologies to transform training practices and enhance patient care is immense, yet it necessitates ongoing collaboration among technologists, educators, and healthcare professionals. This study lays the groundwork for future explorations, aiming to refine these technologies further and expand their application within healthcare education to meet the demands of an ever-evolving clinical landscape.

Acknowledgment. This project has been funded by the Jump ARCHES endowment through the Health Care Engineering Systems Center.

A   Prompt used for Health History scenario conversation

Please generate a script between a nurse and a patient named John, a 26-year-old male admitted to the hospital for Chron's disease. John also suffers from anxiety and depression. The conversation should flow according to the criteria/topic given below. Please use "therapeutic silence" and incorporate similar elements of bedside manner into this script. Include the nurse asking medical-specific questions such as dates of surgeries, dates of last health exacerbation, dosages, names of specialists, etc. Ensure the patient and nurse refer to each other by their first name after introductions. The patient and nurse should not know each other's names until after the introductions.

1. Introduction- The nurse introduces themselves and clarifies how the patient wishes to be addressed.
2. Identifying information/Biographical Data
3. Chief Complaint/Reason for Seeking Care
4. Present Health Status/History of Present Illness
5. Past Health/Past Medical History (Immunizations and Communicable Illnesses, Allergies/Drug Reactions, Hospitalizations/Surgeries, Injuries, Medications)
6. Family History (Illnesses of a Familial Nature)
7. Personal and Social History
8. Review of Systems

B   Prompt used for Ordinary Bedside Conversation

Please generate a script with a patient named Sam Brown who is a 25-year-old male admitted to the hospital after suffering a fall from a ladder. Sam has a broken leg, a broken arm, and a deep abrasion of the skin over the shoulder. John also regularly drinks alcohol. The conversation should flow according to the criteria given below. Please use "*therapeutic silence*" and incorporate similar elements of bedside manner into this script. Include the nurse asking medical-specific questions about how the patient is feeling, current medications being administered, nutrition, if a family has been in to see the patient, along with resources the patient can use in case they need anything like a call light. Ensure both the patient and nurse refer to each other just by their first name after introductions. The patient and nurse should not know each other's names until after the introductions. The nurse tells the patient to wait for a doctor to visit his bed to solve the problems expressed by the patient.

In the later part of the script, the doctor interacts with the patient based on the information collected by the nurse. The goal is to depict a realistic and empathetic interaction between the healthcare professionals and the patient, considering both medical and emotional aspects. Criteria:

1. Introduction- The nurse introduces themself and clarifies how the patient wishes to be addressed.
2. Identifying information/Biographical Data
3. Chief Complaint/Reason for Seeking Care
4. Social conversation
5. Obtaining health and social information that will impact their care
6. Keeping the patient informed about the progress/ Eliciting patient perception about the progress
7. Health Education

References

1. Issenberg, S.B., et al.: Simulation technology for health care professional skills training and assessment. J. Am. Med. Assoc. (JAMA) **282**(9), 861–866 (1999)
2. Ayaz, O., Ismail, F.W.: Healthcare simulation: a key to the future of medical education–a review. In: Advances in Medical Education and Practice, pp. 301–308. Taylor & Francis (2022)
3. Kavanagh, J.M.: Crisis in competency: a defining moment in nursing education. Online J. Issues Nurs. **26**(1), 1–10 (2021)
4. Rubin, V.L., Chen, Y., Thorimbert, L.M.: Artificially intelligent conversational agents in libraries. In: Library Hi Tech, vol. 28, no. 4, pp. 496-522. Emerald Group Publishing Limited (2010)
5. Yang, R., Tan, T.F., Lu, W., Thirunavukarasu, A.J., Ting, D.S.W., Liu, N.: Large language models in health care: development, applications, and challenges. In: Health Care Science, vol. 2, no. 4, pp. 255–263. Wiley Online Library (2023)
6. Luxton, D.D.: Artificial intelligence in psychological practice: current and future applications and implications. In: Professional Psychology: Research and Practice, vol. 45, no. 5, p. 332. American Psychological Association (2014)
7. Kneebone, R., et al.: The human face of simulation: patient-focused simulation training. Acad. Med. **81**(10), 919–924 (2006)
8. Harmon, J., Pitt, V., Summons, P., Inder, K.J.: Use of artificial intelligence and virtual reality within clinical simulation for nursing pain education: a scoping review. In: Nurse Education Today, vol. 97, p. 104700. Elsevier (2021)
9. Brandt, L., Mostowfi, S.: Virtual reality immersion: enhancing physician communication to promote ethical behavior at the bedside. In: Chen, J.Y.C., Fragomeni, G. (eds.) Virtual, Augmented and Mixed Reality. HCII 2023. LNCS, vol. 14027, pp. pp. 419-429. Springer, Cham (2023). https://doi.org/10.1007/978-3-031-35634-6_29
10. Smith, M.B., et al.: The use of simulation to teach nursing students and clinicians palliative care and end-of-life communication: a systematic review. Am. J. Hospice Palliative Med.® 35(8), 1140–1154 (2018). SAGE Publications Sage CA, Los Angeles, CA
11. Deriu, J., et al.: Survey on evaluation methods for dialogue systems. Artif. Intell. Rev. **54**, 755–810 (2021)
12. Jeddi, Z., Bohr, A.: Remote Patient Monitoring Using Artificial Intelligence. In: Artificial Intelligence in Healthcare, pp. 203–234. Elsevier (2020)
13. Adlakha, V., BehnamGhader, P., Lu, X.H., Meade, N., Reddy, S.: Evaluating correctness and faithfulness of instruction-following models for question answering. arXiv preprint arXiv:2307.16877 (2023)
14. Xu, F.F., Alon, U., Neubig, G., Hellendoorn, V.J.: A systematic evaluation of large language models of code. In: Proceedings of the 6th ACM SIGPLAN International Symposium on Machine Programming, pp. 1–10 (2022)
15. American Association of Colleges of Nursing et al.: The essentials: core competencies for professional nursing education (2021)
16. Litman, D.: Natural language processing for enhancing teaching and learning. In: Proceedings of the AAAI Conference on Artificial Intelligence, vol. 30, no. 1. (2016)
17. Albright, G., Adam, C., Serri, D., Bleeker, S., Goldman, R.: Harnessing the power of conversations with virtual humans to change health behaviors. In: Mhealth, vol. 2. AME Publications (2016)

Evaluation of the Effect of Three-Dimensional Shape in VR Space on Emotion Using Physiological Indexes

Takato Kobayashi[✉], Narumon Jadram, and Midori Sugaya

Shibaura Institute of Technology, 3-7-5 Toyosu, Koto-ku, Tokyo 135-8548, Japan
{al20009,nb23107,doly}@shibaura-it.ac.jp

Abstract. Virtual reality (VR) enables a highly realistic experience. In recent years, there has been an increasing demand for VR-based space design, because it is easier to make design changes, saves cost compared to actual construction. When designing a space, it is important to create a comfortable environment for users. Understanding how elements such as color, shape, and materials affect emotions can help in the design process. Previous studies have evaluated the impressions of VR spaces and real spaces. However, the effect of space elements on emotions and impressions is unclear. Therefore, this study aims to investigate the effect of the space elements on emotions in VR space, focusing on the shape of objects. Physiological indexes were obtained during VR viewing using a pulse sensor and a brainwave sensor to evaluate emotions. The Semantic Differential (SD) method was used to evaluate impressions. The results showed the impressions of four types of VR spaces vary greatly depending on their characteristics. The results of the emotions show that spheres in VR space tend to induce relaxation and high arousal, while cones induce tension and high arousal.

Keywords: VR · Shapes · Emotion · Impression

1 Introduction

Virtual reality (VR) enables a highly realistic experience. In recent years, VR has been applied in various fields, such as entertainment, revolutionizing gaming, design, and commerce. In architecture, VR has been used as an evaluation tool to support decision making during the design process [1]. In a space design, designers typically develop and evaluate their designs. However, constructing the actual designs for the evaluation can be costly. In contrast, using VR for the space design allows users to easily change designs. Moreover, VR can save time and costs when evaluating various designs compared to the actual space design on the actual construction. Therefore, the demand for the VR-based space design has been increased.

Design a comfortable space that empathizes with the user's emotions is important in space design [2]. However, to design the comfortable space, there are difficulties to specify the elements of improving the comfortability of the space design. Since the space

© The Author(s), under exclusive license to Springer Nature Switzerland AG 2024
J. Y. C. Chen and G. Fragomeni (Eds.): HCII 2024, LNCS 14706, pp. 213–223, 2024.
https://doi.org/10.1007/978-3-031-61041-7_14

design constitutes various elements, including physical attributes (color, texture, shapes, empty spaces, etc.) and environmental factors (light, sound, temperature, humidity, etc.) [2]. Each element affects emotions differently. It is a challenge for designers to balance the elements to develop a space that empathizes with the user's emotions. Therefore, to design spaces effectively, it is necessary to understand how space elements affect emotions. In addition, the first impression of the space design also needs to be considered, as it could affect the user's interpretation and evaluation of the space. Therefore, evaluating emotions and impressions of a new space designs using VR is necessary to understand how space elements affect emotions and impressions.

Several studies have evaluated emotions and impressions of design spaces using VR. Yokoi et al. used the Semantic Differential (SD) method [3] to compare the impressions of a residential environment in VR and real space [4]. The results showed that the VR space evoked a pleasant mood, and there were differences between the impressions of VR and real space. Furthermore, it was easier to express impressions such as beauty, simplicity, and youthfulness but more difficult to express the impression, which is warmth and individuality in VR space. Yokoi et al. demonstrated that the SD method could evaluate mood and impressions in VR space. However, subjective evaluation methods, such as the SD method questionnaire, cannot provide real-time feedback due to the time required for responses. Therefore, Yokoi et al. did not evaluate the emotional changes experienced while viewing VR spaces. Moreover, it is unclear how elements in the VR space, such as colors, shapes, and textures, affect emotions and impressions.

Shapes are one of the essential design elements that can affect emotions. It can create specific effects, such as stability and weight [2]. Miura et al. investigated the influence of shapes (rectangular, cylindrical, conical, and spherical) using the SD method [5]. As a result, the impression of showiness, pleasantness, strength, warmth, and looseness are emotional factors due to color and shape. Miura evaluated the impression of three-dimensional shapes displayed on the screen. However, it is unclear how three-dimensional shape affects emotions and impressions in VR space.

To satisfy the requirements of the evaluation of the emotion and impressions in VR spaces, we evaluated physiological changes to clarify the change of emotion and evaluate impression using the SD method. Based on the evaluation, we focus on the "object shape," which could affect emotion and impressions in a space design. Since there are few investigations of the effect of different shapes in a VR space, emotion and impressions.

2 Method

2.1 Emotion Map

This study used an "emotion map" [6] to evaluate emotions. This method uses electroencephalogram (EEG) and heart rate variability (HRV) indexes to evaluate emotions based on Russell's circular model of affect [7]. The X-axis represents valence, and the Y-axis represents arousal. The HRV index was used for evaluating the valence level. The EEG index was used for evaluating the arousal level. The emotions of each stimulus were evaluated by mapping the average values of HRV and EEG indexes measured during a stimulus condition. The baseline for the emotion map is determined by the average resting state, which is assigned as the values at an origin point (x = 0, y = 0) on the emotion map. The distance and direction from the origin in both axes on the emotion map visualize the emotion evoked by stimuli. In this study, we used the emotion map to classify emotions into four categories: high valence/high arousal, low valence/high arousal, high valence/low arousal, and low valence/low arousal, as shown in Fig. 1

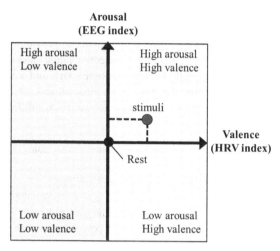

Fig. 1. The emotion map in two dimensions: valence (X-axis) and arousal (Y-axis) classified four categories of emotions. The origin point of emotion map is determined based on the resting state. The red point represents the classified emotion as high valence high arousal.

2.2 Physiological Indexes

To evaluate the emotions experienced while viewing the VR space, we collected physiological signals: EEG and HRV. These signals are highly reliable as they measure human emotions from the central and autonomic nervous systems (ANS) [8, 9]. We used the EEG and HRV indexes to evaluate emotions objectively based on the emotion map method. This method considers the possibility that emotions may not be expressed in facial expressions, as is the case, for example, with a "fake smile". We describe the physiological indexes used in this study as follows.

HRV is generally used to comprehend the autonomic nervous system. In this study, we used a pulse wave sensor (World Famous Electronics llc.) [10] to collected HRV data. We employed pNN50 to evaluate the degree of pleasure or displeasure [11]. pNN50 is a time-domain analysis HRV index, widely used as a parasympathetic index [12]. It is defined as the proportion of successive differences of RRI intervals that differ by more than 50 ms. In this study, a high value of pNN50 is interpreted as comfort, and a low value is interpreted as tension.

We used the High β/High α ratio as the EEG index to evaluate the arousal level [13]. This ratio represents the power spectrum of High β to High α obtained from the brainwave sensor (NeuroSky Inc.'s MindWave Mobile 2) [14]. The summary of the frequency range and interpretations of the EEG obtained from MindWave Mobile 2 is shown in Table 1 In this study, a higher ratio indicates a higher level of arousal.

2.3 Subjective Evaluation

We used the SD method to evaluate impressions of three-dimensional shapes in VR space. The SD is a scale to measure an individual's subjective perception and emotional responses using contrasting pairs of adjectives. In this study, we chose 11 pairs of adjectives to describe impressions of shapes, referring to previous study [5]. In their experiment, factor analysis was performed on 27 adjective pairs, categorized into six factors: showiness, pleasantness, strength, looseness, complexity, and warmth. We selected three significant adjective pairs from the showiness, pleasantness, and looseness factors and one significant adjective pair from the complexity and warmth factors. In addition,

Table 1. EEG frequency bands and related mental states [15].

EEG Index	Frequency Band (Hz)	Related mental states
δ	1–3	Deep sleep without dreaming, unconscious
θ	4–7	Fantasy, imaginary, dream
Low α	8–9	Relaxed, peaceful, conscious
High α	10–12	Relaxed but focus
Low β	13–17	Thinking, aware of self & surroundings
High β	18–30	Alertness, agitation, irritability
Low γ	31–40	Memory, higher mental activity
Mid γ	41–50	Visual information processing

Table 2. The adjective pairs used in this study.

No	SD adjective pairs
1	showy - sober
2	restless - calm
3	beautiful - ugly
4	favorite - dislikable
5	tense - relaxed
6	dark - bright
7	curved - straight
8	simple - complex
9	warm - cool
10	vulgar - refined
11	dynamic - static
12	narrow - wide

we included the narrow-wide pair to account for space-specific expressions. The adjective pairs used in this study are shown in Table 2. Note that the original questionnaire is in Japanese language. The adjective pairs used in this paper is translated version.

3   Experiment

3.1   Experimental Setup

In this experiment, we aim to clarify the effect of three-dimensional shapes on emotions and impressions in VR spaces. We conducted an experiment in which participants viewed four types of VR spaces. Each VR space was arranged with the same three-dimensional shapes but different sizes. In this experiment, we used the head-mounted display (HMD), Meta Quest 2, to view the VR space. To collect EEG and HRV data, we use a pulse sensor and brainwave sensor, as shown in Fig. 2. The Mindwave Mobile2 was chosen as the brainwave sensor for the experiment because it could be attached to the Head-Mounted Display without causing electrode interference. In the experiment, participants were instructed to wear the HMD first, followed by the brainwave sensor. The EEG electrodes were carefully attached to the HMD to avoid interference. Figure 2 shows the experimental scene where the participant wears the HMD and sensors.

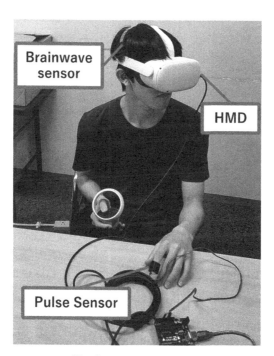

Fig. 2. Experimental scene

3.2   Four Types of VR Spaces Arranged with Different Shapes.

We aimed to clarify how VR spaces with different shapes affect emotions and impressions. Therefore, we focused on the shapes of objects in the VR space. The three-dimensional shapes used in VR space were chosen for their potential to influence emotions and impressions during the VR experience. We created a VR space in Unity with four different three-dimensional shapes arranged (Fig. 3). To focus on the effects of shapes, we standardized the color of the floor and ceiling across all VR spaces. Moreover, we arranged three-dimensional shapes of the same size and position in each VR space. In the experiment, to minimize the effect of color, neutral colors associated with adjectives such as gentle, calm, and comfortable [16] were used for the ceiling, floor, and three-dimensional shapes. The four types of VR spaces arranged with three-dimensional shapes used in the experiment are as follows.

- Type 1: VR space for cubes (Fig. 3(a)).
- Type 2: VR space for spheres (Fig. 3(b)).
- Type 3: VR space for cylinders (Fig. 3(c)).
- Type 4: VR space for cones (Fig. 3(d)).

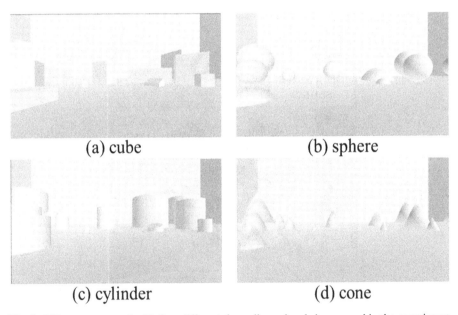

(a) cube   (b) sphere

(c) cylinder   (d) cone

Fig. 3. VR space arranged with four different three-dimensional shapes used in the experiment.

In the resting state, the participant will view a VR space for resting, as shown in Fig. 4. This VR space was created in the same color as the four other VR spaces without arranging any three-dimensional shapes.

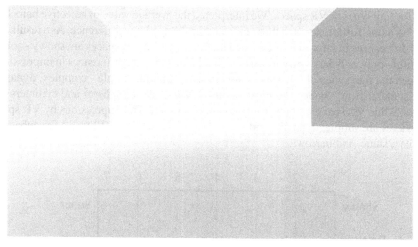

Fig. 4. VR space for resting state used in the experiment.

3.3 Procedure

Seven participants (two females and five males) in their 20s participated in the experiment. The experiment procedure is as follows:

1. Participants were asked to wear the HMD and practice answering a questionnaire using the HMD's interface until they felt familiar.
2. Participants wear the pulse and brainwave sensors.
3. Participants sit and rest for two minutes by looking into the VR space for resting state (Fig. 4).
4. Participants watch and look around the displayed VR space for 1 min.
5. Participants answer the SD-scale questionnaire.
6. Participants rest for one minute by looking into the VR space for the resting state (Fig. 4).
7. Steps 4–6 are repeated for watching VR space types 1 to 4. The VR space was displayed randomly.
8. After the experiment, the participants were asked to answer the questionnaire about the frequency of usual use of VR and the order of preference of the VR space displayed in the experiment.

4   Experimental Results

The results of the emotion maps by EEG and heart rate variability of the seven experimental subjects and the results of the questionnaire using the SD method are described below.

4.1   Result of Subjective Evaluation

We analyzed the value of all adjective pairs from the SD method across all participants to evaluate impressions in each VR space. Figure 5 shows the average values of 12 adjective pairs for four types of VR spaces. We interpreted the average value of adjective pairs less than 1 as a small difference, and those greater than 2.0 as a large difference. As a result, the small differences in impressions between the four types of VR spaces are showy - sober, beautiful - ugly, and dark - bright. On the other hand, the large differences in impressions between the four types of VR spaces are curved - straight, simple - complex, dynamic - static, and narrow - wide. The impressions of VR space for spheres and cylinders are curved, while VR space for cubes and cones are straight. The impressions by VR space for spheres are simple, dynamic, and wide. The impressions by VR space for cubes are complex, static, and narrow.

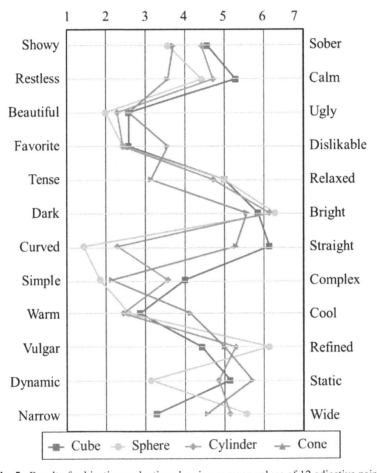

Fig. 5. Result of subjective evaluation showing average values of 12 adjective pairs.

4.2 Result of Emotion Maps

We compared the emotions evoked when viewing the VR space arranged with three-dimensional shapes to the first resting state (rest1). Based on the visualization method described in Sect. 2.1, we plotted the emotion maps using a combination of physiological indexes. The emotion map of each VR space was created using the average of pNN50 and High β/High α from all participants (Fig. 5). We calculated the average physiological index of the first 30 s while viewing the VR space to minimize the effect of feeling tired or bored. Furthermore, we considered the individual differences in participants' physiological indexes by normalizing the average within a range of -1 to 1. Figure 5 show the emotion maps illustrating the classified emotions during the resting state and four type of VR spaces (cube, sphere, cylinder, cone). The number of markers on the emotion map indicates the number of participants. The results of the emotion map of four types of VR space are as follows (Fig. 6).

- The emotion maps of VR space for spheres indicate high valence and high arousal in four out of seven participants.
- The emotion maps of VR space for cones, indicate low valence and high arousal in four out of seven participants. The number of participants that show the low valence are more than the others VR space. Only participant number 5 show high valence.

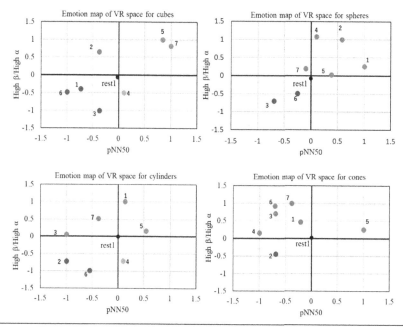

Fig. 6. The emotion map of four types of VR space (cube, sphere, cylinder, cone) for 7 participants. Each participant is denoted by a number from 1 to 7.

5 Discussion

We investigated the effect of four types of three-dimensional shapes (cube, sphere, cylinder, and cone) on emotions and impressions. As the subjective evaluation results, the impressions of four types of VR spaces vary greatly depending on their characteristics. However, there are tendencies of similar impressions. Spheres and cylinders tend to show a curved impression, while cubes and cones show a straight impression. Based on the results shown on the emotion maps (Fig. 5), we found that spheres in VR space tend to induce relaxation and high arousal, while cones in VR space tend to induce tension and high arousal. From the results of the adjective pairs of "tense-relax" (Fig. 5). Sphere show a tendency toward relaxation, while cone show a tendency toward tension. This result matches the emotional map results.

In this study, we observed the effect of spheres and cones on emotions. However, the effects of cubes and cylinders are unclear. Further investigation is necessary. In the future, we will construct VR spaces that are closer to real spaces and evaluate the effect of different shapes arranged in VR on emotions and impressions. Then, evaluate whether there are differences between the real space and the VR space. In addition, since the visual sense is often used in VR, which could potentially affect the activity of the occipital lobe responsible for processing visual information. This study only used EEG indexes obtained from the frontal lobe. Therefore, future studies should consider using EEG indexes obtained from the occipital lobe, which contains the visual cortex, for evaluation.

6 Conclusions

This study aimed to clarify the effect of three-dimensional shape on the emotions and impressions. We used physiological indexes to clarify the change of emotion and evaluate impression using the SD method. In the experiment, participants were asked to view the VR space arranged with four types of three-dimensional shape: cube, sphere, cylinder, cone.

As a results, the impressions of four types of VR spaces vary greatly depending on their characteristics. The results of the emotions show that spheres in VR space tend to induce relaxation and high arousal, while cones induce tension and high arousal. This is supported by the impression results that associate spheres with relaxation and cones with tension.

References

1. Drettakis, G., Roussou, M., Reche, A., Tsingos, N.: Design and evaluation of a real-world Virtual Environment for architecture and urban planning. Presence (Camb.) **16**, 318–332 (2007)
2. Reddy, S.M., Chakrabarti, D., Karmakar, S.: Emotion and interior space design: an ergonomic perspective. Work **41**(Suppl 1), 1072–1078 (2012)
3. Osgood, C.E.: Semantic differential technique in the comparative study of Cultures1. Am. Anthropol. **66**, 171–200 (2009)

4. Yokoi, A., Saito, M.: A study of evaluation on psychological effects of virtual reality in a residential environment. J. Environ. Eng. **78**, 1–7 (2013)
5. Miura, T., Matsuo, K., Taniguchi, T.: Analysis of affective factors of colored three-dimensional shapes. Electron. Commun. Jpn. **92**, 41–54 (2009)
6. Ueno, S., Zhang, R., Laohakangvalvit, T., Sugaya, M.: Evaluating comfort in fully autonomous vehicle using biological emotion map. In: Advances in Human Aspects of Transportation, pp. 323–330. Springer, Cham (2021)
7. Russell, J.A.: A circumplex model of affect. J. Pers. Soc. Psychol. **39**, 1161–1178 (1980)
8. Suzuki, K., Laohakangvalvit, T., Matsubara, R., Sugaya, M.: Constructing an emotion estimation model based on EEG/HRV indexes using feature extraction and feature selection algorithms. Sensors **21** (2021). https://doi.org/10.3390/s21092910
9. Dzedzickis, A., Kaklauskas, A., Bucinskas, V.: Human emotion recognition: review of sensors and methods. Sensors (Basel) **20**, 592 (2020)
10. Pulse Sensor. https://pulsesensor.com/. Accessed 31 Jan 2024
11. Ikeda, Y., Horie, R., Sugaya, M.: Estimating emotion with biological information for robot interaction. Procedia Comput. Sci. **112**, 1589–1600 (2017)
12. Shaffer, F., Ginsberg, J.P.: An overview of heart rate variability metrics and norms. Front. Public Health **5**, 258 (2017)
13. Eoh, H.J., Chung, M.K., Kim, S.-H.: Electroencephalographic study of drowsiness in simulated driving with sleep deprivation. Int. J. Ind. Ergon. **35**, 307–320 (2005)
14. MindWave Mobile 2. https://www.neurosky.jp/mindwave-mobile2/. Accessed 01 Feb 2023
15. Nafea, M., Hisham, A.B., Abdul-Kadir, N.A., Harun, F.K.C.: Brainwave-controlled system for smart home applications. In: 2018 2nd International Conference on BioSignal Analysis, Processing and Systems (ICBAPS), pp. 75–80. IEEE (2018)
16. Yamashita, M.: Colors Associated with Emotions - A Study on Color Design of Facility Spaces for Recuperative Care of the Elderly. Otemae J. **9**, 289–316 (2009)

Affecting Audience Valence and Arousal in 360 Immersive Environments: How Powerful Neural Style Transfer Is?

Yanheng Li[1], Long Bai[2], Yaxuan Mao[1], Xuening Peng[3], Zehao Zhang[4], Antoni B. Chan[1], Jixing Li[1], Xin Tong[5(✉)], and RAY LC[1(✉)]

[1] City University of Hong Kong, Hong Kong, China
{lydia.yh-li,yaxuanmao2-c}@my.cityu.edu.hk,
{abchan,jixingli}@cityu.edu.hk, lc@raylc.org
[2] The Chinese University of Hong Kong, Hong Kong, China
b.long@link.cuhk.edu.hk
[3] University of Florida, Florida, USA
xuening.peng@ufl.edu
[4] The University of Waterloo, Ontario, Canada
z783zhang@uwaterloo.ca
[5] Duke Kunshan University, Suzhou, China
xin.tong@dukekunshan.edu.cn

Abstract. Immersive experiences in Virtual Reality (VR) platforms often require customized content that can be adapted to in-game situations and specific player actions that lead to individualized effects. Controlling the positive-negative emotional valence and the level of arousal of the immersive content allows VR systems to provide situation-specific and action-specific affective influence on players, giving them an experience that is tailor-made for the narrative and interaction espoused by the system. To generate different emotional influences for the same content, we created a system that uses Neural Style Transfer (NST) along with a set of style images with known affective ratings to procedurally generate different versions of the same 360 environments in VR with differing affective influences for players. To explore how the NST-generated VR affects participants' affective perception, we conducted two user studies (N=30 and N=28). Users experienced four separate VR environments with different affective ratings. After each experience, we performed a survey to evaluate their affection, including Emotional Matching Tasks and interviews. Findings suggested that users are more likely to be aware of arousal differences than valence differences, which are mainly perceived by the degree of contrast between color and content of the environment. The stylized features gained from NST that affect the perception of valence are the color tone, the clarity of the texture, and the familiarity of the content for the user. Our work contributes novel insight into how users respond to generated VR environments and provides a machine-learning-based strategy for constructing an immersive environment to influence the affective experience of users, without altering any content and the game mechanism.

© The Author(s), under exclusive license to Springer Nature Switzerland AG 2024
J. Y. C. Chen and G. Fragomeni (Eds.): HCII 2024, LNCS 14706, pp. 224–243, 2024.
https://doi.org/10.1007/978-3-031-61041-7_15

Keywords: Neural Style Transfer · 360 Image Generation · Affective VR · Affective Experience · Human-computer Interaction

1   Introduction

The immersive Virtual Reality (VR) environment can elicit affective responses through simulating different sensory experiences; for example, horrible lighting and sound effects could be used in VR game environments to stimulate users' negative affection [46,55]. In a narrative VR environment, especially VR games, visual design is a significant component of drawing users into specific affective states [59]. When we engage in VR games, observing and evaluating the aesthetic elements is an important means for us to perceive emotions in the game [18]. However, it is challenging to construct an immersive environment by adjusting precise details for particular emotional influence [62]. Some VR designers usually alter the affective states by arranging different game objects in the computer-graphic engine [9], while others import pre-recorded 360 images/video sequences into the engine to build a 360 virtual environment [42]. These approaches may take much time for the designer to prepare the properties.

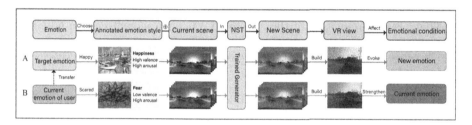

Fig. 1. Emotion-driven affective VR generation system. The *Path A* describes an approach to generate an affective VR environment based on the intention of the designer. For example, the designers want the user to be happy in a future environment; they could choose a series of style images from the datasets annotated with "happy" and then use them to perform Neural style transfer. The output 360 images could be used to construct a VR environment and evoke target emotion after the user experience each time. The emotion resource in *Path B* comes from the current affective condition of users, which may be detected with affective computing or self-report. So the selection of style images is based on the user. After generation, the user will experience the same but a more robust emotional environment to enhance the original emotion.

In non-VR video games, Artificial Intelligence (AI) has provided many benefits for reducing work in game development. Procedural Content Generation (PCG) techniques have been used in the video games industry to generate specific types of content, e.g., sounds, images, game levels, characters, textures, and dialogue [34]. Many Generative AI (GAI) techniques are employed to make the content creation process more effective and accessible. For example, Chat-GPT [40] is helping with brainstorming stories [36] and facilitating dialogue [57];

DALL-E-2 [45] produces images properties allowing users using natural language prompts; Dream Fields is another model using the free-text prompt to achieve 3D object generation [30]. For controlling users' affective experiences, some other studies propose Emotion-Driven Adaptivity, an approach to adjusting the game mechanics to help users improve their in-game behavior after recognizing their affective state [51]. AI acts as an agent in the system to adjust pre-set contents to create new narratives and experiences. Though these GAI techniques are helpful for generating game content more quickly than before, designers may need to take much effort into trying different prompts to figure out the appropriate emotion-specific outcomes. They may also need to assemble all the components in the game engine manually. Thus, in terms of the core problem of emotion-specific VR environment development, an ML-based generation strategy still needs further exploration.

With all these opportunities for creating the adaptive emotional environment procedurally, there is limited research on investigating what exact properties should be adaptively changed for eliciting specific affective experiences, and how these NST-generated VR environments affect users' perception during the experience. Thus, we set the following **research questions**:

- What affective experience can be affected by the ML-based VR environment generation?
- What visual parameters of the generated VR environment can be adjusted to obtain the corresponding affective experience?
- How to control the changes of parameters for eliciting expected affective experience?

In our study, we employed Neural Style Transfer (NST) to generate affective 360 images and created a procedural VR-generating system. To get an environment with a definite emotion, we chose images with different emotional annotations as style images to let the machine learn and transfer the affective features to the 360 content images. We then assigned the generated 360 images to the skybox to build an affective VR environment. After the VR was established, we invited several participants to experience and measure their affective responses using multiple methods, including Emotional Matching tasks (EMT) and interviews. We conducted a formative study in static 360 environments and a formal study in navigated based VR environments. In the pre-study, we built four virtual environments with different valence and arousal values based on a single 360 image, in which the participants can only experience a static environment at a time. We measured the affective states of the participants after each experience. However, their emotional responses in the valence test groups differed from what was expected. Therefore, we modified the VR environments based on the comments provided by the participants in the interviews, and conducted our formal study, where we built the VR environment based on multiple 360 images and a navigation system to make the participant more immersive and thus enhance the affective stimulation.

Using AI to generate a 360-images-based affective VR environment with images of known emotions has many potential applications, which we discuss at the end of this paper. Our **contributions** are:

- We proposed an affective VR generating system using the NST approach (Fig. 1), which could help create affective VR environments without altering content.
- We contributed novel insights about how users responded to generative VR environments by reporting the survey and interview results of formative study (N=30) and formal study (N=28) on how people perceived the affective state of our generated VR environments and what specific visual elements influenced their perception and affective response. The results suggested that our method with discrete emotional word style images dataset could effectively elicit the corresponding affective responses. Transferred color and texture are the key visual elements that took effect. Moreover, generated color and texture have interactive effects when affecting user's affective state in the generated VR environments.
- We ended by discussing the potential applications of our generation system in real VR affective narrative space and game scenarios that automatically alter the affective state of the current environment. We also discussed how our findings of the visual components that affected the emotional expressions of AI-generated images could contribute to the prompt engineering in Artificial Intelligence Generated Content (AIGC) field.

2   Related Work

2.1   Emotion Measurement

A classic example of emotion measurement tools is "six basic emotions" proposed by Ekman: anger, disgust, fear, joy, sadness, and surprise [13]. Dimensional models, on the other hand, attempt to conceptualize human emotions by defining where they lie in multidimensional spaces [43]. For instance, the "circumplex model of affect" developed by James Russell suggests a two-dimensional circular space, containing valence and arousal values [48]. Valence measures the degree of an emotion being perceived as positive and negative; while arousal evaluates how strong the emotion is being felt. Psychologists also use the Positive Activation – Negative Activation (PANA) model [60] to measure self-reported positive and negative affect when testing whether emotions are influenced [25]. However, studies indicate that this model may be limited only to activating emotion states. Positive Activation scores have been found to increase during anger, suggesting that it does not always measure positivity but may be sensitive to approach motivation [26].

Our study applied the EMT instead to deal with the drawbacks of previous methods [37]. This method aims to examine people in emotion perception with multiple experiment components [56]. Different from other evaluations, the EMT considers multi-modal information of emotions, including emotional facial expressions (more than four basic emotional labels) [39], emotional words and emotional situations to compensate for the inaccuracy of positivity measuring in PANA model [2]. Therefore, our study adopted EMT to evaluate human affective states for more accurate and reliable results.

2.2 ML/AI Method for Affective Environment Generation

The use of NST leads to rapid generation and iteration of artwork production. People can use Convolutional Neural Networks (CNNs) to render a content image in different styles [21,22,32]. Based on the new method of image style transfer, the researchers use neural representations learned by CNNs to separate and recombine the content and style of arbitrary images, generating a similar image with the content image, and the style has also been reconstructed simultaneously. They work with the 19-layer VGGNet [52] pre-trained on ImageNet [11], achieved a separation of image content from style, then allowed synthesizing an image that combines the content of one image with style from another [21]. Style Transfer is not only applied in 2D images. For spherical images, researchers address the emerging demand for 3D movies or VR/AR [8]. A feed-forward network is proposed for stereoscopic style transfer [8]. The researchers addresses the challenges of style transfers applied to 360 images by employing a cubic projection to remap the equirectangular projection to a set of six cube faces [47]. The style transfer algorithm is applied to each face of the cube separately, and this methods are time-consuming. Other researches proposes a method directly processing with the stereoscopic images [23], which inspire us to use 360 images to generate VR.

2.3 Affective States Elicitation via VR and Customized Affective Game Experience

To date, numerous studies have already examined applications of VR that have been used to construct real-life scenes with different settings to arouse different human affective status [5,6,16,24,58]. For example, five virtual parks with different scenarios in previous research could elicit a specific affective state respectively (i.e., joy, sadness, boredom, anger, and anxiety) [16]. In contrast, others attempt to induce specific affective status by adjusting the lighting conditions and sounds in real-life virtual scenarios [58].

From those researches, we observed that adjusting the visual elements of a VR environment could effectively alter the perception of the affective state for different scenarios [4,12]. Therefore, inspired by the VR-driven applications of human emotion elicitation, our study aims to verify whether creating a VR environment via 2D panorama images with annotated valence and arousal values could arouse people's diverse affective states, and how the effects differ with respect to altered valence and arousal indexes.

In order to make it easier to develop game environments with different emotional states, customized affective games with smart agents are needed to help quickly and automatically optimize the emotional quality of content for experience when the player enters the environment. In some earlier studies, researchers tended to use AI to automatically adjust the mechanics and dynamics of the game according to the performance of players, thereby changing the gameplay experience to affect the in-game mood [53,54]. In addition to changing the decision tree, recent research on experience-driven procedural content generation framework also focused on the player emotion modelling [61]. Others also change the environment, e.g., text and NPCs. They stimulated alien emotional experiences by producing resemble but novel narratives according to the real-time emotions of players [28].

2.4 Content Generation in Serious Game Application

Serious games, as multimedia learning systems, usually provide players with a variety of games and learning paths to help the growth and advancement of knowledge and experience [3]. Therefore, PCG, as a convenient creative tool, is often used to create personalized game experiences in terms of individual-related background. In the Orange Care, a PCG-serious game for conveying educational content about skin lesions to primary care physicians, the character generation is based on the text describing some physical aspects and the illness condition [41]. The rendering of the appearance of the characters could influence the in-game experience of the users. Shader and texture generation can help the game influence our experience automatically.

Friendly Adaptive Technological Tools Against Cyberbullying (ATTAC) project shows an approach to generating the whole game environment via graphical domain-specific modeling language, which communicates with a computer in an alike natural language [31]. That means semantic emotion words may be used for the affective game space generation in the sense of our project. Meanwhile, Hiramon combines player self-emotional reports and machine learning methods allowing game systems to learn the relationship between player behavior and emotional experience. The game is able to know when the player is experiencing a particular emotion that is undesirable. It will adapt accordingly to make relevant responses and optimize in-game emotional experience [19].

3 Technical Implementation Methodology

We applied the data-driven Arbitrary-Style-Per-Model Fast NSF [22] as a primary method to generate the images with different valence and arousal values. Prior to this, the transformation parameters were needed when changing the style from the original photo to the stylized photo. We employed the style prediction network in [22] to predict the transformation parameters of each style. Therefore, we can change the style of the content image using a single content image and another unlinked style image. In this standard NST model, *Frobenius* norm was used to minimize the difference of Gram matrix associated with the layer activations in style between the generated image and the content image, and $\mathcal{L}_2$-norm was used to minimize the difference of layer activations in style between the generated image and the reference style image.

In our experiment, we employed the pre-trained arbitrary image stylization model[1] [22] to perform fast artistic style transfer that works on arbitrary images. After performing NST and getting a new 360 output image, the 360 images was imported into Unity. Next, the texture shape of this 360 image was set as a cube and used to create a new skybox material. Finally, the material was assigned to the environment's material, thus rendering a panoramic view of the whole Unity scene. The VR camera was placed in the center of the whole scene. Once the scene was running in the VR headset, the users could experience the 360 scenes just like they were standing in a real 3D world.

4   Formative Study: Static 360 Scene Evaluation

4.1   Participants and Procedure

As reported in [33], we recruited 30 participants in this study (10 male, 20 female, from 18 to 38 years old ($M = 22.1$, $SD = 2.28$)). They were labeled with IDs from S1 to S30. The research procedures included a within-subject experiment in which the participants were assigned to four conditions with two different 360 content images (high valence, low valence, high arousal and low arousal VR environments) in random orders to avoid ordering effects. The first group, called the valence group, uses a 360 live performance image as the content image and two style images with inverse valence dimensions (high and low) as the input materials. The output images were imported into the game engine Unity to establish high and low-valence test environments. The other group is called the arousal group, whose content image is a 360 beach site image. Two style images with different arousal values (high and low) were used to influence the arousal condition of the test environment image. Every Participant was asked to watch four 360 outcome images in VR, as shown in Fig. 2. The VR conditions of different test groups were alternatively experienced (for example, high valence first, subsequent low arousal, then low valence, and last high arousal) to avoid decreased sensory perception after seeing two similar images continuously. In each experience, the participants were requested to accomplish an object-searching task in the environment within 4 min, ensuring to look through the whole environment. The objects the participants needed to search for were decided based on the content of the environment. Moreover, we also hoped the searching task would not distract the attention of the emotional experience as much as possible. Precisely, the participants were asked to count the number of people wearing the masks in the valence group because there were a lot of people standing around the participants in the VR environment. However, the arousal test environments contain very little human content but have a beautiful sunset beach view. Therefore, the participants were asked to find a favorite landscape of the environment. After each experience, the participants could have 5 min rest period, in which

---

[1] https://tfhub.dev/google/magenta/arbitrary-image-stylization-v1-256/2.

we conducted a short survey and interview to measure participants' affective states, and understand how NST-generated environments affected their affective experience. The Institutional Human Ethics Committee followed the whole procedures throughout the test.

4.2 Design of Test Materials

In order to test how the images generated by NST affect valence or arousal separately, we set two test groups (valence group and arousal group as shown in Fig. 2). Each group has a high and low-value environment for testing. All four style images were chosen from the Geneva affective picture database (GAPED)[2] [10]. We tried a series of style images with extremely distinct rating to make the outcomes show a striking contrast. For example, for the high-valence environment, we used a style image with a pleasant landscape and a high value (95 out of 100); for the low-valence environment, we used an image of scary spiders and a low valence value (12 out of 100). In our pilot test, we found that the landscape images in the P group (a group of pictures include human and animal babies as well as nature scenes) and the non-sense object images in the N group ((a group of pictures include inanimate objects) in the dataset are more suitable for our style images, because the pictures of other groups in the dataset are related to violence of moral and legal norms.

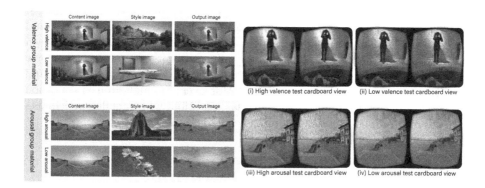

Fig. 2. Image materials for valence test group and arousal test group.

4.3 Formative Results

Discussion on Valence. Those images processed by NST are more likely to evoke negative emotions in the participants because NST introduces **textures that tend to reduce the familiarity and increase the negativity** of these

---

[2] http://www4.ujaen.es/~erpadial/GAPED.html.

content in the images to users. "I feel like the faces of these people in the environment are quite distorted, unlike what I would see in reality". Most participants mentioned this in the interview (take S1, S7, S8, and S9 as cases). People who stay in an unfamiliar environment may have negative emotions such as fear. Brighter colors are considered positive in psychology [27]. However, **the perception of emotions for the environment may be influenced holistically by the combination of visual style (the color and the texture) with the content**. Therefore, the negative content, like scary human faces, makes the brighter color create tenser feelings in this case rather than comfortable. Thus, when using NST to create positive emotions in images, it appears necessary to deal with the visual style of style image that affects the texture to make the content more familiar and positive, which could be related to individual imagination based on emotional memory, the memory of experiences that evoked an emotional reaction. For example, some participants said "The texture looks like Van Gogh's painting, which reminds me of the night he killed himself in the field". Meanwhile, the color also needs to match the content. The emotional responses are also interactively affected by both color and content.

Discussion on Arousal. Unlike the results from the valence test group, which were opposite to our expectations, participants responded high-arousal affective state in the high-arousal environment, while they felt calmer (low-arousal) in the low-arousal environment. **The content of the 360 environments** used in the different tests (arousal vs. valence) caused systematic differences in participants' responses. The content image of the valence test is a crowded indoor view, and the content of the arousal test is an open outdoor sightseeing scenery. The beach landscape, with the sunset and fewer people, makes it easier to recall people with some pleasant memories, so the content will not make them feel gross and scared (the high-arousal affective states). Moreover, the high-arousal condition had a **brighter color** than the low-arousal condition, which made participants have improved arousal levels, according to the interviews.

5   Formal Study: Navigation Based Evaluation

In the formative study, the perception of the valence differences from the participants was not statistically strong due to the blurred human content. We wanted to use the other content images with fewer human and outdoor views, the same as in the previous arousal test. The participants suggested in our formative study that their affective responses were weakened because of the sense of familiarity after looking at repeated content in a short period, which resulted in bias for the test analysis. Therefore, we tried to add more 360 content images as input to build a 360 navigation system like Google Maps, which allows the participants to explore more in a more extended period through rotating and changing their position by interacting with UI button using gaze cursor with the headset [49].

Moreover, navigation benefits the participants in clear recognition of the environment [17], which could help eliminate the unfamiliarity with the textured environment and enhance positive emotional responses.

5.1 Experiment Materials

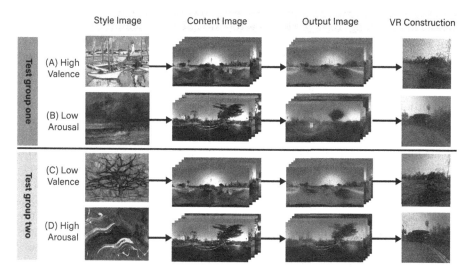

Fig. 3. Four VR environment construction and two test groups. The raw content images are used to build the control environments.

Design of Test Materials. In our formative study, we selected some annotated images from the GAPED dataset [10] as style images. They are mostly real-world landscape images. It is hard to justify what kind of visual elements in the style image have the affective effect that transferred to the 360 images. Therefore, in the formal study, the style images were selected from the WikiArt Emotion dataset[3] [38], which contains paintings from 195 artists. Artistic paintings could evoke an affective response in their viewers, and painters often express their personal emotions through every stroke, just as they imbue affective textures into their paintings [44]. Moreover, the emotion tags in the WikiArt dataset are more specific emotional words (e.g., happiness). As Fig. 3 shows, we randomly select four landscape paintings from the dataset to avoid getting strange textures from specific objects like human faces in some portraits. The emotional labels of these images represent high valence (happiness), low valence (fear), high arousal (fear), and low arousal (sadness). In addition to changing the style images, we add more content images to build a map for navigation in the VR environment.

---

[3] http://saifmohammad.com/WebPages/wikiartemotions.html.

We want to explore how it can influence emotional responses and improve the result by allowing them to experience in longer period and think about the situation.

Measures. Reliable and valid measurements are necessary to assess emotional knowledge with precision [39]. However, due to the complexity and invisibility of human emotions, the subjective choices made by individuals when asked to describe their affective state using a single word may be over-generalized [7]. The Emotional Matching Task (EMT) is a tool designed to facilitate effective communication and adaptive use of emotional expression. It comprises four parts: matching expressions, expression-situation matching, expression labeling, and expression label matching [1,2]. EMT can help participants reflect on their emotions and aid in assessing affective states.

In order to adapt the tasks for adults, we replaced the test materials with validated materials from the Geneva Emotion Recognition Test (GERT) and Geneva Emotion Knowledge Test (GEMOK), which were designed for adults but also assess emotional knowledge in similar task [50], [?]. The simple facial expression images in the first task were replaced with videos in the short version of GERT (GERT-S), which measures the ability to recognize emotions in the face, voice, and body of another person in a performance-based test [50]. Additionally, we provided participants with emotional word packages for the labeling task. Unlike children, adults are able to self-report their experiences verbally without the assistance of others, such as parents or teachers. Therefore, we required participants to self-report in the survey.

Participants and Procedure. We recruited 30 university students from social media interested in this topic (7 males and 23 females between 18 to 25 years old ($M = 21.5$, $SD = 1.23$)) as our participants. Two participants in the second test groups stopped the test due to VR sickness, so their data were not included in the results. We labeled the participants with IDs from P1 to P28. To avoid familiarity with the same content, we separated the participants into 2 test groups and conducted a between-subject experiment to make sure the contents of the environment were different in each group. Therefore, in Study 2, each test group of participants experienced 2 affective environments (Group 1: high valence*content 1 + low arousal*content 2, Group 2: low valence*content 1 + high arousal*content 2), and two control environments (raw 360 environments). The order of environment for each participant were randomized following a Latin square design. We engaged the participants in searching tasks as in formative study, allowing them to experience detailedly. After experiencing one VR environment, they are invited to fill out a questionnaire of EMT and some short answer questions about their related affective experience.

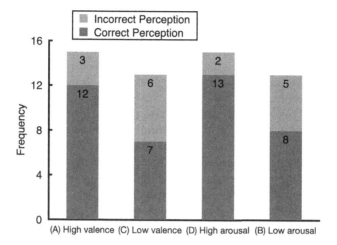

Fig. 4. Bar plot to show the ratio of correct perception in the four test groups. The bar is in order of high and low value for comparison, which is different from the group setting. This figure shows that in formal study, participants can correctly perceive specific emotion conditions, which means the NST approach can generate different emotional VR environments using different emotion-style images.

6 Formal Study Results

6.1 EMT Results Analysis

Each correct answer in the test is awarded one point, while incorrect answers receive zero points. The total score for each participant is calculated by summing up the scores for all the answers in each of the four parts of the test. A score of three or more indicates the successful perception of the expected emotion conveyed by the environment. As shown in Fig. 4, 80.0% of the participants in the high valence (A) group correctly perceived the expected affective condition, while 53.8% of the participants in the low valence (C) group correctly perceived the target emotion. 86.7% of the participants in the low arousal (B) group reported low-arousal affective responses, while those (61.5%) in the high arousal (D) group reported highly intense emotions. These results demonstrate that our generation strategy could effectively alter the participants' affective perception of the environment with annotated emotional style images.

6.2 Affective Stimuli

We list the factors that may influence the emotional responses of the participants for them to choose to help them investigate the concrete type of affective stimuli, including content in the environment, visual element, visual style, and spatial properties. We conducted a chi-square test to identify the differences in affective stimuli among different groups. The chi-square test reveals $x_2 = 3.327, p = 0.344$

(p >0.05), indicating that there are no significant differences among the types of stimuli in each group. It means there may not be one particular type (e.g., visual style) to affect the valence or arousal condition.

However, participants gave us feedback on the specific elements in the environment that evoked accurate affective responses, which can inspire us to perform the future generation.

Transferred texture can reshape the perception of particular game objects, thereby changing the emotional response. P1 mentioned *"water and waves"*, which do not actually exist in the content. However, the transferred chaotic texture changed a blue wall in the environment into a swimming pool full of water. Because of the misinterpretation of the object content, which directly influences the recall of specific emotional memories, the participant felt relief other than negative emotions. This is why some participants reported incorrect perceptions of the low-valence environment. Potentially, we may be able to segment some specific items in the environment images, on which we can perform style transfer separately, letting the texture change the perception of the content, in other words, create new items. We can also recombine the patterns together at last to produce the whole environment.

Dense texture can result in blurred vision and raise the sense of unfamiliarity and high arousal. P3, P4, and P7 said *"I cannot see clearly and get scared"* Clear vision may reduce emotional arousal and increase valence. If we want to generate a scary scene, we can adjust the style parameters to produce more texture.

Complicated texture will narrow the space. More textures will make the space properties more prominent. People may feel the space is blocked and cramped. P8 mentioned *"oil painting, boundary and small space"*. The complicated oil-painting style texture gained from the style image makes the VR environment seem to have an outer frame. The boundary narrows the whole space. The P12 said, *"When I was in B, it felt like being covered... which instantly reduced my positive feeling"*. It inspires us to reduce the clarity of the texture when making negative environments.

Mismatch of the color and content can raise arousal and negativity. P17 told us *"In the D environment, I felt bloody and terrified, and my emotions were intense"*. She also mentioned *"leisure park, contrast color, bright red and incompatible with the content"*. The style image may greatly contrast with the content image for high arousal and negative environments. On the contrary, low arousal and positive environments can use a style image with a more matched and similar color property.

7   Contribution and Future Applications

We employed NST to transform real-world panoramas into VR environments with varying emotional properties. Our study also explored the potential of NST to generate VR environments with affective qualities and identified parameters that impact affective perception. These findings can be valuable references for VR designers and psychologists interested in creating affective VR experiences.

7.1   Manipulate Affective State on VR Psychological Study

In the realm of psychological research, VR has become a popular material used by researchers [20]. VR environments have been developed with the purpose of helping users confront various situations in the real world. For instance, VR has been employed to aid autistic children with affective disorders in learning how to recognize real-world emotions [29]. Additionally, exposure therapy combined with real-world scenarios has been used to assist patients in reducing fear and recovering from anxiety [15]. The primary materials used to create such VR environments include real-life panoramic photographs and specific emotional targets. Thus, the method proposed in this paper could be applied in emotion-based experiments to help psychologists swiftly iterate and identify an appropriate experimental VR space, replacing the conventional method of manual shooting on location. This method could also provide multiple alternatives. Unlike the prior process of constructing a VR environment with a single design goal, the proposed method permits the testing of several design objectives in a short period, while also saving additional environments in case the utilized one fails to meet the expectations.

7.2   Interactive Customization in Emotion-Driven Games

As depicted in Fig. 5, a game development plug-in can be designed. The plug-in can be integrated into the development engine and game system. With this plug-in, game designers can generate a game environment more easily. After pre-selecting the style and content images, designers can input the datasets to the designer side system. The AI agent then quickly generates a library of numerous scenes that game designers can choose to build the storyline and game level. Designers only need to select relevant images based on their narratives through the UI panel. Once designers set the emotion by rating the valence and arousal value using the slider, the system can automatically combine images according to the affective condition and fill in the corresponding position in the storyline and game level. Consequently, game designers can concentrate on creating a good story without spending too much time on technical implementation. Moreover, players can also arrange the stories as their expectations from the UI panel on the player side by adjusting the valence/arousal values. The storylines and scenes are then automatically matched from the library to generate new levels, providing players with more freedom. This marks a significant improvement as compared to the previous PCG games, where the emotional experience could only be continuously enhanced according to the designer's wishes.

7.3   References for Text Prompts

Using a single emotional word in the generation system may not generate the images with appropriate affective visual features, because the AI needs more detailed information to tailor the generated outcomes. We tried to add some

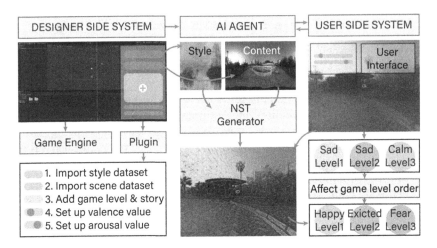

Fig. 5. Game application system hypothesis.

Fig. 6. Left is angry outcome, right is happy outcome.

descriptions of the affective feature we summarized in the prompt in the text-to-image generation system. For example, we prompt "low valence, high intense beach landscape, warm and red color tone, full of texture, blurred people." to generate a scary environment and prompt "high valence high-intensity beach land-scape, bright and relaxed color tone, clear texture, few people." to generate a happy environment. The outcomes are with quite distinct affective conditions, as shown in Fig. 6.

8   Conclusion, Discussion and Limitations

Our formative study justified the particular NST-generated visual elements that affect user's affection, and study two indicated how these elements take effect. The visual parameters that enable people to perceive the affective state of their environment are revealed through self-reports from participants. Typically, upon entering a new environment, people first pay attention to the content within it, such as seeing a park or observing individuals engaged in leisure activities. This content helps individuals quickly establish their understanding and familiarity with the environment. When utilizing NST to generate VR environments, it is important to prioritize the recognizability of the content. Transferred textures can then be used to blur or emphasize specific objects, eliciting either a pleasant or terrifying emotional experience within the environment. The color of an environment can significantly impact its perceived affective state. According to color psychology, red and orange are associated with warmth and cheerfulness, but they may also induce tension in some people [14]. Perception of color in combination with content varies significantly among different individuals. Color tone can directly impact arousal, with warm and strong colors typically resulting in higher levels of arousal [51]. Compared with a game called NEVERMIND [35], which assesses the emotions of the users by bio-sensors and needs to change the visual environment and gameplay mechanics to obtain particular emotional responses, our strategy Allows us only to generate a simple 360 environment with different content and objects to reach the same expectation.

Our study has some limitations. Firstly, the population of participants is not balanced and diverse enough, which may limit the generalizability of the results. Although we included tasks for participants, the VR experience may lack immersion because it is not a real game system that provides adequate interactions. Additionally, our measurement was not an in-game survey, which required participants to take off their headsets to complete the survey outside the VR environment. This interruption might weaken the affective response during the survey and interview. Bio-technologies could greatly help assess the objective and accurate affective state in real-time, providing a more accurate reflection of participants' affective state. Furthermore, our NST model is pre-trained with arbitrary images, which may not be the most effective method for transferring the affective features of annotated emotional style images, although it is effective for affective generation, as indicated by our studies. Therefore, a fine-tuned model with emotional style images may help improve the generation outcomes and affective influence on users.

References

1. Alonso-Alberca, N., Vergara, A.I., Fernández-Berrocal, P., Johnson, S.R., Izard, C.E.: The adaptation and validation of the emotion matching task for preschool children in Spain. Int. J. Behav. Dev. **36**(6), 489–494 (2012). https://doi.org/10.1177/0165025412462154
2. Alonso-Alberca, N., Vergara, A.I., Zappulla, C., Di Maggio, R., Pace, U., Sheffler, K.F.: Cross-cultural validity of the emotion matching task. J. Child Fam. Stud. **29**(4), 1159–1172 (2020)
3. Alvarez, J., Djaouti, D., et al.: An introduction to serious game definitions and concepts. Serious Games simul. Risks Manage. **11**(1), 11–15 (2011)
4. i Badia, S.B., et al.: Toward emotionally adaptive virtual reality for mental health applications. IEEE J. Biomed. Health Inform. **23**(5), 1877–1887 (2018)
5. Baños, R.M., Botella, C., Rubió, I., Quero, S., García-Palacios, A., Alcañiz, M.: Presence and emotions in virtual environments: the influence of stereoscopy. Cyberpsychol. Behav. **11**(1), 1–8 (2008)

6. Baños, R.M., Etchemendy, E., Castilla, D., García-Palacios, A., Quero, S., Botella, C.: Positive mood induction procedures for virtual environments designed for elderly people. Interact. Comput. **24**(3), 131–138 (2012)
7. Berrios, R.: What is complex/emotional about emotional complexity? Front. Psychol. **10**, 1606 (2019)
8. Chen, D., Yuan, L., Liao, J., Yu, N., Hua, G.: Stereoscopic neural style transfer. In: Proceedings of the IEEE Conference on Computer Vision and Pattern Recognition, pp. 6654–6663 (2018)
9. Craig, A.B., Sherman, W.R., Will, J.D.: Developing virtual reality applications: foundations of effective design. Morgan Kaufmann (2009)
10. Dan-Glauser, E.S., Scherer, K.R.: The Geneva affective picture database (gaped): a new 730-picture database focusing on valence and normative significance. Behav. Res. Methods **43**(2), 468–477 (2011)
11. Deng, J., Dong, W., Socher, R., Li, L.J., Li, K., Fei-Fei, L.: ImageNet: a large-scale hierarchical image database. In: 2009 IEEE Conference on Computer Vision and Pattern Recognition, pp. 248–255. IEEE (2009)
12. Dinis, S., Duarte, E., Noriega, P., Teixeira, L., Vilar, E., Rebelo, F.: Evaluating emotional responses to the interior design of a hospital room: a study using virtual reality. In: Marcus, A. (ed.) DUXU 2013. LNCS, vol. 8014, pp. 475–483. Springer, Heidelberg (2013). https://doi.org/10.1007/978-3-642-39238-2_52
13. Ekman, P.: Basic emotions. In: Handbook of Cognition and Emotion, pp. 45–60 (1999). https://doi.org/10.1002/0470013494.ch3, https://onlinelibrary.wiley.com/doi/abs/10.1002/0470013494.ch3, section: 3 _eprint: https://onlinelibrary.wiley.com/doi/pdf/10.1002/0470013494.ch3
14. Elliot, A.J., Maier, M.A.: Color psychology: effects of perceiving color on psychological functioning in humans. Annu. Rev. Psychol. **65**(1), 95–120 (2014)
15. Emmelkamp, P.M., Bruynzeel, M., Drost, L., van der Mast, C.A.G.: Virtual reality treatment in acrophobia: a comparison with exposure in vivo. Cyberpsychol. Behav. **4**(3), 335–339 (2001)
16. Felnhofer, A., et al.: Is virtual reality emotionally arousing? Investigating five emotion inducing virtual park scenarios. Int. J. Hum Comput Stud. **82**, 48–56 (2015)
17. Ferguson, C., Van den Broek, E.L., Van Oostendorp, H.: On the role of interaction mode and story structure in virtual reality serious games. Comput. Educ. **143**, 103671 (2020)
18. Frome, J.: Eight ways videogames generate emotion. In: DiGRA Conference, pp. 831–835 (2007)
19. Frommel, J., Schrader, C., Weber, M.: Towards emotion-based adaptive games: Emotion recognition via input and performance features. In: Proceedings of the 2018 Annual Symposium on Computer-Human Interaction in Play, pp. 173–185. CHI PLAY '18, Association for Computing Machinery, New York, NY, USA (2018). https://doi.org/10.1145/3242671.3242672
20. Gaggioli, A.: Using virtual reality in experimental psychology. Towards Cyberpsychol., 157–174 (2001)
21. Gatys, L.A., Ecker, A.S., Bethge, M.: A neural algorithm of artistic style. arXiv preprint arXiv:1508.06576 (2015)
22. Ghiasi, G., Lee, H., Kudlur, M., Dumoulin, V., Shlens, J.: Exploring the structure of a real-time, arbitrary neural artistic stylization network. arXiv preprint arXiv:1705.06830 (2017)
23. Gong, X., Huang, H., Ma, L., Shen, F., Liu, W., Zhang, T.: Neural stereoscopic image style transfer. In: Proceedings of the European Conference on Computer Vision (ECCV), pp. 54–69 (2018)

24. Guixeres, J., et al.: Effects of virtual reality during exercise in children (2013)
25. Harmon-Jones, C., Bastian, B., Harmon-Jones, E.: The Discrete Emotions Questionnaire: a new tool for measuring state self-reported emotions. PLoS ONE **11**(8), e0159915 (2016). https://doi.org/10.1371/journal.pone.0159915, https://www.ncbi.nlm.nih.gov/pmc/articles/PMC4976910/
26. Harmon-Jones, E., Harmon-Jones, C., Abramson, L., Peterson, C.K.: PANAS positive activation is associated with anger. Emotion **9**(2), 183–196 (2009). https://doi.org/10.1037/a0014959, place: US
27. Hemphill, M.: A note on adults' color-emotion associations. J. Genet. Psychol. **157**(3), 275–280 (1996)
28. Hendrikx, M., Meijer, S., Van Der Velden, J., Iosup, A.: Procedural content generation for games: a survey. ACM Trans. Multimedia Comput. Commun. Appl. (TOMM) **9**(1), 1–22 (2013)
29. Ip, H.H., et al.: Enhance emotional and social adaptation skills for children with autism spectrum disorder: a virtual reality enabled approach. Comput. Educ. **117**, 1–15 (2018)
30. Jain, A., Mildenhall, B., Barron, J.T., Abbeel, P., Poole, B.: Zero-shot text-guided object generation with dream fields. In: Proceedings of the IEEE/CVF Conference on Computer Vision and Pattern Recognition, pp. 867–876 (2022)
31. Janssens, O., Samyny, K., Van de Walle, R., Van Hoecke, S.: Educational virtual game scenario generation for serious games. In: 2014 IEEE 3nd International Conference on Serious Games and Applications for Health (SeGAH), pp. 1–8 (2014). https://doi.org/10.1109/SeGAH.2014.7067106
32. Jing, Y., Yang, Y., Feng, Z., Ye, J., Yu, Y., Song, M.: Neural style transfer: a review. IEEE Trans. Vis. Comput. Graph. **26**(11), 3365–3385 (2019)
33. Li, Y., Bai, L., Mao, Y., Peng, X., Zhang, Z., Tong, X., Ray, L.: The exploration and evaluation of generating affective 360 panoramic VR environments through neural style transfer. In: 2023 IEEE Conference on Virtual Reality and 3D User Interfaces Abstracts and Workshops (VRW), pp. 759–760. IEEE (2023)
34. Liu, J., Snodgrass, S., Khalifa, A., Risi, S., Yannakakis, G.N., Togelius, J.: Deep learning for procedural content generation. Neural Comput. Appl. **33**(1), 19–37 (2021)
35. Lobel, A., Gotsis, M., Reynolds, E., Annetta, M., Engels, R.C., Granic, I.: Designing and utilizing biofeedback games for emotion regulation: The case of nevermind. In: Proceedings of the 2016 CHI Conference Extended Abstracts on Human Factors in Computing Systems, pp. 1945–1951 (2016)
36. McGee, R.W.: Annie Chan: Three short stories written with chat GPT. SSRN 4359403 (2023)
37. Mienaltowski, A., Lemerise, E.A., Greer, K., Burke, L.: Age-related differences in emotion matching are limited to low intensity expressions. Aging Neuropsychol. Cogn. **26**(3), 348–366 (2019)
38. Mohammad, S., Kiritchenko, S.: Wikiart emotions: an annotated dataset of emotions evoked by art. In: Proceedings of the Eleventh International Conference on Language Resources and Evaluation (LREC 2018) (2018)
39. Morgan, J.K., Izard, C.E., King, K.A.: Construct validity of the emotion matching task: preliminary evidence for convergent and criterion validity of a new emotion knowledge measure for young children. Soc. Dev. **19**(1), 52–70 (2010)
40. OpenAI: ChatGPT: a generative model for conversation. OpenAI Blog (2021). https://openai.com/blog/chat-gpt/

41. Pereira, Y.H., Ueda, R., Galhardi, L.B., Brancher, J.D.: Using procedural content generation for storytelling in a serious game called orange care. In: 2019 18th Brazilian Symposium on Computer Games and Digital Entertainment (SBGames), pp. 192–197. IEEE (2019)
42. Pirker, J., Dengel, A.: The potential of 360° virtual reality videos and real VR for education–a literature review. IEEE Comput. Graph. Appl. **41**(4), 76–89 (2021)
43. Posner, J., Russell, J.A., Peterson, B.S.: The circumplex model of affect: An integrative approach to affective neuroscience, cognitive development, and psychopathology. Development and psychopathology **17**(3), 715–734 (2005). https://doi.org/10.1017/S0954579405050340, https://www.ncbi.nlm.nih.gov/pmc/articles/PMC2367156/
44. Prinz, J.: Emotion and aesthetic value. In: American Philosophical Association Pacific Meeting, vol. 15. Kluwer Dordrecht (2007)
45. Ramesh, A., et al.: Zero-shot text-to-image generation. arXiv preprint arXiv:2102.12092 (2021)
46. Riva, G., et al.: Affective interactions using virtual reality: the link between presence and emotions. Cyberpsychol. Behav. **10**(1), 45–56 (2007)
47. Ruder, M., Dosovitskiy, A., Brox, T.: Artistic style transfer for videos and spherical images. Int. J. Comput. Vis. **126**(11), 1199–1219 (2018)
48. Russell, J.A.: A circumplex model of affect. J. Pers. Soc. Psychol. **39**(6), 1161–1178 (1980). https://doi.org/10.1037/h0077714
49. Sauzéon, H., N'Kaoua, B., Arvind Pala, P., Taillade, M., Guitton, P.: Age and active navigation effects on episodic memory: a virtual reality study. Br. J. Psychol. **107**(1), 72–94 (2016)
50. Schlegel, K., Scherer, K.R.: Introducing a short version of the Geneva emotion recognition test (GERT-S): Psychometric properties and construct validation. Behav. Res. Methods **48**(4), 1383–1392 (2016)
51. Schrader, C., Brich, J., Frommel, J., Riemer, V., Rogers, K.: Rising to the challenge: an emotion-driven approach toward adaptive serious games. In: Serious Games and Edutainment Applications : Volume II, pp. 3–28 (2017). https://doi.org/10.1007/978-3-319-51645-5_1
52. Simonyan, K., Zisserman, A.: Very deep convolutional networks for large-scale image recognition. arXiv preprint arXiv:1409.1556 (2014)
53. Smith, G.: Understanding procedural content generation: a design-centric analysis of the role of PCG in games. In: Proceedings of the SIGCHI Conference on Human Factors in Computing Systems, pp. 917–926 (2014)
54. Smith, G., Gan, E., Othenin-Girard, A., Whitehead, J.: PCG-based game design: enabling new play experiences through procedural content generation. In: Proceedings of the 2nd International Workshop on Procedural Content Generation in Games, pp. 1–4 (2011)
55. Somarathna, R., Bednarz, T., Mohammadi, G.: Virtual reality for emotion elicitation – a review. IEEE Trans. Affect. Comput., 1–21 (2022). https://doi.org/10.1109/TAFFC.2022.3181053
56. Sullivan, S., Ruffman, T.: Emotion recognition deficits in the elderly. Int. J. Neurosci. **114**(3), 403–432 (2004)
57. Sun, Y., Xu, Y., Cheng, C., Li, Y., Lee, C.H., Asadipour, A.: Travel with wander in the metaverse: an AI chatbot to visit the future earth. In: 2022 IEEE 24th International Workshop on Multimedia Signal Processing (MMSP), pp. 1–6. IEEE (2022)
58. Toet, A., van Welie, M., Houtkamp, J.: Is a dark virtual environment scary? Cyberpsychol. Behav. **12**(4), 363–371 (2009)

59. Troxler, M., Qurashi, S., Tjon, D., Gao, H., Rombout, L.: The virtual hero: the influence of narrative on affect and presence in a VR game. In: CEUR Workshop Proceedings (2018). http://afcai18.webs.upv.es/index.html, affective Computing and Context Awareness in Ambient Intelligence
, AfCAI ; Conference date: 19-04-2018 Through 20-04-2018
60. Watson, D., Tellegen, A.: Toward a consensual structure of mood. Psychol. Bull. **98**(2), 219–235 (1985). https://doi.org/10.1037/0033-2909.98.2.219, place: US
61. Yannakakis, G.N., Togelius, J.: Experience-driven procedural content generation. IEEE Trans. Affect. Comput. **2**(3), 147–161 (2011). https://doi.org/10.1109/T-AFFC.2011.6
62. Zyda, M.: From visual simulation to virtual reality to games. Computer **38**(9), 25–32 (2005)

Exploring User Preferences for Walking in Virtual Reality Interfaces Through an Online Questionnaire

Ata Otaran[1] and Ildar Farkhatdinov[2,3]([⊠])

[1] Department of Computer Science, Saarland University, Saarbrücken, Germany
[2] School of Engineering and Materials Science, Queen Mary University of London, London, UK
[3] Imperial College of Science, Technology and Medicine, London, UK
`i.farkhatdinov@qmul.ac.uk`

Abstract. This paper presents an overview of human-machine interfaces for walking in virtual reality (VR) and the results of the online survey in which 30 experienced VR users were asked to identify important design aspects and preferable types of interfaces for walking in VR. The survey results provided valuable insight into the experience and preferences of experienced VR users on VR locomotion interfaces. Over 90% of the responders used joysticks and/or "point and teleport" to navigate virtual reality scenes. Approximately 34–44% of the responders used body gestures (walk-in-place, arm swing, hand gesture for flying) to control walking/motion in VR. Less than 30% of the responders used other types of interfaces (treadmill, seated interface with leg gestures, treadmill, slidemill) for walking control. Motion sickness and the use of body-based inputs were selected as important design aspects.

Keywords: virtual reality · locomotion · user evaluation

1 Introduction

More than 30 years of research in the area of virtual reality (VR) locomotion has provided us many different taxonomies to choose from for deciding how to move our avatar inside a VR environment [34,37]. Examples of different types of interfaces to control locomotion in VR that are considered in this study include joystick-based control [32], treadmill walking [51], arm swinging in place [36], slidmills [14], point and teleport method [11], walking-in-place [60], redirected walking [47], seated interfaces with leg tracking [40], hand gestures for floating/flying [49]. Figure 1 demonstrates the examples of such walking in VR interfaces.

There is no clear rule of thumb for deciding which method to use to optimize the locomotion experience with the facilities at hand. Although many taxonomies were evaluated for their advantages and shortcomings in the laboratory environment, many of these interfaces are not widely used by the general public due

© The Author(s), under exclusive license to Springer Nature Switzerland AG 2024
J. Y. C. Chen and G. Fragomeni (Eds.): HCII 2024, LNCS 14706, pp. 244–258, 2024.
https://doi.org/10.1007/978-3-031-61041-7_16

to the slow rate of adoption of VR hardware. The popularity and attainability of basic VR hardware have seen a tremendous rise in recent years which will unavoidably increase the adoption of various locomotion interfaces. In this paper, we present a user survey that compares various locomotion interface design considerations and existing solutions in terms of user preferences. The survey aimed to understand user preferences and important interaction features that can help to design better walking in VR interfaces in the future. The survey was organised online following existing research methods for remote XR studies [45].

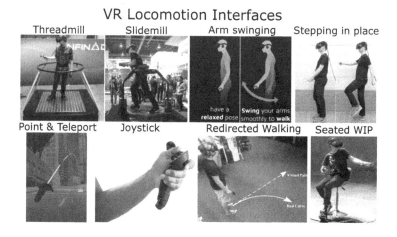

Fig. 1. Locomotion interfaces that are included in the survey

2 Overview of Existing VR Locomotion Interfaces

This section reviews the various categories of VR locomotion interfaces and discusses their overall advantages and disadvantages. We encourage the readers to look into the work of Di Luca et al. [34], which presents a library of locomotion interfaces using various taxonomies. We describe locomotion interfaces in terms of the user input they require and the sensory feedback they provide. The categories we define in Fig. 2 can be further extended, but for brevity we decided to discuss the most common approaches.

2.1 Joystick/keyboard and Mouse-Based Locomotion

Use of joystick and keyboard input based navigation is a method that has long been carried out with screen type visual displays. Keyboard based locomotion provides digital information of whether a key is pressed or not. When controlling the velocity of an avatar, generally a keypress gradually rises the avatar pace towards a specified speed to provide natural gait simulation and better control over the avatar speed. Applications generally allow the use of different keys to switch between different modes of gait, such as natural walking, running or sneaky approaching. Commonly used controllers include analogue sensors to allow better control over the speed of the avatar. These interfaces are compact, cheap and can be used for other interaction tasks with flat screen scenarios. Therefore many users are already proficient in using these interfaces and they are considered the basic choice of hardware with computer systems. Their main shortcoming is the lack of sensory feedback they provide to the user [48,59].

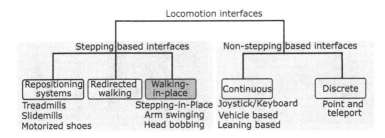

Fig. 2. Interface type categories

General VR controllers use a joystick structure that is accompanied by IMU sensors and motion tracking which allow the use of pointing and gesturing in a 3D setting for providing body-based inputs. This subsection only refers to the traditional use of digital and analogue input capabilities of these interfaces.

Although they suffer from a lack of sensory feedback, as discussed in the survey at the end of the Introduction section, joystick navigation is one of the most used methods of navigation in VR. Studies have shown that non-body based input devices (e.g. joystick or keyboard) can use the addition of stepping related vibrotactile [31,56] or proprioceptive feedback [27] for an improved locomotion experience.

2.2   Magical/Fantastic Approaches

In addition to the methods for controlling natural walking behavior, VR application developers utilise various beyond natural methods. This helps utilize the available controllers in effective ways to inspire and engage users. The point and teleport methods are currently one of the most utilised VR locomotion methods. The point and teleport method is easy to implement and works around the additional sensory requirements of a continuous body movement [12], therefore causes less motion sickness. Other magical or fantastic approaches include flying by like Iron-man by controlling boosters on the hand [4], or swinging like Spider-man between cliffs using grappling hooks [6]. The shortcoming of such dynamic and unnatural movements is that user reviews demonstrate a general complaint on the effects of motion sickness. The magical methods, including teleportation, provide an exciting and alternative method of locomotion; however, they do not provide the natural sensation of walking gait and generally employ the hands of the user.

2.3 Leaning Driven Interfaces

Leaning driven interfaces use the body pose or leaning angle to control the speed of the linear or rotational movement/steering of the avatar. This approach essentially uses the human body as a joystick and relates the avatar control to the whole body movement which provides a more embodied interaction compared to traditional joystick interfaces [22,30].

Guy et al. [20] propose the use of doing one step, bending the knees or bending the trunk forward and backward to animate the avatar's forward and backward movements, and using body rotation or sideways movement (rotating hips or shoulders and sideways leaning of hips or shoulders) for controlling avatar orientation.

Kitson et al. [29] compare locomotion by a traditional joystick and four different seated leaning based methods on a wide range of criteria. The participants found the embodied form of interaction useful but also thought that the traditional joystick was easier for commanding the motion. It should also be noted that some participants found the steering movement to considerably cause motion sickness. This is an important outcome as our interface also currently uses a leaning based rotation strategy, as will be discussed further in detail.

Leaning based interfaces simplify the necessary sensory requirements whilst requiring the movement of a larger portion of the body which can be associated better with walking forward and steering movements when compared to using a joystick. The movement of the body can be captured by using a sensorised chair [8], IMUs, motion capture [20], foot pressure distribution [31] or centre of balance measurement [21]. Body leaning movement sets the hands free for other manipulation tasks and provides an energy-efficient alternative to stepping based interfaces. However, these interfaces do not provide the efferent feedback of the walking interaction and rely on an unnatural locomotion metaphor, leaning induced floating or walking sensation. Another challenge of these interfaces is that pronounced backward leaning may cause the fear of falling [29].

2.4 Stepping Based Interfaces

Using natural walking movements to simulate avatar locomotion is advantageous as it provides a more natural body-based input compared to leaning based systems and provides the opportunity to control the avatar movement more precisely. Below we elaborate further on the advantages and disadvantages of each category of stepping based walking interfaces.

Repositioning type locomotion interfaces refer to systems which physically move the user towards the center of the workspace. Omnidirectional treadmills [16,24] provide the functionality of a treadmill on both horizontal axes enabling movement on all horizontal directions. Position controlled foot platforms are proposed for a reduced inertial load compared to a treadmill [66] and provide vertical movement [18, 26].

Virtusphere [35] proposes placing the human user inside a sphere and animate their VR avatar with revolutions of a passively revolving sphere. The sphere design provides omnidirectional movement but also causes serious instability, especially when the user wants to change speed or direction.

Iwata and Fujii proposed Virtual Perambulator [25], which uses omnidirectional roller-skates and a body harness to allow the user to stay at the same location while performing walking movements. Other similar interfaces propose using a slippery floor and shoes [54] instead of roller skates. These devices present the majority of the commercialised [2, 5] repositioning systems. These interfaces remove the actuation requirement which is the main problem with omnidirectional treadmills and requires relatively less space and money. However, for these systems, the harness not only works to provide safety in case the user loses balance, but the harness constantly applies force against the body that is the same amount as the friction force between the feet and the ground. This causes the user to have an unnatural forward-leaning body posture and the horizontal pressure on the pelvis area of the user may cause discomfort. Although the repositioning systems provide posture and walking kinematics that are close to natural walking, their space and money requirements cause them to be more appropriate for VR gaming arcades rather than home use.

Redirected walking [46] is a method which uses natural walking technique but overcomes the limitations of confined physical spaces by scaling the mapping for translation and rotation in VR. The user is constantly directed towards the center of the workspace by misrepresenting their movement VR and making them adjust their path subconsciously. Naturally, the user can detect if the movements are scaled by high gain value. Therefore, many studies have investigated appropriate gain thresholds and how they may differ depending on the user [13, 19, 64]. Predicting the future path of the user or regenerating the environment depending on the position of the user in the workspace are other factors that can provide a better redirected performance.

Redirection techniques still require plenty of walking area to operate. Therefore, it is either not easy to implement for home use or application developers need to introduce discrete break events to turn the user around if the user gets too close to the end of the workspace and it is not possible to turn the user around without exceeding the detection thresholds.

Walking-in-place (WIP) interfaces use walking-related periodic body movements (gestures or metaphors) to generate a realistic mapping of walking movement in VR. These gestures can be any movement resembling walking, such as marching-in-place, arms swinging, foot sliding/swiping, and head movement. While most of the standing interfaces utilized natural turning most of the seated interfaces resorted to gesture or joystick based methods.

Previous studies used various sensing tools to capture these motion inputs, such as ground force plates [10, 63], a grid of mechanical switch sensors [9], linear encoders on foot sliders [55], rotary encoder rollers attached under shoe [3] or knee exoskeletons [1], motion capture systems [17,36,50,57,62], and wearable inertial measurement units (IMUs) [33,58]. The selection of appropriate sensing technology for gesture based walking interfaces is important as it affects the cost, workspace requirements and ergonomics. High-quality motion capture systems require large workspaces and expensive tools [17,36,62]; on-off type switches or video camera-based motion capture systems do not provide high-frequency kinematic information [9,57]; and IMUs require careful adjustment and calibration for each user [58]. The reliability of the input received from the gesture sensing units is crucially important for capturing and achieving a higher fidelity simulation of the walking motion. If the input signal is available at higher frequencies and lower noise levels, more complex algorithms, offering movement output with more detail and less latency, can be implemented.

The quality of the sensing input and the complexity of the walking algorithm complement each other. While some of the initial algorithms provide a digital ON/OFF output [50,59], as walking or not walking, subsequent works aimed to utilize gesture speed [17,57], amplitude, frequency [62], and the combination of them [7,36].

2.5   Terrain Feedback During Walking in VR

Only few interfaces for walking in VR provide haptic terrain feedback. Such systems mainly recreated footstep haptic sensation [27,28,31,56] to improve a user's navigation awareness during virtual walking. However, those interfaces used manual input devices to generate virtual walking and therefore haptic feedback and locomotion control inputs were non-collocated. In [44,52,53,65] terrain-based haptic feedback was integrated in shoes. Vibrotactile rendering was employed to display different terrain types to a user during walking in VR. The advantage of such haptic feedback shoe systems is the ability to provide natural interactive walking input and feedback as they were integrated with external motion tracking; however, the limitation is the requirement to have a relatively large physical workspace. Another approach for terrain feedback is to use haptic rendering actuators integrated into the floor [15,27,61], but the described floor-integrated feedback methods require additional motion tracking systems and extra workspace for implementing realistic walking inputs. Interestingly, only a few devices for providing kinesthetic feedback for walking in VR have been developed. Large scale robotic exoskeletons [23,43] which provide force feedback to the user's lower limbs during walking in VR were presented; however, these devices were primarily proposed for rehabilitative locomotion training. An end-effector type force feedback device that can provide terrain-related feedback was presented in [26]; however, its main disadvantage is the large workspace requirement. Additionally, existing robotic end-effector feedback devices and wearable lower limb exoskeletons are complex in design and control, costly, and therefore less suitable for generic VR applications.

3   Methods for the Online Survey

An online survey was created using *Google Forms* service and distributed through multiple mailing list targeting virtual reality and computer gaming users. The survey included open-ended, multiple choice, rating questions and Likert scale ranking questions. The survey included the following questions with multiple choice answer options:

- **Q1.** How frequently do you use VR applications?
- **Q2.** Which of the below VR locomotion interfaces have you experienced before?
- **Q3.** Please order the interfaces/methods below in the order of your preference.
- **Q4.** If you have tried VR locomotion interfaces, could you please explain your experience with locomotion in VR so far?
- **Q5.** Agree/disagree with the statement: I prefer using body based inputs (arms/legs/trunk movements) compared to joystick or keyboard input.
- **Q6.** Agree/disagree with the statement: I would like to have a standing body posture rather than seated.
- **Q7.** Agree/disagree with the statement: I would like my hands to be free for manual tasks during locomotion.
- **Q8.** Agree/disagree with the statement: I would like the interface to offer me sensation (haptic feedback) of the terrain during walking
- **Q9.** Agree/disagree with the statement: I would like my body to be stable and balanced without needing of additional support during walking in VR (harness or other support).
- **Q10.** Agree/disagree with the statement: I would like to be able to rotate my whole body for turning in VR.
- **Q11.** Rate the features in the order of importance for you.

Additionally, the survey included questions on user preferences on both VR locomotion interface features, which play a major role in the decision process while designing a VR locomotion interface, and also specific VR locomotion interface categories. The features we selected to query on were the following:

- Using body-based inputs (arms/legs/trunk movements) compared to joystick or keyboard input.
- Standing vs. seated body posture
- Using hands for locomotion vs. keeping hands free for manipulation at all times
- Whether haptic terrain sensation is important or not
- Keeping body stable through additional support vs not risking instability during walking in VR
- Whole-body rotation vs using cues without performing full rotation for steering in VR.

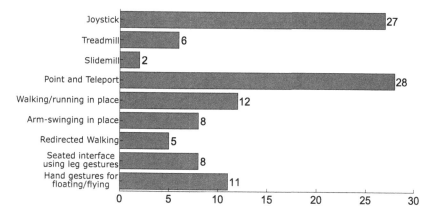

Fig. 3. Number of participants who experienced the locomotion interfaces, (out of the 30 participants).

4   Results

Participants and their Experience. Out of 30 participants who took part in the survey, 11 tried VR several times, 10 used it frequently (every week), 8 used it sometimes (every month), and 1 person used VR daily (Question **Q1**).

We asked the participants if they have experienced the VR locomotion interfaces listed below (Question **Q2**). The results are shown in Fig. 3. Since we were primarily concerned with walking-based locomotion interfaces our query included several popular methods (first three methods on the list) and various walking-based methods (rest of the list). As expected, the use of joystick input and point and teleport methods were the most widely utilized method among the available interfaces.

Selected Features. We asked the participants to rate the importance of selected VR locomotion interface features on a 7-point Likert scale (Questions **Q5-Q10**). The results are presented in Fig. 4. According to the responses, most of the participants (63%) find it very important to be able to rotate their bodies to induce turning movement. A significant number of the participants also dislike the requirement of additional support (harness) with locomotion interfaces. Many of the participants found it important for locomotion interfaces to use body-based inputs, however several of them also did not think they were important, meaning they favoured joystick-like lower sensory feedback modalities for VR locomotion. A similar outcome occurred for terrain sensation where 66% considered it was important or very important but few people considered it to be not necessary. Although more participants choose standing posture over seated, a considerable amount of participants (one-third) were indifferent to having a seated or standing posture for VR locomotion.

We also asked users to rank the above concepts to observe how participants prioritize one feature of a VR locomotion interface over another (Question **Q11**). For this questionnaire, we also added motion sickness and space requirements as

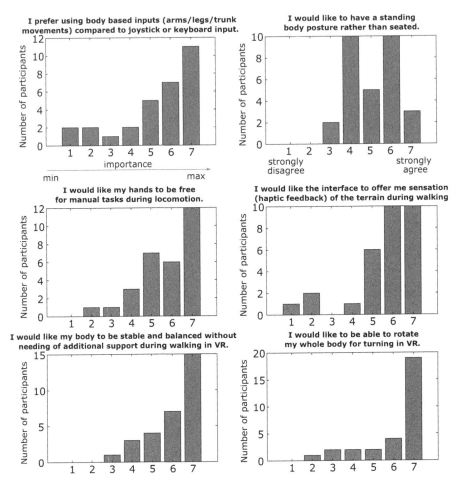

Fig. 4. Bar plots presenting the results of participant rating (7 point Likert scale) on the importance of VR locomotion interface features for a better VR locomotion experience.

interface features to be ranked. We omitted these in the rating question since we did not think participants would be indifferent to or supporting against having less motion sickness or space requirements.

Figure 5 presents the results of the interface feature ranking survey question. The plot shows the rankings on the top four positions on the right side of the central line and the last four positions on the left side of the line. The results show that the most important feature for the majority of users is reducing motion sickness. Using body-based inputs and small space requirements comes next in terms of the number of participants who rank them in the top four positions. Terrain feedback and standing posture can be considered as the two overall least preferred features. In fact, other than motion sickness, none of the features

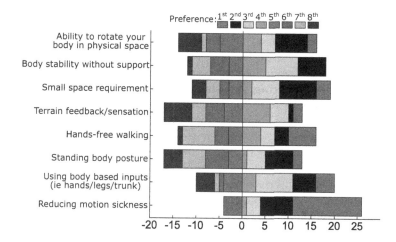

Fig. 5. Results of the ranking questionnaire, where participants are asked to rank VR locomotion interface features with respect to their importance. 1st denotes the most important feature and higher numbers denote less important features. The width of each rectangular region refers to how many users preferred the locomotion interface for the ranking corresponding to the colour of the rectangle

	Percent comparison scores (%)									Cumulative scores	N/A
	AS	HG	J	PT	RW	SLG	SM	TM	WIP		
Arm-swinging in place (AS)		50	75	46	29	85	30	60	64	4.39	17
Hand gestures for floating/flying (HG)	50		43	58	40	57	33	67	29	3.77	15
Joystick (J)	25	57		38	13	50	33	50		2.65	2
Point and Teleport (PT)	54	42	63		39	77	36	64	53	4.27	2
Redirected walking (RW)	71	60	88	61		83	50	44	55	5.12	19
Seated interface using leg gestures (SLG)	15	43	50	23	17		13	25	33	2.19	19
Slidemill (SM)	70	67	67	64	50	88		71	57	5.33	22
Treadmill (TM)	40	33	50	36	56	75	29		25	3.44	18
Walking/running in place (WIP)	36	71	100	47	45	67	43	75		4.84	12

Fig. 6. Results of the ranking questionnaire, where participants are asked to rank VR locomotion interface categories concerning their importance. 1st denotes the highest preference. The selection of "NA" is represented as circles of sizes proportional to the number of participants who wanted to keep the interface out of the raking. The percentage comparison scores denote the percentage of the time the interface on the row is selected over the interfaces on the column of the specific box by the same user. The cumulative scores are computed by adding row percentage scores of each interface.

dominates over or falls behind others, as even terrain feedback and standing body posture are each considered as the most important feature by a couple of users. We can deduce that there is a high variation in the user preferences on interface features. This may be due to many reasons such as variety in VR application experience, subjective perceptual differences or lack of experience with different VR locomotion interface types.

Preferences for Walking Interfaces. Just like the interface features, we asked the participants to rank the locomotion interfaces in the order of their preferences (Question **Q3**). The participants had an option to select "Not Available (N/A)" for interfaces they have not experienced but we did not strictly enforce this option for systems that they are not experienced with. Since participants of the survey did not try many of the interface options, the method used for the presentation of interface features ranking may not be very informative for this ranking survey question. Instead, we use a different method to present this ranking task. Figure 6 shows how users prioritize the locomotion interfaces. The percentage comparison scores present the pairwise comparison of the row and column interfaces. The values in each cell refer to the percentage of time a user ranked the row interface higher than the column interface. The results of each row are summed up to get a cumulative score for each interface. The results show that although joystick type interfaces are used by most participants when compared pairwise many users tend to select the other available interface over the joysticks. The point and teleport method, another widely used method that does not provide much multisensory feedback, ranks quite well against the other interfaces. However, the best two pairwise comparison results are achieved by redirected walking and slidemill type interfaces both of which require close to normal walking kinematics as the user movement. This is aligned with the high rating of the use of body-based inputs in the feature ranking survey question. Walking-in-place type systems also scored third both on the cumulative scores and the number of people who have not been selected (N/A).

5   Conclusion

Over 60% of the respondents used VR software and hardware at least once every week or every month. Over 90% of the responders used joysticks and/or "point and teleport" to control motion in VR scenes. Approximately 34–44% of the responders used body gestures (walk-in-place, arm swing, hand gesture for flying) to control walking/motion in VR. Less than 30% of the responders used other types of interfaces (treadmill, seated interface with leg gestures, treadmill, slidemill) for walking control. Therefore, using hand joysticks for motion control (including the "point and teleport" function) is a primary way to navigate in VR scenes. The survey indicated that there are three preferred methods to navigate in VR: hand joysticks, "point and teleport" and "walking/running in place", as summarised below (% of respondents who selected particular methods as 1st, 2nd or 3rd choice/preference): joysticks: 26% as 1st choice, 21% as 2nd choice, 21% as 3rd choice; point and teleport: 17% as 1st choice, 35% as 2nd choice, 17%

as 3rd choice; walk/run in place: 13% as 1st choice, 26% as 2nd choice, 5% as 3rd choice.

The survey results provided valuable insight into the experience and preferences of experienced VR users on VR locomotion interfaces. It showed that the users' preferences on the interface types and features show large variations over participants. Especially about the user posture, we believe that there is a serious divide in the user preferences but fewer participants think it is better to be seated than standing. Users attach high importance to reducing motion sickness and the use of body-based inputs for locomotion. The terrain feedback is considered an important feature by all but does not rank high against other interface features. The authors take into account the results of the survey into their work on designing seated walk-in-place interface for VR [38,39,41,42].

Acknowledgment. This work was supported by the UKRI EPSRC grant EP/V035304/1 (Q-Arena).

References

1. Agilevr by mechatech. https://www.mechatech.co.uk/. Accessed 20 June 2021
2. The cyberith virtualizer. https://www.cyberith.com. Accessed 20 June 2021
3. Cybershoes. https://www.cybershoes.io/. Accessed 20 June 2021
4. Echovr. https://www.oculus.com/echo-vr/. Accessed 20 June 2021
5. The virtuix omni. https://www.virtuix.com. Accessed 20 June 2021
6. Windlands2. https://www.windlands.com. Accessed 20 June 2021
7. Allison, R., Harris, L., Jenkin, M., Pintilie, G., Redlick, F., Zikovitz, D.: First steps with a rideable computer. In: Proceedings IEEE Virtual Reality 2000 (Cat. No.00CB37048), pp. 169–175 (2000)
8. Beckhaus, S., Blom, K.J., Haringer, M.: Intuitive, hands-free travel interfaces for virtual environments. In: In New Directions in 3D User Interfaces Workshop of IEEE VR 2005, pp. 57–60 (2005)
9. Bouguila, L., Florian, E., Courant, M., Hirsbrunner, B.: Active walking interface for human-scale virtual environment (2005)
10. Bouguila, L., Hirsbrunner, B., Sato, M., Iwashita, M.: Virtual locomotion interface with ground surface simulation. In: ICAT (2003)
11. Bozgeyikli, E., Raij, A., Katkoori, S., Dubey, R.: Point & teleport locomotion technique for virtual reality. In: Proceedings of the 2016 CHI Play (2016)
12. Bozgeyikli, E., Raij, A., Katkoori, S., Dubey, R.: Point & teleport locomotion technique for virtual reality. In: Proceedings of the 2016 Annual Symposium on Computer-Human Interaction in Play, CHI PLAY 2016, pp. 205–216. Association for Computing Machinery, New York (2016)
13. Bruder, G., Interrante, V., Phillips, L., Steinicke, F.: Redirecting walking and driving for natural navigation in immersive virtual environments. IEEE Trans. Visual Comput. Graphics **18**(4), 538–545 (2012)
14. Cakmak, T., Hager, H.: Cyberith virtualizer: a locomotion device for virtual reality. In: ACM SIGGRAPH 2014 (2014)
15. Cirio, G., Marchal, M., Lécuyer, A., Cooperstock, J.R.: Vibrotactile rendering of splashing fluids. IEEE Trans. Haptics **6**(1), 117–122 (First 2013)

16. Darken, R.P., Cockayne, W.R., Carmein, D.: The omni-directional treadmill: a locomotion device for virtual worlds. In: Proceedings of the 10th Annual ACM Symp. on User Interface Software and Technology, pp. 213–221. NY, USA (1997)
17. Feasel, J., Whitton, M.C., Wendt, J.D.: LLCM-WIP: low-latency, continuous-motion walking-in-place. In: 2008 IEEE Symposium on 3D User Interfaces, pp. 97–104, March 2008
18. Fukushima, H., Noma, H., Iwata, H., Yano, H.: Circulafloor: a locomotion interface using circulation of movable tiles. In: IEEE Virtual Reality 2005, pp. 223–230. IEEE Computer Society, Los Alamitos March 2005
19. Grechkin, T., Thomas, J., Azmandian, M., Bolas, M., Suma, E.: Revisiting detection thresholds for redirected walking: combining translation and curvature gains. In: Proceedings of the ACM Symposium on Applied Perception, SAP 2016, pp. 113–120. Association for Computing Machinery, New York (2016)
20. Guy, E., Punpongsanon, P., Iwai, D., Sato, K., Boubekeur, T.: Lazynav: 3d ground navigation with non-critical body parts. In: 2015 IEEE Symposium on 3D User Interfaces (3DUI), pp. 43–50 (2015)
21. Harris, A., Nguyen, K., Wilson, P.T., Jackoski, M., Williams, B.: Human joystick: Wii-leaning to translate in large virtual environments. In: Proceedings of the 13th ACM SIGGRAPH International Conference on Virtual-Reality Continuum and Its Applications in Industry, VRCAI 2014, pp. 231–234. Association for Computing Machinery, New York (2014)
22. Hashemian, A., Lotfaliei, M., Adhikari, A., Kruijff, E., Riecke, B.: Headjoystick: Improving flying in VR using a novel leaning-based interface. IEEE Trans. Visualization Comput. Graph., 1–14 (2020)
23. Hidayah, R., Chamarthy, S., Shah, A., Fitzgerald-Maguire, M., Agrawal, S.K.: Walking with augmented reality: a preliminary assessment of visual feedback with a cable-driven active leg exoskeleton (c-alex). IEEE Robot. Autom. Lett. 4(4), 3948–3954 (2019)
24. Iwata, H.: The torus treadmill: realizing locomotion in VES. IEEE Comput. Graphics Appl. 19(6), 30–35 (1999)
25. Iwata, H., Fujii, T.: Virtual perambulator: a novel interface device for locomotion in virtual environment. In: Proceedings of the IEEE 1996 Virtual Reality Annual International Symposium, pp. 60–65 (1996)
26. Iwata, H., Yano, H., Nakaizumi, F.: Gait master: a versatile locomotion interface for uneven virtual terrain. In: Proceedings IEEE Virtual Reality 2001 (2001)
27. Jayakumar, R.P., Mishra, S.K., Dannenhoffer, J.F., Okamura, A.M.: Haptic footstep display. In: 2012 IEEE Haptics Symposium, pp. 425–430 (2012)
28. Kato, G., Kuroda, Y., Kiyokawa, K., Takemura, H.: Force rendering and its evaluation of a friction-based walking sensation display for a seated user. IEEE Trans. Visual Comput. Graphics 24(4), 1506–1514 (2018)
29. Kitson, A., Hashemian, A.M., Stepanova, E.R., Kruijff, E., Riecke, B.E.: Comparing leaning-based motion cueing interfaces for virtual reality locomotion. In: 2017 IEEE Symposium on 3D User Interfaces (3DUI), pp. 73–82 (2017)
30. Kitson, A., Riecke, B.E., Hashemian, A.M., Neustaedter, C.: Navichair: evaluating an embodied interface using a pointing task to navigate virtual reality. In: Proceedings of the 3rd ACM Symposium on Spatial User Interaction, SUI 2015, pp. 123–126. Association for Computing Machinery, New York (2015)
31. Kruijff, E., et al.: On your feet! enhancing vection in leaning-based interfaces through multisensory stimuli. In: Proceedings of the 2016 Symposium on Spatial User Interaction, SUI 2016, pp. 149–158. Association for Computing Machinery, New York (2016)

32. Langbehn, E., Lubos, P., Steinicke, F.: Evaluation of locomotion techniques for room-scale vr: Joystick, teleportation, and redirected walking. In: Laval Virtual (2018)
33. Lee, J., Ahn, S.C., Hwang, J.I.: A walking-in-place method for virtual reality using position and orientation tracking. Sensors 18(9), 2832 (2018)
34. Luca, M.d., Seifi, H., Egan, S., Gonzalez Franco, M.: Locomotion vault: the extra mile in analyzing VR locomotion techniques. In: ACM CHI, May 2021
35. Medina, E., Fruland, R., Weghorst, S.: Virtusphere: walking in a human size vr "hamster ball". Proc. Hum. Factors Ergon. Soc. Annual Meeting 52(27), 2102–2106 (2008)
36. Nilsson, N.C., Serafin, S., Nordahl, R.: The perceived naturalness of virtual loco-motion methods devoid of explicit leg movements. In: Proceedings of Motion on Games, MIG 2013, pp. 133:155–133:164. ACM, New York (2013)
37. Nilsson, N.C., Serafin, S., Steinicke, F., Nordahl, R.: Natural walking in virtual reality: a review. Comput. Entertainment (CIE) 16(2), 1–22 (2018)
38. Otaran, A., Farkhatdinov, I.: Modeling and control of ankle actuation platform for human-robot interaction. In: Althoefer, K., Konstantinova, J., Zhang, K. (eds.) TAROS 2019. LNCS (LNAI), vol. 11649, pp. 338–348. Springer, Cham (2019). https://doi.org/10.1007/978-3-030-23807-0_28
39. Otaran, A., Farkhatdinov, I.: A cable-driven walking interface with haptic feedback for seated VR. In: IEEE World Haptics Conference (2021)
40. Otaran, A., Farkhatdinov, I.: Haptic ankle platform for interactive walking in vir-tual reality. IEEE Trans. Visualization Comput, Graph (2021)
41. Otaran, A., Farkhatdinov, I.: A short description of an ankle-actuated seated vr locomotion interface. In: 2021 IEEE Conference on Virtual Reality and 3D User Interfaces Abstracts and Workshops (VRW), pp. 64–66. IEEE (2021)
42. Otaran, A., Farkhatdinov, I.: Walking-in-place foot interface for locomotion con-trol and telepresence of humanoid robots. In: 2020 IEEE-RAS 20th International Conference on Humanoid Robots (Humanoids), pp. 453–458. IEEE (2021)
43. Pan, C.T., et al.: Design of virtual reality systems integrated with the lower-limb exoskeleton for rehabilitation purpose. In: IEEE International Conf. on Applied System Invention, pp. 498–501 (2018)
44. Papetti, S., Fontana, F., Civolani, M., Berrezag, A., Hayward, V.: Audio-tactile display of ground properties using interactive shoes. In: Nordahl, R., Serafin, S., Fontana, F., Brewster, S. (eds.) HAID 2010. LNCS, vol. 6306, pp. 117–128. Springer, Heidelberg (2010).https://doi.org/10.1007/978-3-642-15841-4_13
45. Ratcliffe, J., Soave, F., Bryan-Kinns, N., Tokarchuk, L., Farkhatdinov, I.: Extended reality (XR) remote research: a survey of drawbacks and opportunities. In: Pro-ceedings of the 2021 CHI Conference on Human Factors in Computing Systems, pp. 1–13 (2021)
46. Razzaque, S., Kohn, Z., Whitton, M.C.: Redirected walking. In: Eurographics 2001 - Short Presentations, pp. 289–294 (2001)
47. Razzaque, S., Swapp, D., Slater, M., Whitton, M.C., Steed, A.: Redirected walking in place. In: EGVE, vol. 2. Citeseer (2002)
48. Ruddle, R.A., Lessels, S.: For efficient navigational search, humans require full physical movement, but not a rich visual scene. Psychol. Sci. 17(6), 460–465 (2006)
49. Shiratuddin, M.F., Wong, K.W.: Non-contact multi-hand gestures interaction tech-niques for architectural design in a virtual environment. In: Proceedings of 5th International Conference on Information Technology & Multimedia (2011)

50. Slater, M., Usoh, M., Steed, A.: Taking steps: The influence of a walking technique on presence in virtual reality. ACM Trans. Comput.-Hum. Interact. **2**, 201–219 (1995)
51. Sloot, L.H., Van der Krogt, M.M., Harlaar, J.: Effects of adding a virtual reality environment to different modes of treadmill walking. Gait Posture **39**(3), 939–945 (2014)
52. Son, H., Gil, H., Byeon, S., Kim, S.Y., Kim, J.R.: Realwalk: Feeling ground surfaces while walking in virtual reality. In: Extended Abstracts of the CHI Conference on Human Factors in Computing Systems, pp. D400:1–D400:4. ACM (2018)
53. Strohmeier, P., Güngör, S., Herres, L., Gudea, D., Fruchard, B., Steimle, J.: Barefoot: generating virtual materials using motion coupled vibration in shoes. In: Proceedings of the 33rd Annual ACM Symposium on User Interface Software and Technology, UIST 2020, pp. 579–593. Association for Computing Machinery, New York (2020)
54. Swapp, D., Williams, J., Steed, A.: The implementation of a novel walking interface within an immersive display. In: 2010 IEEE Symposium on 3D User Interfaces (3DUI), pp. 71–74 (2010)
55. Templeman, J.N., Sibert, L.E., Page, R.C., Denbrook, P.S.: Pointman - a new control for simulating tactical infantry movements. In: IEEE Virtual Reality Conference, pp. 285–286, March 2007
56. Terziman, L., Marchal, M., Multon, F., Arnaldi, B., Lecuyer, A.: The king-kong effects: improving sensation of walking in VR with visual and tactile vibrations at each step. In: 2012 IEEE Symposium on 3D User Interfaces (2012)
57. Terziman, L., Marchal, M., Emily, M., Multon, F., Arnaldi, B., Lécuyer, A.: Shake-your-head: revisiting walking-in-place for desktop virtual reality. In: VRST (2010)
58. Tregillus, S., Folmer, E.: VR-STEP: Walking-in-place using inertial sensing for hands free navigation in mobile VR environments. In: CHI (2016)
59. Usoh, M., Arthur, K., Whitton, M.C., Bastos, R., Steed, A., Slater, M., Brooks, F.P.: Walking > walking-in-place > flying, in virtual environments. In: Proceedings of 26th Ann. Conf. on Computer Graphics and Interactive Techniques. ACM, USA (1999)
60. Usoh, M., et al.: Walking¿ walking-in-place¿ flying, in virtual environments. In: 26th Annual Conference on Computer Graphics and Interactive Techniques (1999)
61. Visell, Y., et al.: A vibrotactile device for display of virtual ground materials in walking. In: Ferre, M. (ed.) Haptics: Perception, Devices and Scenarios, pp. 420–426. Springer, Heidelberg (2008)
62. Wendt, J.D., Whitton, M.C., Brooks, F.P.J.: GUD-WIP: Gait-understanding-driven walking-in-place. In: IEEE Virtual Reality Conference 2010, pp. 51–58 (2010)
63. Williams, B., Bailey, S., Narasimham, G., Li, M., Bodenheimer, B.: Evaluation of walking in place on a wii balance board to explore a virtual environment. ACM Trans. Appl. Percept. **8**(3), 19:1–19:14 (Aug 2011)
64. Williams, N.L., Peck, T.C.: Estimation of rotation gain thresholds considering fov, gender, and distractors. IEEE Trans. Vis. Comput. Graph. **25**(11) (2019)
65. Yokota, T., Ohtake, M., Nishimura, Y., Yui, T., Uchikura, R., Hashida, T.: Snow walking: motion-limiting device that reproduces the experience of walking in deep snow. In: Proceedings of the 6th Augmented Human International Conference, AH 2015, pp. 45–48. ACM, New York (2015)
66. Yoon, J., Ryu, J.: A novel locomotion interface with two 6-dof parallel manipulators that allows human walking on various virtual terrains. Int. J. Robot. Res. **25**(7), 689–708 (2006)

"Not in Kansas Anymore" Exploring Avatar-Player Dynamics Through a Wizard of Oz Approach in Virtual Reality

Adam Palmquist[1,2]([✉]) [iD], Izabella Jedel[3] [iD], Chris Hart[1],
Victor Manuel Perez Colado[1], and Aedan Soellaart[1] [iD]

[1] Faculty of Social Sciences, Nord University, Bodø, Norway
`adam.palmquist@nord.no`
[2] Department of Applied IT, University of Gothenburg, Gothenburg, Sweden
[3] Faculty of Education and Arts, Nord University, Bodø, Norway

Abstract. Virtual reality (VR) gaming has the potential to offer more immersive and realistic environments for players. Recent developments in VR technology and gaming have resulted in more advanced game controllers and the development of more nuanced games. Despite the vast potential behind VR games in enhancing the player experience, there is a lack of frameworks and methodologies that specifically address the player experience in opposition to the user experience. Therefore, the present study aimed to develop and assess a proof-of-concept technology based on a Wizard of Oz (WOz) methodology to evaluate the player experience in VR games. The WOz approach provides a tool for evaluating player-avatar interactions in the preliminary stages of VR game development. We present the WOz approach and an initial exploratory qualitative study in the present study. The study's results highlight the importance of technical aspects, interaction design, and authenticity in player-avatar interactions. The resource-efficient prototype enables practitioners and researchers to investigate different forms of player-avatar interactions in the preliminary stages of VR-game development. Avenues for further research to conduct experimental studies through the prototype are discussed.

Keywords: Virtual Reality · Game Design · Game Development · Player-Avatar Interaction · Wizard of Oz · User Experience · Player Experience

1 Introduction

VR games have the potential to offer a higher sense of presence and interaction by immersing the player in three-dimensional virtual environments [1]. Consequently, the video game experience is transformed through new dimensions of realism and play [2]. These technical possibilities highlight VR's growing role in shaping future entertainment and interactive experiences. At the same time, the evolving VR gaming landscape driven by gamers' changing needs has brought forth technological advancement in VR technology. The synergy has led to enhanced VR controllers, integrating detailed hand

© The Author(s), under exclusive license to Springer Nature Switzerland AG 2024
J. Y. C. Chen and G. Fragomeni (Eds.): HCII 2024, LNCS 14706, pp. 259–276, 2024.
https://doi.org/10.1007/978-3-031-61041-7_17

movements and haptic feedback [3]. The indie gaming community has also played a pivotal role in VR game creation, driving technological innovation and priming the industry for broader commercialization [2]. Despite the vast possibilities of VR gaming, several factors can hinder its adoption, including subpar design and development frameworks [4].

To create high-quality, immersive VR gameplay, establishing better principles and reliable guidelines and evaluation methods is crucial [5]. Researchers and practitioners have made several advancements in evaluating the VR Game experience. For instance, player locomotion in VR games [5] and the distinction between varied interaction spaces in VR gameplay [6].

Contemporary VR evaluation methodologies can be dichotomized into two primary categories: inspection methods and user testing [5]. Inspection Methods involve assessing a VR system against established design principles or performance models, such as heuristics. Its key characteristic is its independence from user engagement, relying on expert analysis to determine compliance with these guidelines. Recent decades have seen substantial efforts to develop heuristic lists tailored for VR, addressing its unique usability challenges [5]. For example, Wang et al. [7] identified 672 distinct usability issues in a function-oriented VR application, finding that 77% aligned with Nielsen's heuristics, thereby affirming their relevance in VR contexts. Beyond heuristics, this evaluation extends to interaction and cognitive processing models. Fitts' Law has been applied in VR to study input performance concerning geometry displacement and texture rendering. However, Schwind et al. [8] found that depth cues did not significantly affect input performance, suggesting different dependencies in VR. Moreover, adaptations of the Goals, Operators, Methods, and Selection Rules (GOMS) model for VR, such as H-GOMS, have been developed [9]. User Testing involves user interaction with the VR system and focuses on user experience metrics, including performance, behavior, and subjective responses. In their comprehensive chapter on XR environments, Stanney et al. [5] mention two forms common for user testing of VR systems: formative, quantifying user interactions like speed and accuracy, and summative, comparing systems using quantitative data. Methods include explicit measures (e.g., task performance indicators) and implicit measures (e.g., visual attention and physiological responses).

Inspection methods and user testing can be useful for evaluating general VR-systems. However, there is a notable gap in the literature concerning evaluation methods that address the unique characteristics of VR-games. This is a concern since user experience (UX) and specific player experience (PX) methods are needed to evaluate games sufficiently. Traditional UX evaluations, which focus on usability and functionality, are insufficient for assessing PX, which revolves around the experience of play and the emotional responses elicited by players [10, 11]. UX, while broader, differs from PX, particularly in VR gaming, where immersive experiences necessitate a deeper understanding of PX [12]. Therefore, the prevalent use of traditional UX techniques does not fully capture the essence of VR games, indicating a need for VR-specific evaluation methods. Furthermore, cost-effective evaluation methods are needed to support the indie gaming communities and game developers with fewer financial resources. These would enhance understanding of PX in VR environments, contributing to VR game design advancements and ensuring emotional resonance for players. The aim of the present study was to develop and assess a proof-of-concept technology based on a Wizard of Oz (WOz) methodology for evaluating the dimensions of the PX in VR games. Specifically, the technology provides a tool for evaluating the player-avatar dynamics in VR games. Based on an initial qualitative evaluation, we identified initial factors that contribute to the player-avatar interaction in VR-gaming and provided avenues for further research in terms of evaluating the VR-gaming PX.

2 Methodology

The VR-evaluation technology was based on a WOz methodology to explore player-avatar interactions in VR gaming. The present section outlines the WOz methodology used for the analog and technical setup and describes the methodology for the qualitative study conducted as a first step to evaluate player-avatar dynamics in VR games.

2.1 The Wizard of Oz Methodology

In HCI, the WOz is a research methodology designed to emulate a fully functional interactive system [13]. However, this apparent functionality is an illusion; the system is operated manually by a concealed human operator known as the "wizard." The primary advantage of this approach is its ability to collect valuable user behavior data without the need to build a fully functional, automated system. During the approach, participants are led to believe they are interacting with an automated computer system – such as a voice-activated assistant, a recommendation engine, or even a sophisticated robot. Unbeknownst to them, a human operator discreetly orchestrates the system's responses, thereby simulating advanced functionalities like natural language comprehension that the system does not genuinely possess. The WOz technique simulates functionalities in an interface application that has yet to be developed. Users believe they interact directly with the system, but their responses come from another human [14].

The WOz approach has been utilized in diverse applications studies involving human-robot interactions and AI system research [15], from analyzing gestures [16] to examining human dialogues with virtual agents [17]. The WOz demonstrates value when actual functionality is overly costly to develop or when the preferred technological solution is still not a common commodity, providing a way to evaluate prospective interfaces [18]. Given its efficiency and cost-effectiveness, this method is also beneficial for gauging feasibility and assessing concepts before committing to complete system development [18].

We developed a WOz prototype in a VR-gaming context in the present study. Our objective was to attain high avatar realism without requiring extensive financial backing or partnerships with major technology companies. The design of the WOz prototype involved a person covertly controlling the avatar in the VR experience, unbeknownst to the participant, allowing for observing genuine user responses to avatars. Therefore, The WOz prototype included both analog and digital setups. The technology enables the systematic manipulation of avatar characteristics, allowing for insights into the attributes that contribute to the PX when interacting with avatars in VR.

2.2 Research Design

Study Sample. The participants selected to evaluate the WOz proof-of-concept were recruited through a convenience/purposive sampling [19]. The approach allowed us to reach out to a small group of individuals with domain expertise in media and digital technology. Their feedback was expected to provide rich and nuanced insights across technical and experiential components of the proof-of-concept technology. Three field expert participants were included in the study. All participants were adult men of various European descent.

Data Collection. Participants interacted with the WOz prototype for around 10 min. Semi-structured interviews were conducted with participants following their interaction with the VR avatar. Participants were taken to another room during the interviews, which lasted around 30 min. Utilizing semi-structured interviews allowed us to adapt to participants' responses and reflections about their experiences. The exploratory nature of our study guided our decision to use this method. A fixed set of questions structured into five categories (Table 1) was used to understand the player's experience when interacting with the avatar. The interviewee was allowed to ask follow-up questions and pursue alluring topics, asking participants to elaborate on specific actions or decisions they made during the experience.

Table 1. Interview Guide

Category	Example question
Overall Experience	*Describe the overall experience?/What did you think of the avatar interaction?*
Novelty	*Have you experienced something similar?*
Appreciation & Aversions	*What aspects of the interaction did you consider gratifying/disturbing?*
Improvements	*Do you have any recommendations for enhancing the experience?*

Data Analysis. After the WOz session, each interview was manually transcribed and analyzed separately using thematic analysis [20]. Thematic analysis identified and reported patterns or "themes" within the participants' responses. The thematic analysis allowed for a flexible approach to examining and synthesizing qualitative data. Five main steps were followed (Table 2). Employing this approach allowed us to organize the qualitative data into a coherent structure, making it easier to understand participants' experiences and identify areas for improvement.

Ethical Considerations. Ethical guidelines were adhered to in the data collection process [21]. Participants received a comprehensive briefing about the study's purpose, including the possibility of simulated functionalities by a researcher. They were made aware of their involvement, potential risks, discomforts, and the deceptive elements of the 'WOz' approach. Obtaining written informed consent, which detailed their understanding of these elements, was crucial to maintaining the research's integrity and respecting

Table 2. Thematic Analysis Phases

Phase	Example question
Data Familiarization	The responses from each participant were reviewed to understand the content and context
Coding	Specific points made by participants were identified and coded. E.g. comments about "eyecontact not meet" were coded under "Visual Realism > Facial Features."
Identify themes	The codes were grouped under broader categories - initial themes - (e.g., Level of Visual Realism, Degree of Social/Emotional interaction)
Reviewing themes	Each theme was reviewed to represent the data accurately. Definitions and sub-themes were created to provide more depth to each theme
Interpretation	The data was synthesized and interpreted to provide a comprehensive view of participant feedback and offer actionable insights

participants' autonomy and confidentiality. Participants were thoroughly debriefed and allowed to withdraw their data. This process ensures ethical integrity and addresses any potential discomfort or mistrust resulting from the procedures' deception. The WOz approach presents unique ethical challenges, notably involving deception, where participants might believe they are interacting with an autonomous system while some functionalities are manually controlled. This deception necessitates careful consideration of the psychological impact on participants and the trust between the researcher and participants. Deception can erode this trust, potentially impacting the broader research community. As highlighted in the literature, a thorough debriefing is critical to address potential adverse psychological effects and dependence issues that might arise from a WOz study [13, 15, 22]. Such debriefing should elucidate the necessity of deception and disclose the true objectives of the study to mitigate any potential psychological harm and distrust. Moreover, previous research has underscored the potential for increased societal trust issues and suspicions towards AI innovations due to a lack of transparency about whether interactions are with an algorithm or a human [23]. Ethical considerations have been prioritized to address participants' uncertainties about interacting with a human actor versus an AI. Transparency regarding the nature of the interaction is thus crucial in fostering positive relationships with emerging technologies. Moreover, the use of deception could impact participants' impartiality, influencing both the outcomes of the research and their future perceptions of VR avatars. Consequently, all participants were informed and debriefed about the WOz setup following their interaction, ensuring clarity, and addressing any misconceptions.

3 Result

The present section details the setup of the WOz prototype in the analog and digital environment and the results from the qualitative exploration.

3.1 WOz Prototype

Setup in the Analog Environment. Building on previous research (McDonnell et al., 2012), we have implemented a professional actor sporting a motion capture suit endowed with high-precision tracking systems for the body and face; this suit empowers us to record each subtle motion of the actor in real-time. For the optimal execution of the procedure, our laboratory is carefully partitioned into two distinct sections: the Actor/Motion Capture Area and the Participant/VR Area. This thoughtful setup enhances our methodology by ensuring an accurate and efficient transference of motion data from the actor to the virtual avatar. In the Actor/Motion Capture Area, an actor dons a motion capture suit and performs actions translated into a virtual environment. An avatar mirrors these actions in real-time. In the Participant/VR Area, a human participant interacts with the avatar wearing an XR 3 Varjo headset, providing a pathway into the virtual environment where the avatar resides (Fig. 1).

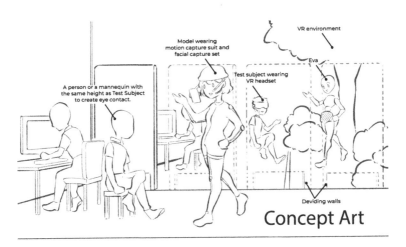

Fig. 1. Setup in the analog environment.

Setup in the Digital Environment. The WOz prototype was designed to evaluate player-avatar interactions within a VR context and offered multimodal experiences, highlighting the nuances of the environment and the embodiment of avatars within the VR setting. It facilitates an exploration of the depth and breadth of interactions in a digitally simulated environment, specifically focusing on the dynamics of player-avatar interaction. This section explains the technical architecture and setup process of the WOz prototype. A comprehensive digital environment was established to explore the intricacies of VR gaming players' experience using Unreal Engine 5 (see Appendix 1. For a guide towards setting up the environment). In the virtual environment, WOz participants engage with the actor-directed avatar Bella (Fig. 2). The sophisticated modeling and rigging in the WOz prototype facilitated a realistic and interactive player experience within the VR setting. This was crucial for the project's aim of crafting an evaluation method for avatar-human interaction, allowing for an in-depth analysis of the dynamics and nuances of these interactions in a simulated environment.

Fig. 2. LHS: The Avatar, Bella. RHS: the actor who recreates Bella.

The setup (Fig. 3) is divided into two different machines (running Windows 11) connected using a WiFi router with the addition of a mobile handheld device (iPhone X). The first computer's task (from now on, capturing computer) is to capture the different motions of the actor that is going to control the player-avatar and thus play the role of the "wizard" in the setup. The core of our motion capture (MoCap) system comprised the Movella Xsens MVN Awinda suit (Fig. 2, right), selected for its precision in capturing intricate movements. This motion capture suit includes 17 XSens tracking points that must be attached to the actor at specific body locations. This setup is critical for capturing accurate body movements transferred to the VR environment through the Xsens MVN Animate software, facilitating the process of digitizing and synchronizing the actor's position and motion capture into our WOz setup. The facial capture is captured using facial recognition software using an iPhone X. Apple's ARKit is used in this project due to its high fidelity compared to analog ARCore techniques (Android software). This device was mounted on a head-mounted phone holder (Fig. 2, right), ensuring the front-facing camera aligned correctly with the actor's face. The Live Link Face app, downloaded on the iPhone, enabled real-time facial motion capture, integrating seamlessly with the Unreal Engine setup.

Conversely, the second computer (hereafter the rendering computer) oversees the environment and interactive experience. This environment was crafted using Unreal

266   A. Palmquist et al.

Engine 5, chosen for its advanced capabilities in rendering realistic VR scenes. The project was initiated in Unreal Engine using the Virtual Reality template. The scene was designed to include human-scale 3D objects, ensuring users could orient themselves easily within the virtual space. A Player Start Actor was positioned at the center of the scene, approximately two meters above the ground, serving as the initial point of interaction for users in the VR environment. In a location nearby to the player, there is the actor's avatar. In terms of character setup, an Unreal MetaHuman base was utilized. A detailed 3D robot character asset, inspired by the AI character from 'Ex Machina,' was then downloaded and retargeted onto this MetaHuman skeleton (Fig. 2, left). This process was crucial to ensure the character was equipped with blend shapes compatible with our facial recognition capabilities (ARKit), enabling a more nuanced and lifelike facial expression in VR. The smartphone device (iPhone X) in charge of emitting facial capture information used the Live Link Face app, and within the Unreal Engine project, plugins such as Apple ARKit, Apple ARKit Face Support, and Live Link were activated. The Live Link Face app was then launched, and the IPv4 addresses of both computers were input into the app's target fields, ensuring synchronization between the facial capture data and the VR environment.

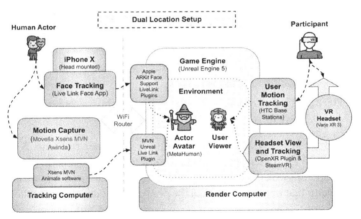

Fig. 3. Diagram of the technical setup involved in creating the prototype. The diagram shows two different actors and avatars and three different devices interconnected. The render computer receives all the signals using the plugins and controls the avatar and VR Headset.

Finally, connected to the rendering computer, the periscope to this WOz configuration was set up by using the Varjo XR-3 Mixed Reality Headset, renowned for its high fidelity and mixed reality capabilities. It is worth noting that the Varjo XR3 is a costly and resource-consuming headset, but it is the most suitable option for this experiment due to its visual accuracy. The Varjo XR3 requires external outside-in tracking stations to track the player's motion data. Two HTC SteamVR Base Station 2.0s were strategically positioned within the setup. The precision enabled by these base stations plays a vital role in the effectiveness of the WOz prototype, facilitating a higher level of immersion and accuracy in the interactions with the actor. Setting up the VR system required careful placement of the HTC SteamVR Base Stations, installation of the Varjo Base application, and enabling the Varjo OpenXR plugin within Unreal. To streamline the experience, SteamVR was run in the background while Oculus VR and SteamVR plugins were turned off in favor of OpenXR.

A local area network (LAN) was established for the inter-computer connection using 5 GHz WiFi connectivity for better performance in real-time interaction and responsiveness in the VR environment. This setup facilitated communication and data transfer between the two computers and the smartphone, which were in a single-location setup, using the same space separated by a physical barrier. The same technological framework can be used in a two-location setup if the rooms are nearly located, promoting a more isolated experience at a limited cost on both ends.

Running the VR project involved compiling all shaders in the Unreal Engine to ensure a smooth and seamless VR experience. The project was then launched in VR Preview mode on the computer connected to the VR headset. This step was crucial to ensure that the VR environment was rendered correctly and that the participant could interact with it as intended. The other computer, not directly connected to the VR headset, was used to monitor and manage the environment, remaining in editor mode.

The final aspect of the setup involved establishing effective communication between the VR user and the actor. This was accomplished by placing noise-cancelling wireless headphones with microphones on both individuals. External devices, such as smartphones, were used to connect the headphones and set up a voice call, enabling clear and uninterrupted communication during the VR experience.

As a result, the setup enables the test subject to engage with the Bella avatar in a fully immersive and lifelike experience. This was crucial for the project's aim of crafting an evaluation method for avatar-human interaction, allowing for an in-depth analysis of the dynamics and nuances of these interactions in a simulated environment. The setup provides a technical framework for performing WOz-like studies. Thanks to the lifelike and highly controlled setup, it allows for the embodiment of an actor in a VR scenario and offers an interaction that transcends the boundaries of what has previously been evaluated to study VR interaction and its implications further. Elements such as the body language of the actor, the various expressions that the avatar's face can convey, the extent of eye contact, and the quality and tone of the avatar's voice are some of the aspects that are controlled in this setup and could become variables to research VR interaction. In addition to those, the system can also provide a window into quantitative data extracted from the different devices (including motion and gaze tracking for both actor and participant and face tracking of the actor) and from the actual embodiment in the digital environment (e.g., what specific part of the actor's avatar is the participant looking at). In the following sections, we explore the proof-of-concept pilot done as part of the present study. This pilot study aimed to evaluate the practicalities of the interactive experience that the WOz prototype setup provides as a framework for VR research.

3.2 Factors Affecting the Avatar-Human Interaction in VR Gaming

Based on the interview, three main themes emerged that can play a vital role in the avatar-human interaction experience in VR gaming.

Technical Improvements for Satisfactory Experiences Human-Avatar Interaction. The first theme concerns technical improvements to meet the participants' expectations. Our investigation into the technical dimensions of player immersion within virtual environments yielded significant findings, particularly in the realm of avatar realism. The first theme harbors four sub-themes: *Avatar Height and Orientation Discrepancies, Significance of Eye Contact and Facial Realism, Body Language and Synchronization,* as well as *Technical Requirement's for Player Immersion.*

Avatar Height and Orientation Discrepancies. An outcome of our WOz was identifying recurrent issues related to avatar height and orientation. Participants reported a consistent sensation of feeling looked down upon due to mismatches in human-avatar height and perspective alignment. This phenomenon was observed across the participant spectrum, indicating a widespread challenge in meeting player spatial expectations within virtual environments.

Significance of Eye Contact and Facial Realism. The critical role of eye contact in player-avatar interactions emerged as a prominent theme. Players experienced a detachment during these interactions, attributed to latency in the prototype system, which hindered the authenticity of eye contact. The unanimous participant feedback underscored the need for enhanced realism in eye contact, suggesting it is a key area for technical refinement. Furthermore, the specificity of participants' comments on the necessity for improved facial tracking algorithms, particularly for eye movements, highlighted the importance of facial realism in enhancing player engagement and immersion. The capacity of the avatar to convey emotions emerged as a variable aspect of the virtual experience. While one participant noted the engaging nature of the avatar's facial expressions, there was an overall sentiment that Bella's facial emotional expressiveness should be further developed.

Body Language and Synchronization. An aspect of the participants' feedback pertained to the avatars' body language, with hand and arm movements characterized as "unnatural". This critique highlights a broader challenge in achieving naturalistic motion in virtual characters, suggesting that current animation techniques fail to replicate human movements' fluidity. Issues such as speech desynchronization and visual glitches were also mentioned, indicating that minor yet impactful elements detracted from the immersive experience.

Technical Requirements for Player Immersion. The findings from WOz underscore the imperative for advanced technical solutions to address the identified issues. Enhancing avatars' visual and behavioral realism, achieving spatial congruence, reducing system latency, and ensuring behavioral authenticity emerged as critical areas for development. These technical enhancements are essential for bridging the gap between player expectations and the current capabilities of virtual environments, thereby fostering a more immersive and engaging PX.

The first theme sheds light on the role of technology in augmenting immersion within virtual environments, with a particular focus on the realism of avatar representation. The identified discrepancies in avatar height and orientation, alongside the crucial need for realistic eye contact and facial expressions, underscore the necessity for continued research and development in this domain. Addressing these technical challenges is fundamental to advancing and enhancing the overall quality of virtual experiences for users.

Advancing Interaction Design for Deeper Engagement. The second theme concerns the necessity of a more developed interaction design concerning the breadth and depth of human-avatar interaction. The participants' feedback on the current state of interactive design and outlines avenues for enriching the virtual experience. This theme has three sub-themes *Varied Interactive Options, Environmental Interactivity and Engagement,* as well as *Perceived Social and Emotional Avatar Attributes.*

Varied Interactive Options. An insight from the early stage of WOz was the participants' desire for a more diversified range of interactive opportunities. The feedback highlighted a consensus that the virtual experience should transcend basic conversational exchanges, indicating a need for a more dynamic and multifaceted interaction landscape. The current environment was perceived as static, merely as a backdrop rather than an integral, interactive component of the experience. This perception underscores the potential for enhancing engagement by incorporating more interactive elements within the virtual setting.

Environmental Interactivity and Engagement. The participants' comments on the virtual environment's passive function in the virtual experience suggest a missed opportunity for deeper immersion. Participants asserted that transforming the environment into an active interaction element, proposing that such a shift could unveil new dimensions of engagement. This feedback indicates a direction for future development: enriching the environmental design to foster a more interactive and immersive virtual space.

Perceived Social and Emotional Avatar Attributes. One participant stated that during the human-avatar interaction session, he started forming "some kind of friendship" with the Avatar, underscoring the potential for virtual interactions to elicit a sense of social connection. Although the specific participant did not mention attributes such as empathy, curiosity, humor, and enthusiasm, they were subtly inferred throughout the interview conversation. The result, although indirect, suggests social and emotional competencies as a latent potential for human-avatar interaction. To embody these characteristics more explicitly in the game, Avatars might enhance the relational dynamics within the virtual experience.

Insights from the second theme highlight the impact of interaction design in VR environments on the interaction between humans and avatars. Diversifying interactive options, integrating the environment as an active participant in the experience, and deepening avatars' emotional and conversational capabilities can significantly enhance player engagement and satisfaction. These findings point towards a comprehensive approach to interaction design, emphasizing the importance of environmental interactivity, emotional expressiveness, and depth in creating more meaningful and immersive PX.

Improving Authenticity in the VR Avatar. The third theme involves adding a layer of realism to the VR Avatar and Environment. This theme encapsulates two sub-themes *Avatar Apparel and Graphical Glitches* and *Potential Enhancement for Immersion.*

Avatar Apparel and Graphical Glitches. Our early WOz study displays the critical aspect of realism in avatars, as identified by participants' feedback on the visual and motion characteristics of the Avatar. Participants pointed out specific elements that detracted from the visual realism of avatars, particularly in terms of clothing and hair.

Two participants described Bellas' attire as " cartoony" and exaggerated, indicating a disparity between participants' expectations for realism and the current graphical representation of the avatar. Furthermore, graphical glitches in animations were noted as distracting, undermining the overall verisimilitude of the avatar's appearance. These observations underscore the necessity for improved graphical fidelity and animation smoothness in depicting avatars.

Potential Enhancement for Augmenting Immersion. When asked, the participants gave no certain remarks on specific human visual traits besides height, such as skin, eye color, or body proportions, suggesting that these aspects may already possess a satisfactory level of realism in the WOz. Although this indicates that while certain foundational elements are adequately represented, there remains a significant opportunity for refining the animation and synchronization techniques to enhance the overall realism of avatar interactions. The participants reveal that the WOz VR environment and avatar hold promise but require comprehensive attention across multiple domains to elevate the player experience. Enhancements in facial tracking, body orientation, speech synchronization, and dynamic expressiveness are areas for improvement. The PX could transition from merely "interesting" or "fascinating" to fostering immersive and compelling virtual interactions by addressing these aspects.

The insights from the third theme elucidate the importance of realism in avatar design and behavior for enhancing the immersive quality of VR environments. Addressing the identified challenges in graphic representation and motion realism presents a pathway to enrich the PX interaction with avatars. Advancing the fidelity of clothing and hair animations, aiming for a more naturalistic body language, and refining synchronization techniques might elevate engagement and satisfaction within virtual interactions, moving closer to a seamless blend of virtual and real-world experiences.

4   Discussion

4.1   Main Contribution

The WOz prototype presented in the current work demonstrates a promising resource-effective alternative for completing a dynamic, pragmatic, and interactive evaluation procedure for player-avatar interactions in VR game environments. Compared to previous evaluation methods in VR environments, which have focused on the UX of VR [5, 6], the present work contributes a cost-efficient approach to evaluating the PX in VR-games. Such evaluation procedures for VR games can be useful for indie game studios and university environments with limited resources, which play a key role in game creation [5, 6]. Despite its limited resources, the prototype showcases a cutting-edge realistic and immersive simulation supported by the Varjo XR3 headset and Unreal Engine 5. This high-fidelity environment can be used to observe and quantify variables ranging from the emotive perspective, including facial expressions, and acting information, to the physical data or latency information.

Potential improvements could be implemented to the setup presented here. The introduction of an inside-out tracking solution is a common feature in recent headsets that eliminates the requirement of external outside-in trackers (in our current setup, provided by the HTC Base Stations) and improves the user experience of VR users. The newly released devices with inside-out tracking, such as the Varjo XR4, could bring such advancements and simplification without sacrificing any visual fidelity - and even improve it. Other features that the Varjo XR4 could improve include 3D spatial audio and noise-cancelling microphones that provide a more comfortable experience for the wearer. Introducing a finger-tracking solution for the actor like the Xsens Metagloves could improve hand motion fidelity at a small cost.

Finally, when latency can become a determining factor, the current setup could be simplified to a single computer setup that combines both the capturing and rendering computer, potentially reducing synchronization issues. However, this setup (Fig. 4) has the cost of doing the procedure in an individual location, limiting the use of pure VR experiences, and can suffer from different participant sensory leaks. While several motion-tracking solutions could replace the one chosen for this prototype, challenges were encountered with the accuracy of the initial motion capture data during the development process. The solution to this issue was switching from the Perception Neuron Axis mocap suit to the Xsens MVN Awinda, which proved less susceptible to interference from magnetic fields. While this change reduced the error induced, to fully remove any contamination from magnetic inference and sound, setting up the capturing computer in an adjoining studio will be required. The outcome of the WOz development process underscores the importance of comprehensive hardware and software integration, accurate motion, and facial capture. These insights are beneficial for further developing and refining the WOz prototype and further evaluations with a similar setup.

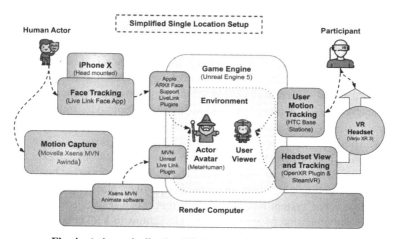

Fig. 4. A theoretically simplified setup with just one computer.

The findings from the qualitative evaluation also illuminate several critical areas for improvement that could elevate PX in VR virtual reality gaming toward engaging and immersive environments. By addressing technical challenges such as height adjustment and spatial audio, the experience can match the user's natural expectations, thereby boosting immersion. Additional layers of engagement can be added by providing structured processes and diverse interactive options. Including dynamic elements and a more life-like avatar can make the experience feel less like a static interaction and more like a vibrant, shared space. A feedback mechanism is crucial to ensure these improvements align with user expectations. By acting on these insights, a promising opportunity exists to create a more interactive, immersive, and user-friendly virtual reality experience. The current iteration of the VR experience shows promise, though multiple areas require attention. Addressing the above-mentioned issues will improve the avatar's visual realism and social competence. Moreover, making these enhancements could significantly improve user engagement and immersion, creating a more compelling and realistic virtual experience.

4.2 Limitations and Further Research

The convenience sample targeting domain experts presented the possibility of gaining more in-depth responses about the player experience. However, it also presents a set of limitations. The generalizability of the findings is constrained due to the specialized nature of the participant selection and the few participants (n = 3); the results may not extend beyond the specific context and to people with less VR experience. Moreover, the potential for observer bias is heightened, as the selected experts might not typically represent the average level of skill or knowledge in the field. The circumstance suggests that the WOz outcomes should be interpreted cautiously. Future investigations should incorporate a more diverse sampling approach. The WOz prototype presented in the current work can be used to explore several different avenues in further research related to player-avatar interaction in VR gaming. For example, the avatar's behavior, personality, facial expression, and body language could easily be manipulated by the person controlling the avatar to distinguish how different avatar characteristics influence PX. This would allow for experimental testing of factors that might be important in the player-avatar interaction. With extensive data tracking features, it would also be possible to gain objective and subjective measures of the experience, providing the possibility of data triangulation. This approach involves using multiple data sources to confirm or refute a particular observation, thereby increasing the credibility and reliability of the results. Another avenue for further research would be to investigate how VR literacy impacts participants' perceptions and may influence perceptions and experiences of player-avatar interactions. In addition, it would be intriguing to examine how interaction patterns change when an AI controls an avatar, potentially replacing a human actor with an on/off AI-powered system resembling a chatbot. Such investigation could further enhance our comprehension of avatar-human interactions in VR. In addition, it would be intriguing to examine how interaction patterns change when an AI controls an avatar compared to a human. Another potential avenue for further research would be to switch between an AI-controlled avatar and a human-controlled Avatar and investigate how participants' perceptions change.

4.3 Conclusion

WOz approaches can be used to evaluate the PX in VR-gaming cost-effectively. In the present work, we presented one such approach in which a human actor controls the avatar. The resource-efficient approach enables practitioners and researchers to evaluate different forms of player-avatar interactions qualitatively and quantitatively in VR games. Based on an exploratory qualitative environment, we identified three main factors that can contribute to a positive PX: 1) technical improvements, including aligning users' perception to their height and eye contact, 2) interaction design improvements, including providing a rich interaction between the player and the avatar and scripting meaningful conversations, and 3) authenticity improvements including making body movements natural and including credible physical features. Due to the limitations of the present study, these factors need to be explored further in future studies. The WOz prototype presented in the study could be used for further exploratory and experimental studies to understand the mechanics of player-avatar interaction in VR gaming.

Acknowledgements. This research was financially supported by the Centre of Excellent IT Education (EXCITED). The authors declare no conflicts of interest related to the study.

Appendix 1.

Prerequisites

- Unreal Engine 5
- Two Windows 11 computers with the minimum specification requirements for development with Varjo XR3 and in Unreal Engine 5.
- Movella Xsens MVN Awinda motion capture suit and recording and docking station (referred to as MoCap suit in this article)
- Xsens MVN Animate software (referred to as MoCap software in this article)
- Varjo XR-3 Mixed Reality Headset (referred to as VR Headset in this article)
- Varjo Base software
- Varjo OpenXR Plugin for Unreal
- Two HTC SteamVR Base Station 2.0s (To ensure a smoother VR experience for the headset wearer)
- SteamVR client software
- iPhone X (the first iPhone generation compatible with ARKit) [referred to as 'phone' in this article]
- Live Link Face app on the iPhone X
- A head-mounted phone holder mounted to the real life actor's head, with the iPhone's front-facing camera facing the wearer.
- Router (5Ghz WiFi preferred over 2.4Ghz for faster communication speed between the phone and two computers)
- Two noise-cancelling wireless headphones with microphones

Step 1 - Set up the virtual environment

1. Download the Epic Games Launcher

2. Install Unreal Engine Version 5.0.0 (version 5.0.0 is the earliest supported by the Varjo OpenXR plugin.)
3. Launch the installed Engine Version. Select the category Games, and the project template Virtual Reality, choose a project location on the disk drive and click Create.
4. Build a virtual environment in-engine tools such as Quixel Bridge so that the scene contains 3D objects that are to human scale, such as foliage on a flat ground, so the user with the VR headset can orient themselves easier.
5. Add a Player Start Actor in the centre of the scene, positioned approximately 2 m above the flat ground.

Step 2 - Set up VR

1. Mount the two base stations diagonally, at opposite corners of your space, 2 or more metres from the floor, both at least 0.5m away from the VR headset user.
2. On the computer, install the Varjo Base application
3. Download and Enable the Varjo OpenXR plugin from the Unreal Marketplace
4. Install and Launch SteamVR so it is running in the background.
5. In the Unreal Engine project, disable OculusVR and SteamVR plugins, leaving only OpenXR switched On.

Step 3 - Set up character

1. Download an Unreal MetaHuman as a base.
2. Download a 3D character asset with bones and rigging. In our case: a robot character inspired by the AI character from Ex Machina.
3. Retarget the chosen character onto the Unreal MetaHuman skeleton. Make sure the character is set up with a set of blend shapes that match the facial blend shapes produced by ARKit's facial recognition.

Step 4 - Set up motion capture

1. Attach all 17 XSens points to the actor in the required spots on the body.
2. Launch Xsens MVN Animate software.

Step 5 - Set up facial capture

1. Connect the iPhone and the computers to the same WiFi network.
2. Install Live Link Face by the creator Unreal Engine from the Apple App Store.
3. In the Unreal Engine project, activate the Apple ARKit, Apple ARKit Face Support and Live Link plugins.
4. Launch the Live Link Face app.
5. Choose Live Link (ARKit).
6. Identify the IPv4 addresses of both computers and put both addresses into the app's two Target fields.

Step 6 - Connect both computers to each other

1. Using the local IPv4 addresses, connect the two computers via LAN.

Step 7 - Run the project in-engine on both computers

1. Make sure the Unreal Engine project has finished compiling all shaders to ensure a smoother experience.
2. In the computer connected to the VR headset, Select VR Preview play mode and click Play to see the scene inside the headset. The other computer can remain out of Play mode, just with the editor open.
3. In the editor during play, adjust the height of the VR user's actor to be more accurate to their real life distance to the ground.

Step 8 - Set up a Call Between the User and the Actor. Place noise-cancelling wireless headphones with microphones on both the actor and the VR headset user. Using external devices like two smartphones, connect the headphones respectively and set up a voice call between them.

References

1. Bodzin, A., Junior, R.A., Hammond, T., Anastasio, D.: Investigating engagement and flow with a placed-based immersive virtual reality game. J. Sci. Educ. Technol. **30**, 347–360 (2021). https://doi.org/10.1007/S10956-020-09870-4
2. Korkut, E.-H., Surer, E.: Visualization in virtual reality: a systematic review. Virtual Real. **27**, 1447–1480 (2023). https://doi.org/10.1007/S10055-023-00753-8
3. Zhu, M., et al.: Haptic-feedback smart glove as a creative human-machine interface (HMI) for virtual/augmented reality applications. Sci Adv. **6**, (2020). https://doi.org/10.1126/SCIADV. AAZ8693
4. Madary, M., Metzinger, T.K.: Real virtuality: a code of ethical conduct. Recommendations for good scientific practice and the consumers of VR-technology. Front. Robot. AI. **3**, (2016). https://doi.org/10.3389/FROBT.2016.00003
5. Stanney, K.M., Nye, H., Haddad, S., Hale, K.S., Padron, C.K., Cohn, J.V.: Extended reality (XR) environments. In: Handbook of Human Factors and Ergonomics, pp. 782–815 (2021). https://doi.org/10.1002/9781119636113.CH30
6. Hartmann, J., Holz, C., Ofek, E., Wilson, A.D.: Realitycheck: blending virtual environments with situated physical reality. In: Proceedings of the 2019 CHI Conference on Human Factors in Computing Systems.•dl.acm.org. (2019). https://doi.org/10.1145/3290605.3300577
7. Wang, W., Cheng, J., Montreal, P.M., Canada, Q., Guo, J.L.C.: Usability of virtual reality application through the lens of the user community: a case study. In: Extended Abstracts of the 2019 CHI Conference on Human Factors in Computing, 2019•dl.acm.org. (2019). https://doi.org/10.1145/3290607.3312816
8. Schwind, V., Knierim, P., Haas, N.: Using presence questionnaires in virtual reality. In: CHI Proceedings of the 2019, p. 19. ACM (2019). https://doi.org/10.1145/3290605.3300590
9. Zhou, X., Teng, F., Du, X., Li, J., Jin, M., Xue, C.: H-GOMS: a model for evaluating a virtual-hand interaction system in virtual environments. Virtual Real. **27**, 497–522 (2023). https://doi.org/10.1007/S10055-022-00674-Y
10. Wiemeyer, J., Nacke, L., Moser, C., Floyd, F.: Player experience. In: Foundations, Concepts and Practice, pp. 243–271. Springer (2016). https://doi.org/10.1007/978-3-319-40612-1_9
11. Isbister, K., Schaffer, N.: Game Usability: Advancing the Player Experience. Morgan Kaufman Publishers, Massachusetts (2008)
12. Ip, I., Sweetser, P.: Investigating player experience in virtual reality games via remote experimentation. In: Extended Abstracts of the 2021 Annual Symposium on Computer-Human Interaction in Play, pp. 146–151. ACM, New York (2021). https://doi.org/10.1145/3450337. 3483462

13. Lazar, J., Feng, J.H., Hochheiser, H.: Research methods in human-computer interaction. Morgan Kaufmann Publishers (2017). https://doi.org/10.1016/b978-0-12-805390-4.00014-5
14. Dahlbäck, N., Jönsson, A., Ahrenberg, L.: Wizard of Oz studies. In: Proceedings of the 1st International Conference on Intelligent User Interfaces - IUI '93, pp. 193–200. ACM Press, New York (1993). https://doi.org/10.1145/169891.169968
15. Preece, J., Sharp, H., Rogers, Y.: Interaction design: beyond human-computer interaction. John Wiley & Sons (2015)
16. Henschke, M., Gedeon, T., Jones, R.: Touchless gestural interaction with Wizard-of-Oz: Analysing user behaviour. OzCHI 2015: Being Human - Conference Proceedings, pp. 207–211 (2015). https://doi.org/10.1145/2838739.2838792
17. Fialho, P., Coheur, L.: ChatWoz: chatting through a wizard of Oz. In: ASSETS 2015 - Proceedings of the 17th International ACM SIGACCESS Conference on Computers and Accessibility, pp. 423–424 (2015). https://doi.org/10.1145/2700648.2811334
18. Thomas, J., Bell, M., Lindenau, T.: Behind the curtain. ACM SIGGROUP. Bulletin **31**, 42–43 (2003). https://doi.org/10.1145/1052829.1052854
19. Campbell, S., et al.: Purposive sampling: complex or simple? research case examples. J. Res. Nurs. **25**, 652–661 (2020). https://doi.org/10.1177/1744987120927206
20. Braun, V., Clarke, V.: Using thematic analysis in psychology. Qual. Res. Psychol. **3**, 77–101 (2006)
21. Myers, M.D., Venable, J.R.: A set of ethical principles for design science research in information systems. Inf. Manage. **51**, 801–809 (2014). https://doi.org/10.1016/j.im.2014.01.002
22. Rea, D., Geiskkovitch, D.: Wizard of awwws: exploring psychological impact on the researchers in social HRI experiments. dl.acm.org. 21–29 (2017). https://doi.org/10.1145/3029798.3034782
23. Ivarsson, J., Lindwall, O.: Suspicious minds: the problem of trust and conversational agents. Comput. Support. Coop. Work **32**, 545–571 (2023). https://doi.org/10.1007/S10606-023-09465-8

The Correlations of Scene Complexity, Workload, Presence, and Cybersickness in a Task-Based VR Game

Mohammadamin Sanaei, Stephen B. Gilbert$^{(\boxtimes)}$, Nikoo Javadpour, Hila Sabouni, Michael C. Dorneich, and Jonathan W. Kelly

Iowa State University, Ames, IA 50010, USA
{asanaei,gilbert}@iastate.edu

Abstract. This investigation examined the relationships among scene complexity, workload, presence, and cybersickness in virtual reality (VR) environments. Numerous factors can influence the overall VR experience, and existing research on this matter is not yet conclusive, warranting further investigation. In this between-subjects experimental setup, 44 participants engaged in the Pendulum Chair game, with half exposed to a simple scene with lower optic flow and lower familiarity, and the remaining half to a complex scene characterized by higher optic flow and greater familiarity. The study measured the dependent variables workload, presence, and cybersickness and analyzed their correlations. Equivalence testing was also used to compare the simple and complex environments. Results revealed that despite the visible differences between the environments, within the 10% boundaries of the maximum possible value for workload and presence, and 13.6% of the maximum SSQ value, a statistically significant equivalence was observed between the simple and complex scenes. Additionally, a moderate, negative correlation emerged between workload and SSQ scores. The findings suggest two key points: (1) the nature of the task can mitigate the impact of scene complexity factors such as optic flow and familiarity, and (2) the correlation between workload and cybersickness may vary, showing either a positive or negative relationship.

Keywords: virtual reality experience · scene complexity · workload · presence · cybersickness

1 Introduction

In recent years, the rapid progress in Virtual Reality (VR) technology has propelled its integration into diverse fields. In education and training, it offers immersive and safe learning environments for users to have effective learning outcomes [1]. Within the healthcare industry, VR provides potential benefits in medical practice, such as improving surgical skills, enhancing the patient experience, and facilitating efficient training for healthcare professionals [2]. Also, VR's immersive power in game industry can contribute to users' satisfaction in many cases such as presence, immersion, interactivity, and feedback [3].

© The Author(s), under exclusive license to Springer Nature Switzerland AG 2024
J. Y. C. Chen and G. Fragomeni (Eds.): HCII 2024, LNCS 14706, pp. 277–289, 2024.
https://doi.org/10.1007/978-3-031-61041-7_18

This widespread adoption of VR applications in the mentioned domains underscores the growing need to gain a deeper understanding of the elements that shape user interaction and experiences within VR environments. Previous research has shown that VR environments may be different from video conferencing and face to face conditions in terms of social-related factors [4], task-related factors [5], and even performance [6]. These results necessitate new research to evaluate the relationships between different variables in the VR field to offer insights that could assist industry designers in creating better VR environments.

Several factors contribute to a person's overall VR experience: hardware, individual characteristics, and software [7]. Hardware factors refer to technology limitations of the device, such as screen resolution and field of view, along with customizable headset options, which can notably affect the experience [8]. Previous research also shows that individual characteristics such as age [9] and personality [10] can also affect VR experience.

Software factors, including scene complexity and the level of detail of the environments can also affect the engagement of the experience [11]. Virtual spaces with intricate and interactive content can provide a more realistic and compelling experience compared to simpler environments [12]. However, scene complexity can also impact the VR experience negatively; Fichna et al. [13] showed that high scene complexity can lead to increased cognitive load and visual clutter.

The significance of the relationship between scene complexity and VR experience is particularly pronounced in the domain of training, businesses, and virtual reality gaming, where users are not only entertained but are also presented with challenges that require the exertion of cognitive and motor skills. Thus, it is essential to study scene complexity in the game context and explore the relationship between scene complexity and other variables to help maintain user satisfaction in VR environments.

This research endeavored to explore the impact of scene complexity on participants' task-based VR gaming experiences, with a specific focus on four variables: scene complexity, workload, presence, and cybersickness.

2 Related Work

The relationship between scene complexity and workload could depends on multiple factors, such as the user's familiarity with the environment [14], the user's cognitive abilities [15], or time [16] High scene complexity can overwhelm users and cause cognitive load, making it difficult for them to understand and navigate through the environment [17, 18]. However, if users are adequately trained and adapted to the scene, they may become more efficient and experienced, leading to lower workload over time [14]. On the other hand, low scene complexity can result in a boring or less desirable experience [12]. So, the relationship between scene complexity and workload and their effects on VR experience can be non-trivial and dynamic. Therefore, in this study, the authors sought to contribute insight into how scene complexity and workload interact.

Another factor that might affect the users' VR experience could the relationship between scene complexity and presence [19, 20]. Although some studies have concluded that parameters of scene complexity like display resolution and texture mapping may not have a high influence on the sense of presence [21, 22], the findings of Witmer & Singer [23] and Welch et al. [20] on pictorial realism indicated that the higher level of details and realism in VEs led to an increased level of presence. Designing more complex scenes to have a better sense of presence may lead to higher possibility of cybersickness due to an associated increased perception of vection [19]. So, comprehending the dynamics of the relationship between scene complexity and presence is important for optimizing the VR gaming experience.

Understanding the relationship between workload and cybersickness has become another key research focus that could affect VR experience. Prior research has suggested that engaging in a task (higher workload) may contribute to reduced cybersickness in VR settings [24, 25]. Nevertheless, a recent study studying various workload levels and their impact on cybersickness indicated that participants in the higher workload condition had a significantly higher SSQ score and higher level of dropout due to cybersickness [26]. Because the results seem conflicting, it's important to take another look at how workload and cybersickness are connected.

Presence is defined as observers' feeling of psychologically transitioning from the real world to the virtual world [27]. Understanding the relationship between presence and cybersickness has been one of the primary goals in achieving a successful virtual reality experience [28]. Some investigations have found a positive relationship between the presence level in VR and cybersickness [29, 30]. For instance, in a virtual grocery shopping task where participants were looking for a specific item, a strong correlation between presence and cybersickness were found [30]. Also, some studies have reported a null correlation [31, 32]. But the overall weight of evidence suggests that presence and cybersickness are negatively related [28]. As an examples, Sepich et al. (2022) showed that there is a significantly negative correlation between presence and cybersickness in one of the conditions of that study. Another study on an immersive multisensory environment, aiming to improve presence, found that subjective presence was negatively associated with participants' discomfort [33].

In addition, literature has sometimes shown a correlation between presence and task workload. A virtual pipe-cutting task designed by Draper & Blair [34] showed a significant positive correlation between presence and workload scores [34], which aligned with a Ma & Kaber [35] study, where higher presence led to higher workload levels. On the other hand, some research offered contrasting outcomes. For example, Riley & Kaber [36] showed a potential negative relationship between presence and mental workload. In this particular study, however, it might have been due to the high difficulty of the task, leading participants to report high frustration levels through NASA-TLX. The high workload led participants disengaged and some left the task unfinished [36]. Also, earlier research has suggested that there is minimal to no correlation between these two factors [26, 37].

3   Experiment Design

Based on the independent variable in this study, scene complexity, the Pendulum Chair had two different scenes, which were called simple scene and complex scene (Fig. 1). These scenes are different in two key aspects: optic flow and scene familiarity. Based on the measurements of Lucas & Kanade [38] algorithm used across the first 10-s duration of 20 participants in the simple scene and complex scene, the complex scene had roughly 10 times the optic flow of the simple scene. Also, regarding the familiarity, in a separate study, 53 participants completed a pairwise comparison survey that posed the question "Which of these scenes is more familiar?" for all possible pairings of four images from the simple scene and four images from the complex scene. Then, using the Bradley-Terry [39] and an independent samples t-test among familiarity strength of those eight pictures, participants rated that the familiarity of the complex scene is statistically significantly higher than a simple scene, $t(6) = -7.785, p < .001, d = -5.50$.

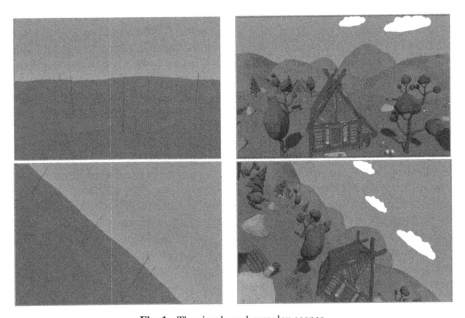

Fig. 1. The simple and complex scenes.

Upon receiving approval from the Institutional Review Board (IRB), the researchers conducted their Pendulum Chair study data collection at Iowa State University. The study involved 44 participants consisted of 26 women, 16 men, one non-binary, and one preferred not to answer aged 18–53 ($M = 24.2, SD = 6.8, Mdn = 22.0$). All the participants had no history of photosensitive seizure disorders or vision problems, were fluent in English, and were at least 18 years of age. All the data was gathered from the first-person virtual reality (VR) game, Pendulum Chair, as described in Sanaei et al. (2023).

Half of the participants experienced the simple scene, while the other half experienced the complex scene. When participants arrived at the laboratory, they completed a pre-survey that included demographic information. Then, after having their interpupillary distance measured and the headset adjusted accordingly, each participants started to play the Pendulum Chair game [40]. In Pendulum Chair, the player sits in a chair atop an inverted pendulum and uses a joystick to prevent the chair from falling and hitting the ground (Fig. 2). While the maximum of game play was 650 s, participants could exit the environment whenever they wanted. After playing the game, the researcher asked participants to fill in the post survey consisted of SSQ, NASA-TLX, and Presence questionnaires.

Fig. 2. Participants' posture (left) and an external view of Pendulum Chair, showing the chair atop a pole that acts as an inverted pendulum. The goal is to stay balanced.

This study measured three variables as dependent variables in the Pendulum Chair. Post SSQ [41] was used to measure the cybersickness. The SSQ questionnaire contains 16 Likert scaled questions ranging from zero (no symptoms) to three (severe symptoms). To measure the workload that participants experienced, the authors used the NASA-TLX questionnaire [42] in the post survey. NASA-TLX consists of six questions which analyze participant's mental, physical, temporal demands, effort, performance, and frustrations in a 21-point scale for each of variables. Additionally, participants' feeling of presence in the Pendulum Chair was measured with an immersion questionnaire [43]. The immersion questionnaire consisted of 31 questions for which participants rated each using a 5-point Likert scale.

4   Hypotheses

The first hypothesis is written based on the Faure et al. [17] 's study, in which driving in more complex environments and performing a secondary task increased drivers' mental workload, as evidenced by higher blink rates and smaller pupil diameters. So, H1 is that participants will experience higher workload in the complex environment. The second hypothesis is based on a study by Stanney et al. [19]. Stanney et al. [19] found that more complexity of the scene (in terms of more texture and details) enhanced the sense of presence for users, so H2 would be that participants experience a higher sense of presence in the complex scene. Next, per Sepich et al. [26]'s study where they found that more cognitive workload led to more sickness, the authors suggest in H3 that the higher workload participants experience, the more sickness they will have in the environment. Per Weech et al. [28]'s study, which conducted a comprehensive literature search about the relationship between presence and cybersickness and suggested a negative relationship between presence and cybersickness, H4 says that the higher sense of presence participants have, the less sickness they will experience in the environment. The last hypothesis is based on Draper & Blair [34] study, in which they found that higher presence led to higher workload levels; H5 predicts a positive relationship between workload and presence.

5   Results

Independent sample t-tests were used to analyze if there is any difference between the dependent variables based on condition (simple scene vs. complex scene). The assumptions of the t-test were analyzed by using inspection of a boxplot for assessing the outliers, Shapiro-Wilk's test for assessing the normality, and Levene's test for assessing the homogeneity of variances. Effect size for each comparison was measured using Cohen's d to measure the effect size as large ($d = 0.8$), medium ($d = 0.5$), and small ($d = 0.2$) [44]. For correlations, a Pearson's correlation was used unless it was uncertain that the variable relationships were monotonic, in which case a Kendall's tau-b correlation was used.

If the two means in a comparison were very close, with a high p-value and a low effect size, an equivalence test was run to explore whether the two distributions were statistically equivalent. The two one-sided test (TOST) equivalence approach was used with independent sample t-tests [45] the null hypothesis was tested by setting the α level at .05. The key to equivalence testing is setting the upper and lower bounds for the equivalence range, or similarly, setting the smallest effect size of interest (SESOI). There are several different approaches to setting these bounds or SESOI. They include 1) basing them on a known standard or benchmark in the experimental domain, 2) basing them on an objectively measurable just-noticeable-difference, or 3) basing them on a subjective judgment of what difference would be of interest for a particular domain, as well as other approaches [46]. For example, in the domain of pharmaceutical drug equivalence, the U.S. Federal Drug Administration has designated that a generic drug must have no more than a 20% change from the original drug's mean efficacy to be deemed equivalent [47].

The present analysis used the last approach, as the authors conducted a thought experiment by asking themselves the question for each variable, "If someone said they had an intervention that would change [the variable] by X amount, how big does X need to be for the intervention to be of interest?" Multiple authors suggested that a 10% change from the mean would be worth noting and merit further exploration of this hypothetical intervention. Another viewpoint is that a change of 10% of the maximum value of the variable could be appropriate. Because of the subjectivity of this approach, strong claims about equivalence are not made, but equivalence testing was used as a tool for further exploring the relationship between the simple and complex scene data.

5.1   Workload

All t-test assumptions were met except that there was one outlier in the simple scene data. Analysis continued with the outlier because omitting the outlier did not change the result of the t-test (sensitivity analysis). There was no significant difference between mean of participants' workload experienced in the simple scene (10.89 ± 3.20) and mean of participants' workload experienced in the complex scene (10.55 ± 3.40), $t(42) = .342, p = .734, d = 0.103$. Then, using bounds at 10% of the mean, ± 1.07 did not yield a significant equivalence test ($p = .234$). However, using bounds at 10% of the maximum amount of possible workload, ± 2.1, an equivalence test showed that workload in both simple and complex scenes was statistically significantly equivalent ($p = .042$) (see Fig. 3).

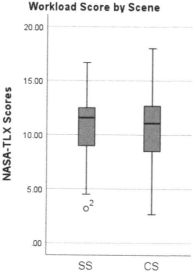

Fig. 3. Boxplots of NASA-TLX workload scores for participants in the simple scene ($n = 22$) vs. complex scene ($n = 22$). Using 10% of the max NASA-TLX value for bounds yielded a significant equivalence.

5.2   Presence

All t-test assumptions were met. There was no significant difference between mean of participants' presence experience in the simple scene (98.54 ± 13.48) and mean of participants' presence experience in the complex scene (101.09 ± 19.17), $t(42) = .509$, $p = .613, d = 0.154$. Using bounds at 10% of the mean, ± 9.98, yielded a near significant equivalence test ($p = .073$). However, using ± 12.4 (10% of $155 - 31$, the maximum and minimum presence score) yielded statistical equivalence ($p = .028$). The threshold 12.4 was 10% of the maximum amount of possible presence (Fig. 4).

Presence Score by Scene

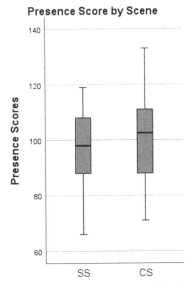

Fig. 4. Boxplots of presence scores for participants in the simple scene ($n = 22$) vs. complex scene ($n = 22$). 10% of the max presence value for boundaries yielded a significant equivalence.

5.3 Cybersickness

The assumptions of the t-test were met. The result showed no significant difference between mean of SSQ score in simple (64.77 ± 40.53) and complex (52.02 ± 32.38)

Post-SSQ Score by Scene

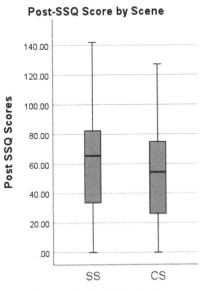

Fig. 5. Boxplots of SSQ scores for participants in the simple scene ($n = 22$) vs. complex scene ($n = 22$). 13.6% of the max SSQ value for boundaries yielded a significant equivalence.

scenes, $t(42) = -1.153, p = .256, d = -0.35$. The closeness of the means of the Post-SSQ score across the simple and complex scenes suggested that it could be worthwhile to run a two one-sided test (TOST) equivalence test. Using an upper and lower bound of 10% of the mean (± 5.8), the distributions were not statistically equivalent ($p = .733$). However, the distributions were similar enough that using an upper and lower bound of ± 32, 13.6% of the max SSQ value, yielded a significant equivalence effect ($p = .045$) (see Fig. 5).

5.4 Correlations

There was a significant moderate, negative correlation between workload and SSQ scores, $\tau_b = -.38, p = .001$. The correlation between presence and SSQ scores was not significant, $\tau_b = -.87, p = .417$. The correlation between workload and presence was not significant, $\tau_b = -.05, p = .63$.

6 Discussion

H1 (higher workload in complex) and H2 (higher presence in complex) were not supported. Despite marked differences in optic flow and familiarity (scene complexity) between the simple and complex scenes, the observed equivalency, particularly within the 10% boundaries of the maximum possible workload and presence, prompts consideration of an additional influencing factor. The equivalent workload and presence in both scenes could be attributed to the uniformity of the task across environments. The presence of the same task in both the simple and complex scenes may result in comparable levels of workload and presence, potentially overshadowing the effects of optic flow and familiarity (scene complexity). This result suggests that the presence of a task, independent of scene content, has the potential to neutralize the impact of scene complexity factors.

H3 (higher workload correlated with greater sickness) and H4 (higher presence correlated with lower sickness) were not supported. Like optic flow and familiarity effects, similar outcomes may extend to the realm of cybersickness, where the observed equivalency hints at the potential dominance of factors beyond scene complexity, specifically workload and presence. Prior investigations have established correlations between cybersickness and workload [26] as well as cybersickness and presence [28]. The documented relationship between optic flow, a scene complexity factor, and cybersickness [7] indicates that increased optic flow often correlates with heightened cybersickness. Intriguingly, in the present study, despite significant differences in optic flow, no corresponding difference in cybersickness was observed. This could imply that the equivalency in workload and presence, stemming from the uniform task across scenes, might overshadow the impact of varying optic flow. It raises the possibility that the influence of presence and workload variables might outweigh the impact of optic flow in influencing cybersickness. A future focus on these variables could refine VR experiences, enhancing both user enjoyment and comfort.

Furthermore, the observed negative correlation between workload and cybersickness in the present study suggests that a higher workload imposed by the virtual environment may correlate with a reduced likelihood of experiencing cybersickness. While some studies have reported contradictory outcomes [26], Sepich et al. [26] demonstrated that increasing workload up to a certain limited threshold might result in decreased cybersickness—an alignment with our study's findings. The authors posit that the results of our study fall within this threshold, with the task potentially diverting individuals from cybersickness cues. These results underscore the need for future research to consider workload analysis, particularly exploring the maximum workload threshold that minimizes cybersickness.

The results did not reveal a significant correlation between presence and cybersickness. This lack of significance could potentially be attributed to the modest sample size in our study. It's plausible that with a larger sample size, the large negative correlation value could become statistically significant, aligning with existing literature that posits a negative relationship between presence and cybersickness. Moreover, the lack of support for H5 is consistent with findings from some previous studies that revealed minimal to no correlation between these two factors [26, 37]. This observation highlights the need for further investigation into this correlation in future research efforts.

7 Conclusion

In this study, the aim was to investigate the interplay between scene complexity, workload, presence, and cybersickness. Surprisingly, the results unveiled no significant distinctions between simple and complex scenes across any dependent variables. Equivalence testing, when considering 10% of the maximum variable value, further revealed statistical equivalence in workload and presence between both scenes. Cybersickness also demonstrated equivalence when employing 13.6% of the maximum SSQ value. As discussed in the discussion section, our findings suggest that the dynamics of scene complexity, workload, presence, and cybersickness may depend on the nature of the task users engage in within the VR environment. When users perform a task that is unrelated to the scene, scene complexity factors seem to be disregarded. Moreover, our study proposes that workload and presence might exert more influence than traditional factors such as optic flow in shaping cybersickness experiences. Despite significant differences in optic flow, our study found no substantial difference between simple and complex scenes when workload and presence were measured equal in both scenes. Intriguingly, these results challenge existing literature by indicating that an increase in workload correlates with a decrease in cybersickness, contrary to previous findings.

Future research should prioritize task considerations when examining cybersickness variables, as the nature of the tasks may potentially override the effects of other variables. Lastly, exploring various levels of workload in relation to cybersickness is a valuable avenue for further investigation. Such exploration can illuminate the threshold at which workload distracts users from cybersickness cues and may identify the workload conditions that may exacerbate the feeling of sickness in VR environments.

References

1. Xie, B., et al.: A review on virtual reality skill training applications. Front. Virtual Reality **2** (2021). https://doi.org/10.3389/frvir.2021.645153
2. Javaid, M., Haleem, A.: Virtual reality applications toward medical field. Clin. Epidemiol. Glob. Health. **8**, 600–605 (2020). https://doi.org/10.1016/j.cegh.2019.12.010
3. Checa, D., Bustillo, A.: A review of immersive virtual reality serious games to enhance learning and training. Multimed. Tools Appl. **79**, 5501–5527 (2020). https://doi.org/10.1007/s11042-019-08348-9
4. Sanaei, M., Machacek, M., Eubanks, J.C., Wu, P., Oliver, J., Gilbert, S.B.: The effect of training communication medium on the social constructs co-presence, engagement, rapport, and trust: explaining how training communication medium affects the social constructs co-presence, engagement, rapport, and trust. In: Proceedings of the 28th ACM Symposium on Virtual Reality Software and Technology, pp. 1–3 (2022)
5. Sanaei, M., Machacek, M., Gilbert, S., Wu, P., Oliver, J.: Comparing perceptions of performance across virtual reality, video conferencing, and face-to-face collaborations. In: 2023 IEEE Conference on Systems, Man, and Cybernetics (2023)
6. Sanaei, M., Machacek, M., Gilbert, S., Eubanks, C., Wu, P., Oliver, J.: The impact of embodiment on training effectiveness. In: 2023 11th International Conference on Information and Education Technology (ICIET), pp. 44–50. IEEE (2023)
7. Tian, N., Lopes, P., Boulic, R.: A review of cybersickness in head-mounted displays: raising attention to individual susceptibility. Virtual Reality **26**(4), 1409–1441 (2022). https://doi.org/10.1007/s10055-022-00638-2
8. Rebenitsch, L., Owen, C.: Review on cybersickness in applications and visual displays. Virtual Reality **20**(2), 101–125 (2016). https://doi.org/10.1007/s10055-016-0285-9
9. Rey, M.C.B., Clark, T.K., Wang, W., Leeder, T., Bian, Y., Merfeld, D.M.: Vestibular perceptual thresholds increase above the age of 40. Front. Neurol. **7** (2016). https://doi.org/10.3389/fneur.2016.00162
10. Jasper, A., Doty, T., Sepich, N., Dorneich, M.C., Gilbert, S.B., Kelly, J.W.: The relationship between personality, recalled cybersickness severity, and recalled cybersickness recovery time. Proc. Hum. Fact. Ergon. Soc. Ann. Meeting **65**(1), 206–210 (2021). https://doi.org/10.1177/1071181321651185
11. Luo, X., Kenyon, R., Kamper, D., Sandin, D., DeFanti, T.: The effects of scene complexity, stereovision, and motion parallax on size constancy in a virtual environment. In: 2007 IEEE Virtual Reality Conference, pp. 59–66 (2007). https://doi.org/10.1109/VR.2007.352464
12. Handali, J.P., Schneider, J., Gau, M., Holzwarth, V., vom Brocke, J.: Visual complexity and scene recognition: how low can you go? In: 2021 IEEE Virtual Reality and 3D User Interfaces (VR), pp. 286–295. IEEE (2021)
13. Fichna, S., Biberger, T., Seeber, B.U., Ewert, S.D.: Effect of acoustic scene complexity and visual scene representation on auditory perception in virtual audio-visual environments. In: 2021 Immersive and 3D Audio: from Architecture to Automotive (I3DA). pp. 1–9. IEEE (2021)
14. Rostami, S., Shenfield, A., Sigurnjak, S., Fakorede, O.: Evaluation of mental workload and familiarity in human computer interaction with integrated development environments using single-channel EEG. In: Proceeding of PPIG 2015–26th Annual workshop (2015)
15. Hernandez, R., Jin, H., Pyatak, E.A., Roll, S.C., Schneider, S.: Workers' whole day workload and next day cognitive performance. Curr. Psychol. (2023). https://doi.org/10.1007/s12144-023-04400-y
16. Hertzum, M., Holmegaard, K.D.: Perceived time as a measure of mental workload: effects of time constraints and task success. Int. J. Hum.-Comput. Interact. **29**, 26–39 (2013). https://doi.org/10.1080/10447318.2012.676538

17. Faure, V., Lobjois, R., Benguigui, N.: The effects of driving environment complexity and dual tasking on drivers' mental workload and eye blink behavior. Transp. Res. Part F: Traffic Psychol. Behav. **40**, 78–90 (2016). https://doi.org/10.1016/j.trf.2016.04.007

18. Lyu, N., Xie, L., Wu, C., Fu, Q., Deng, C.: Driver's cognitive workload and driving performance under traffic sign information exposure in complex environments: a case study of the highways in China. Int. J. Environ. Res. Public Health **14**, 203 (2017)

19. Stanney, K.M., Kingdon, K.S., Graeber, D., Kennedy, R.S.: Human performance in immersive virtual environments: effects of exposure duration, user control, and scene complexity. Hum. Perform. **15**, 339–366 (2002). https://doi.org/10.1207/S15327043HUP1504_03

20. Welch, R.B., Blackmon, T.T., Liu, A., Mellers, B.A., Stark, L.W.: The effects of pictorial realism, delay of visual feedback, and observer interactivity on the subjective sense of presence. Presence Teleoperators Virtual Environ. **5**, 263–273 (1996)

21. Hettinger, L.J.: Illusory self-motion in virtual environments. In: Handbook of Virtual Environments, pp. 511–532. CRC Press (2002)

22. Snow, M.P., Williges, R.C.: Empirical models based on free-modulus magnitude estimation of perceived presence in virtual environments. Hum. Factors J. Hum. Factors Ergon. Soc. **40**(3), 386–402 (1998). https://doi.org/10.1518/001872098779591395

23. Witmer, B.G., Singer, M.J.: Measuring immersion in virtual environments. ARI Technical Report 1014. Alexandria, VA: US Army Research Institute for (1994)

24. Farmani, Y., Teather, R.J.: Evaluating discrete viewpoint control to reduce cybersickness in virtual reality. Virtual Real. **24**, 645–664 (2020)

25. Mittelstaedt, J., Wacker, J., Stelling, D.: Effects of display type and motion control on cybersickness in a virtual bike simulator. Displays **51**, 43–50 (2018). https://doi.org/10.1016/j.dis pla.2018.01.002

26. Sepich, N.C., Jasper, A., Fieffer, S., Gilbert, S.B., Dorneich, M.C., Kelly, J.W.: The impact of task workload on cybersickness. Front. Virtual Real. **3**, 943409 (2022). https://doi.org/10.3389/frvir.2022.943409

27. Sadowski, W., Stanney, K.: Presence in virtual environments. In: Handbook of Virtual Environments, pp. 831–846. CRC Press (2002)

28. Weech, S., Kenny, S., Barnett-Cowan, M.: Presence and cybersickness in virtual reality are negatively related: a review. Front. Psychol. **10** (2019). https://doi.org/10.3389/fpsyg.2019.00158

29. Ling, Y., Nefs, H.T., Brinkman, W.-P., Qu, C., Heynderickx, I.: The relationship between individual characteristics and experienced presence. Comput. Hum. Behav. **29**, 1519–1530 (2013)

30. Liu, C.-L., Uang, S.-T.: Effects of presence on causing cybersickness in the elderly within a 3D virtual store. In: Jacko, J.A. (ed.) HCI 2011. LNCS, vol. 6764, pp. 490–499. Springer, Heidelberg (2011). https://doi.org/10.1007/978-3-642-21619-0_61

31. Mania, K., Chalmers, A.: The effects of levels of immersion on memory and presence in virtual environments: a reality centered approach. Cyberpsychol. Behav. **4**, 247–264 (2001). https://doi.org/10.1089/109493101300117938

32. Seay, A.F., Krum, D.M., Hodges, L., Ribarsky, W.: Simulator sickness and presence in a high field-of-view virtual environment. In: CHI '02 Extended Abstracts on Human Factors in Computing Systems, pp. 784–785. ACM, Minneapolis Minnesota USA (2002). https://doi.org/10.1145/506443.506596

33. Cooper, N., Milella, F., Cant, I., Pinto, C., White, M., Meyer, G.: The effects of multisensory cues on the sense of presence and task performance in a virtual reality environment (2015)

34. Draper, J.V., Blair, L.M.: Workload, flow, and telepresence during teleoperation. In: Proceedings of IEEE International Conference on Robotics and Automation, pp. 1030–1035. IEEE (1996)

35. Ma, R., Kaber, D.B.: Presence, workload and performance effects of synthetic environment design factors. Int. J. Hum.-Comput. Stud. **64**, 541–552 (2006). https://doi.org/10.1016/j.ijhcs.2005.12.003

36. Riley, J.M., Kaber, D.B.: Utility of situation awareness and attention for describing telepresence experiences in a virtual teleoperation task. In: Proceedings of the International Conference on Computer-Aided Ergonomics and Safety, pp. 88–93 (2001)

37. Nenna, F., Zanardi, D., Gamberini, L.: Effects of presence on human performance and workload in simulated VR-based telerobotics. In: Proceedings of the 16th International Conference on PErvasive Technologies Related to Assistive Environments, pp. 47–52. ACM, Corfu Greece (2023). https://doi.org/10.1145/3594806.3594856

38. Lucas, B.D., Kanade, T.: An iterative image registration technique with an application to stereo vision. Vancouver (1981)

39. Bradley, R.A., Terry, M.E.: Rank analysis of incomplete block designs: I. Method paired comparisons. Biometrika **39**, 324–345 (1952). https://doi.org/10.2307/2334029

40. Sanaei, M., Perron, A.J., Gilbert, S.B.: Pendulum chair: a research platform for cybersickness. Proc. Hum. Fact. Ergon. Soc. Ann. Meeting **67**(1), 1837–1843 (2023). https://doi.org/10.1177/21695067231192456

41. Kennedy, R.S., Lane, N.E., Berbaum, K.S., Lilienthal, M.G.: Simulator sickness questionnaire: an enhanced method for quantifying simulator sickness. Int. J. Aviat. Psychol. **3**, 203–220 (1993). https://doi.org/10.1207/s15327108ijap0303_3

42. Hart, S.G., Staveland, L.E.: Development of NASA-TLX (Task Load Index): Results of empirical and theoretical research. In: Human Mental Workload, pp. 139–183. Elsevier (1988). https://doi.org/10.1016/S0166-4115(08)62386-9

43. Jennett, C., et al.: Measuring and defining the experience of immersion in games. Int. J. Hum.-Comput. Stud. **66**, 641–661 (2008)

44. Cohen, J.: Statistical power analysis for the behavioral sciences Lawrence Earlbaum Associates, 20th (1988)

45. Dixon, P.M., Saint-Maurice, P.F., Kim, Y., Hibbing, P., Bai, Y., Welk, G.J.: A primer on the use of equivalence testing for evaluating measurement agreement. Med. Sci. Sports Exerc. **50**, 837 (2018)

46. Lakens, D., Scheel, A.M., Isager, P.M.: Equivalence testing for psychological research: a tutorial. Adv. Methods Pract. Psychol. Sci. **1**, 259–269 (2018)

47. Federal Drug Administration, H.: Orange book: approved drug products with therapeutic equivalence evaluations. USA US Food Drug Adm. (2013)

The Influence of the Level of Detail and Interactivity of 3D Elements on UX in XR Applications

Maurizio Vergari[1]([✉]), Maximilian Warsinke[1], Tanja Kojić[1],
Sebastian Möller[1,4], Jan-Niklas Voigt-Antons[3], Osama Abboud[2],
and Xun Xiao[2]

[1] Quality and Usability Lab, TU Berlin, Berlin, Germany
`maurizio.vergari@tu-berlin.de`
[2] Advanced Wireless Technologies Lab - Munich Research Center, Huawei
Technologies Duesseldorf GmbH, Munich, Germany
[3] Immersive Reality Lab, Hamm-Lippstadt University of Applied Sciences,
Lippstadt, Germany
[4] German Research Center for Artificial Intelligence (DFKI), Berlin, Germany

Abstract. In the realm of extended reality (XR) applications, a significant challenge lies in the resource-intensive rendering of 3D models, which often demand high computational power, creating a need for optimization. However, not all elements within a 3D environment are equally important for the user experience (UX). Recognizing and effectively addressing this could greatly enhance the performance of XR applications. How can manipulating the level of detail (LOD) increase the overall quality of user interactions? It was hypothesised that there would be no significant effect on participants' perception of the reduction of LOD for non-interactive objects, thereby forming the null hypothesis for H_1. Additionally, a second hypothesis was proposed: The reduction of LOD of non-interactive objects would not significantly affect the game enjoyment, forming the null hypothesis for H_2. A virtual reality (VR) survival game was developed in Unreal Engine to test these hypotheses. The virtual environment contained two types of objects: interactive objects (e.g., barrels and weapons) and non-interactive objects (e.g., pallets and shelves). Using interactive objects, players must defend themselves against multiple enemies. Users had to play through different conditions with a decreasing LOD of non-interactive objects and answer a post-session questionnaire. Only 5 out of 53 participants noticed a difference in quality. Furthermore, the majority of participants reported equal game satisfaction for every condition. These findings indicate that a decrease in the LOD of non-interactive objects is not significantly perceptible and does not significantly affect the UX.

Keywords: Extended Reality · Level of Detail · User Experience · Virtual Reality · Gaming

© The Author(s), under exclusive license to Springer Nature Switzerland AG 2024
J. Y. C. Chen and G. Fragomeni (Eds.): HCII 2024, LNCS 14706, pp. 290–300, 2024.
https://doi.org/10.1007/978-3-031-61041-7_19

1   Introduction

XR technology continues to gain popularity. Due to the novel and affordable head-mounted devices (HMDs), XR entertainment has reached a wider audience and is becoming increasingly established in the consumer market. Most new headsets are designed to function independently, allowing games and apps to run directly on the device. The redundancy of powerful gaming computers for playing VR games made the technology more accessible to a broader audience. However, standalone devices cannot offer the same computational power as externally connected PCs. This development creates a need for performance optimization to provide a comparable visual quality and reduce battery consumption, thereby increasing the duration of usage. This trade-off between device limitations and optimal performance can be regarded as a key challenge in current XR devices.

In the area of gaming, a performance-costly factor is the handling and visualization of 3D objects within the virtual environment. Many practices have been established in game development to guarantee high-performance applications, such as culling, LOD adjustments, or texture and shader techniques. Because VR games are even more dependent on high frame rates, dynamic quality adjustments are even more important. When implementing LOD adjustments, it is common to examine where players pay attention to. Respectively, visual present objects should be prioritized and receive the highest performance allocations. These tend to be objects with which players interact, such as items or 3D characters. Therefore, it was assumed that non-interactive objects, receiving less attention, have a greater tolerance for low LOD without negatively impacting the players' UX.

To test this assumption, a VR shooting game was developed for the user study. The player had to use several interactive objects to defend against approaching enemies. The genre offers highly interactive gameplay, requiring the user to shoot, aim, dodge, and navigate in the virtual world. Approaching enemies are a constant threat that focuses the attention on the action. During the game, the LOD of the non-interactive objects decreases with each of the four game rounds. After completing the level, each participant answered a questionnaire to gather insights into their perceptions. The goal of the experiment was to determine if the quality reduction of the non-interactive objects was noticeable and if the reduction had an impact on the enjoyment of the game. Therefore, the following two hypotheses were formulated:

Hypothesis 1 (H_1): In a VR survival game, the reduction of the LOD of non-interactive objects is significantly noticeable for participants.

Hypothesis 2 (H_2): In a VR survival game, the reduction of the LOD of non-interactive objects significantly affects the game enjoyment.

The qualitative and quantitative answers from the post-game questionnaire, given by 53 participants who took part in the experiment, suggest that there is not enough evidence to reject the null hypothesis for both H_1 and H_2. Hence, in the specific game that was developed, the reduction in the LOD of non-interactive objects was neither significantly noticeable nor did it significantly impact the UX.

If this result can be translated to other genres and game situations, the results could confirm that non-intractable objects offer the potential for performance optimization in VR gaming.

2   Related Work

2.1   UX in VR Gaming

According to the International Organization for Standardization, UX refers to a person's perceptions and responses that result from the use or anticipated use of a product, system, or service [7]. When discussing UX in digital games, additional dimensions of the experience must be considered. Games often require the fulfilment of a specific challenge that players must overcome. In this regard, influencing factors such as the competence and experience of a player can determine the enjoyment of the game [10]. The concept of *flow* describes the state of a person who is in the perfect equilibrium of the difficulty of a task and his abilities to overcome it [3]. In VR gaming, two unique aspects deserve more attention for UX: the presence and immersion of VR technology and the accompanying condition of cybersickness.

The terms *presence* and *immersion* are commonly used to describe VR experiences, but it is important to distinguish between the two. According to Slater and Wilbur, immersion describes the objective aspects of the VR system (e.g. display resolution) while presence is the subjective quality induced in the user (feeling present in a virtual environment) [14]. In a subsequent publication, Slater further specified the term presence [12]. Proposed is a distinction between Place Illusion (PI) "being there" and Plausibility illusion (Psi) referring to the fantasy that the virtual scenario is actually occurring. In the most recent update from 2022, Slater argued that a separate reality can be created if PI and Psi are imposed on participants concurrently [13].

Cybersickness is a form of motion sickness that occurs when users immerse themselves in a VR environment [9]. Symptoms, among others, are eye strain, headache, and nausea, and the causes are not fully understood [9]. The most common theory for its origin is the sensory mismatch between visual and vestibular inputs (users see themselves moving through a virtual space without actually moving in an analogue space) [5]. The appearance and strength of cybersickness symptoms seem to be influenced by multiple factors, such as predispositions from users, hardware, and the content of the experiences [2].

2.2   Visual Attention and LOD Management

The human vision is limited to 135° vertically and 160° horizontally and fine details are only perceived within a central circle of 5° [6]. Consequently, in computer games, only the central circle and foveal zone would have to be rendered with a high LOD. Watson et al. demonstrated that peripheral resolution could be diminished by nearly 50 percent with no significant decline in perception [15]. It has been shown that eye movement patterns differ among different game genres. El-Nasr and Yan's eye-tracking experiment with 3D games revealed that players in first-person shooter games predominantly focus on the center of the screen, where the crosshair is located, while the player's visual attention in action-adventure games is distributed across the entire screen [4].

However, gaze-based LOD management can lead to artifacts when updating the display after rapid eye saccades [8]. Furthermore, anticipating eye movements is challenging because attention is influenced by low-level image features (e.g., luminance, contrast) and higher-level cognitive phenomena.

According to Reddy, the attention of a game object can be determined by criteria such as distance, size, eccentricity and speed of the objects [11]. Adaptive LOD approaches reduce the number of polygons in a virtual scene by selecting an appropriate instance of polygon complexity for 3D models, depending on the current game situation. But also in non-adaptive games, the allocation of triangle counts is a common practice. Objects that are crucial for the game objective, such as characters and interactable objects, usually possess a much higher LOD than decorative, non-intractable objects. The LOD of a 3D object is primarily defined by its texture quality and number of vertices [1].

3 Methods

3.1 Game Design

A VR shooter game was developed to test the hypotheses formulated in Sect. 1. This genre offers high interactivity and a strict focus of attention. The player stands in a warehouse setting with the objective of defending against approaching enemies (e.g., melee fighters, ranged fighters, flying drones). The enemies' behavior follows a basic pattern: they advance towards the player until reaching a specific proximity, at which point they execute an attack maneuver. If a weapon or projectile collides with the player character, it leads to a decrease in "life points". To evade these attacks, the player can dodge with the HMD. Apart from this method of movement, the player remains stationary, in the analog lab room and within the virtual world to prevent cybersickness during the experiment. For defence, the player can use either weapons (e.g. gun, knife) or objects that are incorporated in the game environment. All objects were grouped into two distinct categories:

– **Interactive objects:** Barrels, walls, weapons, enemies
– **Non-interactive objects:** Pallets, bricks, shelves, sand mounds etc.

The enemies arrive in four rounds that mirror the four conditions in this experiment. With each round, the LOD of non-interactive objects is reduced. A round ends if the last enemy is defeated and after four rounds, the game ends.

3.2 Technology and Tools

The HMD chosen was the Meta Quest 2, which was connected through the Meta Link cable to a gaming computer. The game was developed with Unreal Engine

5.1.1[1] with the usage of the Quixel Megascans[2] library that offers a large amount of 3D assets. Conveniently, 3D objects are already available at different quality levels, thus being well suited for the experimental conditions. The game environment was built using geometry meshes from the Unreal Editor and by using suitable assets, with the goal of creating an authentic-looking factory building (Fig. 1). The finished level consisted of over 13,000 game objects. The 3D models and animations for the enemies were obtained from the Unreal Engine marketplace and were available free of charge.

Fig. 1. Warehouse as game environment

Level of Detail. Following the experimental design, the non-interactive objects had to have four different quality settings. For the manipulation of LOD, the texture resolution and triangle count of the 3d model should serve as primary factors for quality reduction. The Quixel Megascans already provided a high-triangle and low-triangle version, that was complemented by manual reduction of texture quality. This led to an average reduction of triangles by 95,9% (Fig. 3) and four different levels of texture resolution, namely 4096 × 4096, 1024 × 1024, 512 × 512, and 256 × 256 pixels, reducing the total number of pixels by 99,6% (Fig. 2). Combining both variables allowed the creation of four distinct quality levels (Fig. 4), which were applied to the non-interactive objects in each successive game round.

---

[1] https://www.unrealengine.com/.
[2] https://quixel.com/megascans/.

The following quality levels were used for the conditions (i.e., game rounds):

– LOD 0 (High quality): 4096x4096 pixel, 14804 triangles
– LOD 1 (Medium quality): 1024x1024 pixel, 500 triangles
– LOD 2 (Low quality): 512x512 pixel, 500 triangles
– LOD 3 (Really low quality): 256x256 pixel, 500 triangles

Fig. 2. Wooden pallet textures with 1024x1024 pixel and 256x256 pixel

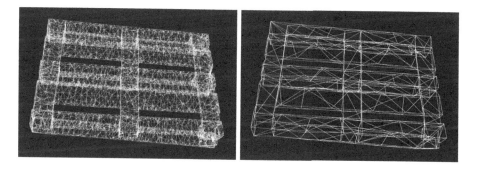

Fig. 3. Wooden pallet wireframes with 14804 triangles and 500 triangles

3.3 Study Procedure

Due to the uncertainty of the number of participants, a within-subject design
was chosen to increase statistical power. The experiment was conducted in a

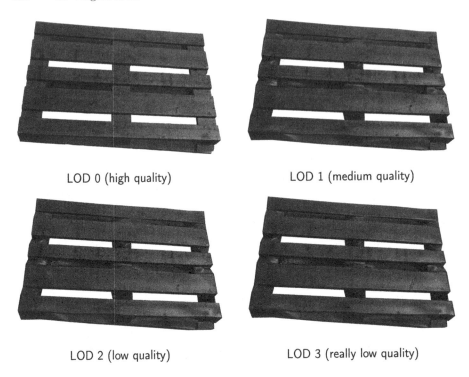

LOD 0 (high quality)   LOD 1 (medium quality)

LOD 2 (low quality)   LOD 3 (really low quality)

Fig. 4. Wooden pallet LOD conditions

university laboratory. Each participant was greeted by an instructor and introduced to the HMD. The game was explained in advance. The experiment consisted of one continuous game session, divided into four game rounds. Each game round the LOD of non-interactive objects decreased according to the description in Sect. 3.2. After the game was finished, participants were asked to complete an online questionnaire on an additional laptop, requiring both qualitative and quantitative answers. The quantitative questions were rated on a 5-point Likert scale. The questionnaire included questions concerning demographics, vision impairments, and previous experiences with both gaming and VR technology. The questions regarding the game experience were as follows:

- Q1: What is your overall game satisfaction?
- Q2: Briefly describe your choice in the previous question.
- Q3: Which round of the game did you enjoy the most?
- Q4: What game objects did you find most engaging?
- Q5: Have you noticed any differences in the quality of the same game objects?
- Q6: When have you noticed a difference in the quality of the same game objects?
- Q7: What difference in the quality of the same game objects have you noticed?

3.4   Participants

The 53 participants for the study were mainly acquired through advertisements on the social networks of the researchers. The average age was 23 ($SD = 2.79$), and the gender distribution was 62.3% male and 35.8% female.

50 of the 53 participants indicated no visual impairment, 2 persons were shortsighted, and 1 had red-green color blindness. Notably, only 26 persons reported requiring any optical aids, such as glasses or contact lenses. This discrepancy raises the possibility that questions regarding visual impairment might have been misinterpreted by some participants.

The average general familiarity with video games on a Likert scale from 1 to 5, was 3.64 ($SD = 1.30$), with an average frequency of playing video games of 3.03 ($SD = 1.25$). The preferred game genres were shooters with 41.2% of the participants, action with 29.4%, strategy with 9.8%, and puzzle with 7.8%. Among the participants, 11.3 % claimed to have different favorite video game genres.

The average general familiarity with VR on a Likert scale from 1 to 5, was 1.69 ($SD = 0.86$), with an average frequency of using VR applications of 1.45 ($SD = 0.53$). Notably, 79.2% reported that they had never used a VR device before, 7.5% tried PlayStation VR, 7.5% Meta Quest 2, and 5.6% other Meta devices.

3.5   Data Analysis

The post-study questionnaire was evaluated by examining the descriptive statistics of the quantitative data. For more information regarding the reasoning behind certain answers, qualitative answers were added to the analysis. For hypothesis testing, a one-proportion z-test was used to ascertain whether the proportion of given answers held statistical significance.

4   Results

4.1   Perception of LOD

Of the 53 participants surveyed, only 5 (9.4%) stated that they noticed a difference in the quality of objects between all four conditions (Q5). No difference was found for 29 (54.7%) participants and 19 (35.8%) were not sure. The qualitative question Q7 revealed that among the five participants who perceived a difference, only one could describe that there was a reduction in the LOD.

When removing the uncertain answers from the question of noticed difference, the proportions were 5 participants who noticed a difference against 29 who could not see a difference, showing a new percentage of 14.71% against 85.29%. When performing a one-proportion z-test, this proportion revealed a statistically significant difference ($z = 5.81$, $p < 0.01$). This suggests that the observed variations in responses are not likely due to random chance.

4.2   Game Enjoyment

The mean overall satisfaction (Q1) of the 53 participants throughout the 4 rounds was 3.77 ($SD = 0.81$). When asked for the most enjoyable game round (Q3), 34 of the 53 participants claimed that they enjoyed all rounds equally (64.2%), 8 preferred round 4 (15.1%), 7 preferred round 3 (13.2%) 3 preferred round 2 (5.7%) and 1 person preferred round 1 (1.9%). The distribution is shown in Fig. 5.

To assess the significance of these proportions, a one-proportion z-test was performed to compare the 34 answers of equal enjoyment and all 19 other answers (non-equal enjoyment), revealing a statistically significant difference ($z = 2.27$, $p < 0.05$). This suggests that the observed variations in responses are not likely due to random chance.

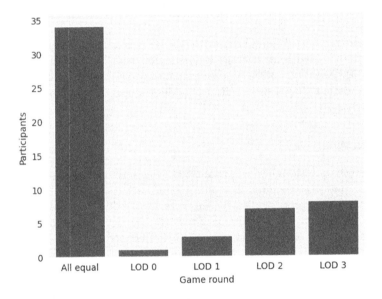

Fig. 5. Distribution of answers for Q3

5   Discussion and Conclusion

With only 5 out of 53 participants who were certain to have perceived a difference in quality between the game rounds, there is not enough evidence to reject the null hypothesis for H_1. This result suggests that there is room for LOD optimization in VR shooting games, particularly when considering that only one participant could identify the exact difference. If a pixel reduction of 99.6% in the texture resolution and a triangle reduction of 95.9% of non-interactive objects are not greatly perceived by players, new possibilities for performance optimization arise.

With 19 out of 53 participants who did not enjoy all game rounds equally, there is not enough evidence to reject the null hypothesis for H_2. If the answers for non-equal enjoyment were examined, instead of a reduction of enjoyment for each round (i.e., a reduction of LOD), the opposite trend occurred; the most enjoyable round was the last for 8 participants. However, from the experimental design, this effect cannot be attributed to the change in LOD; rather, it is much more likely that the participants became more proficient with the game mechanics with each successive round, thus increasing the enjoyment through their gained experience.

34 participants claimed that they enjoyed all rounds equally, suggesting that the reduction of LOD for non-interactive objects does not significantly impact the UX in VR shooting games. This result supports the possibility of optimizing the performance by reducing the quality of 3D assets that are not the focus of attention. The average overall satisfaction of 3.7 out of 5 confirmed that the game offered some enjoyment, thus being a game experience comparable to existing shooter games.

5.1 Limitations and Future Work

It's important to acknowledge that the results cannot be translated into all game genres without hesitation. In addition, within the genre of shooter games, the results would solely apply to sequences where the player is stationary and engaged in direct action. As soon as movement within the virtual environment is allowed, non-interactive objects could get more attention just by approaching them. This could depict an opportunity to explore adaptive LOD changes, according to the gameplay. Further, it should be noted that the assessment of game enjoyment in this study is an initial value of exploration and should be investigated and unraveled with distinct questions. In the following experiments, comprehensive aspects of the UX, such as presence, immersion or flow should be surveyed to improve the understanding of the relationship between game enjoyment and quality reduction for optimization. Despite these limitations, the study results can serve as a starting point for further research and optimization efforts to improve the UX of XR applications. Future studies on this topic could consider a randomized order of conditions and a comparison with LOD reduction for interactive objects. Explorations with different game genres and scenarios could lead to fruitful results.

Acknowledgements. This work would not have been possible without the effort of Annalena Wittig, Denys Babenko, Ella Danay, Lin Son Cheung, Milos Denck, Shao-Chieh Lee, Colin Schreiber, and You-Jin Kim, who contributed to the design and development of the shown solution. This work was partly funded by the Federal Ministry of Education and Research (BMBF) and the state of Berlin under the Excellence Strategy of the Federal Government and the Länder.

References

1. Buhr, M., Pfeiffer, T., Reiners, D., Cruz-Neira, C., Jung, B.: Echtzeitaspekte von VR-Systemen. Springer Vieweg (2013). https://doi.org/10.1007/978-3-642-28903-3
2. Chang, E., Kim, H.T., Yoo, B.: Virtual reality sickness: a review of causes and measurements. Int. J. Hum.-Comput. Interact. **36**(17), 1658–1682 (2020). https://doi.org/10.1080/10447318.2020.1778351
3. Csikszentmihalyi, M.: Flow: the psychology of optimal experience. HarperPerennial, New York, 1. harperperennial ed edn. (1991)
4. El-Nasr, M.S., Yan, S.: Visual attention in 3D video games. In: Proceedings of the 2006 ACM SIGCHI international conference on Advances in computer entertainment technology, p. 22. ACM, Hollywood California USA (2006). https://doi.org/10.1145/1178823.1178849
5. Gallagher, M., Ferrè, E.R.: Cybersickness: a multisensory integration perspective. Multisensory Res. **31**(7), 645–674 (2018). https://doi.org/10.1163/22134808-20181293
6. Guenter, B., Finch, M., Drucker, S., Tan, D., Snyder, J.: Foveated 3D graphics. ACM Trans. Graph. **31**(6), 1–10 (2012). https://doi.org/10.1145/2366145.2366183
7. International Organization for Standardization: ergonomics of human-system interaction - part 210: human-centred design for interactive systems (formerly known as 13407). Tech. Rep. ISO 9241-210:2010, International Organization for Standardization, Genf (2010)
8. Koulieris, G.A., Drettakis, G., Cunningham, D., Mania, K.: C-LOD: context-aware material level-of-detail applied to mobile graphics. Comput. Graph. Forum **33**(4), 41–49 (2014). https://doi.org/10.1111/cgf.12411
9. LaViola, J.J.: A discussion of cybersickness in virtual environments. ACM SIGCHI Bulletin **32**(1), 47–56 (2000). https://doi.org/10.1145/333329.333344
10. Möller, S., Schmidt, S., Beyer, J.: Gaming taxonomy: an overview of concepts and evaluation methods for computer gaming QoE. In: 2013 Fifth International Workshop on Quality of Multimedia Experience (QoMEX), pp. 236–241 (2013). https://doi.org/10.1109/QoMEX.2013.6603243
11. Reddy, M.: Specification and evaluation of level of detail selection criteria. Virtual Reality **3**(2), 132–143 (1998). https://doi.org/10.1007/BF01417674
12. Slater, M.: Place illusion and plausibility can lead to realistic behaviour in immersive virtual environments. Philos. Trans. Royal Soc. B: Biol. Sci. **364**(1535), 3549–3557 (2009)
13. Slater, M., Banakou, D., Beacco, A., Gallego, J., Macia-Varela, F., Oliva, R.: A separate reality: an update on place illusion and plausibility in virtual reality. Front. Virtual Real. **3** (2022). https://www.frontiersin.org/articles/10.3389/frvir.2022.914392
14. Slater, M., Wilbur, S.: A framework for immersive virtual environments (FIVE): speculations on the role of presence in virtual environments. Presence: Teleoperators Virtual Environ. **6**(6), 603–616 (1997)
15. Watson, B., Walker, N., Hodges, L.F., Worden, A.: Managing level of detail through peripheral degradation: effects on search performance with a head-mounted display. ACM Trans. Comput.-Hum. Interact. **4**(4), 323–346 (1997)

Exploration of Cultural IP Image and Common Pattern Gene Extraction in Virtual Reality Design Interaction

Junyu Zhou[1][✉] and Ruiyang Chen[2]

[1] Department of Visual Communication, Nanjing Normal University, Nanjing 210098, China
12210617@njnu.edu.cn
[2] Art Education Major, Nanjing Normal University, Nanjing 210098, China

Abstract. This paper first studies the origin and flow of IP images from the interactive perspective of design, explores the definition and rules of IP in the form of knowledge graph based on semiotics, and puts this problem into the background of the current wave of AI and virtual reality, and raises the following questions: - The definition of IP in virtual reality and the original IP in the network? What is the way forward? Based on the AI data era background of IP business image for induction automation design processor, to achieve better IP cultural communication and exchange.

The author selected the female ethnic characteristic clothing of Hui 'an area of Fujian Province as the representative object of design. In this realization part, the article first takes Hui 'an women's ethnic clothing as an example to explore the characteristics of ethnic clothing induction methods - structure multi-modal form and cross-comparison analysis of horizontal multi-cultural pattern design and extract the elements. Then, according to the formula points summarized, the virtual IP image is designed with the characteristic ethnic dress of women in Hui 'an area of Fujian Province, China.

According to the cultural gene and regional characteristics contained in the regional ethnic image, the pattern factors are decomposed reconstructed, and applied to the IP image design under the meta-structure virtual reality technology. On this basis, the VR system of the minority cultural IP generator is built. It allows users to generate IP images of featured nationalities in a more immersive environment through shapes, colors, lines, etc., summarized by patterns.

Finally, the team tested the VR system. According to the five aspects of "whether the generated IP image is more vivid/whether it can integrate national characteristics/whether it is more immersive/whether it is more memorable/whether it is easier to understand", a total of 20 members participated in the evaluation. In the answer, we finally find that through this VR system, we can more intuitively and immersive feel the integration of culture and national memory in a new form, construct a new mode of cultural transmission in the meta-universe era, and promote cultural exchange and cultural memory storage.

Keywords: IP image design · National characteristic pattern finishing · Virtual reality interaction

© The Author(s), under exclusive license to Springer Nature Switzerland AG 2024
J. Y. C. Chen and G. Fragomeni (Eds.): HCII 2024, LNCS 14706, pp. 301–311, 2024.
https://doi.org/10.1007/978-3-031-61041-7_20

1 Introduction

The wave of China's modernization has promoted the innovative return of traditional intangible cultural heritage. China's intangible cultural heritage has a large number, fine categories, mixed classification, each with its own characteristics, with a strong national color. Since the outbreak of COVID-19, China, as a major resource country, has faced increasingly serious problems such as lack of space, disconnection from reality and difficulty in sustaining intangible cultural heritage in the development process [1]. The brocade pattern in the national intangible cultural heritage is a very momentous part of it.

At the same time, since the rapid development of intelligent technology in this century, the concept of meta-universe came into being and was widely discussed by all walks of life. AI and digital art enable the diversification, modernization, innovation, productization and commercialization of intangible cultural heritage. Intangible cultural heritage can be revitalized in the new era.

IP image design is an important connotation of visual culture image. At present, IP design has become the mainstream under the direction of multimedia and multi-symbol visual image, and now the multicultural needs make IP image in urgent need of further design and research. Visual culture communication needs to occupy the high ground and play a new image with IP image design as the leading banner in the new era. And the meta universe suddenly arrived, breaking the traditional IP image cognition. The appearance of virtual human shows the diversity and representativeness of IP in the meta-universe. Tsinghua University digital people "Hua Zhibing", Baidu AI digital people "Du Xiaoxiao", and so on, the endless digital people have become the new IP image in the new era of the meta-universe. More intangible cultural heritages promote cultural tourism by creating virtual digital human IP images. Virtual digital human technology has been applied in many Chinese museums to make the explanation of cultural relics and the popularization of historical science more vivid. At the same time, the use of VR devices allows users to have a more in-depth immersive experience.

Based on this background, our team hopes to promote the design and publicity of traditional national images through a more immersive meta-universe virtual IP design. Team to Hui 'an female as a classic representative. Hui 'an women is the female name of Hui 'an City, Fujian Province, China. They are deeply rooted in the hearts of the people with the image of hard-working and virtuous Fujian women. This article takes the image of Hui 'an woman in Fujian province as a case design. In general, the article takes "the origin of IP - characteristic analysis of ethnic clothing patterns - construction of VR image design system" as the idea, and proposes a conceptual model for the IP design of other ethnic images with characteristics, which has the significance of cross-era and cross-space.

2 The Integration of IP Source Sink

2.1 The Redefinition of IP from the Perspective of Source and Design

Under the wave of information age, the enterprise group appears "IP" to represent the image and content. "IP" is now in various industries and the first set off IP line for the electronic information industry, meaning electronic address. In the legal profession, IP comes from "Intellectual Property", which refers to intellectual property or intellectual property. Then, it is introduced to the design industry to convey the images needed to represent enterprises and cities with interesting, wide communication and excellent expression, and convey the core of design thinking based on the narrative of culture and corporate communication needs. The author used python arithmetic to search application website data crawling, since the "IP" appeared once in 2011, IP design has formed a new demand for design, to 2015 the search volume reached a peak, the phenomenon of hot words are now in the public eye (Table 1).

Table 1. "IP" search versus peak information.

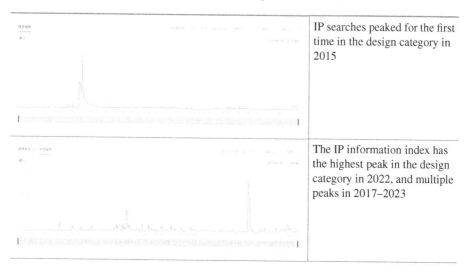

	IP searches peaked for the first time in the design category in 2015
	The IP information index has the highest peak in the design category in 2022, and multiple peaks in 2017–2023

Later, IP not only refers to cultural property, but more generally refers to everything that can represent a certain thing. Under this vision, the IP visual image design needs to redefine the IP image with the meaning of "mascot" in the design field, and enshrine its image cultural connotation, which is not limited to visual representation but deep into its essence. From the perspective of new design, IP should integrate visual, behavioral and spiritual aspects of regional culture into visual, behavioral and spiritual aspects to extend and reproduce cultural visualization [2].

The purpose of IP design is to convey the demand-oriented content represented by enterprises, governments, brands, etc., which is in line with the design intention. As a vocabulary, IP should be redefined from the perspective of new design disciplines, integrating the basic system framework of design with it, and acting as a representative of new cultural development under the necessity of image construction. To "easy to see, easy to understand, diverse, great beauty" as the demand goal of design, show the new era of regional culture in the new requirements (Fig. 1).

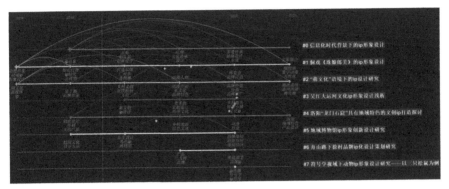

Fig. 1. A figure is an analysis chart of keywords and core articles in IP-related literature

2.2 Necessity and Logic Chain of IP Image Design Under Virtual Reality Technology Background

Virtual reality creates a virtual environment with advanced software and hardware systems, and realizes immersive, interactive and multi-perception experience by simulating vision, hearing, touch and even a variety of human senses. Virtual reality breaks through time and space to build a multi-end access data system, and its own characteristics provide a wide range of exposure to culture. It constructs virtual fields to incorporate users into them, presenting the real space composed of digital information that can be perceived by users, aiming to eliminate users' reality cognition and immerse themselves in the virtual environment.

With the rapid development of technology, virtual reality penetrates into many fields and bears the important responsibility of contemporary translation of traditional culture. Based on innovation-driven development strategy and new smart city development goals, it is imperative that virtual reality technology be integrated into urban IP shaping.

The development of information technology promotes the diversification of demand, and the digital communication mode urgently needs to become the mainstream communication path. Digital city IP can effectively promote the wide dissemination and recognition of urban culture. With the support of digital media, we can innovate the popularization and modernization mode of urban civilization. Virtual forms enrich design expression, revitalize abstract concepts, and transform regional culture into universally accepted images that are young and not limited to vision. Virtual reality will connect traditional and modern, material and virtual, local and global in a new attitude, and help upgrade the aesthetic image of the city.

3 Design Factor Construction Analysis of Huian Woman and Model Construction

3.1 Huian Women's Wear in Fujian Culture, Tradition of the Foundation

Huian women, often living in Huidong Peninsula, Huian County, Quanzhou City, Fujian Province, and Putian Nanri Island, narrowly refers to the main scope of activities in the east of Huian County, Fujian Province Chongwu town, Shanxia town, Jingfeng town and Xiaozuoian town area of the Min women, known for their hard-working, gentle, simple and virtuous quality. In May 2006, Huian women's clothing was selected into the first batch of national intangible cultural heritage list, and Shanhui women's folk customs have become five major tourism brands in Fujian Province.Based on the Chinese theology and mystic culture quadrant of coastal Mazu, Huian women gradually evolved from regional humanism to a symbol of spiritual civilization in Fujian, which is a symbol of Fujian women's virtues such as worship virtue to good, hard work and progress. The Fujian cultural identity constructed by Hui 'an female has even become the Fujian cultural brand, which leads to the inner circulation of culture and the outer circulation of external communication.

3.2 Huian Daughter and Historical Provenance: The Importance of Modern Conservation

In the field of academic research, a total of 344 journals, academic disserations, conferences and newspapers were searched with the keyword "Hui 'an Women", and 124 related research papers were actually published. The existing materials have few studies on Hui 'an women's habits clothing, and there is a lack of extension exploration on its modern innovative IP design. "The overall style of Hui 'an women's clothing was shaped in the Tang Dynasty, gradually mature to the Song Dynasty, and after the late Ming and early Qing Dynasties, there were more obvious changes, that is, formed the basic characteristics of strange style, unique decoration, color coordination, and gorgeous decoration." At the beginning of the 20th century, with the gradual broadening of cultural life and vision, Hui 'an women's clothing continued to develop and improve, thus becoming a highly regional characteristics of clothing folk culture phenomenon." [3] Quanzhou Cultural Bureau, Quanzhou Xinhai Road Minnan Cultural Protection Center, edited. Bibliography of Quanzhou Intangible Cultural Heritage [M]. Fuzhou: Straits Literature and Art Publishing House, 2007. Mindi multi-ethnic and the vast, in addition to the Hui 'an female there are still Meizhou female, Pu female folk fisherman The most valuable research significance of Huinu lies in its image research and development. It has important research value and design innovation significance in the past of feudal traditional folk custom, the present of imminence and the change of times, and the future of innovative innovation, so it is more necessary to study Huinu's image IP (Fig. 2).

3.3 Hui 'an Women and Other Areas of Minjiang Dress Comparison

Mekong women, Hui 'an women, Pu women three major fishing women settlement in Fujian and Huian women still have a high influence, the corresponding dress style is more widely spread. Meizhou women's dress system is the same as the upper and lower system, and its upper shirt color is bright dark blue, the lower body wears black wide pants, and likes to braid hair in the back of the head to do "comb" Mazu head, supplemented by scattered flowers. Pu female is located in Quanzhou ancient purple harbor, surrounded by the sea on three sides, there is a folk song saying "field snail head, flower hairpin, big train shirt, wide leg pants, rooster shoes" for the Pu female, the most obvious feature of the head with flowers - the long hair is coiled to the head, with a wooden pin up, collecting flowers will be implicated, around the head After many

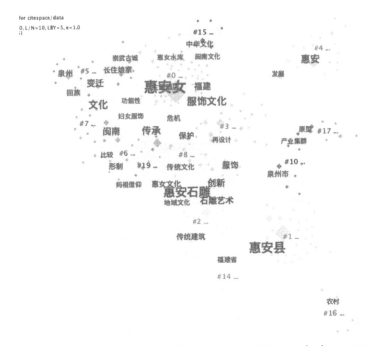

Fig. 2. A figure caption is Fujian paper research keywords cluster research map

years, under the change of time, the existence of Meizhou women, Poa women has gradually been erased, and non-gathering large-scale temple fairs or ancestor worship are almost not featured While Huian women's clothing is still changing in time and space, IP design is also to let Huian women exude the comfortable vitality of modern meaning. The different distribution of Huian female zone makes it different. The dress and costume pairs are shown (Table 2).

3.4 Huian Women Dress Shape Composition

The shape of Huian women's clothing is based on the shape of traditional Chinese clothing, with the "upper and lower" truncated shape as the main way, with "yellow hat, flowered headscarf, short jacket, wide pants, silver waist chain" [4]. Constitute the basic shape and decoration. The special shape of Huinu is influenced by its geological appearance and historical origin. Huizuanchangchang lives in Huanhai Peninsula, Fujian Province, with the towns of Xiaozuo, Shanxia, Dongqiao, Dongling, Chongwu, Tuzhai, and Jingfeng seven as the main active areas. Affected by monsoon, the annual precipitation ranges from 1400 mm to 2000 mm during the same period of rain and heat, and is attached to a subtropical Marine monsoon climate. Within the island, the mountains and hills are piled, and the face is surrounded by the sea, and the light is abundant all year round. Based on the special climate and geomorphic conditions, as well as the actual use needs of field work as an example, Hui 'an women's clothing system requires the above part of the short shirt and the lower part of the wide pants - the upper part of the

Table 2. Huian women in different regions of different styles of jewelry

District headwear	Legend	Font size and style	Graphic design method	Origin of ethnic elements
Chongwu, Shanxia area headwear		Roll pattern	Repetition, symmetry, combination	Yi nationality elements
Daozuo and Jingfeng area collar chain		Flower pattern, "s" pattern	Symmetry, continuity, combination	Miao and Dai nationality elements
Silver bracelet in Xiaozuo and Jingfeng area		Geometric pattern, lantern pattern, cirrus cloud	Repetition, symmetry, continuity, combination	Yao nationality elements

short shirt is exposed to the navel, which ADAPTS to the variability of monsoon climate and Marine climate; And the lower half of the wide pants serve the requirements of farming.Since a hundred years ago, Hui woman at the end of the Qing Dynasty, wearing a sleeved shirt, under the large fold pants, waist scarf [5],After more than 100 years of custom changes to the current dress style of top and pants. (Fig. 3).

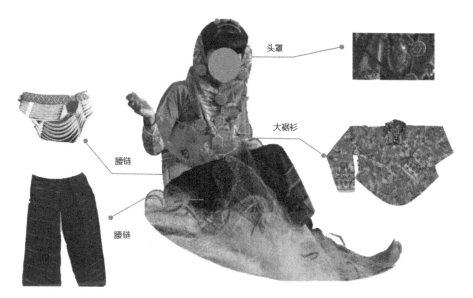

Fig. 3. A figure is Huian women's clothing style

4 Huian Women Applied IP Clothing Pattern and Color Factor Analysis

4.1 Huian Women Clothing Pattern Category Analysis

Table 3. Huian women's different styles of dress in different regions

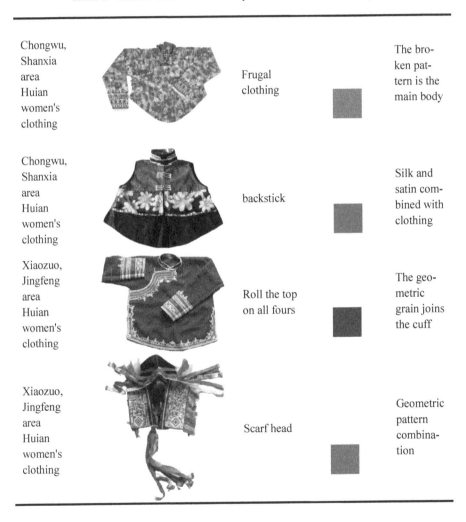

Chongwu, Shanxia area Huian women's clothing		Frugal clothing		The broken pattern is the main body
Chongwu, Shanxia area Huian women's clothing		backstick		Silk and satin combined with clothing
Xiaozuo, Jingfeng area Huian women's clothing		Roll the top on all fours		The geometric grain joins the cuff
Xiaozuo, Jingfeng area Huian women's clothing		Scarf head		Geometric pattern combination

Huian women's clothing is different because of different living areas and trial production. Chongwu, Shanxia area of Huian women's clothing is divided into two styles, one with floral patterns for clothing patterns, with bright and colorful colors, such as fresh powder, bright red, bright orange. The cuff and neckline of the saving shirt are matched with the sleeve edge formed by repeated combination of geometric patterns such as diamond shape, matching the saving shirt style. Color Use contrasting cool colors to help highlight the main tone and pattern. The second of the Huian women's clothing in Chongwu and Shanxia areas is mainly composed of cool colors, with bright colors on the edge of the clothing, and black and other colors as the main color. Its patterns are mostly based on the patterns of items in daily life, close to the lives of fishermen, showing Fujian customs (Table 3).

Table 4. Huian female pattern collation map

Collar embroidery fish and shrimp aquarium pattern local		asymmetric
Collar embroidery fish and shrimp relative grain area		symmetry

4.2   Huian Women's Clothing Colour Extraction and Matching

Colour in Hui'an women's clothing is of great significance, and it is also one of the important extracts of the pattern factor. Hui'an women's dresses have high purity of colour and are good at orange-red, bright blue and red as the main colours, highlighting the tattoos to show the tension, attracting others with bold, provocative and brilliant colours, and at the same time, showing the passionate and lively folklore of the Min land. Take the above shirt as an example, the overall colour of the garment is orange, red, blue and other main tones, at both ends of the cuffs are sewn with a white base, with patterned style, patterned colours are dominated by red, surrounded by green leaves to match, and often embellished with blue patterns in two-thirds of the calibre, making the cuffs delicate and chic, which is just like "flowers are like brocade". Brightly coloured tops and Huinu navel skin tone of white, show Huinu surplus of a waist posture, Chu Chu can be attractive. There is a reason for the application of high purity colours to Hui-nu, in theology and religion, the bright colours are often used to expel foreign enemies in the culture of A-Ma-Zu in the Min belt, and more environmentally, it is the bright and natural environment of Min that creates the virtuous and beautiful Hui-nu between the sea and the mountains (Table 4).

Table 5. Comparative colour map of Hui'an women

Pattern morphology	Extract color		Color proportion

5 Huian Women Applied IP Clothing Pattern and Color Factor Analysis

5.1 New Patterns and Characteristics of Pattern Genes in Virtual Reality

Virtual reality changes the traditional pattern creation environment and puts the creation process into the virtual environment. The "anything is possible" characteristic of virtual world makes the creation process free from the restrictions of tools and materials, forming the reconstruction of design form language, breaking through traditional aesthetic and innovating artistic style. The concept of noise is put forward in Defler's interactive process model, and it is believed that noise will affect the quality of information transmission. The immersive experience of virtual reality can effectively reduce the effect of noise on the content expressed by designers (Table 5).

Visually, virtual reality broadens the user's perspective and strengthens the visual impact and immersive feeling of the pattern. Let the digital information fall back into the real situation to enrich the visual information. In terms of hearing, it innovates the transmission form of sound, makes the cultural information contained in the pattern concrete, and creates a unique artistic atmosphere of the city. In virtual reality, users will change their visual and static understanding of patterns, enrich their understanding of the history and humanity behind patterns in a multi-sensory experience, and deepen their memory of patterns and culture.

In virtual reality, pattern is no longer a simple "product", but a "scene". Users harvest a unique memory of Hui 'an in the unique sensory feast, and realize the understanding and identification of urban culture.

6 Peroration

Recently, IP image design has gradually drawn the attention of the public. Taking the IP image design of Huian urban area as an example, the IP image design conveys the excellent scheme of IP design in many aspects such as artistic aesthetics and cultural attainments. At the same time, IP involves the investment of Fujian's famous brands, and can be applied to the plane, multimedia and even the province's visual image system to give satisfactory answers. In this study, Huian IP design, all use Huian has a certain mass base and brand planning power. Its image color suggests the image of Huian women - simple and simple, hardworking and serious, gentle and gentle. Then, the study of the pattern of Hui 'an women's clothing, combing the changes of the shape, color, basic deformation and the final variation of Hui 'an women's clothing, so that Hui 'an women in the face of the situation of cultural inheritance fault constantly actively break the situation, so that it has continued to adhere to the right innovation from the Qing Dynasty and the modernization of Hui 'an women's inheritance more confident. In daily life, brand design is indispensable and has profound influence on people. Excellent urban brand image design can promote the aesthetics of urban people and enhance people's sense of belonging and pride.

References

1. Chengdu, W., Ying, W.: Making intangible cultural heritage "alive": new thoughts on the meta-universe and the development of intangible cultural heritage in China. Yuejiang J. (3), 148–157 (2022)
2. Weishang, L., Zhuo, L., Jialin, Q : The regional culture and agriculture regional brand image fusion of IP strategy research. J. package. Eng. (18), 262–268 (2021). https://doi.org/10.19554/j.carolcarrollnki.1001-3563,2021.18.031
3. Quanzhou Cultural Bureau, Quanzhou Xinhai Road Minnan Cultural Protection Center edited. Bibliography of Quanzhou intangible Cultural Heritage. Fuzhou: Straits Literature and Art Publishing House (2007)
4. Xiangqun, J.: Hui 'an County, Fujian: Building cultural characteristics and building a strong humanistic county. Party Build. **311**(11), 51 (2013)
5. Hui 'e, L., Tianqi, S.: The influence of natural geographical environment difference on costume color: a case study of folk costume in Jiangnan and Southern Fujian. Art Des. Res. **74**(04), 27–32 (2016)

Author Index

© The Editor(s) (if applicable) and The Author(s), under exclusive license
to Springer Nature Switzerland AG 2024
J. Y. C. Chen and G. Fragomeni (Eds.): HCII 2024, LNCS 14706, pp. 313–316, 2024.
https://doi.org/10.1007/978-3-031-61041-7